Emerging Nodes in the Global Economy: Frankfurt and Tel Aviv Compared

The GeoJournal Library

Volume 72

The titles published in this series are listed at the end of this volume.

Emerging Nodes in the Global Economy: Frankfurt and Tel Aviv Compared

edited by

DANIEL FELSENSTEIN

Department of Geography,
Hebrew University of Jerusalem, Israel

EIKE W. SCHAMP

Department of Economic and Social Geography,
Johann Wolfgang Goethe University,
Frankfurt am Main, Germany

and

ARIE SHACHAR

Department of Geography,
Hebrew University of Jerusalem, Israel

KLUWER ACADEMIC PUBLISHERS
DORDRECHT / BOSTON / LONDON

A C.I.P. Catalogue record for this book is available from the Library of Congress

ISBN 1-4020-0924-0

Published by Kluwer Academic Publishers,
P.O. Box 17, 3300 AA Dordrecht, The Netherlands.

Sold and distributed in North, Central and South America
by Kluwer Academic Publishers,
101 Philip Drive, Norwell, MA 02061, U.S.A.

In all other countries, sold and distributed
by Kluwer Academic Publishers,
P.O. Box 322, 3300 AH Dordrecht, The Netherlands.

Printed on acid-free paper

Printed in the Netherlands.

TABLE OF CONTENTS

SECTION IV: CONSUMER-DRIVEN ACTIVITIES

SECTION V: CONCLUSIONS

CONTRIBUTORS

Hanan Barkai is an MA student in the Department of Geography and the Institute of Urban and Regional Studies, Hebrew University of Jerusalem.

Yaron Ergas is a PhD candidate in the Department of Geography, Hebrew University of Jerusalem and Director of Tourism Planning at the Israeli Ministry of Tourism, Jerusalem.

Daniel Felsenstein is a Senior Lecturer in the Department of Geography and Director of the Institute of Urban and Regional Studies, Hebrew University of Jerusalem.

Alexander Grimm is a PhD candidate in Human Geography and research assistant in the Department of Geography, Friedrich Schiller University, Jena.

Michael H. Grote is a PhD candidate and research assistant in the Department of Economics, Johann Wolfgang Goethe-University, Frankfurt am Main.

Amir Mossek is an urban planner and MA student in the Department of Geography and the Institute of Urban and Regional Studies, Hebrew University of Jerusalem.

Ursula Rachor-Hagelueken is a geographer and was head of the EU coordination office for Academic Organizations in Bonn.

Holger Rudolph is a geographer currently working in the corporate communications division of a private bank, Frankfurt am Main.

Eike W. Schamp is Professor of Economic Geography in the Department of Economic and Social Geography, Johann Wolfgang Goethe University, Frankfurt am Main.

Arie Shachar is the Leon Safdie Professor of Urban Studies in the Department of Geography, Hebrew University of Jerusalem.

Noam Shoval is a Lecturer in the Department of Geography, Hebrew University of Jerusalem.

Ralph Steinert is a geographer currently working in the research division of an international hotel corporation, Munich.

TABLES

FIGURES

DANIEL FELSENSTEIN, EIKE W. SCHAMP
AND ARIE SHACHAR

1. EMERGING NODES IN THE GLOBAL ECONOMY: AN INTRODUCTION

1.1 NODES, NETWORKS AND FLOWS IN THE GLOBAL ECONOMY

The 'global economy' is increasingly perceived as a catch-all phrase. It evokes vastly divergent emotions ranging from resentment and anger over poverty and sustainability to pride and admiration over technological progress and human ingenuity. For all its fuzziness (Markusen, 1999), globalization does however convey two major shifts that pervade much of the economic and spatial change taking place in the world economy. The first relates to the notion of scale. Whether distance has died or simply been minimized (Cairncross, 1997), globalization has redrawn the limits on spatial interaction. The second relates to the seamlessness of the world economy. Globalization has led to the obliteration or neglect of borders. A truly global economy implies the unfettered flows of people, goods and services for whom regional or national boundaries are increasingly irrelevant.

Both of these processes impact on places. Paradoxically, they lead to the glorification of some, such as the global or world cities, and the demise of others. At one and the same time, the uniqueness of some locations is highlighted while the identities of many others are merged into an amorphous mass. But just how different is this to the 'global economy' of previous eras? Did not previous rounds of globalization, from the Renaissance to the Industrial Revolution have similar effects both on the scale of interactions and the flows between locations and on the fortunes of those places in which they originated?

The answer to this question underlies the motif of this volume. While the contemporary global economy may be doing very much the same as in the past but at greater intensity, the nature of relations between the places comprising the global economy has changed radically. The rise to prominence of Florence in the Renaissance period or Manchester in the Industrial Revolution simply served to elevate these locations within the given hierarchy of global places. The role, fate and fortune of places was determined by their place in this hierarchy. The implicit theme of this book is that the perception of the global economy as an hierarchical structure is of limited utility. While hierarchies have formed the mainstay of explanatory frameworks in economic geography ranging from central place theory, through location theory and core-periphery relations, we suggest that this construct breaks down when faced with phenomena that are structured as networks. Many of the

D. Felsenstein et al. (eds.),
Emerging Nodes in the Global Economy: Frankfurt and Tel Aviv Compared, 1–8.

contemporary processes driving the global economy are inherently network-based. The network metaphor therefore forms the main unifying concept of this volume.

While the network has been used increasingly as an explanatory framework in studies of social, economic and spatial relations (Cooke, 1988; DeBresson and Amesse, 1991; Powell, 1990), less attention has been focused on the functions of the nodes that comprise the network. Our conception of the roles of cities in global networks differs from that adopted in recent studies. For us, these nodes are not 'mid-level' places in a global hierarchy (Sassen 2002) or 'second-tier' cities beyond the metropolitan area (Markusen, Lee and DiGiovanna 1999). Rather, they are temporal and volatile forms of engagement with the global economy conducted from key locations. Due to the network structure in which they are organized, the same place can function at one and the same time as global node and a parochial location.

Our central thesis is that in the current round of globalization, places (cities, metropolitan areas or city-regions) selectively function as nodes within networks. In this respect, we draw on the network paradigm that sees synergetic relations between places in a manner similar to those between firms (Camagni, 1993; Camagni and Salone, 1993). We do not attempt to formalize the resultant network topography but in common with this literature we recognize that the network relations of places are not independent of the firms located in these places (Taylor, 2001). Consequently, our approach is to analyze the process of network formation through in-depth studies of leading sectors in two different contexts. On this basis we extract more general insights into the operation of networks and the functioning of nodes, for example, network formation drawing on the case of high tech nodes (Chapter 6).

The notion of a 'node' implies constant interaction with other units such as places, firms, households etc. The value of a node lies in its connectivity with other nodes. The denser the level of inter-connectedness the more receiving, transmitting and processing the node can accomplish. Underlying this conceptualization of places as nodes, is the recognition that places come to be characterized by the specialized economic function that they fulfill in the global economy.

The implications of this perspective are far reaching. First, this view suggests a relational view of the global economy (Beaverstock, Smith, Taylor, Walker and Lorimer, 2000). The importance and centrality of a node is defined by its relations to other nodes. The upshot of this view, is that static rankings based on leading indicators while highly prevalent in the literature, are less than adequate. Instead, it is more useful to look at interaction between nodes by observing the flows between them. Movement of capital, telecommunications traffic, international investment, market information, cultural goods and highly skilled labor can all be used to proxy these flows. The boundaries of these flows define the topography of the network. The efficiency gains derived from organizing interaction as a network rather than as a hierarchy, derive from the increasing returns that network organization affords. This point is developed further below (Chapter 6). However, at this juncture it is poignant to note that proximity is not a sine qua non of network formation and there is even empirical evidence that supports the contention that geographical dispersion makes for greater network efficiency (Kilkenny, 2000). A further important theme arising from a network perspective is that node centrality in a network derives from relations with other nodes. The more the interaction, the more central the node. This emphasis on the role of returns to scale should hardly be ignored. It links network formation to a burgeoning literature that emphasizes the role of increasing returns in urban and metropolitan development (Krugman, 1991).

Second, we posit a high degree of flexibility and temporality in the economic functioning of places. The prominence (or decline of a node) is not necessarily contingent on the attributes of the node itself. Nodes assume different levels of importance over time determined by their interactions with other nodes. Thus places functioning as nodes are less likely to be subject to the vagaries of technological lock-in and path dependence than places whose centrality is determined by their position in the urban hierarchy. This is not to say that historic accidents and idiosyncratic events cannot trigger off a unique growth process of a node in a given place. Rather, we are simply asserting that in a network configuration, the chances of a whole system locking-in to a sub-optimal form of operation is much less likely than in a tightly structured and hierarchical chain of interactions.

Third, the network approach broadly ascribes to the 'space of flows' thesis (Castells, 1989, 1996). The level, frequency and intensity of flows between nodes, defines their place in the global economy. Places are defined by "what flows through them, rather than what is fixed within them" (Beaverstock *et al.*, 2000, p.47) These flows can relate to skilled labor (Chapter 6), international finance (Chapter 5), foreign direct investment (Chapter 4) and so on. It is important however, not to over-state the role of flows. Nodes are also real places with distinctive characteristics, development histories and attributes that distinguish them from each other. Their emergence on the global arena is as likely to affect their urban development as it is their economic development. As both a repository of flows and a very real location, a tension can exist in the emerging node. In certain instances the flow aspect dominates, as argued for example in the Israeli high tech case (Chapter 6). In other instances, the concrete place function determines the character of the node, as in the case of activity grounded in physical movement of goods (Chapters 7,9) or the consumption of tourism or cultural amenities (Chapters10-12).

Fourth, a stress on nodes suggests multi-positioning in the global economy. If networks govern the interaction between places, then places can be global in one respect and local in another. The same location can engage in multiple roles, functioning as a global node in a given network but as a parochial center in other aspects of its economic development. It is this potential dualism that gives nodes their particular identity despite the global forces fashioning (and homogenizing) them. Given the process-led focus of our investigation, we treat Frankfurt and Tel Aviv as the prism through which these developments can be viewed. For this reason we are less interested in accurately delimiting the spatial boundaries of the nodes. In general we adopt the metropolitan region or city-region definition as the spatial unit of analysis (Scott, 2001). Our focus on process rather than particular city development per se, also highlights the direction of causality in the relationship between globalization and node emergence. On the one hand, we recognize the primordial relationship in which global forces cause the emergence of nodes and view nodes as a reflection of these forces. On the other hand, cognizant of nodes as concrete locations, we acknowledge that they can also play an active role in shaping future rounds of globalization.

1.2 FRANKFURT AND TEL AVIV AS EMERGING NODES

In terms of static indicators of centrality, Frankfurt and Tel Aviv share some common features within their national economies. The Frankfurt metropolitan region (the city of Frankfurt and the Rhein-Main area) houses 4.7 million people and over 1.7 million employees. The city itself has 650,000 inhabitants and 450,000 workers and serves as the center of a grid-like network of urban sub-centers. These span an area of 5,000 sq. km. stretching from Giessen in the north to Darmstadt in the south and from Mainz in the west to Hanau in the east. This area accounts for about 3 percent of Germany's total land cover and contains roughly 6 percent of both national population and employment. The Frankfurt region, including the cities of Frankfurt, Offenbach and Darmstadt, accounts for over 7 percent of Germany's GDP (Eurostat 1999). While Frankfurt has successfully repositioned itself as a central node both at the national and European scale (Chapter 2), its centrality as a business and commercial center is increasingly challenged by other German cities, primarily Hamburg and Munich and potentially, Berlin (Beaverstock, Hoyler, Pain and Taylor, 2001)

Compared to Frankfurt, the Tel Aviv metropolitan enjoys an even more primate position within the Israeli economy. Metropolitan Tel Aviv spans an area of over 1,500 sq. km. and administratively comprises the Tel Aviv district, the Central district and the smaller Ashdod area. Again, this area is a poly-nucleated urban network with Tel Aviv at its center and surrounded by a string of medium sized cities from Netanya in the North to Ashdod in the South and Kfar Saba and Modiin in the east. The over-riding dominance of the Tel Aviv metropolitan region is reflected in its share of the national economy. Comprising less than 7 percent of the land coverage, it nevertheless houses 43 percent of population and 54 percent of the labor force (CBS, 2001). While regional GDP figures are not available, estimates of Tel Aviv and Central district GDP for 2000, based on imputing from long-term extrapolations (Mazor and Sverdlov, 1997), suggest that the two areas together account for close to half of national GDP.

On the basis of size and global profile, Frankfurt and Tel Aviv would seem to have very little in common. Frankfurt features prominently on global lists of 'places rated' and is grounded in a vast hinterland market. Tel Aviv on the other hand, has been described as located at the 'deadend of the global economy' (Kipnis, 2001) and its global presence is based on penetrating global networks in order to compensate for a miniscule local market. A definitive inventory of global cities lists Frankfurt as a second level location (behind London, Paris, Tokyo and New York) and on a par with the likes of Chicago, Hong Kong Los Angeles Milan and Singapore (Beaverstock, Smith and Taylor, 1999). In contrast, Tel Aviv is six rungs below on the global cities ladder on equal footing with places such as Athens, Dublin, Helsinki New Delhi Philadelphia and Vienna. However, in view of the process orientation of this volume, highlighting the differences in static attributes across the two locations, would seem to miss the point. We are more interested in how places generate a selective global presence and hook into worldwide networks. As such, this book consciously presents examples of nodes at different stages in their emergence.

A consequence of this approach is that our interest in Frankfurt and Tel Aviv relates less to their present or future ranking on the global cities roster and more to the process in which they develop 'global' profiles. Despite the spate of recent interest in 'global' cities (Beaverstock, 2002; Marcuse and van Kempen, 2000; Moulaert, 2000; Sassen, 2002; Short and Kim, 1999), the approach of this volume is not to focus on the two cities per se, but to use them as a filter for observing how conditions of globalization cause metropolitan change. Intra-urban change and micro-geography are important as consequences of the workings of global networks.

We characterize Frankfurt and Tel Aviv as 'emerging' nodes. This is in keeping with our stress on defining nodes via their flow characteristics. It conveys the idea that the ascendancy of a node within a network is both dynamic and temporal. Flows of information, capital and investment are inherently volatile. An important node location can easily be by-passed in a network structure and the flows re-routed. In addition nodes can adopt multi-functions exhibiting global profiles in some economic activities and particularly local growth trajectories, in others. Both Frankfurt and Tel Aviv aptly illustrate this dualism. In contrast, truly global places, such as New York and Tokyo exhibit global profiles across a whole range of activities. Emerging node status is thus a stage rather than a permanent state. Recent interest in 'mid-range' global cities such as Shanghai, Sao Paulo and Hong Kong (see Sassen, 2002) or 'second tier cities' such as Taejon or Seattle (Markusen et. al., 1999) generally relates to the function of a place within a fixed urban hierarchy. The approach posited here, suggests alternatively, that places operate simultaneously in a variety of organizational structures, many of them loose, horizontal and in a state of constant flux.

Finally, given the foregoing, the case for labeling Frankfurt and Tel Aviv as 'nodes' should now be apparent. Despite the obvious differences in urban scale and level of development, both places exhibit the attributes necessary to qualify for node status. Both are driven by leading sectors that area heavily flow-based. In both instances, the temporality and volatility of their present leading economic functions are evident (Keil and Ronneberger, 2000; Schamp, 2001, 2002; Kipnis, 2002). Furthermore, the present status of both Frankfurt and Tel Aviv has been fashioned by both flow attributes and concrete place-based attributes and unique historical and institutional conditions. In the case of Frankfurt, the vast strides towards European integration have served to bolster the city's position as a global financial node. In the case of Tel Aviv, the development of military industries and the close synergies between army and civilian industry within the city, have helped consolidate its high tech node status. Finally, both places exhibit the attribute of multi-positioning, exhibiting both global and parochial features.

1.3 THE ORGANIZATION OF THIS BOOK

The genesis of this book was in a three-year collaborative research program on 'Emerging Nodes in a Global System: Internationalization and Urban Development in the Tel Aviv and Rhine-Main (Frankfurt) Areas'. This was funded by the German Israeli Foundation for Scientific Research and Development (GIF) and brought together research teams from the Department of Economic Geography, University of Frankfurt and the Department of Geography, Hebrew University of Jerusalem. The result was a unique opportunity to explore a key issue in globalization utilizing diverse methodological approaches and research styles. All the findings reported below represent original work conducted within the framework of this project.

The volume is organized around a series of leading themes associated with globalization and all impacting on the development of emerging nodes. At the outset, Section I examines the metropolitan structure of the emerging node and the relationship between urban development and economic development. Inevitably, this involves some form of economic restructuring that leaves an imprint on the physical development of the metropolitan area. The drivers of the node economy are then analyzed in Section II. While this section stresses the processes operating, such as the entry of foreign direct investment and the development of international finance, the sectoral expression of these processes is also given due attention. Leading sectors are intimately associated with the emergence of a node economy and the process of globalization. With respect to Frankfurt, this is particularly evident in the banking and airport sectors. In the case of Tel Aviv, high tech has been the vanguard sector for entry into global networks. The tertiarization of the node economy forms the next major area for examination and is presented in Section III. Sassen (1991, 1994) has stressed the characterization of global cities through producer-driven services and especially advanced producer services (such as accounting, management consulting, advertising, and logistics activities). The role of these sectors as entry points to global networks, is illustrated in the case of Frankfurt and Tel Aviv.

Finally, echoing the arguments of the 'consumer city' thesis (Glaeser, Kolko and Saiz, 2001), we address the question of reciprocity between economic globalization and consumption-driven globalization in Section IV. This complementarity is illustrated by highlighting incipient globalization in the arts and cultural sector in Tel Aviv and amenity-led tourism in both Frankfurt and Tel Aviv. The later refers not just to the origin of visitors to both cities, but to globalization and homogenization processes occurring within the tourism sector such as the internationalization of hotel chains and of the convention and trade fair markets.

While the volume is inherently comparative in approach, no attempt has been made to produce 'mirror image' pieces for each of the case study cities. Rather than force the issues into an analogical straight-jacket, we have chosen those processes and the sectors in which they are manifest, in order to highlight complimentary and sometimes contradictory outcomes. In certain instances, this leads itself to natural comparisons, as in the case of global trends in the tourism sector in both Frankfurt and Tel Aviv (Chapters 10 and 11). In other instances, entry into global networks is so heavily identified with unique 'flagship' sectors such as banking in Frankfurt

(Chapter 5) and high tech in Tel Aviv (Chapter 6), so as to render any form of comparison futile. Sometimes, the issue at stake may be comparable (such as metropolitan restructuring) but its spatial scale in the two locations is very different (Chapters 2 and 3). Even when sectoral comparisons may ostensibly be evident, their expression in each of the two nodes can diverge dramatically. This is the case with respect to the delivery of market information. In Frankfurt this is expressed in the concrete existence of the node as a market place and logistics hub (Chapter 9). For Tel Aviv it is reflected in a flurry of merger and acquisition activity amongst the leading producer service firms eager to access global markets (Chapter 8). The very different historical circumstances, institutional contexts and market environments, as outlined above, therefore make for a rich, yet eclectic, collection of research issues. This is also reflected in the varied research styles employed, combining both qualitative and quantitative methods. The juxtaposition of two rather different emerging nodes is not for the purpose of deriving universal generalities with respect to node emergence. Rather, it serves to highlight the multiple routes that generate node formation and development and allows for the systematic examination of differences between the different pathways taken.

Finally, the production of a volume such as this involves no small measure of international co-ordination. Despite the availability of facilitating technologies that allow for problem-free file transfer between academic nodes, the human element is still decisive in ensuring the smooth management of material and its up-grading to camera-ready copy. To that end, we are indebted to many individuals who assisted along the way. Geremy Forman style-edited many of the manuscripts and Sara Höfler translated some of the German texts. Heike Bertram and Helmut Nuhn provided valuable input to Chapter 7, Daniel Freeman assisted with the input-output estimates that appear in Chapter 12 and Vivien Lo contributed some important suggestions for Chapter 13. Finally, Michal Stern efficiently handled all file conversions and formatting of the final manuscript and Tamar Sofer of the cartographic laboratory in the Department of Geography at Hebrew University conceived and executed the cover design.

REFERENCES

Beaverstock, J.V., Smith, R.G. & Taylor, P.J. (1999). A roster of world cities. *Cities, 16,* 445-458.

Beaverstock, J.V., Smith, R.G., Taylor, P.J., Walker, D.R.F. & Lorimer, H. (2000). Globalization and world cities: Some measurement methodologies. *Applied Geography, 20* , 43-46.

Beaverstock, J.V., Hoyler, M., Pain, K. & Taylor, P. (2001). *Comparing London and Frankfurt as world cities: A relational study of contemporary urban change.* London: Anglo-German Foundation for the Study of Industrial Society.

Beaverstock, J.V. (2002). *The global city.* UK: Arnold.

Cairncross, F. (1997). *The death of distance: How the communications revolution will change our lives.* MA: Harvard Business School.

Camagni, R.P. (1993). From city hierarchy to city network: Reflections about an emerging paradigm. In T.R. Lakshmanan & P. Nijkamp (Eds.), *Structure and change in the space economy* (68-87). Berlin: Springer-Verlag.

Camagni, R.P. & Salone, C. (1993). Network urban structures in Northern Italy: Elements for a theoretical framework. *Urban Studies, 30 (6),* 1053-1064.

Castells, M. (1989). *The informational city: Innovation technology, economic restructuring and the urban-regional process.* Oxford: Blackwell

Castells, M. (1996). *The rise of the networked society*. Oxford: Blackwell.

CBS (2001). *Statistical abstract of Israel, No. 52*. Jerusalem: Central Bureau of Statistics.

Cooke, P. (1988). Flexible integration, scope economies and strategic alliances: social and spatial mediations. *Society and Space, 6*, 281-300.

DeBresson, C. & Amesse, F. (1991). Networks of innovators: A review and introduction to the issues. *Research Policy, 20*, 363-380.

Glaeser, E.L., Kolko, J. & Saiz, A. (2001). Consumer city. *Journal of Economic Geography, 1*, 27-50.

Kilkenny, M. (2000). *Community networks for industrial recruiting*. Presented at conference on 'Entrepreneurship, ICT and Local Policy Initiatives: Comparative Analyses and Lessons', May 22-23, 2000, Amsterdam.

Kipnis, B.A. (2001). *Tel Aviv, Israel - A world city in evolution: Urban development at a deadend of the global economy*. GaWC Research Bulletin 57. Available: http://www.lboro.ac.uk/gawc/rb/rb57.html

Kipnis, B.A. (2002). *The impact of globalization on the boom and crisis of Israel's high-tech industry*. GaWC Research Bulletin 72. Available: http://www.lboro.ac.uk/gawc/rb/rb72.html

Krugman, P. (1991). Increasing returns and economic geography. *Journal of Political Economy, 99 (3)*, 483-499.

Marcuse, P. & van Kempen, R. (Eds.) (2000). *Globalizing cities: A new spatial order?* Oxford: Blackwell.

Markusen, A. (1999). Fuzzy concepts, scanty evidence, policy distance: The case for rigor and policy relevance in critical regional studies. *Regional Studies, 33 (9)*, 869-994.

Markusen, A.R., Lee, Y.S. & DiGiovanna (Eds.) (1999). *Second tier cities: Rapid growth beyond the metropolis*. Minneapolis, MN: University of Minnesota Press.

Mazor, A. & Sverdlov, E. (1997). *Israel 2020: Options, alternatives and evaluation*. Master Plan for Israel in the 21st Century, Haifa: Technion (Hebrew).

Moulaert, F. (2000). *Globalization and integrated area development in European cities*. Oxford: Oxford University Press.

Powell, W.W. (1990). Neither market nor hierarchy. In B. Straw & L.L. Cummings (Eds.), *Research in organizational behavior* (295-336). Greenwich, CT: JAI Press.

Keil, R. & Ronneberger, K. (2000). The globalization of Frankfurt am Maine: Core, periphery and social conflict. In P. Marcuse & R. van Kempen (Eds.) (2000), *Globalizing cities: A new spatial order?* (228-248). Blackwell, Oxford.

Sassen, S. (1991). *The Global City*. Princeton: Princeton University Press.

Sassen, S. (1994). *Cities in world economy*. London: Pine Forge Press.

Sassen, S. (Ed.) (2002*) Global networks, linked cities*. London: Routledge.

Schamp, E.W. (2001). Der Aufstieg von Frankfurt/Rhein-Main zur europäischen Metropolregion. *Geographica Helvetica 56 (3)*, 169-178.

Schamp, E.W. (2002). Globalization and the restructuring of a metropolitan knowledge system: The case of research and development in Frankfurt/Rhein-Main, Germany. In R. Hayter & R. Le Heron (Eds.), *Knowledge, industry and environment: Institutions and innovations in territorial perspective*. Avebury: Ashgate (forthcoming).

Scott, A.J. (Ed.) (2000). *Global city-regions: Trends, theory and policy*. Oxford, Oxford University Press.

Short, J.R. & Kim, Y.H. (1999). *Globalization and the city*. London: Longman

Taylor, P.J. (2001). Specification of the world city network. *Geographical Analysis, 33 (2)*, 181-194.

SECTION I:

METROPOLITAN STRUCTURE AND RESTRUCTURING

EIKE W. SCHAMP

2. FROM INDUSTRY TO SERVICES: THE CHANGING BASIS OF THE FRANKFURT/RHEIN-MAIN METROPOLITAN ECONOMY

2.1 URBAN ECONOMY AND THE DISSOLUTION OF THE CITY IN THE AGE OF GLOBALIZATION

Since the beginning of industrialization, the growth of most of Europe's larger cities has been linked to the growth of industry. Cities have partially evolved into the cores of larger economic areas that prospered with industrial growth. Due to the simultaneous transition to the 'second industrial divide' (Piore and Sabel, 1985) and to a society that produces more income and employment from services than from manufacturing, the economic base of cities has changed. De-industrialization and tertiarization of cities have therefore become quasi 'normal' processes of European city-reconstruction in recent decades, and new city trajectories have emerged, based in part on cities' historic (industrial) roots. Wherever economic actors rebind cities to the process of globalization or, as we will argue, the Europeanization of urban economic regions, the trajectory of these cities must be reinterpreted. This chapter will address the process of redefining the economic basis of the Frankfurt/Rhein-Main region in the age of globalization

The city, however, can no longer be regarded as a quasi-closed urban economic region, as its economic activity has increasingly come to extend outside its territorial borders. In particular, activities contributing to the globalization of the urban economy result in an increased demand for locations and space, which can no longer be fulfilled by smaller cities. Just as industries once left the city looking for wide-open spaces, physical infrastructure (like international airports), office complexes and huge logistics companies are also heading for the hinterland today. This is especially true of Frankfurt am Main. The city has less than 650,000 inhabitants, and, unlike other German cities, such as Berlin, Munich and Cologne, was unable to substantially expand its territory. Important elements of infrastructure that serve global economic actors are no longer located within the city's political and administrative territory. With Frankfurt's growing importance as a globalizing city, essential economic activities have moved into its hinterland, as well as into neighboring cities like Wiesbaden, Mainz and Darmstadt. While Frankfurt am Main is not the only city experiencing this process of "the dissolution of the city into its region" (Läpple, 1999), it is leading the way. Regarding the city's economic

D. Felsenstein et al. (eds.),
Emerging Nodes in the Global Economy: Frankfurt and Tel Aviv Compared, 11–34.

globalization, the term 'metropolitan region' appears to be decisively more appropriate than 'metropolitan city', for only when the surrounding Rhein/Main Region is taken into account does Frankfurt become a powerful metropolitan region with more than 4 million inhabitants.

Many studies assign great importance to this region as a 'second tier global city' (see, for example, Friedman, 1995; Keil and Ronneberger, 2000). The metropolitan region, however, is economically defined - not politically. Attempts to facilitate the political institutionalization of the Frankfurt/Rhein-Main Region have been made repeatedly and are being intensified today. Whether or not political institutionalization will serve to improve the metropolitan region's economic competitiveness remains an open question, and will not be addressed here (see Schamp, 2000).

In this chapter, the term 'Frankfurt/Rhein-Main metropolitan region' refers to a region that has been demarcated according to economic criteria for the purpose of analysis (Figure 2.1). The region possesses no political legitimization, most notably because the economic region straddles the borders of two neighboring federal states. This demarcation is partially legitimized by the fact that the regional Chambers of Commerce, which represent business interests in Germany, banded together under the name "Rhein-Main Forum" in the early 1990's.

This chapter will describe the reconstruction of this city-regional economy, and its evolution from an economy of national importance to one of international importance. Reconstruction is a long-term, path-dependent process that is influenced by powerful actors from both inside and outside the region. Two things result from this. Firstly, the historical growth of the region's economic structure plays a central role in the remodeling of its economic basis. The economic basis of cities and their surrounding regions often reflects an historically-based specialization that is no longer able to withstand the pressures of global competition. In this way, the Rhein-Main Region constituted one of Germany's most important industrial production regions for quite some time. This chapter will examine the influence of the retreat of industrial production on the metropolitan region's future role. Considerable differentiation, however, emerges among the individual industrial clusters, and, with the arrival of new services in the region, new areas of specialization also emerge, redefining the role of Frankfurt/Rhein-Main within the European city-system. In other words, the new role of the region would be insufficiently defined if limited to a financial center alone (see Chapter 5).

Secondly, newly emerging actors in the region, as well as the strategies of already established actors that must always be regarded as responses to current changes in the world, have a definite impact on the path of development. Foreign companies, particularly in the industrial sector, have been active in the Frankfurt/Rhein-Main region for quite some time, without causing massive changes in the role of the city and its region in the national and European contexts. These companies changed their strategies, and new companies with innovative strategies entered the scene, due purely to the circumstances of the 1980's and 1990's. These circumstances were related to increasing Europeanization within the context of creating one integrated European economic region. In reaction to this change in context, companies took steps that were partially anticipatory. The single European market discussed in the 1980's and implemented in the 1990's totally changed the institutional arena of business for many companies.

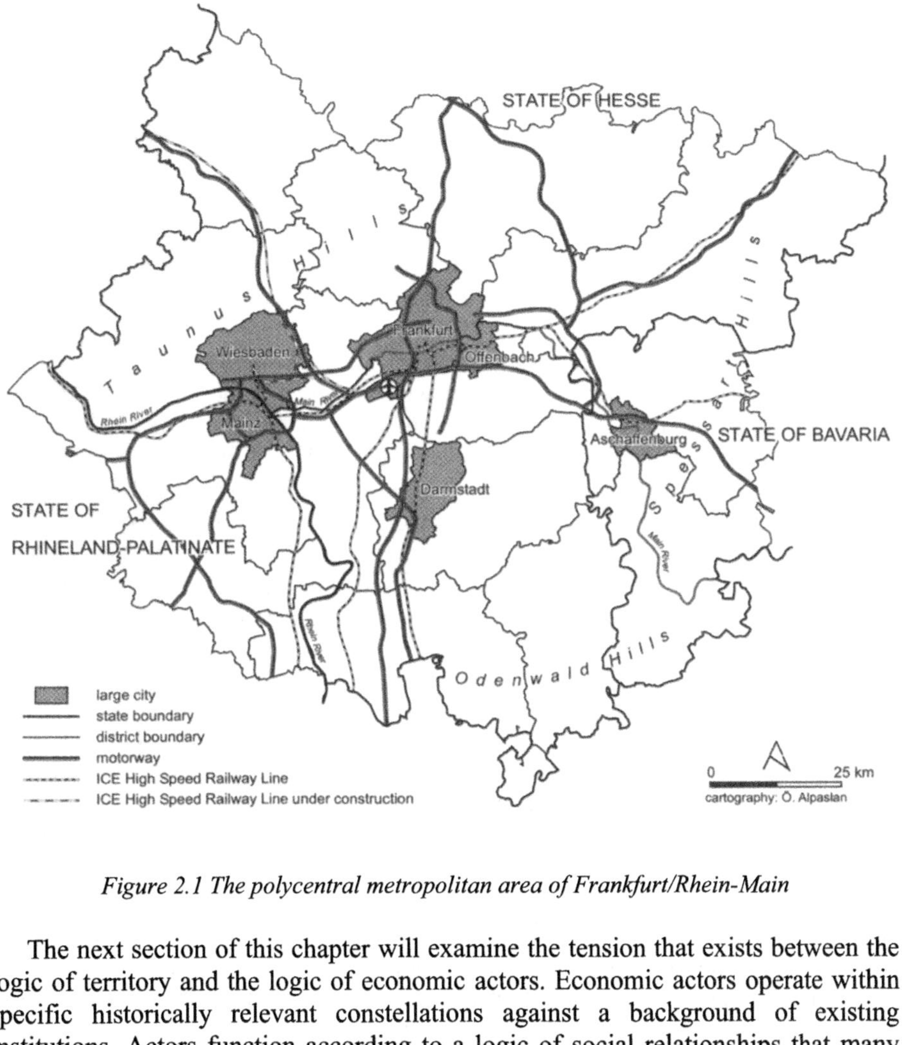

Figure 2.1 The polycentral metropolitan area of Frankfurt/Rhein-Main

The next section of this chapter will examine the tension that exists between the logic of territory and the logic of economic actors. Economic actors operate within specific historically relevant constellations against a background of existing institutions. Actors function according to a logic of social relationships that many researchers define as a network. While some institutions may be understood as being territorially bound - especially if they have been codified for a certain territory, networks are generally characterized by ranges that cross territorial borders. This is especially true of internationalized companies, as well as foreign companies investing in the region. One of the theses of this chapter is that the process of redefining regional structures has been considerably accelerated by the actions of globally operating actors. This has resulted in social and political tensions within the city-region that have yet to be resolved (Keil and Ronneberger, 2000).

Even though the city's economy is generally characterized by heterogeneity and diversity, a degree of specialization is still visible. Porter's concept of geographic clusters of companies that share one value chain is useful for analyzing the restructuring of the economic basis of the Frankfurt/Rhein-Main region (Porter, 1990, 1996). This concept also facilitates additional possibilities for argumentation. Firstly, it is based on competition, a mechanism of economic coordination strengthened by changes in institutional frameworks, like the initiation of a single European single market. This concept also asserts that the specialization of one territory's economic base increases the competitiveness of the companies involved. In turn, their success contributes to the prosperity of the region as a whole. In contrast to specialized industrial districts, however, a plurality of diverse clusters is to be expected in a metropolitan region, in both secondary and tertiary sectors, as well as in old and new sectors. A major problem involved with reconstructing a metropolitan region's economic basis is that 'old' specialization patterns may be superceded by 'new' ones.

Porter's concept of clusters has seen much utilization and much criticism. For regional analysis, it offers a heuristic framework for in-depth description of changes taking place in regional business structures. In addition, integration of the dimensions of power and regional coherence can enhance this framework. Some actors, especially larger companies operating in the region, wield enormous power in their value chains and have great influence on the cluster's formation. In this way, they contribute to the unique nature of the regional cluster's internal coherence, which, in turn, impacts important areas of local politics, like the regional labor market, the regional supply market and regional tax yield. Altogether, these fields determine what may be referred to as the socioeconomic endurance of the region.

Porter's concept of the value chain implies both dynamism and competition. Competition also exists between different clusters within a metropolitan region - for example, to gain access to regionally available resources. The dynamic of clusters impacts upon the metropolitan region's path of long term economic development. This conception of a dynamic of old and new clusters should, heuristically, be used for the analysis of the retreat of manufacturing from the Frankfurt/Rhein-Main region. This retreat may be regarded as the result of a complex process involving the intersection of three dimensions. The first dimension encompasses basic changes made to industrial organization. These have taken place over the past few decades in industrialized countries in terms of the restructuring of Fordist structures into the as of yet undefined structures of the future (Keil and Ronneberger, 2000). The second dimension is the region's new role as an 'emerging node' in the world system. These first two dimensions, in turn, result in a third dimension: the redefinition of the region's internal spatial structures, and the 'dissolution' of the city. This process leads to social tensions that may also have an impact on the role of the region as a node in the world system. The latter aspect, however, falls outside of the scope of this chapter, and will therefore not be further examined here (Keil and Ronneberger, 2000).

The remainder of the chapter will address various aspects of the subject at hand. The second section will look at the restructuring of the region's economic base that has taken place over the past 25 years, and, to this end, will make use of employment statistics. The third section will attempt to provide a quantitative assessment of the future impact of foreign capital flow into the region, as well as the impact of regional investment in foreign countries, on globalization in the region. We will only, however, be able to consider macroeconomic data, and this will reveal the 'old' specialization pattern of the Frankfurt/Rhein-Main region and its contradictory restructuring.

In order to discuss the role of specific actors in the transformation of the region's economic basis, an in depth examination of individual clusters is necessary. We argue that actors in Fordist industries, operating according to extremely diverse restructuring strategies, continue to constitute the primary factors influencing the restructuring of the Frankfurt/Rhein-Main region into a node within the world system. The chapter's fourth section will focus on the restructuring of two of the region's traditionally Fordist industrial clusters. Detailed examination of both clusters will reveal a fundamental difference between the chemical industry, which was regarded as the 'core industrial competency' of the region, and the region's automobile industry, including its suppliers. The fifth section will discuss attempts to create a 'new' specialization pattern to enable the region to gain importance in the world economy. While political actors strive to encourage a new industrial manufacturing cluster based on the 'old' competencies of the industrial economy (like biotechnology, for instance), an additional large cluster of marketing and market-related activities is also evolving. It should be noted that these activities are transforming the Frankfurt/Rhein-Main region into a central hub within the logistical systems of central Europe (see Chapter 9). Finally, the sixth and concluding section will offer some thoughts on the region's new economic basis - services. In terms of total numbers of jobs, the financial sector accounts for only a small portion of this sector.

2.2 THE TRANSFORMATION OF THE REGION'S ECONOMIC BASIS: 1975-1998

The Frankfurt/Rhein Main region was, and continues to be, one of Germany's most important manufacturing regions. The region employs more than 1.7 million people, and its unemployment rate has been far lower than the German average for over two decades. This was particularly true after the unification of Germany, when the region became an important destination for people immigrating westward.

For more than 25 years, industrial employment within German cities has been experiencing serious decline. This process had an especially swift impact on the Frankfurt/Rhein-Main region during the 1990's (see Figure 2.2). While the inner city of Frankfurt employed approximately 135,000 people, or 29.5 percent of the workforce, in industry in 1975, this number sank to approximately 79,000 people, or 17 percent of the workforce, by 1998. Despite this decline throughout the region as a whole, industrial employment still accounted for 470,000 jobs, or 27 percent. This reflects the fact that the general de-industrialization process impacting the region, along with the rest of the nation, was accompanied by a process of relocation to outside of the region's center.

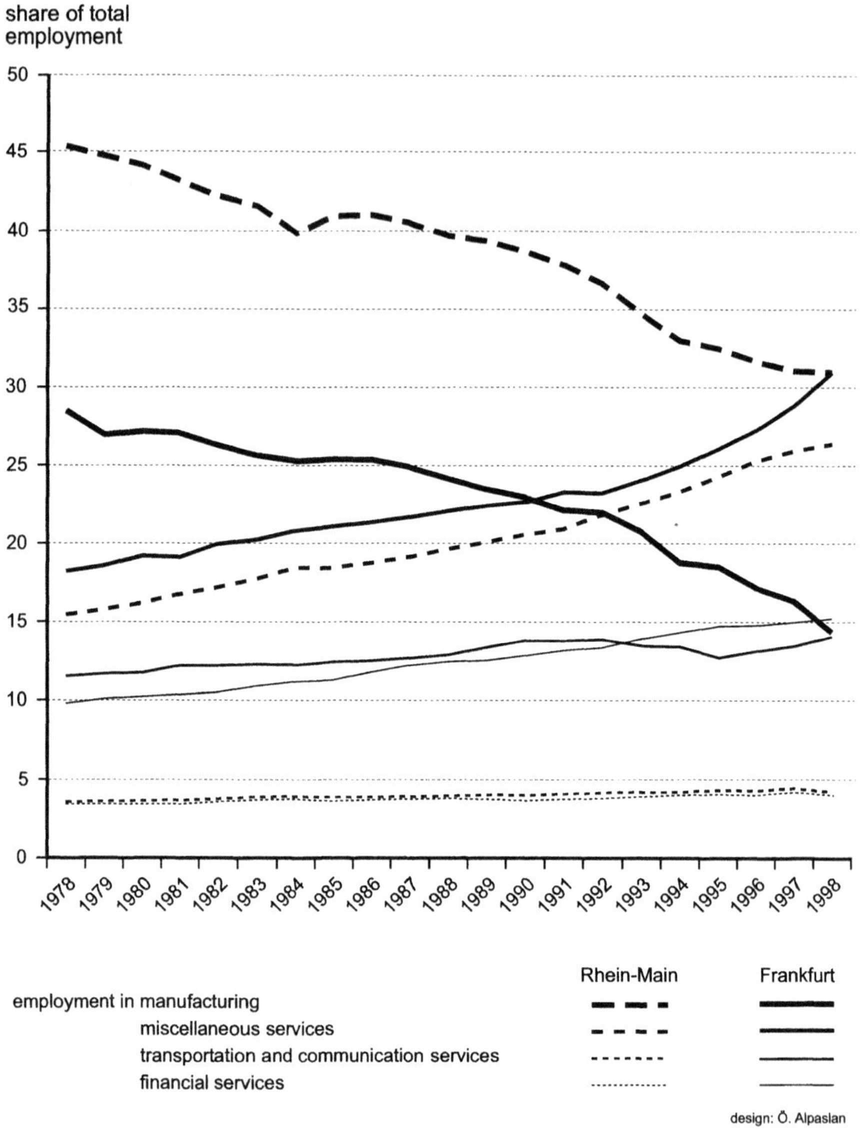

Figure 2.2 Employment development in selected sectors of the City of Frankfurt and the Rhein Main Region, 1975-1998

This process is not new, and has served to strengthen the expansion of industry in the region since its beginnings. Even today, territorial structures of the 19th century continue to determine the geographic distribution of the region's industrial production. While the city resisted industrialization during the last part of the 19th century, due to its traditional role as a trade and banking center, outlying areas welcomed the evolution of a differentiated and spatially specialized industry (Dünzl, 1995). Such an attitude was not uncommon for city dwellers at that time, and the towns and hamlets surrounding many German cities were the site of early industrialization. The same went for other cities of the modern metropolitan region such as Wiesbaden, which also situated its chemical production, mechanical engineering and construction in the city's surrounding area. The territorial changes that occurred within large cities during the 20th century due to new municipal restructuring brought many of these older industries back into the city. Still, they later relocated further out. A new wave of industrial suburbanization began as early as the 1950's, and is still in effect today (Freund, 1995). The city of Frankfurt became a metaphor for the new German economic wonder (Keil and Lieser, 1992) and, at the same time, a spearhead of structural change in Germany.

The breathtaking decline in industrial employment in cities, to about half of what it had been in 1975, undoubtedly caused a major change in employment structure. This phenomenon was also accompanied by a general shift in jobs out of the city center and into the more peripheral areas of the metropolitan region (Figure 2.3). In the city centers of Frankfurt and Offenbach, total employment experienced an absolute decline over the past 25 years, while the number of jobs in the entire region - after the 'unification boom' of the early 1990's - increased 12 percent, from approximately 1.5 million to 1.7 million. In this case, the 'dissolution of the city' can clearly be discerned. In fact, this process has not only effected the city of Frankfurt, but all large cities in the region. The cities' neighboring communities have gained new jobs, primarily in the service sector, and more remote communities have seen an increase in job numbers within the industrial sector. In light of these spatial changes, the traditional geographical concept of a city's center and periphery is now of only limited use. The metropolitan region has become a heterogeneous space with important dimensions of globalization settling in, especially along its borders (Keil and Ronneberger, 1994).

Frankfurt and the surrounding region retained its primary industrialization drive from the late 19th century until the beginning of the 20th century. The chemical industry led the way, followed by electrical engineering, mechanical engineering and the auto industry. These sectors together form the industrial profile of the region. The main industrial clusters in the Rhein-Main region today are therefore the heirs of the third Kondratieff cycle and, at the same time, an expression of the era of Fordist organization. What is true for Germany as a whole is also true for the Frankfurt/Rhein-Main region in particular: its production structure has been less determined by high technology sectors than by sectors representing a mature middle technology (Naschold *et al.*, 1998). The region's export strength, similar to that of the rest of the Federal Republic, lies in mechanical engineering, electrical technology, vehicle construction and the chemical industry. All of these sectors have experienced crises in recent decades and are therefore presently undergoing major restructuring.

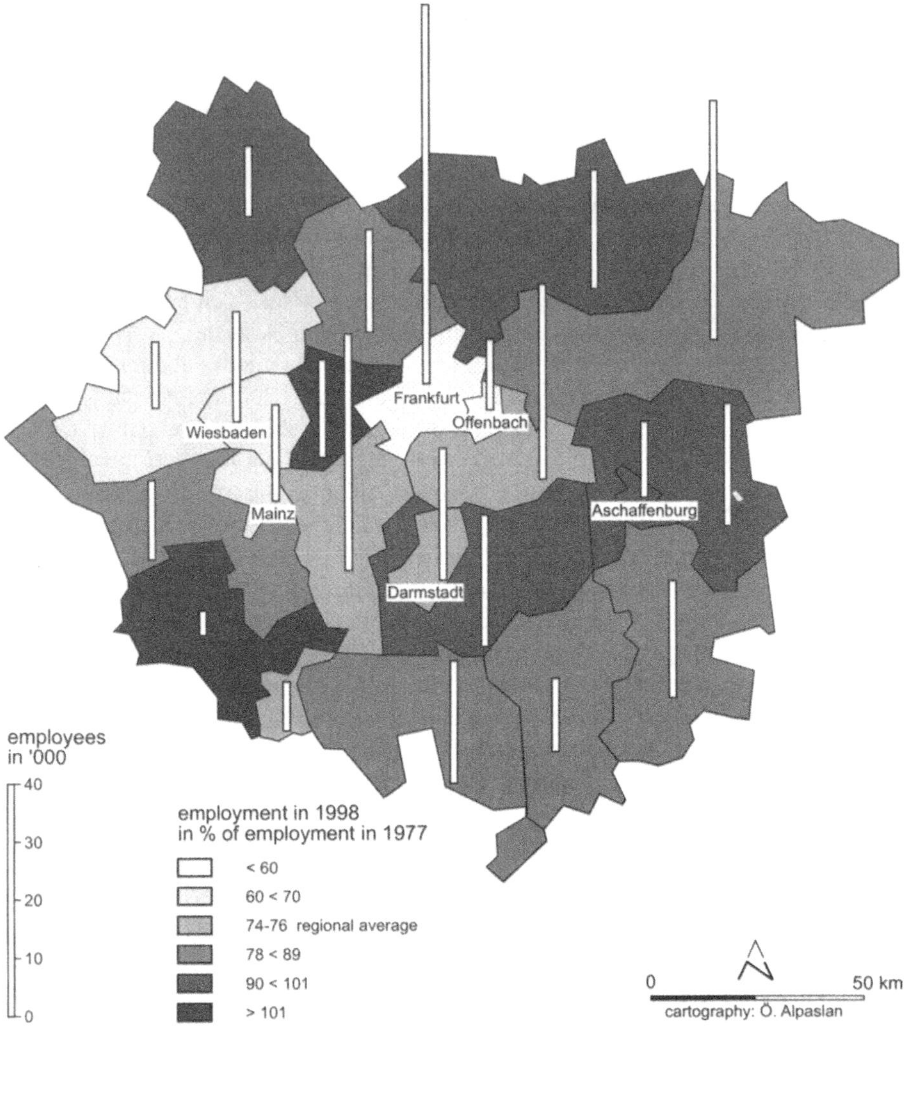

Figure 2.3 The spatial shift of industrial employment in the metropolitan region, 1977 - 1998

On the other hand, employment in the service sector, particularly in 'miscellaneous services', including business oriented services, has increased dramatically. This sector is on the rise throughout Germany, and service-related employment growth in the city of Frankfurt has compensated for the decrease in industrial manufacturing employment. This has not been true only in Frankfurt, however. In the district of Offenbach, 'miscellaneous services' employment increased by 13,600 jobs between 1975 and 1998, from a total of 8,400, while employment in industry decreased by 10,600 during the same period. 'Miscellaneous services' constitutes a fundamental sector of the region's economy, with 490,000 jobs (28% of the total) (UVF, 2000).

The macro-data presented here provides only superficial representation of regional development. The sectoral nature of statistics can capture neither the economic clusters of Porter nor internal company job shifts from manufacturing to services. The shift from implementation activities to coordination and control, which has characterized the globalization of cities, cannot be measured with these statistics, and neither can the effects of foreign capital on the economic basis of the region. Before analyzing the restructuring of individual economic clusters, we briefly turn our attention to the importance of foreign companies in the region, as well as the foreign investments of German companies.

2.3 THE DEVELOPMENT OF CROSS-INVESTMENT WITH FOREIGN COUNTRIES IN THE METROPOLITAN REGION

Foreign companies started to play a role in the economic development of the region long before globalizing cities became an issue of discussion. For example, Adam Opel AG was acquired by General Motors (GM) in 1929, and proceeded to develop into one of the most important German, European and even international auto manufacturers. Even today, the assembly center at Rüsselsheim constitutes the largest industrial business in the state of Hessen. On the other hand, local businesses also evolved into global players by investing in foreign companies at an early stage, and this was especially true for the chemical industry. World wars, however, consistently stripped this industry of its foreign locations, and for this reason the history of foreign investment in Germany only really begins after the Second World War. The amount of capital networking from the metropolitan region to foreign countries is difficult to assess. The Federal Bank provides sectoral statistics on incoming and outgoing foreign direct investment (FDI), but only on the level of federal states. In addition, the Federal Bank has often changed its parameters for measuring FDI. For example, the mandatory investment registration threshold was lowered from 25 percent of a company's shares to 20 percent in 1990, and again to 10 percent in 1999. Such data can only be used in order to estimate development in a specific region. For the relatively small federal state of Hessen, such use may be justified, as three fourths of Hessen's economic strength derives from the Rhein-Main region. Furthermore, the Rhein-Main region is the most important target, in relative worth, of foreign investment in Germany, with the highest ratio of direct investment per employee throughout Germany as a whole. In addition, the number of people employed in the region by foreign companies is the highest in Hessen.

While German investment in foreign countries has exceeded foreign investment in Germany since 1980, foreign investment in the state of Hessen has grown at the same rate as foreign investment by Hessen-based companies abroad. The Frankfurt/Rhein-Main metropolitan region has remained attractive for new foreign investment longer than Germany did itself, in contrast to complaints regarding the decreasing attractiveness of 'Standort Deutschland' (for example, see Gaebe, 1994).

Foreign investment began to stagnate only in the 1990's, while regional investment in foreign countries continued to rise (Figure 2.4).

From a sectoral perspective, development corresponds to a region's specialization and therefore differs greatly from average German direct investments (Dicken, 1998). The chemical industry leads cross-investment with foreign countries. For decades, more investment left the state of Hessen destined for foreign countries than vice-versa, and the rate of growth continued to increase during the 1990's. Substantial growth of foreign investment in Hessen began in the 1990's. Cross-investment with foreign countries is relatively low in most industrial sectors, the only exception being the auto industry. No spectacular structural changes have taken place however. While outgoing FDI from Germany in the automobile sector exceeds incoming FDI by 10 to 1, the Frankfurt/Rhein-Main boasts a ratio that is completely the opposite - 0.6 to 1 (Table 2.1). Does this over-abundance of outgoing direct investment in contrast to incoming direct investment undermine the role of the region as a coordination and control center (as the unions feared), or does it strengthen it? Foreign companies made considerable new investment in the chemical and auto industry in the early 1990's. Was this a reflection of the 'unification boom' and expectations of a larger market in Germany, or merely the result of a shift in statistical investigation procedures? In services, two sectors stand out: the finance industry and retail trade. Although foreign investment in retail trade has been entering Hessen for quite a while - increasing since the early 1990's, the relationship between incoming and outgoing investment in the financial sector had evened out at a low level by the end of the 1980's. Since the beginning of the 1990's, outgoing direct investment has increased especially rapidly, and this means that German financial companies have internationalized more quickly than international financial companies seeking to come to Frankfurt (Figure 2.4).

Table 2.1 FDI in the primary economic sectors of the state of Hessen, 1998

	FDI abroad (a)		*FDI from abroad (b)*		*proportion*
	in billion DM	*%*	*in billion DM*	*%*	*a / b*
All Sectors	109.3	100.0	79.2	100.0	1.4: 1
Chemical Industry	18.7	17.1	12.3	15.5	1.5: 1
Auto Industry	1.5	1.4	2.6	3.3	0.6: 1
Retail Trade	1.3	1.1	10.4	13.1	0.1: 1
Financial Services	47.4	43.5	17.1	21.6	2.8: 1

Source: Landeszentralbank in Hessen 2000: Vierteljahreszahlen - 2. Quartal 2000, 11/12.

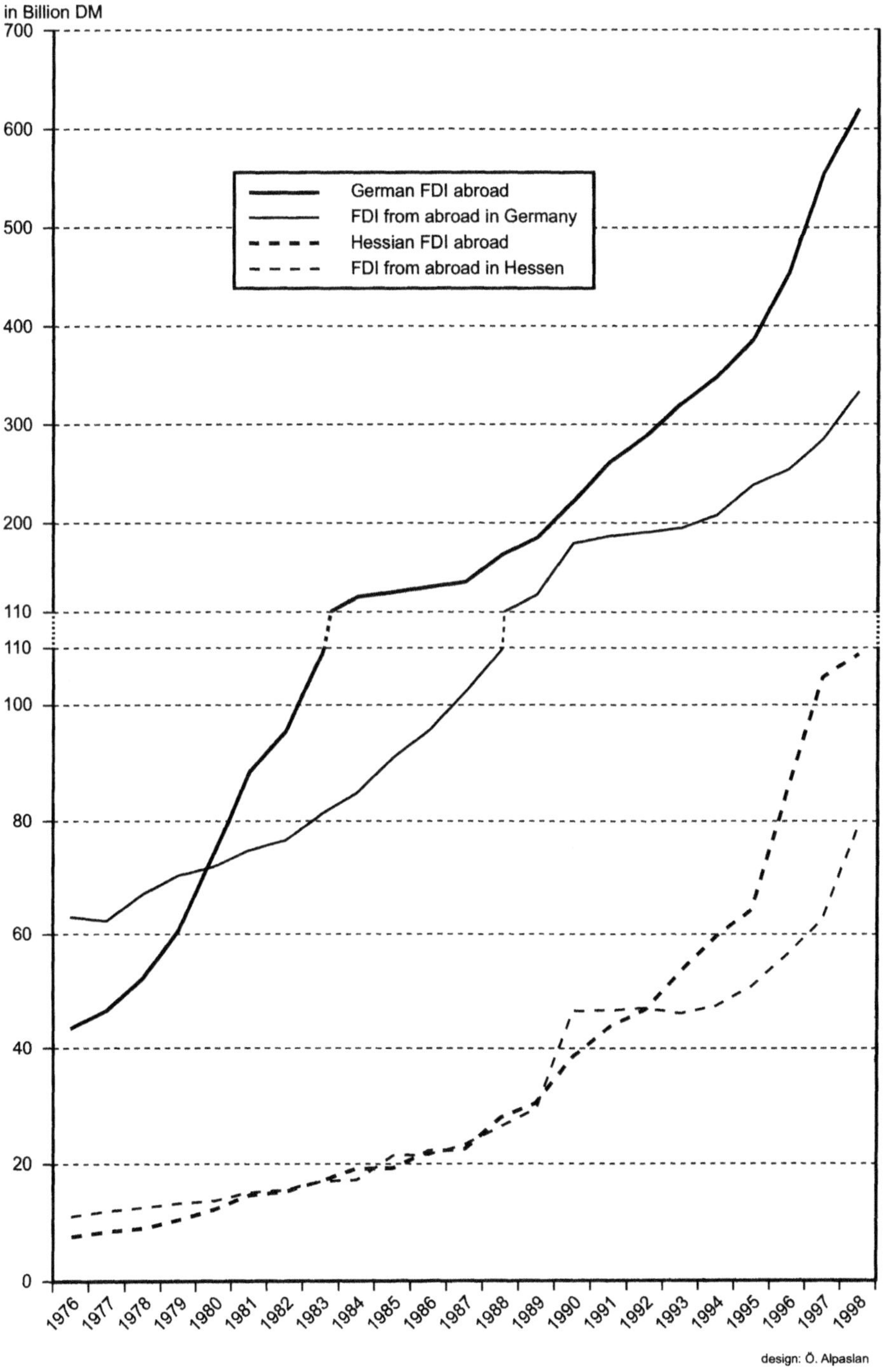

Figure 2.4 The growth of cross-investment with foreign countries - a comparison of Hessen and Germany

American companies in particular have dominated incoming direct investment in Hessen for several decades. It was not until the mid-1990's that Hessian direct investment in the United States exceeded American investment in the state of Hessen. It should be noted, however, that the weight of capital exchange has also been in favor of European Union (EU) countries since the beginning of the 1990's. German FDI in other EU countries has experienced a marked increase, and the investment of EU countries in the state of Hessen has grown as well, matching the total volume of American FDI. Even if it is not yet of great importance in absolute numbers, German direct investment in the transition states has seen exponential growth since the early 1990's (Figure 2.5).

FDI statistics reflect the new role assumed by Hessen and the Frankfurt/Rhein-Main region since 1990 as a node of cross-investment in Europe. It also appears that the region functions more as a source of foreign direct investment than as a destination region. One explanation for this unequal investment flow lies in structural changes that have occurred within the region. While in manufacturing (in the chemical industry, for example), production activities require high investment, activities of control and coordination generally require less investment per job or turnover unit. When German industries transfer production to foreign countries and foreign companies simultaneously enter the region with service operations, an absolute inequality in investment flow is to be expected. In this way, the contribution of foreign companies to the region's transformation in a European, if not global, system cannot be sufficiently represented through such statistics.

Additional attempts to represent a complete picture of multinational companies and their strategies in the region have tended to fail, due to a lack of extensive information. Still, an understanding of this full picture is necessary for a thorough understanding of the globalization of the metropolitan region. We therefore present below the strategies of some of the most important actors in various clusters. Quantitative assessment of FDI alone, however, indicates that foreign companies do indeed have a considerable influence on the region's structure and global network.

2.4 THE RESTRUCTURING OF FORDIST PRODUCTION SYSTEMS

Even though the city of Frankfurt itself has experienced a radical de-industrialization in recent decades, the region as a whole remains an important German industrial production region. Frankfurt's relationship with European, as well as global production and consumption systems is determined primarily by two factors. Firstly, dominant industrial clusters differ according to their restructuring trajectory. This has various effects on the region's importance in an international context. Secondly, dominant industrial clusters differ according to their function within the regional headquarters economy. Thus, while the chemical industry is of primarily national origin and has internationalized from Frankfurt in the past, auto industry companies and their suppliers have been in the hands of foreign companies for quite a while. Each has been dominated by one focal company - one German and the other American. Each of their strategies has influenced the Frankfurt/Rhein-Main region's restructuring as an international node in different ways.

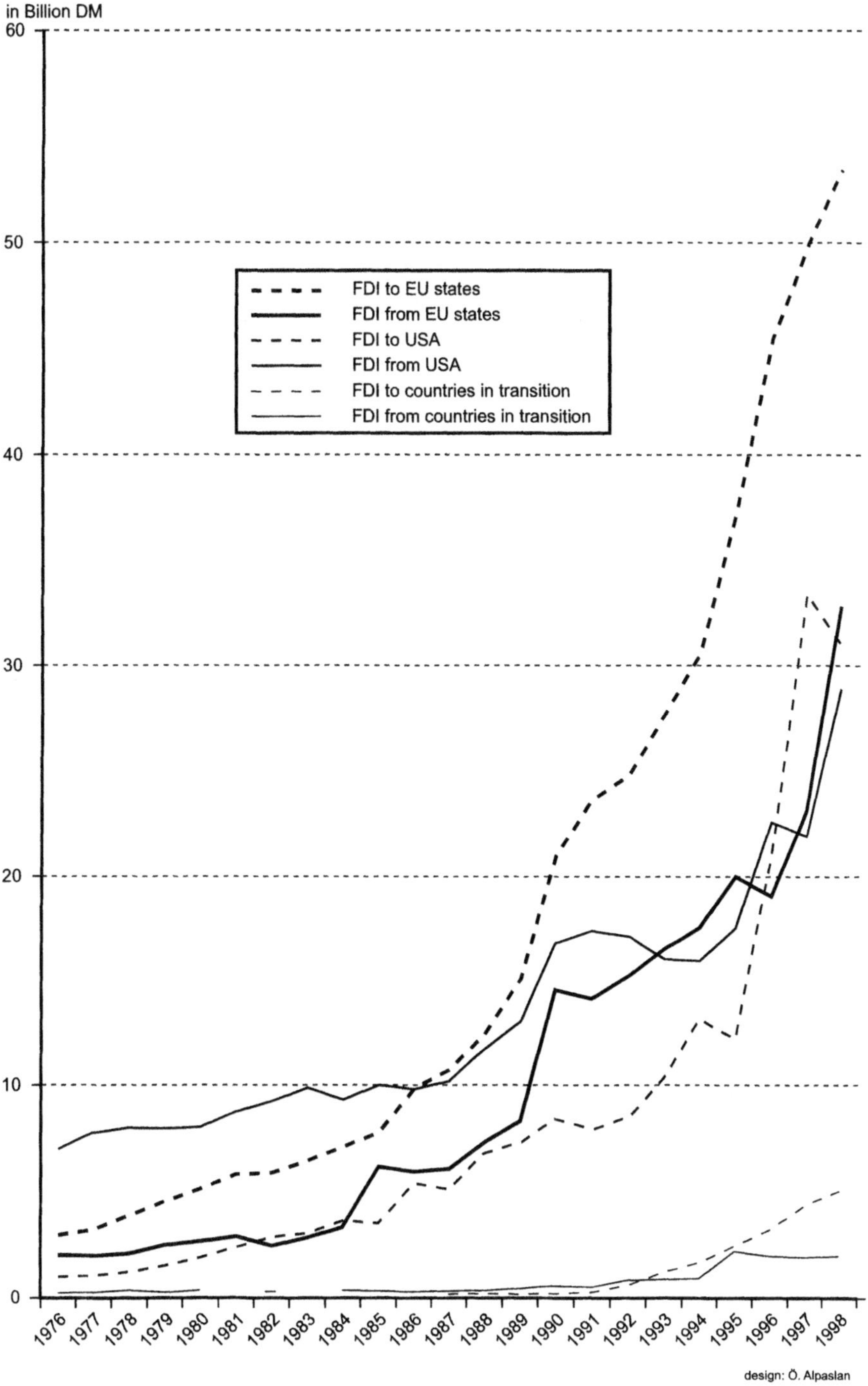

Figure 2.5 FDI in Hessen according to destination and source, 1976 - 1998

Clusters that were directed by national companies alone experienced crises at an earlier stage and were in danger of going under. Such clusters, including mechanical engineering, electrical engineering and construction, were often dominated by mid-size companies. Due to this dynamic, only the restructuring of the industrial clusters of the chemical and auto industries will be presented here.

2.4.1 The Migration of the Chemical Industry

Germany's export base still lies in the chemical industry, and the Frankfurt/Rhein-Main region remains one of the four most important chemical production regions in Germany, after Rheinland, Rhein-Neckar and Hamburg (Bathelt, 1997). Hoechst, Bayer and BASF are the leading companies of the first three regions, which together compose the most important global players in the chemical industry (Bathelt, 1995). Nevertheless, at the beginning of the 1990's, the Frankfurt/Rhein-Main region's chemical industry accounted for 19 percent of industrial employment, and was the largest industrial sector in the region. At the same time, the chemical sector is extremely research intensive: while the sector had an average of 8.7 percent of its employees in R&D, the Frankfurt/Rhein-Main region averaged 13.1 percent. The Hoechst company was especially responsible for this, employing a full 36 percent of the 13,000 R&D employees of the region's chemical industry. With approximately 37,000 employees, Hoechst was the largest industrial employer in the region (Specht, 1999) and made up the 'core' of its chemical industry. At the same time, the chemical industry of the Frankfurt/ Rhein-Main region was intensely differentiated and only loosely connected, with concentrations of paint and dye companies, as well as companies from the pharmaceutical and cosmetics sector (Bathelt, 1997). Despite their size and global operations, many of these companies still belong to the German 'Mittelstand'.

Chemical companies were the first in Germany to internationalize and were led by Hoechst, amongst others. As long as company structures were centralized and hierarchical, the region was strengthened both in terms of world headquarters and research and production centers. In contrast, foreign chemical companies played only a minor role in the region. Bathelt (1997) has shown that the restructuring of Fordist organization structures in the chemical industry took place very slowly, becoming clearly visible only with the shift from mass production to specialized products (Becker and Schumm, 2001). The crisis facing the chemical industry's traditional integrated system of production in the 1980s was solved by Hoechst, which by that point was already less integrated than other German chemical companies, with a further reduction of integration. Earlier than its competitors, the company transferred some production operations to other parts of the world (Ronneberger, 1995) and reoriented other operations, particularly R&D, towards the United States (Bathelt, 1995; Becker and Schumm, 2001; Specht, 1999).

Recently, the company has dismantled its former organizational structure and re-established itself as a completely new company. Since changing CEO's in 1994, it has followed a course of capital market-oriented reorganization (Becker and Schumm, 2001). First, the company was transformed into a holding company in

1997. Then, at the end of the 1990's, its production unit was dismantled, and sold in part to competitors like the Swiss joint venture Clariant and in part on the stock exchange. The remainder was fused with Rhône Poulenc of France, as a new 'Life Sciences' company, and then transferred as a new company named Aventis to Strasbourg, France (Becker and Schumm, 2001). With this, fundamental decision making ability regarding production, investment, and R&D were removed from the Frankfurt/Rhein-Main region. The pharmaceutical-sector of Aventis, however, has remained in Frankfurt.

Hoechst's radical restructuring in the recent past has marked a clear turning point in the regional development of the chemical sector. Due to the sheer size of the company within the region, the move has contributed greatly to the region's de-industrialization. This has had significant impact on the region. For one, chemical industry employment in the city of Frankfurt has been dropping, with the number of employees decreasing from 40,000 to about half that number within 25 years. The company's original plant lost 25% of its jobs during the 1990's, and has been transformed into the "Hoechst Industrial Park", housing some of the holding companies as well as new and foreign companies. Research and development now belongs to Aventis (France); LII Europe has taken over the traditional production of chlorine, caustic soda and hydrochloric acid; Clariant (Switzerland) has taken over the production of fine chemicals; Celanese Chemicals (United States) has assumed the production of basic chemicals; and Grillo (Germany) produces inorganic sulfur chemicals (Schwarz, 2000). Approximately 40 companies currently operate in the industrial park, including a few young companies and a number of foreign companies. A Hoechst joint venture under the name "Infraserv" has emerged as the industrial park's service and management company.

In this way, a completely new organization of a traditional production location emerged. The strict locational dependence on a central R&D laboratory with primary production abilities is especially typical of German transnational companies (Specht, 1999). While Hoechst had previously set up a decentralized, internationally networked production and R&D organization, the company's reorganization into a holding company signified the end of the local production complex. The results of this process are clearly reflected in the realm of R&D. In 1970, Hoechst spent only 5 percent of internal R&D expenditures in foreign countries, while by 1995 the figure had climbed to 53 percent. During the same year, Frankfurt was still the largest R&D location. But, after a 30 percent reduction in employees, it employed only approximately one-fourth of all company R&D employees (Specht, 1999). New research competencies were set up in other locations, for example a genetic research center near Munich. As of the year 2000, Frankfurt no longer had a central research lab.

What consequences will this have on the Frankfurt/Rhein-Main region, aside from effects related to change in size? One answer is found in the assumption that large companies' Fordist organization hindered the emergence of a regionally networked 'island of competency' in which the company, research and vocational training units might have worked together (Schamp, 2002). Just as in production (Bathelt, 1997), virtually no regional cooperation existed among companies involved in the chemical industry (Specht, 1999). This means that foreign companies located in Frankfurt/Rhein-Main also find no evidence of a regional center of innovation, and it is no wonder that they only rarely undertake R&D in the region. In a study of 45 foreign companies involved in chemicals, Specht (1998) found that only seven maintained their own R&D centers locally. These centers had one goal in particular: local development for adjusting to national markets, particularly for the pharmaceutical sector. However, these companies have also recently started reducing their research facilities in the region as well. The Japanese companies Takeda and Otsuka, which are both active in pre-clinical and clinical research, have either moved their R&D establishments or closed them altogether. In 1992, the American company DuPont de Nemours invested DM 30 million in a new European research lab for composite materials at their German headquarters. In 1997, however, they closed it down and moved its components to other locations. Despite the fact that the German headquarters of the American conglomerate Procter & Gamble are located in Frankfurt/Rhein-Main, the company moved its R&D lab to Great Britain after acquiring a local cosmetics company. Some foreign chemical companies still have R&D facilities in the Frankfurt/Rhein-Main region, but they are not part of a technology oriented internationalization strategy. While R&D continues after the acquisition of companies, these takeovers are not aimed at acquiring know-how, rather at gaining access to German and European markets. When foreign firms do continue to undertake R&D in the region, the departments are small and often designed for market observation and product modification for the national market.

With the chemical industry's reduction of R&D capacities in Frankfurt/Rhein-Main, the selection mechanisms of R&D networks of global companies are becoming increasingly obvious. When a region loses its specific comparative advantage, it loses its ties to the industry's international R&D establishment and becomes replaceable. Different studies have revealed the region's weaknesses in the field of technology within the chemical industry (Biehler, 1992; Specht, 1999) in both local research and training infrastructures. These same reasons were behind the decision of Hoechst's board of directors to shift research to another location.

2.4.2 New Competencies in the Auto Industry

Automobile production is part of the core of the German economy and impacts its international competitiveness (Porter, 1990; Schamp, 1995; Naschold *et al.*, 1998). German auto production companies have been planning globally for quite some time, and were the first to restructure their Fordist production structures. Philosophies of restructuring spread, quickly in the global sense. They also, however, were adapted to suit the goals and conditions of individual companies. Some authors therefore refer to a 'hybridization' of modern production concepts. Decentralization strategies have caused a considerable spatial reorganization of auto production. This has strengthened some local centers of auto development and production, but has also simultaneously integrated them more closely into global networks. This, in turn, has resulted in the development of both internal company networks, among assembly plants on different continents, and external networks, emerging with suppliers in specific regions.

The auto industry cluster in the Frankfurt/Rhein-Main region is bound to these global tendencies, but also possesses its own historical development path. The foundation of the auto and auto supply industries' current importance in the region was established in the late 19th and early 20th centuries, with the production of bicycles and sewing machines. The industry was led by Adam Opel AG in Rüsselsheim, which in the 1920's grew to be the largest bicycle manufacturer in the world. At the beginning of WWI, the company began manufacturing automobiles as well. By the early 20th century, the American companies Ford and GM were looking for a way to enter European markets, which became increasingly closed after 1913. In 1929, GM took over the leading German auto manufacturer: Adam Opel AG. Opel was an early imitator of the American system of assembly line manufacturing and developed relatively early into a volume manufacturer (Lompe *et al.*, 1991).

Frankfurt/Rhein-Main became the leading auto producing region in Germany prior to the Second World War (Lompe *et al.*, 1991), and not only because of Opel . The regional industrial structure of the mechanical and electrical engineering sectors, along with the growth of the bicycle industry, resulted in the evolution of a diverse supply industry in the region, initiated primarily by local business. This, however, remains virtually impossible to prove in a quantitative manner. Firstly, the supply industry is extremely heterogeneous and has roots in many sectors. Secondly, the size and structure of the supply industry has experienced major changes over the decades, due to changes in both the organization of auto production (lean production) and vehicle technology (for example, electronics and plastics). Thirdly, since the inception of the European single market, there has been a considerable selection process concerning company takeovers, reselling and market entry and exit (Sadler and Amin, 1995), and the structure of the supply industry has been subject to constant changes. Despite the fact that Frankfurt/Rhein-Main lost its leading position as an auto manufacturing area for the Stuttgart and Bavaria regions following the Second World War, it remains one of Germany's leading supply regions (Lompe *et al.*, 1991).

In contrast to regions competing in auto manufacturing today, Frankfurt/Rhein-Main became the most important destination for foreign, primarily American, auto supply investment very soon after the war. Closely related to the overall importance of Frankfurt as an American location in Germany (as the headquarters of American troops and the German-American Board of Trade), many American companies quickly started taking over mid-size suppliers in the region. The importance of large auto manufacturers as focal companies for the structuring of local clusters is well known. Suppliers are motivated by their powerful customers to make foreign investments, and the Meritor company is a useful example of this phenomenon. In 1972, the American technology company Rockwell International took over a German supplier founded in Frankfurt in 1872, developing it into a large scale manufacturer of sun roofs, not only for Opel, but for other European auto manufacturers as well. This resulted in the establishment of a European system of branch plants that stretched all the way to Eastern Europe by the 1990's. At the end of the decade, Rockwell decided to sell its automotive division as an independent company called Meritor. Frankfurt thus became a global 'center of expertise' for sunroofs, influencing developments in even the United States and Japan. On the other hand, total employment numbers for production in Frankfurt have diminished in favor of locations like Great Britain, Eastern Europe and Spain.

The dominant position of American suppliers was clearly reflected in a nationality-based survey on auto suppliers in the region. According to this survey, of 163 supply companies located in the region, 96 are German, 33 are American subsidiaries, 6 are Japanese and 28 are from other European countries. Among American suppliers are world market leaders like the Lear Corporation, AMP, Allied Signal, ITT and TRW. The concentration of their German headquarters in the Frankfurt/Rhein-Main region cannot be explained by the presence of Opel alone, as all first tier suppliers deliver to almost all auto manufacturers in Europe. Rather, it is the result of a combination of factors, including: the initial advantage of the region due to GM, the availability of German companies for acquisition, the intercontinental accessibility facilitated by the airport, and the fact that the location itself is so well known due to the presence of American troops and companies.

The fate of the auto production cluster in Frankfurt/Rhein-Main will depend a great deal on the strategies that GM adopts regarding Opel. Various strategy changes have caused increasing integration of the Rüsselsheim plant into a global network. First of all, the various GM locations in Europe were integrated into one group at the end of the 1970's. The Rüsselsheim Opel plant stood in the middle, and witnessed the concentration of development of all models for Europe, and later for all parts of the world except North America. A new division of labor among GM plants in Europe was also instituted at about the same time, situating additional production operations, especially of larger models of automobiles, at Rüsselsheim. However, in the 1980's, Rüsselsheim lost a number of functions for two reasons. Firstly, GM combined and expanded its suppliers into the Automotive Components Group (later Delphi) in Paris. Secondly, the company headquarters were moved to Zurich in 1986 (Lompe *et al.*, 1991).

In the process of restructuring, manufacturing operations in Rüsselsheim were reduced and development operations increased. Production was concentrated on assembly of the largest models - the Vectra and the Omega, while more and more components were acquired from suppliers. Because Opel has been less successful over the past few years, extreme pressure has emerged in the company to reduce the number of employees. Growing competition, however, makes it mandatory to increase the speed at which models are modified and to improve the development of vehicles. For this reason, Opel's International Technology and Development Center in Rüsselsheim has grown considerably, now employing 9,000 people, with an additional 2,300 added in the independent development units for software and engines.

As in the case of Meritor, first tier suppliers have also enhanced their research and development activities in the region. Due to the fact that product development is currently organized according to a division of labor similar to production, a local cluster of large and small technical consulting firms has developed since the early 1990's. Outsourcing of engineering plays an increasingly important role in the strategies of auto manufacturers: wherever central auto industry R&D labs are located, new clusters of auto supply R&D labs and technical consulting appear. New large technical consulting companies geared towards the auto industry have been established, setting up branch offices 'right by the front door' of the auto manufacturers (Rentmeister, 2001). In Germany, they are still primarily national companies. Their internationalization, however, is expected to take place soon. Since the end of the 1980's, some Japanese auto manufacturers, like Honda, Mazda, Mitsubishi, Subaru, and Isuzu, have finally set up R&D labs in the region. These labs began as small market research units located at German market business centers and were initially responsible for market research, such as the research of technological trends in Germany and production tests, or activities closely related to the national market (Park and Schlunze, 1991). The labs received new responsibilities for model development in the 1990's, in part serving as development labs for new models aimed for the European market. This was especially true of Honda, as described by Mair (1994), as well as for Mazda (Specht, 1999).

In result, the region witnessed the evolution of a 'knowledge cluster' for automotive development, which is internationally networked in many ways: first, through the organizational networking of global companies; second, through cooperative networking in R&D, for example with software companies in Munich or designers in northern Italy; and, finally, through international supply networks.

This type of organization of production and development within the auto industry, which is often referred to as 'neo-Fordist' has resulted in diverse consequences for the Frankfurt/Rhein-Main region. The region has continued to lose production activities, because companies are experiencing 'internal' de-industrialization. On the other hand, they are also acquiring new service operations with the goal of gaining better access to the national and European markets, whose customers are becoming increasingly demanding.

2.5 CAN POLITICS CREATE NEW CLUSTERS?

While the most important industrial clusters, at least in terms of the regional labor market, are converting into service operations, other industrial sectors are in danger of vanishing. The endangered sectors include electrical engineering, mechanical engineering and the construction industry, all of which were considered important regional employers at the beginning of the 1990's. The leading electrical engineering firm, AEG, was initially restructured after its takeover by Daimler-Benz, but was eventually liquidated (Biehler, 1992), and the traditional Frankfurt based production of office communications came to a halt. After Olivetti's acquisition of the office communications company Triumpf-Adler, production in Frankfurt was halted in 1990. Other companies were relocated out of Frankfurt and used relocation as an opportunity for rationalization and reorientation: towards the automobile sector, for example. With the exception of the unique printing press sector, the crisis that hit German mechanical engineering at the beginning of the 1990's forced several older companies to shut down. Mid-sized companies have exported more and more, but have not internationalized themselves. Finally the construction sector belongs to those failing clusters in the Rhein-Main area, which, with companies like Philip Holzmann, had been integral to the region's former importance as a location of many global players of German construction. As these sectors, which had traditionally been the backbone of Germany's export strength, were facing de-industrialization, politicians in the region began in the 1990's to search for new technological fields to ensure the region's future as a production region.

Due to these circumstances, the city of Frankfurt and Umlandverband Frankfurt initiated a study together in the 1990's about the possibilities of new technological fields capable of replacing old production structures. The Umlandverband - founded as a public authority in 1975 and dismantled in 2001 - was a public body representing numerous municipalities in the central Frankfurt/Rhein-Main metropolitan region. Biotechnology was identified among other possibilities, and it is indeed this field of technology on which local politicians are currently concentrating. Steps taken in this direction include: future city investment in a biotechnology park; the establishment of a venture capital fund in March 1999 by the federal state of Hessen and Hoechst; and modernization of the university's biotechnological research efforts, and concentration of institutions in a biotechnological campus. Political action is directly aimed at local start-ups and appears to hardly include already existing larger companies. The extent to which these great attempts of local politics will be successful is still unclear. In any case, the Frankfurt/ Rhein-Main region was unsuccessful in the BioRegio contest announced by the German government during the 1990's. In this context, the German government was looking for the 'best' biotechnology regions in Germany, in order to promote them and transform them into new competence centers. The Frankfurt/Rhein-Main region failed due to the almost total absence of networking among companies, politics and science, as well as the fact that the majority of biotechnological companies are more service oriented than production oriented (Dohse, 2000; Schamp, 2002).

Another high-tech cluster is surprisingly less visible, probably because it is located in Darmstadt, which is not considered part of the Frankfurt metropolitan region (see Figure 2.1). A software industry cluster has evolved in Darmstadt around the technical university and the research facilities of German Telecom (previously state owned), which has long been dominated by a few larger companies like Software AG and American Computer Associates. Darmstadt's lost its role as the 'secret software capital of Germany' in the 1980's to Munich (Sternberg and Tamásy, 1999). Software AG experienced another crisis with their mainframe products as well. However, they began experiencing a new era at the end of the 1990's. 70 percent of the more than one thousand IT companies around Darmstadt were founded within the last 5 years, mostly as small service oriented companies. One reason for this was the deregulation of the telecommunication market in Germany, and another was the success of the Internet. Even if close proximity to Germany's central internet node in Frankfurt has no technical importance, it is psychologically attractive. This development was also related to new venture capital sources. Recently, an internet start-up park was set up in Frankfurt in the so called 'venture lab'.

Local politicians in Darmstadt are taking advantage of this development in order to bring about a public awareness of telecommunications technology. They have employed the following method: a local community of companies and banks establish a start-up park, the city tries to promote a vision of a 'scientific city' in the eyes of the public, and the technical university develops new courses of study. While branches of the IT sector are essentially growing in an environment of global competition, the large and small companies of the Darmstadt area are still only important on the regional and national levels. Still, it currently appears that this is the only technology cluster in the metropolitan region that may contribute to strengthening the region's future role in the European and world economies.

2.6 NEW SERVICES IN THE REGION

De-industrialization of the Frankfurt/Rhein-Main region is inevitable. In traditional sectors, which are still listed in statistics as manufacturing sectors, production operations are being replaced by services. New industry sectors are turning out to be either purely or predominantly service oriented. The percentage of employees in service oriented companies is growing at a fast rate. By the 1980's, the city of Frankfurt had the second highest percentage of service oriented employment out of all major cities in Germany (second only to Hamburg) (Biehler, 1992); in 1998, this figure stood at 83%.

The dissolution of the city of Frankfurt into its metropolitan region is represented more and more by the spatial distribution of the service sector (Table 2.2). Primarily urban service activities, or those in the larger cities, fall into the finance, transportation and non-profit sectors. While the figures analyzed include the cities of Darmstadt, Wiesbaden and Mainz as well, the city of Frankfurt nonetheless occupies a dominant position. Trade, on the other hand, has moved into the region, and even 'other services', which include advanced producer services, are distributed equally among urban and non-urban communities across the region.

Table 2.2 Urban and non-urban employees in the service sectors of the Frankfurt/Rhein-Main region, 1998

Sector	Urban (thousands)	%	Non-Urban (thousands)	%	Total
Retail	94.5	37.0	158.2	63.0	252.7
Transport	80.6	62.3	48.7	37.7	129.3
Finance	93.0	74.0	32.7	26.0	125.7
Other Services	258.5	53.0	226.6	47.0	488.1
Non Governmental Organizations	34.7	64.0	19.5	36.0	54.2
Public Authorities*	54.4	50.7	52.8	49.3	107.2
Total	615.5	53.2	541.8	46.8	1,157.3

Note: * state government in Wiesbaden, Federal organisations in Frankfurt, among others.

Statistics for services must be examined with the same reservations as for industry: heterogeneous clusters cannot be measured. However, Porter's cluster concept does hold validity for services as well. The importance of the region's financial cluster as a European node is presented in Chapter 5. For example, financial service providers need the support of highly valuable services such as legal consulting, software development, corporate consulting, market research, general information services, a training and continuing education infrastructure, as well as technical support (system backup, data organization, city net-provider). This financial cluster is concentrated in Frankfurt's Westend, but it is also expanding into several other locations in the metropolitan region (Lo and Schamp, 2001).

The same can be said for the region's transportation cluster, which allows the metropolitan area to function as a central transportation node for international air traffic in continental Europe (see Chapter 7). It also partially represents the region's new role as a logistical hub and a central gateway for the German market (see Chapter 9). Both clusters extend significantly beyond Frankfurt's city limits and expand into the surrounding region.

The reduction of industrial employees in production and the growth of R&D activities, in conjunction with rising employment in finance, traffic and logistic clusters, suggests that the entire metropolitan Frankfurt/Rhein-Main region is losing its traditional industrial economic base. It is, however, gaining a new basis in specific service clusters, and this is enabling the region to evolve into a central node of the European city structure. The trend in competition between European metropolitan regions points to both a growing hierarchy and to specialization. Such specialization of the region's economic clusters may result in dynamic agglomeration and growth effects (Gordon, 1999). Bonneville (1994) named three fields of specialization in the internationalization of European cities: first, 'technological cities'; second, 'interfaces between the world economy and their regions', and; third, 'cities with international regional functions'. Actual specializations may develop as hybrids of this typology. While the Frankfurt/Rhein-Main metropolitan region is gaining international importance in comparison to other German city regions, its specialization is based on its function as a point of market entry and as a financial steering center. In this way, city politicians and economic leaders find themselves in competition with other metropolitan regions of Europe, which are moving along similar trajectories. Depending on the context, such cities include London and Paris in the financial sector and Amsterdam in traffic and logistics.

While the Frankfurt/Rhein-Main metropolitan region is faced with increasingly less competition from within Germany - Munich is becoming 'Technology Region Number One' (Sternberg and Tamásy, 1999), Berlin, perhaps, is becoming the city of government and culture - its role as a financial and trading center in the European city system has been disputed, despite the great advantages that it enjoys over other places. It is located in the center of both the largest market of the European Union and the urban prosperity belt of Europe, stretching from Southeast England to Northern Italy. The advantage of being able to reach markets, however, can only be exploited when general conditions for social well being and dynamic economic development are fostered and maintained through politics on the national level, as well as on the level of the European Union.

REFERENCES

Bathelt, H. (1995). Global competition, international trade, and regional concentration: The case of the German chemical industry during the 1980s. *Environment and Planning C: Government and Policy 13,* 395-424.

Bathelt, H. (1997). *Chemiestandort Deutschland. Technologischer Wandel, Arbeitsteilung und geographische Strukturen in der Chemischen Industrie.* Berlin: edition sigma.

Becker, St. & Schumm, W. (2001). Begrenzte Vernetzung. Restrukturierung von Großunternehmen der chemischen und pharmazeutischen Industrie in der Region Rhein-Main. In J. Esser & E.W. Schamp (Eds.), *Metropolitane Region in der Vernetzung. Der Fall Frankfurt/Rhein-Main* (105-130). Frankfurt: campus.

Biehler, H. (1992). *Industriestandort Frankfurt im Strukturwandel. Perspektiven der Investitions- und Verbrauchsgüterindustrie für die 90er Jahre.* München: Imu-Studien.

Bonneville, M. (1994). Internationalization of non-capital cities in Europe: Aspects, processes and prospects. *European Planning Studies 2,* 267-285.

Dicken, P. (1998). *Global shift. Transforming the world economy* (3rd ed.). London: Paul Chapman.

Dohse, D. (2000). Technology policy and the regions - the case of the BioRegio contest. *Research Policy 29,* 1111-1133.

Dünzl, H.J. (1995). Die Geschichte des Industriestandorts Frankfurt-Darmstadt. In VDI (Ed.), *Technischer Fortschritt und wirtschaftliche Entwicklung. Beiträge zur Geschichte des Industriestandorts Frankfurt-Darmstadt* (19-63). Frankfurt/M.: Societäts-Verlag.

Freund, B. (1995). Die Suburbanisierung von Betrieben im Rhein-Main-Gebiet. In G. Meyer (Ed.), Das Rhein-Main-Gebiet. Aktuelle Strukturen und Entwicklungsprobleme. *Mainzer Kontaktstudium Geographie 1* (45-54). Mainz: Geographisches Institut der Johannes Gutenberg-Universität.

Friedman, J. (1995). Where we stand: a decade of world city research. In P.L. Knox & P.J. Taylor (Eds.), *World cities in a world-system* (21-47). Cambridge: Cambridge Univ. Press.

Gaebe, W. (1994). Standort Deutschland. Attractiveness for German and foreign investors is decreasing. In W. Gaebe & E.W. Schamp (Eds.), *Gateways to the European market: Case studies from the Netherlands and Germany* (103-119). Münster: Lit.

Gordon, I. (1999). Internationalisation and urban competition. *Urban Studies 36,* 1001-1016.

Keil, R. & Lieser, P. (1992). Frankfurt: Global City - Local Politics. In M.P. Smith (Ed.), *After modernism. Global restructuring and the changing boundaries of city life* (39-69). London: Transaction Publishers.

Keil, R. & Ronneberger, Kl. (1994). Going up the country: internationalization and urbanization on Frankfurt's northern fringe. *Environment and Planning D: Society and Space 12,* 137-166.

Keil, R. & Ronneberger, Kl. (2000). The globalization of Frankfurt am Main: Core, periphery and social conflict. In P. Marcuse & R. van Kempen (Eds.), *Globalizing Cities. A New Spatial Order?* (228-248). Oxford: Blackwell.

Läpple, D. (1999). Die Ökonomie einer Metropolregion im Spannungsfeld von Globalisierung und Regionalisierung. Das Beispiel Hamburg. In G. Fuchs, G. Krauss & H.G. Wolf (Eds.), *Die Bindungen der Globalisierung* (11-47). Marburg: Metropolis.

Landeszentralbank in Hessen (2000). *Vierteljahreszahlen 2. Quartal.* Frankfurt/M.: Landeszentralbank in Hessen.

Lo, V. & Schamp, E.W. (2001). Finanzplätze auf globalen Märkten - Beispiel Frankfurt/Main. *Geographische Rundschau 53,* 26-31.

Lompe, K., Müller, T., Rehfeld, D. & Blöcker, A. (1991). *Regionale Bedeutung und Perspektiven der Automobilproduktion. Die Beispiele Südostniedersachsen und Südhessen.* Düsseldorf: Hans-Böckler-Stiftung.

Mair, A. (1994). *Honda's global local corporation.* New York: St. Martin's Press.

Naschold, F., Soskice, D., Hancké, B. & Jürgens, U. (Eds.) (1998). Ökonomische Leistungsfähigkeit und institutionelle Innovation - Das deutsche Produktions- und Politikregime im globalen Wettbewerb. *WZB Jahrbuch 1997.* Berlin: edition sigma.

Park, S. & Schlunze, R. (1991). Forschungs- und Entwicklungsmanagement japanischer Konzerne in der Bundesrepublik Deutschland. In S.J. Park (Ed.), *Japanisches Management in der Bundesrepublik* (147-182). Frankfurt/M.: campus.

Piore, M.J. & Sabel, Ch.F. (1984). *The second industrial divide. Possibilities for prosperity.* New York: Basic Books.

Porter, M.E. (1990). *The competitive advantage of nations*. New York: Free Press.

Porter, M.E. (1996). Competitive advantage, agglomeration economies, and regional policy. *International Regional Science Review 19*, 85-94.

Rentmeister, B. (2001). Vernetzung wissensintensiver Dienstleister in der Produktentwicklung der Automobilindustrie. In J. Esser & E.W. Schamp (Eds.), *Metropolitane Region in der Vernetzung. Der Fall Frankfurt/Rhein-Main* (154-180). Frankfurt: campus.

Ronneberger, Kl. (1995). Von High-Tech-Regionen lernen? *Jahrbuch sozialwissenschaftliche Technikberichterstattung 1995* (19-78). Berlin: edition sigma.

Sadler, D. & Amin, A. (1995). 'Europeanisation' in the automotive components sector and its implications for state and locality. In R. Hudson & E.W. Schamp (Eds.), *Towards a new map of automobile manufacturing in Europe? New production concepts and spatial restructuring* (39-61). Berlin: Springer.

Schamp, E.W. (1995). The German automobile production system going European. In R. Hudson & E.W. Schamp (Eds.), *Towards a new map of automobile manufacturing in Europe? New production concepts and spatial restructuring* (93-116). Berlin: Springer.

Schamp, E.W. (2000). Globalization, the European market, and the urban regions: The case of Southern Germany. In M. Vellinga (Ed.), *The dialectics of globalization. Regional responses to world economic processes: Asia, Europe, and Latin America in comparative perspective* (257-278). Boulder, Col.: Westview.

Schamp, E.W. (2002). Globalization and the reorganization of a metropolitan knowledge system: The case of R&D in Frankfurt/Rhein-Main, Germany. In R. Hayter & R. Le Heron (Eds.), *Knowledge, territory and industrial space* (forthcoming).

Schwarz, Ch. (2000). Industriepark Höchst. Ende der Gemütlichkeit. *Wirtschaftswoche* no. 9, 24.2.2000, 102-109.

Specht, J. (1998). *Internationalisierung des Forschungs- und Entwicklungsstandortes Rhein-Main*. Manuscript, Department of Economic and Social Geography, Goethe-University Frankfurt/Main.

Specht, J. (1999). *Industrielle Forschung und Entwicklung: Standortstrategien und Standortvernetzungen*. Münster: Lit.

Sternberg, R. & Tamásy, Ch. (1999). München as Germany's No.1 high technology region: Empirical evidence, theoretical explanations and the role of small firm/large firm relationship. *Regional Studies 33*, 367-377.

UVF (Umlandverband Frankfurt) (2000). Region Frankfurt RheinMain. *Statistik-Trends 10/00*.

ARIE SHACHAR AND DANIEL FELSENSTEIN

3. GLOBALIZATION PROCESSES AND THEIR IMPACT ON THE STRUCTURE OF THE TEL AVIV METROPOLITAN AREA

3.1 INTRODUCTION

The chapter deals with processes of change in the functional structure of the Tel Aviv Metropolitan Area (TAMA) in the wake of economic globalization processes of the 1980s and 1990s. Of all the components making up the spatial organization of the TAMA, the chapter focuses on the development of two Central Business Districts (CBD) in metropolitan Tel Aviv: the traditional central city business arena and a new emerging center. Rather than heralding the formation of a polycentric urban structure, the new Tel Aviv CBD represents a real-estate led response at generating a new center of gravity for economic activity in Tel Aviv. The new center therefore competes vigorously with the established center. A further unique feature of the developing metropolitan structure is the ex nihilo nature of the new development. Instead of following the well-known pattern of incremental CBD expansion via new building at the margins of the established center, the new Tel Aviv business district represents an attempt at re-directing growth to a new location altogether.

Traditionally, the Tel Aviv CBD developed in the southern area of Tel Aviv in the location of the original site of the first neighborhood of the city of Tel Aviv, the Ahuzat Bayit quarter established in 1909. It grew consistently and systematically to become the managerial and financial center of the metropolitan area and in many instances served as the nerve-center of the entire Israeli economy, a role which it still fulfills today. Over the last decade or two however, the growth of the CBD stabilized and its areal extent changed only slightly.

Challenging the established CBD, a secondary center emerged in an area that was sparsely occupied by industrial workshops, garages and a municipal swimming pool. In terms of jurisdictional responsibilities the new center is located outside the Tel Aviv city limits and within the neighboring municipal jurisdiction of the city of Ramat Gan. Its most significant locational advantage is its proximity to the major highway of the metropolitan area (Netivei Ayalon – Highway No. 2), which is the backbone of the transportation system for the entire region (Figure 3.1). This new CBD has emerged in direct proximity to the Diamond Exchange (Bourse) which is the control center of the entire diamond industry in Israel. All import and export flows of diamonds and other precious stones are transacted via the Ramat Gan location. The Diamond Exchange is located about three kilometers to the north-east

D. Felsenstein et al. (eds.),
Emerging Nodes in the Global Economy: Frankfurt and Tel Aviv Compared, 35–53.

of the traditional CBD and has become the focal point for the development of the alternative CBD attracting much of the high-rise office development in the metropolitan area of Tel Aviv. While the initial buildings near Diamond Exchange were of medium height (15 to 30 stories), later construction built in the 1990s rose to heights of 50 to 60 floors. At present, the area of the new CBD is developing outwards in a north-east direction as a collection of post-modern, high-rise office buildings. While the new center does still not match the old CBD in terms of total floor space and number of employees, it nevertheless has accumulated a critical mass of office, research and design space serving some of Israel's leading firms in high-tech and the producer services sector.

This chapter analyzes whether there are significant differences in terms of composition of the economic sectors between the two CBDs and tests the hypothesis that the new CBD is strongly related to economic globalization processes, which occurred in Israel during the 1980s and 1990s. Two different but inter-related aspects of Tel Aviv's functional structure are considered in the analysis that follows. The first deals with the emergence of a new CBD alongside an established center as a response to the needs of a metropolitan economy undergoing processes of globalization. The second outlines the emergence of a new socio-spatial residential structure which is a direct result of the growing number of foreign workers occupying the lowest level neighborhoods in Tel Aviv. A highly segregated micro-geography has emerged as a further urban response to the challenges of globalization and a distinct enclave of foreign workers of significant size and particular way of life has been formed.

3.2 THE TWO CBDS OF THE TEL AVIV METROPOLITAN AREA

In order to highlight the role of governance structure affecting functional structure in metropolitan Tel Aviv, we first broadly sketch the jurisdictional limits of the TAMA and the role of the planning authorities that serve this area. We then highlight the different tax regimes operating across the different jurisdictions that comprise the metropolitan region. In purely administrative terms, the metropolitan area is composed of three territorial units (defined by the Israel Central Bureau of Statistics). These are the Tel Aviv District and the Central District and the smaller Ashdod natural area at the southern border of the Central District (Figure 3.1). The population of the TAMA was 2.65 million (2001), which comprised 42 percent of Israel's total population (CBS, 2001). The TAMA has grown around the historical core of the city of Tel Aviv-Yafo over the past fifty years to comprise at present more than 25 towns, 33 local authorities, and 13 regional councils, which include 198 villages. Tel Aviv is the central city of the metropolitan area. It is surrounded by rings of built-up area of descending density and declining intensity of commuting streams to the metropolitan core - the city of Tel Aviv.

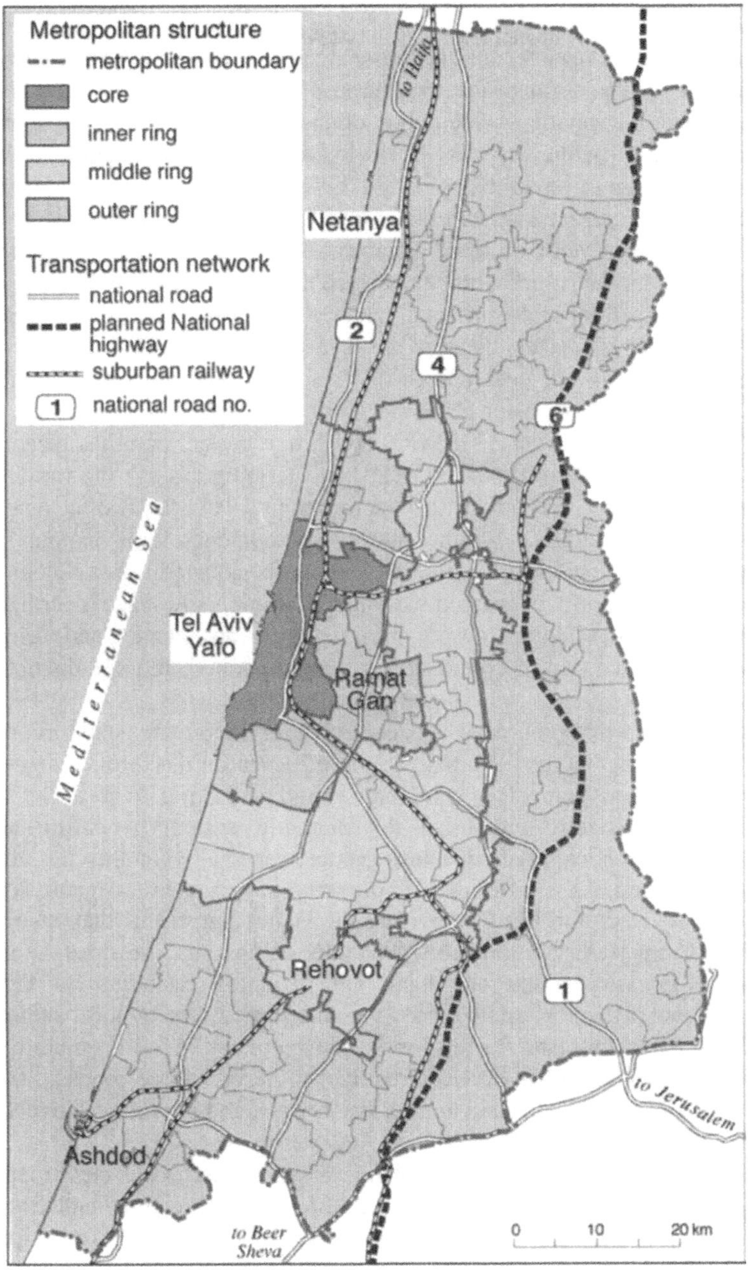

Figure 3.1 Tel Aviv-Yafo metropolitan area: basic structure and main transportation network

While the metropolitan area roughly comprises a functional economic unit and a composite spatial labor market, it is highly segmented politically. No metropolitan governance structure operates and at present, the TAMA exists as a geographical-administrative entity defined for the purpose of statistical analysis. There are however several metropolitan-wide public organizations with sectoral responsibility for the provision of public services. These are single-task organizations comprising of ad-hoc groupings of jurisdictions within the metropolitan area. The geographical extent of these organizations varies by service provided and there is no spatial correspondence of several of these organizations. Thus there is little attempt at creating organizational coordination on a metropolitan-wide basis.

The land-use pattern of the metropolitan area is partially fashioned by a planning system that prepares master plans at the district level. As the metropolitan area combines two districts, its development is thus influenced by two different spatial plans. Over the 1990s a master plan was formulated and approved for the Central District (District Master Plan 3 - DMP3) and a new master plan has recently been completed for the Tel Aviv District (DMP5) and is going through the various stages of approval at present. According to Israeli planning law, the district master plan provides the major outlines for the future development of the region. Detailed planning is the responsibility of each city, local authority, and regional council. The district planning authority is charged with the fine-tuning and spatial coordination of individual local plans. Major transportation networks are planned and designed by the Ministry of Transportation and they are incorporated into the district master plans.

Despite the seeming bureaucratic control exerted by the statutory planning system, a competing source of initiative and influence on the form of metropolitan development comes from the commercial and industrial real estate market. Municipalities constantly pressurize the planning system to ensure adequate provision of land for real estate development and especially commercial, office and industrial premises. As non-residential property tax provides a major source of independent revenue for local authorities, it is not surprising that metropolitan development represents the outcome of the competing pressures exerted by property-led growth on the one hand and planning restraints on the other. Commercial and office real estate projects are often perceived by local authorities as 'cash cows'. Allocating land for this kind of development yields revenues over four times the value of the urban services required to service these projects, facilitates intensive use of the land allocated to high-rise towers, and imposes relatively limited environmental problems.

This combination of a regulative planning system and local tax structure was expected to provide an answer for the huge demand for commercial floor space which occurred in the Tel Aviv metropolitan area from the mid-1980s until the year 2000. This unprecedented demand for commercial floor space was strongly affected by two processes of economic globalization. The first was the establishment of a very large number of new firms in knowledge-based sectors (see Chapter 6). Most of these new firms searched for accommodation in office-type buildings. The more advanced technologically they were, the more they looked for 'smart' buildings offering the most modern facilities which were unavailable in office buildings prior the 1980s. These particular demands for 'smart' buildings channeled the locational search to newly built high-rise office buildings, which were not in abundance in Tel Aviv, especially in the old CBD. The agglomeration economies of these new firms required that they be located in complexes comprising several new buildings to allow for a threshold number of firms to operate in close spatial proximity. The old CBD area of Tel Aviv could not provide the ready supply of land necessary for the development of large office tower complexes.

While the old CBD of Tel Aviv has undergone a slow process of renewal and renovation with older and smaller buildings replaced by office towers, than has not been a sufficient response to meet the demand for office property generated by the globalization processes affecting the Tel Aviv economy. Furthermore, this response is limited in scope because of the specific historical geography of the area and the consequent planning policy towards its renovation. The old CBD is located on the site of the first neighborhood of modern Tel Aviv constructed at the beginning of the twentieth century. The area includes of buildings of historical and architectural significance thereby limiting its potential for commercial development. The Tel Aviv-Yafo Municipality has enacted a strict policy of historical preservation, which means that many old buildings are protected and cannot be demolished or radically changed. Large scale development of the old CBD in order to meet the needs of a modern property market has therefore not been possible. For example, planning permission for a new office tower on the Rothschild Boulevard (the main axis of the traditional CBD) was made conditional on the replanting of one of the historical buildings from its original site to a nearby site only twenty meters away. The direct outcome for developers is a slow process of obtaining planning permits and an increase in total development costs on top of the very high cost of land in the old CBD. Another problem in the development process of the old CBD is small lot size. This is a legacy of an antiquated system of land parcelation. Modern development requires consolidation of very small land parcels as a precondition for commercial and office projects. In other cases building facades have been listed for preservation necessitating the intact freezing of the exterior structure while tearing down the buildings behind the preserved facade. Thus, any redevelopment in the old CBD incurred greater costs and proceeded at a slower pace than similar projects at alternative locations in different parts of the Tel Aviv or even outside its limits. These limitations meant that only offices able to pay the highest rents would be likely to occupy the any new office space, to be built in the old CBD. In practice, this has resulted in the concentration of firms in the financial and business service sector such as headquarters of banks and insurance companies, prestigious legal offices and international accounting firms in the old CBD (Charney, 1997).

The second globalization-related outcome has been the tremendous growth in demand for office space created by the dramatic increase in the producer services sector (see Chapter 8). The number of employees in the finance and business services in Israel almost doubled in the decade between 1988-1998 from 148,000 to 293,000, out of the latter 23.5 percent were concentrated in the city of Tel Aviv (CBS, 2000). The rapid expansion of producer services of all sorts could not be accommodated within the existing CBD of Tel Aviv. The problem was accentuated by the fact that the large firms in the various branches of producer services looked for offices in buildings, which carried with them an aura of prestige, affluence, and modernity. Very few buildings within the old CBD could match these requirements despite attempts to up-grade existing buildings. This new floor space created could not accommodate the exploding demand of the large producer services firms.

Thus in the mid 1980s the stage was set for a major expansion of office space either in Tel Aviv or in one of the municipalities within its vicinity. This opportunity was seized by the Municipality of Ramat Gan, which is Tel Aviv's neighbor to the east. Applying well-known measures in interurban competition, Ramat Gan offered attractive incentives for the development of office towers. The first was a waiver on height limits for office blocks allowing for intense exploitation of floor space. It took the Tel Aviv-Yafo Municipality more than ten years to follow up with the same relaxation of height limits. Israeli planning law allows for each municipality to enact its own regulations and by-laws, independent of those in neighboring municipalities. The District Planning Commission approved of Ramat Gan's planning policy cognizant of the growing demand for new floor space, which could not be met in Tel Aviv because of its planning restrictions. The second measure was reduced property taxes for non-residential land uses. For big firms utilizing large areas of floor space this was a substantial incentive. Together these two measures combined to attract land development and large-scale office and commercial property construction. A collection of over 20 high-rise buildings rapidly emerged at the western-most tip of Ramat Gan by the end of the 1990s. This 'top location' was created outside the boundaries of Tel Aviv over a relatively short period, featuring all the characteristics of a CBD in terms of the intensity of development and type of firms occupying the new office development (Kipnis, 1998).

Over the period 1995-2000 the Israeli economy benefited from a continuous stream of foreign investment aimed to a great extent at local high-tech industry and a multitude of start-up companies established at that time (Chapter 4). Aware of the demand for large scale property development to serve high-tech firms part of the inflow of foreign investment was channeled into land development. Bank of Israel figures point to \$183 million of foreign capital in land development in 1996 in \$191 million in 1998, \$221million in 1999 and \$192 million in 2001 (Bank of Israel, 2001). The geographical destination of this investment is not available but it can be assumed with a high degree of certainty that the majority was directed to the Tel Aviv metropolitan area. No surprisingly, most of the office towers in the new CBD were joint ventures between foreign and Israeli entrepreneurs. The free flow of capital, a major characteristic of the global economy, therefore had a direct impact on the changing functional structure of the metropolitan area.

In addition to the land development incentives, the rapid and unplanned development of a second CBD in Tel Aviv was facilitated by changing patterns of accessibility in the metropolitan region. Over a period of almost twenty years a major highway was constructed in the center of the built-up area of the metropolitan region aligned in a north-south direction, starting at the southern entrance into Tel Aviv and terminating outside the northern boundary of the city (Figure 3.2). This highway (Highway No. 2, called 'Netivei Ayalon') created an efficient and high-

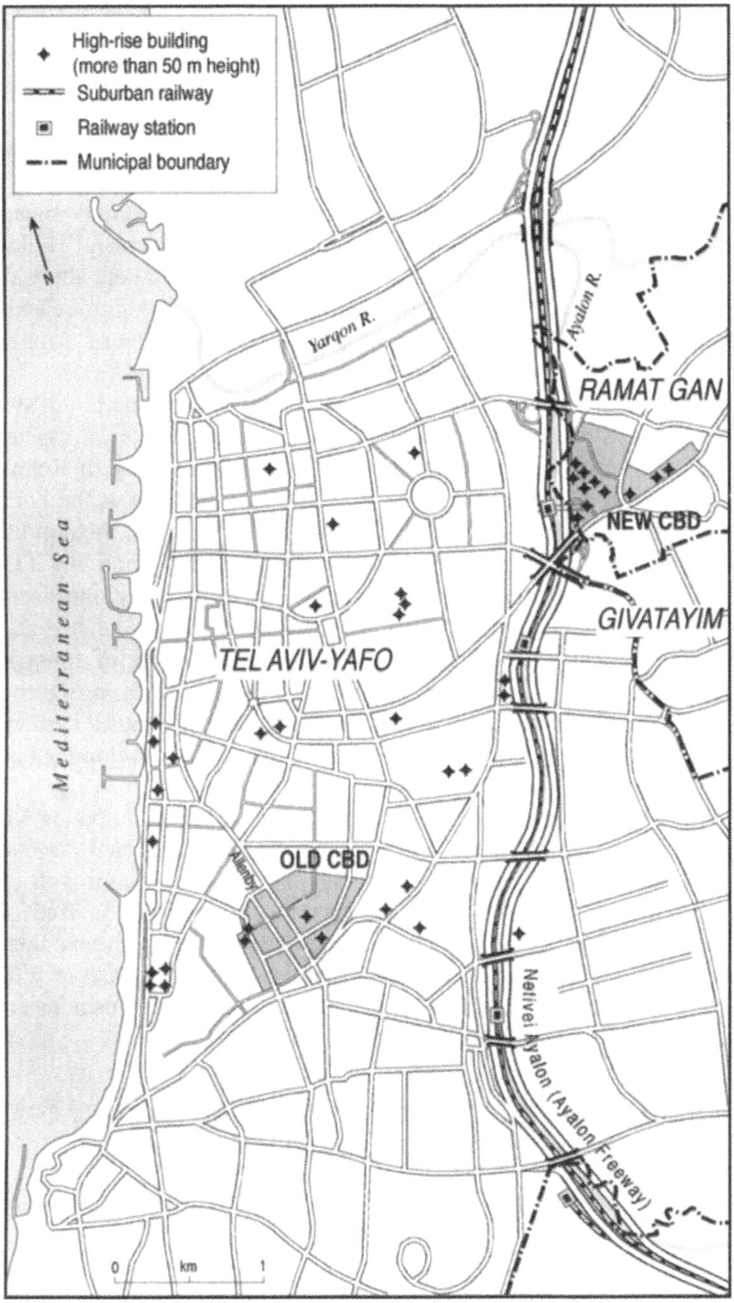

Figure 3.2 The old and new central business district in Tel Aviv-Yafo and Ramat Gan, 2000

speed transportation corridor and rapidly developed as the backbone for the car transportation network. All areas adjacent to the highway became accessible for passengers and goods arriving from all parts of the metropolitan region and even beyond it. Fortuitously, the new CBD was adjacent to Highway 2 and therefore could reap the benefits of the rapid accessibility to the highway. Two exits from the highway funnel vehicles directly toward the new CBD. The proximity of the CBD to the northern rail and bus station located within the municipal boundary of Tel Aviv but adjacent the concentration of office towers in Ramat Gan, further enhances CBD accessibility. In contrast, the old CBD does not enjoy the benefits of Highway 2 and a lack of lateral connections in an east-west direction has kept the old CBD in relative isolation from any major transportation networks. This significant difference in accessibility could also account for the different composition of firms in the two centers.

Recently a further component has been added to the transportation system with the initial construction of the first lines of the TAMA commuter rail system known as the 'suburban train'. This is scheduled to run from the city of Rehovot at the southern edge of the metropolitan area to the city of Netanya at the northern end. The commuter train runs parallel to Highway 2, traversing the metropolitan region from north to south. As this new component is not yet fully operational it is too early to evidence a rise in the volume of passengers to Tel Aviv in any significant manner. Nevertheless, anecdotal evidence suggests that it already is having an effect in increasing the Tel Aviv area labor-shed with a large number of commuters from Rehovot, Netanya, and even Zichron Yaakov to the north using the system. Eventually with extensions added in all directions, this mass transit system will give a tremendous locational advantage to the new CBD and to development adjacent to Highway 2.

The emergence of a new CBD located in Ramat Gan and competing with the old CBD in Tel Aviv has caused a major change in the functional structure of the metropolitan area. It is assumed that the establishment and the growth of the new CBD are an outcome of the new demands for floor space spurred on by the economic globalization of the metropolitan economy. We hypothesize therefore that the composition of the new CBD, which has grown in response to globalization processes, will be rather different to that of the traditional business center. The following section attempts to establish this proposition.

3.3 EXAMINING THE CONNECTION BETWEEN LOCATION AND GLOBALIZATION IN THE OLD AND NEW CBD AREAS OF TEL AVIV

3.3.1 Survey and Method

The objective of this section is to analyze the characteristics of the firms located in both the new and old CBD's of Tel Aviv with a view to ascertaining the relationship between their locational choice and globalization processes. The causality of this relationship is generally considered reciprocal: globalization determines location and the characteristics of location further impact on the process of globalization (Short and Kim, 1999). The case of business services however is conditioned by rather different factors to those governing the globalization of other highly agglomerative activities, such as high tech production (see Chapter 6). Business service firms tend to cluster in very specific locations within the central city (downtowns or CBD's). Central business areas tend to exist alongside high quality commercial premises at density levels unknown even at the most successful high tech production centers. In the classic monocentric conception of urban structure, CBD location is favored by those activities whose production functions most effectively allow the substitution of capital and labor for land (Mills and Hamilton, 1994). The result of competitive bidding amongst different activities is a rent gradient that falls off sharply with distance from downtown. Business services are amongst the most competitive of activities for CBD locations due to their ability to effectively operate in high-rise, high-density environments. The result is the symbiotic agglomeration of corporate offices, financial services, business and professional services in office-based facilities in relatively small areas. Constant pressure on CBD areas has caused their physical expansion, relocation and the development of subsidiary CBD's throughout the 1990's, such that the idea of a 'walking downtown' has increasingly become eroded (Guiliano and Small, 1991).

The localization economies to be gained from business service clustering lie in the externalities that proximity affords (labor pooling, information flows etc, specialized services etc). In a growing CBD, the marginal gains from these externalities must outweigh the marginal costs of accessibility and congestion in the CBD area.

Sassen (1991) has stressed the demand for knowledge-rich environments as the primordial factor governing the formation of intensive business service clusters in select global locations. Global liberalization and merger activity, the need for intensive interaction with clients and advances in IT have all made for global business service firms with voracious needs for information (see chapter 8). In addition, many of the factors driving the agglomeration of economic activity (Quigley, 1998) are pertinent to the case of business services.

While CBD clustering may not offer advantages in terms of scale economies in production and the ability to attain large plant size, it does allow those located in downtowns to realize economies of scale in consumption promoting a large range and full access to a whole host of public goods available in the CBD. Another advantage of central city clustering relates to sharing inputs. The evidence of shared inputs in production in the business services sector is meager (Bogart, 1998). However, on the consumption side much of the 'consumer city' thesis is predicated on the joint provision of amenity-based inputs (such as theaters, restaurants and the like) that serve a variety of producers in the CBD (Glaeser, Kolko and Saiz, 2001). Transactions costs savings from downtown agglomeration is realized both on the production and consumption sides. In the case of the former it is expressed through labor market pooling. In the case of the latter it is evidenced via the joint provision of shopping and commercial facilities within business districts. Finally, the 'law of large numbers' (urbanization economies) also provides a further advantage for CBD clustering. This results in 'statistical economies' in production and consumption. The sheer volume and magnitude of business activity, visitors and people in the

CBD serves to mitigate the effects of fluctuations in the economy. Thus while an individual producer may be feeling the effects of a cyclical downturn others will not and the overall effect on the CBD economy is one of statistical stability.

In the present context, an interesting question is whether the clear spatial tendency towards CBD clustering is also related to globalization. Do the more 'global' firms produce a particular geography? What are the particular marginal gains from clustering that accrue in the case of globalizing firms? Are they any different from the standard sources of localization economies?

In considering the case of Tel Aviv and its distinctive urban structure comprised of a new and old CBD, a further list of issues emerge. For firms that decide to relocate to the new CBD from elsewhere, a definite gain at the margin must be occurring. The question arises as to whether this gain is related to globalization tendencies of the firm. Furthermore, an emerging node location such as Tel Aviv is basically a small open economy trading with other economies worldwide. This poses the question as to the advantage to be gained from trading from a particular location such as the new CBD. In the context of Tel Aviv and its relocated CBD we are also interested in examining the extent to which firms in the new CBD of Tel Aviv are more global than firms in the old CBD. Has relocation enhanced globalization? While we will not be able to address all these questions, examining the interface between globalization and locational choice forces us to confront them.

The spatial pattern of two specific business service sectors within metropolitan Tel Aviv (accountancy and advertising), are dealt with later (see Chapter 8). At this juncture we are more interested in the micro-geography of the CBD and specifically, the connection between locational patterns and globalization. The explicit hypotheses underlying this examination suggest that the globalization tendencies of business service firms are conditioned by firm attributes (age, size, sector, organizational status), agglomeration economy factors (with firms tending to seek out the localization economies of a particular place) and the entrenching role of micro-location in this process.

To examine these issues, we present the result of a comprehensive survey of firms in both the old and new CBD areas of Tel Aviv. The same survey instrument was administered to over 330 business service firms in the new CBD area and 220 in the old CBD area. While this does not represent a full census of all businesses operating in the two areas, and to some extent is a self-selecting sample, it still does account for some 60 percent of businesses operating in the 'core' sections of the two CBD areas. The composition of the businesses surveyed in the two areas is rather different. In the new CBD roughly one quarter of firms are law firms and a further quarter offer computer and communications services. The rest are real estate, financial services and accounting firms. In the old CBD, 28 percent are law firms, 18 percent offer financial services and another 25 percent are either insurance firms or accounting offices.

In order to determine the level of globalization in the business, firms were asked whether they had a major client abroad. Sixty two percent of the firms in the new CBD and 35 percent in the old, answered positively to this question. This binary variable served as the dependent variable in the statistical testing that follows. Using a linear logit model, we attempt to estimate the probability of a business service firm having global connections, as a function of a string of firm attributes. This relationship is estimated three times: first for the firms in the new CBD (model 1), then for the firms in the old CBD (model 2) and finally for all firms with firm location (new/old CBD) acting as a predictor variable (model 3). Data limitations prevent us from using the identical model in each case but key variables do feature in each of the three estimations.

The variables used in the analysis below and their hypothesized relationships, are as follows:

AGE: this is a continuous variable that captures business experience. We expect this to be positively related to globalization with experience giving firms an edge in forging links with firms abroad.

FLOORSPACE: this is a continuous variable that proxies for firm size. The direction of this relationship is indeterminate: larger firms could on the one hand be more oriented to the local market and on the other hand, size could be correlated with age and impact on globalization as a result of this connection.

INDEPENDENT FIRM: this categorical variable juxtaposes all independent firms with all other forms of organizational structure (branch offices, subsidiaries etc). We anticipate that independent firms will have more freedom in pursuing clients abroad than firms that are part of larger business structure.

RE-LOCATION TO CBD: this binary variable attempts to capture the agglomeration economies associated with a CBD location. All re-locators to the new CBD from another location are compared with non-mover firms who were either established in the CBD, never moved in their business history, ore moved within the CBD. We expect that those firms actively looking for the benefits of CBD localization economies, to also be more active in the area of global linkages.

NEW CBD LOCATION: this categorical variable (0,1) identifies firm location as either in the new or old CBD. In line with the hypothesis offered above, we anticipate that firms in the new CBD will tend to have more global connections than firms in the old CBD.

SECTOR: this identifies firms as either computer or communications firms or something else, which incorporates, law, real estate insurance and accounting firms. The direction of this relationship is hard to specify. On the one hand, those law and accounting firms that choose a CBD location are likely to have more global business relations than other similar business service firms. On the other hand, the reality of the computer and communications sector in Israel is that it is one of the main drivers behind the internationalization of business in Israel.

In the estimations that follow, not all variables appear in each model due to problems of either data paucity or multi-colinearity between the explanatory variables. In addition we are not looking for the most parsimonious model. Rather we are more interested in the direction and strength of the relationship between each of the independent variables and the tendency to have a major client abroad.

3.3.2 Results

Regression results are reported for each of the three models (Table 3.1). As a probability estimation method is used, the regression coefficients are not readily interpretable. In the results reported below, significant coefficients are transformed into P values (see Note 1, Chapter 4 for full derivation). These specify the probability change at the mean for a unit change in the independent variable. As many of the latter are categorical variables, the P's indicate the effect of a category move in *x* on the mean probability of *y*.

From the first panel in Table 3.1 we can see that older firms are more likely to have global clients, although the same cannot be said for larger firms (measured in terms of floorspace). The most significant relationship is that of firm organizational status. The probability of global links rises the more the firm is independent. A categorical change in the independent variable will elicit a probability rise of 3 percent in the mean value of the dependent variable. Our hypothesis about the agglomeration economy effect of locating the in the CBD (as captured in the re-locators) is not upheld. While the direction of the relationship is as predicted, the coefficient is not significant. Sectoral affiliation has some effect on the likelihood of having a major client abroad with more law, real estate and accounting firms and more likely than computer and communications firms. The latter would seem to be service companies serving the domestic market and not the classic profile of the Israeli export-oriented, high tech firm (see Chapter 6).

The model relating to the tendency to globalize amongst business service firms in the old CBD area, suffers from less observations and less variables that are statistically significant (Table 3.1, model 2). While the signs on the age and ownership variables match our expectations, the coefficients themselves are not significant. Firm organization is the only variable that appears as having any significant effect in what is otherwise a weak model. Thus with respect to the firms in the old CBD, the only significant factor explaining the tendency to have a major client abroad is firm organizational independence. This finding does not lend itself to any intuitive explanation. The main overall finding is that the tendency to globalize is weaker amongst firms located in the old CBD, although a convincing causal explanation as to why this is so, is not so obvious. There is also no real indication in this model of any agglomeration benefits from location in the old CBD. This does not mean that they do not exist. Rental and business density levels would seem to indicate that at one time, firms were prepared to pay a premium for some perceived advantage of being in the old CBD. We simply have not been able to capture this in our survey and the advent of the new CBD has in all likelihood, served to erode this advantage.

Our third model, attempts to establish the link between intra-metropolitan location and globalization (Table 3.1, model 3). Here we introduce location (new/old CBD) as an explicit determinant. This factor is not significantly correlated with the agglomeration economy effect (as captured by re-location) and thus both enter the model independently. Along with firm organizational status, these two variables are significant and with signs in the direction expected. Firms relocating to the new

Table 3.1 Determinants of globalization: Tel Aviv CBD firms

	Dependent Variable: Existence of Major Client Abroad		
Independent Variables	Model 1	Model 2	Model 3
Constant	-3.012** (1.124)[2]	-2.735** (.773)[2]	-1.482** (.396)[2]
AGE (years)	.023* (.013) [.0002][3]	.691 (.445)	.007 (.009)
INDEPENDENT FIRM (OTHER: SUBSIDIARY, BRANCH OFFICE ETC.)[1]	1.478** (.457) [.030]	1.492* (.804) [.031][3]	.813** (.293) [.051][3]
RE-LOCATION TO CBD (OTHER: LOCAL ETC)[1]	.020 (.437) [.036]		1.040** (.290) [.047]
FLOORSPACE (m^2)	-.0007 (.0004)		
SECTOR: COMPUTERS and COMMUNICATIONS (OTHER SECTORS)[1]	-.867* (.464) [.027]		
ISRAELI OWNERSHIP (FOREIGN)[1]		-.825 (.464)	
NEW CBD LOCATION (OLD)[1]			.572* (.315) [.038]
n	262	173	472
Mean, Dependent Variable	.62	.35	.48
-2 x log likelihood	175.8	135.1	352.1
^{2} values for model / d.f.	18.6/5**	7.9/4*	22.6/4**
Percentage correctly predicted	88.2	85.5	86.4

* logit coefficient significant at p<.10 level
** logit coefficient significant at p<.005 level
1. Dummy Variable; reference group in parenthesis
2. Standard Error in parenthesis.
3. P_i probability change estimated at mean, for unit change in independent variable.

CBD from elsewhere are more likely to have global connections implying some relationship between the agglomeration economy effect and globalization. Relocating to the new CBD from any alternative location, increases the probability of having global clients by nearly 5 percent at the mean. In addition, all other things equal, business service firms in the new CBD are more likely to have global clients than others. A categorical change from the old CBD to the new, increases the mean likelihood of global links by close to 4 percent.

This finding may serve to hint at the self-entrenching process of globalization based on location in the new CBD. Once a firm decides on locating in the new CBD, this increases the probability that it will develop connections with global clients. Thus, we can use these results to suggest that firms looking for the agglomeration advantages of the CBD will tend to be more globally oriented. Once they locate in the new CBD, this tendency may strengthen. This hints at the 'increasing returns' explanation of urban agglomeration (Krugman, 1991).

Finally, as noted earlier, the vexing question of causality in the relationship between globalization and intra-metropolitan location, still remains. Does location in the new CBD make firms more global or do the more global firms seek out the new CBD? The findings presented have assumed a uni-causal direction with location in the new CBD reinforcing the tendency to globalize. However, there could be a process of self-selection at work, whereby the globalization tendency of the firm is an attribute that explains location in the new CBD.

3.4 RESTRUCTURING THE RESIDENTIAL PATTERN OF THE CITY OF TEL AVIV

Most developed countries encountered the social-geographical phenomenon of foreign workers migrating to their large cities in order to provide cheap labor, predominantly in those sectors in which local labor is not willing to participate (Sassen, 1999). Over the period 1967-1990 the demand for foreign labor in Israel was met by Palestinian workers who commuted daily in large numbers from the West Bank and Gaza to parts of the country and especially to the Tel Aviv metropolitan area. At the beginning of the 1990s the geographical pattern of Palestinian commuting was radically transformed. Because of rising political tensions resulting from the first *Intifada* (Palestinian up-rising), only a small number of Palestinian workers were allowed to work in Israel. Over a very short period of time they were replaced by foreign workers arriving to Israel from various parts of the world. The main countries of origin were: Romania, the Philippines, Thailand, and certain Central American countries. To illustrate the fast growth in the number of foreign workers, we can note that in 1993 the number of foreign workers in Israel was 16,000. By 1995 this figure was 60,000 (Bar Tzuri, 1996) and a year later it was110,000. In 1997 their number diminished to 90,000. These figures relate to foreign workers who entered the country legally. In parallel, a secondary market of illegal workers developed and their number was estimated in 1997 to be 150,000 (more than the legal workers at that time). Since then, the number of foreign workers, legal and illegal, seems to have stabilized at about 250,000 accounting for about 10 percent of the Israeli labor force. Foreign workers live in a highly concentrated and segregated pattern. With the exception of the Thai workers who specialize in agriculture, all the others are located within the cities of Israel and adjacent to major construction projects.

Of the large number of foreign workers in the Israeli labor market, about 60,000-70,000 reside and work in the city of Tel Aviv-Yafo. At present they comprise 15 percent of the total population of the city. This high concentration can be related directly to the globalization processes that shaped the Tel Aviv economy and its spatial structure during the 1990s. It is instructive to trace the relationship between globalization and residential restructuring in Tel Aviv.

The first source of extensive demand for foreign workers is the growing affluence of the upper middle class. They occupy the expensive residential districts of central and northern Tel Aviv. Their ability to accumulate capital is a direct outcome of rising income levels in the wake of the economic boom of the 1990s. Demographic change and the 'graying' of Tel Aviv has created demand for personal health care workers for an affluent and aging population that can afford it. In addition, the rising share of women in the Israeli labor force has created demand for household help. This demand was has been filled, in the main, by foreign workers from the Philippines. A second source of demand has been the construction boom of the 1990s especially the high-rise office tower complexes in the two CBDs. Local labor supply has not been sufficient to meet demand for construction workers. As a result, this demand has been met by foreign workers from Romania and more recently, China. The third influence on demand has been the development of a market for workers in the area of maintenance, cleaning, and security of the numerous commercial and office buildings in the two CBDs. Foreign labor from African and Central American countries have filled this particular demand.

The large number of foreign workers in Tel Aviv has not only transformed the structure of the labor market but has also significantly changed the spatial structure of the housing market in Tel Aviv. On arrival in Tel Aviv, foreign workers invariably search for cheap accommodation as close as possible to the center of the city where most employment opportunities can be found and where public transportation is readily available allowing for easy access to most of the metropolitan area. Residential accommodation of this type is available at the edge of the CBD that borders on the poorer housing neighborhoods of south Tel Aviv.

Since its birth as a modern city, Tel Aviv has been characterized by a north-south divide that has seen upper and middle-income residential neighborhoods develop in the northern part of the city initially populated by immigrants of European origin. In contrast, the southern part of Tel Aviv has been associated with lower income housing occupied by non-professional and working-class households of South-Western and Central Asian and North African origins. This striking division was a direct outcome of the political and security tension between Jewish Tel Aviv and Arab Jaffa (Yafo), located to the south of Tel Aviv. All neighborhoods built in the southern part of Tel Aviv from the 1920s onward were considered less attractive due to their proximity to the invisible but strongly effective boundary with the city of Jaffa. These disparities perpetuated and deepened after the establishment of the State of Israel in 1948 and the amalgamation of Tel Aviv and Yafo into one municipal jurisdiction.

From the beginning of the 1990's some of the residential neighborhoods in south Tel Aviv underwent an urban renaissance. Demand for these neighborhoods generated by two distinct populations caused a significant turn-around in the prospects for these once- decaying areas. The first significant social group to revive this area was the young urban, new middle-class, many of them related to high-tech industry and to newly expanded producer services. These young couples were looking for an area that would maximize the benefits of proximity to the amenities and cultural activities of central Tel Aviv. In particular the Neve Tzedek neighborhood southwest of the old CBD, became a magnet for those wanting to capitalize on the consumption opportunities of the central city and proximity to place of work. A once-deteriorating neighborhood was regenerated through the demand for a typically urbane lifestyle. A second distinct social group that has generated demand for south Tel Aviv residential neighborhoods is the immigrant population originating from the former USSR. Akin to the experience in other large cities, these first time arrivers tended to gravitate to the lower income southern neighborhoods, especially the Neve Shaanan and Shapira quarters. Cheap housing in these areas was nevertheless highly accessible to centers of employment. Most immigrants from the former Soviet Union looked on these areas as a stepping-stone in upward social mobility and progression in the housing market (Nachmias and Menahem, 1997).

By the mid-1990s the Neve Tzedek neighborhood was almost completely colonized by young, affluent, middle-class gentrifiers. In contrast, an opposite process of neighborhood depopulation occurred in those quarters that had served the Russian immigrants as points of entry to the Tel Aviv labor and housing markets. Over time, the migration balance of many Tel Aviv neighborhoods south of the old CBD became negative. Highest negative rates were recorded for the Neve Shaanan (-69.4 per 1,000 inhabitants in 1993 and -83.9 per 1,000 inhabitants in 1994) and the Shapira Quarter (-84.0 in 1993 and -76.9 in 1994). Thus by the mid-1990s many lower income neighborhoods of southern Tel Aviv were characterized by depopulation and very high vacancy rates.

The opportunity for accessing cheap housing in close proximity to the city center was seized by the considerable flows of foreign workers coming into Tel Aviv and whose numbers peaked in the mid 1990's. Over a period of three to four years most of the southern neighborhoods became repopulated by foreign workers, initially single males followed by households moving in at a later stage. The Neve Shaanan area became home to more than 5,000 foreign workers out of a total population of 7,200 (close to 70 percent) (Schnell, 1999). Over sixty percent of apartment buildings in this neighborhood had foreign worker occupancy rates of more than 50 percent. Neve Shaanan became known as the core area in the newly emerging micro-geography of foreign workers residential choice. The neighborhoods due south of this core experienced a similar phenomenon but to a lesser degree (Figure 3.3).

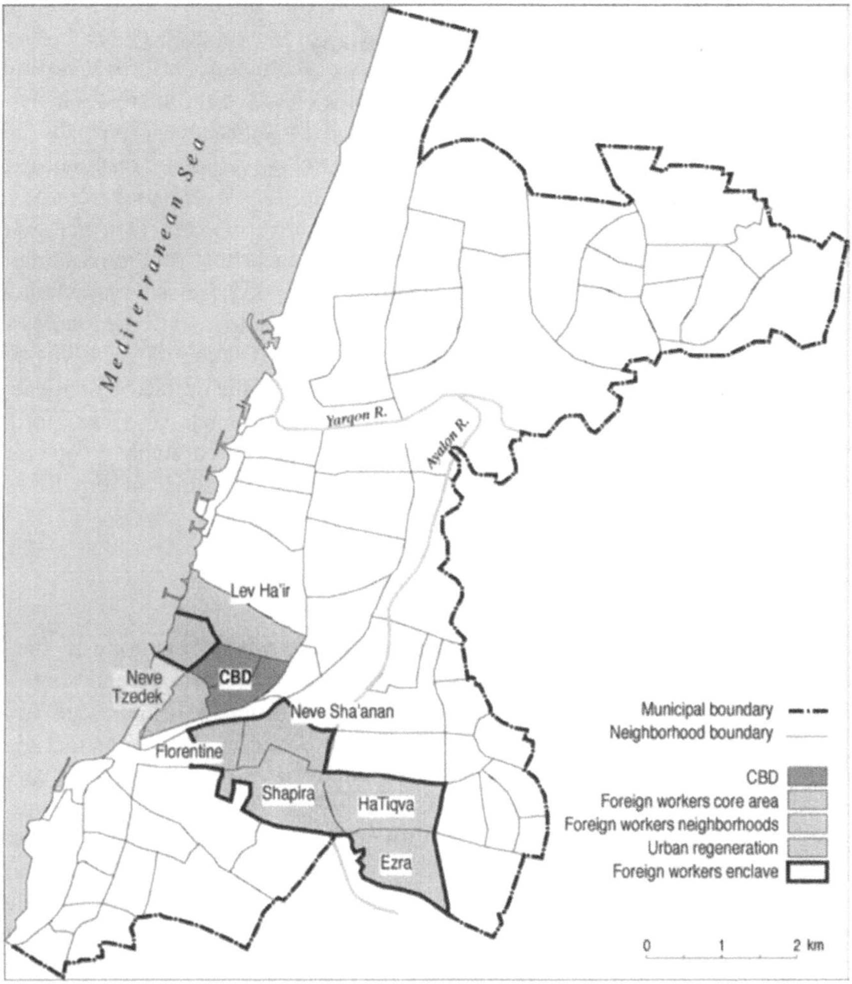

Figure 3.3 Foreign workers neighborhoods in Tel Aviv-Yafo, 1998

These foreign workers neighborhoods have recently begun to consolidate as communities. Local commercial change reflects the social change in the area: many stores and restaurants have changed hands and accommodate the tastes of the foreign workers, mainly from African countries and South-East Asian. A large number of bars, pubs, and massage parlors cater to the entertainment needs of the single, male foreign worker. Small international telephone calling centers cater to the demand for communication with countries of origin. Communal institutions have began to take root reflected in the large number of churches of all denominations, which serve not only as places of worship but also as community centers. Over time this process can be expected to intensify fed by family reunification and new foreign worker household formation which in turn will increase the demand for community services and institutions. While the southern Tel Aviv neighborhoods are invariably perceived as fluctuating and lacking a unifying social structure, efforts at institution building by the various foreign worker communities have contributed an element of permanence to an area traditionally characterized by transience. Thus, the urban consequences of globalization imply residential as well as economic restructuring.

Finally, it should be noted that the reverse side of the globalization coin has left its imprint on the residential structure of the affluent areas of north Tel Aviv as well. Parallel to the urban renaissance and rejuvenation in the select southern quarters of the city, the northern neighborhoods underwent a cycle of large-scale new building. These new housing developments reflected the rising standard of living across the different residential areas north of the Yarkon River. By the end of the 1990s urban restructuring was almost complete. The spatial result was the de facto emergence of the two cities of Tel Aviv - the affluent, veteran Israeli, modern northern neighborhoods juxtaposed with the poorer, highly segregated south composed of foreign workers, aging low-income Israelis and some remnants of the flows of immigrants from the former Soviet Union.

3.5 CONCLUSIONS

This chapter has reviewed two major processes of urban restructuring in the Tel Aviv metropolitan area. The first dealt with the emergence of a second new CBD and the development of a 'top location' outside the municipal boundaries of Tel Aviv-Yafo. This new CBD was statistically characterized by having distinct global features reflecting the rapid change the economic base of the metropolitan area in response to globalization processes. The second process was the polarization of the city of Tel Aviv's residential structure caused by the housing choices of a very large number of foreign workers engaged in community-building in the southern part of the city. In turn this is creating a significant spatial watershed between the affluent north and the deprived south of the city. Globalization processes have therefore served to accentuate existing divides at both the intra-urban and intra-metropolitan scales.

REFERENCES

Bank of Israel (2001). *Annual Report*. Jerusalem: Bank of Israel (Hebrew).

Bar Tzuri, R. (1996). Foreign workers in Israel. In R. Natanson (Ed.), *A new world of work in an era of economic change*. Jerusalem: Office of Economic Planning (Hebrew).

Bogart, W.T. (1998). *The Economics of Cities and Suburbs*. NJ: Prentice Hall.

CBS (2000). *Statistical abstract of Israel, No. 51*. Jerusalem: Central Bureau of Statistics.

CBS (2001). *Statistical abstract of Israel, No. 52*. Jerusalem: Central Bureau of Statistics.

Charney, I. (1997). *Financial services in Tel Aviv-Yafo: Patterns and spatial processes*. Jerusalem: The Floersheimer Institute for Policy Studies (Hebrew).

Glaeser, E.L., Kolko, J. & Saiz, A. (2001). Consumer city. *Journal of Economic Geography, 1*, 27-50.

Guiliano, G. & Small, K. (1991). Subcenters in the Los Angeles region. *Regional Science and Urban Economics, 12*, 163-182.

Quigley, J.M. (1998). Urban diversity and economic growth. *Journal of Economic Perspectives, 12 (2)*, 127-138.

Kipnis, B.A. (1998). Location and relocation of Class A office users: A case study in the metropolitan CBD of Tel Aviv. *Geographical Research Forum, 18*, 64-82.

Krugman, P. (1991). Increasing Returns and Economic Geography. *Journal of Political Economy, 99 (3)*, 483-499.

Mills, E.S. & Hamilton, B.W. (1994). *Urban Economics* (5th ed.), fifth edition. New York: Harper Collins.

Nachmias, D. & Menahem, G. (Eds.) (1997). *Social processes and public policy in Tel Aviv-Yafo*. Tel Aviv: Ramot (Hebrew).

Sassen, S. (1991). *The Global City*. Princeton: Princeton University Press.

Sassen, S. (1999). *Globalization and its discontents*. New York: The New Press.

Schnell, I. (1999). *Foreign workers in south TelAviv-Yafo*. Jerusalem: The Floersheimer Institute for Policy Studies (Hebrew).

Short, J.R. & Kim, Y.H. (1999). *Globalization and the City*. London: Longman.

SECTION II:

'GROWTH ENGINES' OF THE NODE ECONOMY

DANIEL FELSENSTEIN AND YARON ERGAS

4. INVESTING IN AN EMERGING NODE: FOREIGN-OWNED COMPANIES IN THE TEL AVIV ECONOMY

4.1 INTRODUCTION

This chapter investigates Israel's role as an 'emerging node' in the global economy through the prism of foreign direct investment (FDI). Empirically, we investigate the probability that a foreign-owned firm will locate in Tel Aviv. Foreign ownership is taken here as representing one facet of globalization. While we are aware that globalization processes encompass much more than the presence of foreign investors in the domestic economy and should also include some investigation of Israeli firms operating abroad, this topic will be touched on, inter-alia, through the analysis of patterns of FDI. As will be noted, much of this latter process is bound up with FDI in that many Israeli, technologically advanced, firms that try to break into global markets do so through by being incorporated or traded abroad (see chapter 6 and also Haaretz, 2000; Red Herring, 2000). A presence abroad is therefore linked to some form of foreign control over local firms and thus the two facets of globalization are inter-linked.

While this chapter deals explicitly with 'globalization', it also has implications for urbanization. As will be seen, foreign presence in a local firm is inextricably connected with a metropolitan location and invariably this is the Tel Aviv metropolitan region. As such, globalization processes under-pin processes of urbanization and metropolitan growth and expansion. The life-style and housing choices of many of the employees of the more advanced sectors of the Israeli economy, that have attracted a foreign presence, make for increasing pressure on the metropolitan land market. Firms decentralize to outer-metropolitan industrial parks and demand for suburban living means increasing consumption of land and expansion of the metropolitan area. As such, globalization finds expression in urbanization and metropolitan expansion.

The aim of this chapter is to suggest a stylized process by which foreign investment enters an emerging node economy, its impact on metropolitan growth and the way in which the node is integrated with the world economy through these two processes. Due to limits of data availability, our analysis will be confined to investigating those processes for which we have been able to collect empirical data. We are aware of the sterility of the term 'foreign direct investment' and of the fact that a foreign presence in a local firm can be expressed in a multitude of new forms of contractual arrangements. These include arrangements such as research and marketing agreements, limited partnerships, OEM agreements, joint ventures, licensing and franchising and the like. However, we do not have detailed data on all

D. Felsenstein et al. (eds.),
Emerging Nodes in the Global Economy: Frankfurt and Tel Aviv Compared, 57–80.

these forms of foreign presence. We therefore supplement our aggregate findings with some more qualitative information on these new forms of contractual arrangements but this remains at most, anecdotal.

A major hypothesis underlying our approach is that the motives for a foreign presence in a node economy characterized by high tech industry and sophisticated services are very different to those 'classic' factors that characterized FDI in the past. While incentives, cheap labor, infrastructure investment and good labor relations are all part of the collective wisdom as to what attracts foreign investment, our approach is that these factors are much less relevant when it comes to a node economy characterized by technologically advanced activities. Investigating this hypothesis means focusing special attention on the high technology and advanced financial services sectors and in the analysis, these activities merit special attention. The nature of the Tel Aviv high technology economy is also dealt with separately (see Chapter 6). In place of the traditional FDI-inducing factors, we posit a variety of alternative motives that attract FDI. These include, the presence of small firms, the presence of considerable R&D activity in these companies, the relative employment stability of highly skilled labor in these firms and so on. Again, our data do not always allow us the direct measurement of these factors but our results at least allow for drawing conclusions by implication, with respect to this hypothesis.

In the sections that follow, we outline the theoretical and conceptual background on the emergence of a 'node'-type economy and the way FDI is a part of this process. We then describe the process of foreign investment in the Israeli economy from the beginning of the 1990's analyzing the trends and exploring some of the motives and anomalies in the behavior of Israeli firms that seek foreign investment abroad. Following-on from that we will present a simple model of the process of foreign investment as a two-stage (nested) process. This can be viewed conceptually and modeled empirically as either an hierarchical structure, in which the decision to invest abroad and the scope of this investment are executed first followed by the locational decision, which in our case is a binary or categorical choice. Alternatively, the process can be modeled as a simultaneous system where the output of one decision becomes the input to another. The data sources and main variables are then presented as a prelude to the discussion of the empirical findings.

4.2 FDI AS A STRATEGIC CHOICE

A voluminous literature exists on the motivations for foreign direct investment (FDI). Much of this evidence points to factors such as the size of the local market, the existence of incentives, the presence of cheap labor and the union climate as determinants of FDI (Glickman and Woodward, 1989; Dicken and Quevit, 1994). This literature puts the stress on the behavior and motives of the investing companies. Less attention has been focused on the behavior of the companies that are the object of this investment. They are assumed to be the passive recipients of externally dictated events. This chapter suggests that in the case of a node economy looking to break into global markets, becoming the object of FDI (i.e. facilitating whole or partial acquisition by foreign interests), might be a strategic choice (Chapman, 1999; Dicken, 2000).

This is a very different perspective on FDI, to the view traditionally taken. It implies that the imperatives of globalization are encouraging a new form of firm behavior. The volume of foreign investment in a domestic economy is one manifestation of the existence of global networks. The traditional form this takes is through the 'classic' FDI route; i.e. foreign companies acquiring shares in domestic producers. This can lead to either horizontal or vertical integration between the foreign and the domestic interests (Dunning, 1993). Another route to integrating in global networks is through forging shorter-term alliances with foreign interests such as OEM agreements, joint R&D collaborations, limited partnerships, franchises, marketing agreements and the like. This gives rise to 'diagonal integration' between the domestic and the foreign companies (Ahern, 1993). A further strategy for breaking into global networks, and the focus of the present chapter, is for local firms to actively look to FDI (via direct investment, portfolio investment, mergers and acquisitions, venture capital investments etc) as a route to integration into the global economy. While in terms of national accounts this is no different to 'classic' FDI, from a network perspective, its' significance is rather revealing.

This form of behavior is often used as an active strategy consciously pursed by firms in high-risk sectors where market visibility is paramount. For example, recent research from Israel suggests that high technology companies that are largely unknown in the market will issue offerings abroad as a 'signaling' strategy (Blass and Yafeh, 2001, see also Chapter 6). This way they indicate to markets and investors that they should be taken seriously. These firms often face the well-know 'Macmillan Gap' that faces small high risk firms i.e. the trade off between relinquishing control and raising capital. By encouraging foreign investment, the firm may have to forfeit some control but is gaining global investor recognition in the process.

This behavior also calls into question the classic rational for FDI. Foreign investment in domestic firms in this instance is not a result of local cheap labor pools or incentives. Rather, FDI prompted by the desire to enter global networks, presupposes a very different rationale. Earlier work has suggested that this form of investment is attracted to a country like Israel because of factors such as the relative stability of local high skilled labor and the concentration of R&D in small firms (Felsenstein, 1997). This is taken to indicate that the local economy is playing a node-type role in global networks.

A similar trend is discernible in with respect to other economies where the need to establish a high tech presence in foreign markets, is acute. In the Canadian economy for example, while inward investment has traditionally been dominated by the establishment of branch plants of large multinationals operating in primary production, since the early 1990's a new trend has emerged. This is characterized by a shift towards higher value-added, technology-based inward investment and by mergers and equity holdings rather than new plant construction (MacPherson, 1996). In terms of volume of inward investments, acquisitions and stock issue accounted for nearly 90 of all foreign investment activity which totaled over $8bn in 1990. Canadian-based foreign controlled firms account for the majority of inward investments and are more likely to be in advanced, high value-added sectors than inward investment stemming from other sources (McNaughton, 1992). Like the experience of the Israeli high technology sector, the growing importance of technology intensive exports means that Canadian firms are looking to financial institutions in the US (such as NASDAQ) as both a source of capital and international recognition. For Canadian small and mid-sized high-tech firms this is of particular importance as capital constraints put them at a disadvantage with respect to foreign high tech plants operating in Canada (Britton, 1996).

In the case of the UK, the case has been made that local firms and institutions use multi-national investment in the local or regional economy as a method for linking into complementary but geographically distant networks. Cantwell and Iammarino (2000) show a self-perpetuating and symbiotic relationship in the pattern of multinational R&D investments in UK regions. This FDI seeks out particular places with pre-existing technological advantages. Once rooted in these places, FDI further serves to enhance local competences, endogenizing the growth dynamic and making select locations even more attractive to further rounds of investment.

4.3 SURVEYING RECENT TRENDS IN FOREIGN INVESTMENT IN ISRAELI INDUSTRY

This analysis charts the growth in foreign presence in the Israeli economy since the early 1990's using annual aggregate data published by the Controller for Foreign Currency at the Bank of Israel. FDI (defined as a 5 percent controlling interest in real (asset-based) investment) as a percentage of industrial investment has grown from an average of 1-1.5 percent at the start of the decade to 7-8 percent today. Until the early 1990's, the combination of geo-political instability and small market-size were probably the main factors explaining the limited foreign interest, although empirically, the former has been shown to be less of a potent factor in explaining US overseas investments, than commonly imagined (Thrall, 1984). This fast rate of growth over the last decade, has allowed Israel to start approaching FDI volumes in other comparable similar sized countries such as Holland, Denmark and Belgium, where FDI shares of 9-10 percent are commonplace (Chapman, 1999). The dollar volume of this activity however is limited. At the beginning of the decade, foreign direct investment was less $500m. It only reached a plateau of over $1bn in the second half of the 1990's when the first fruits of the 'peace dividend', the liberalization of local capital markets, deregulation and structural reform in local markets and the growth of the high tech boom, began to simultaneously materialize. FDI grew to $1.8bn in 1998, $2.8bn in 1999 and to $4.4bn in 2000 (Bank of Israel, 2000) (Figure 4.1). In parallel, foreign investment in listed securities portfolios (which is not included in our strict definition of foreign 'direct' investment) also increased, from roughly $0.3bn at the beginning of the decade to $2.5bn in 1998 and $4.0bn in 2000. However, the combination of the worldwide economic slowdown plus a worsening security situation in Israel brought a stark turnaround in these trends in 2001 with direct foreign investment shrinking by 34 percent to a total of $2.7bn.

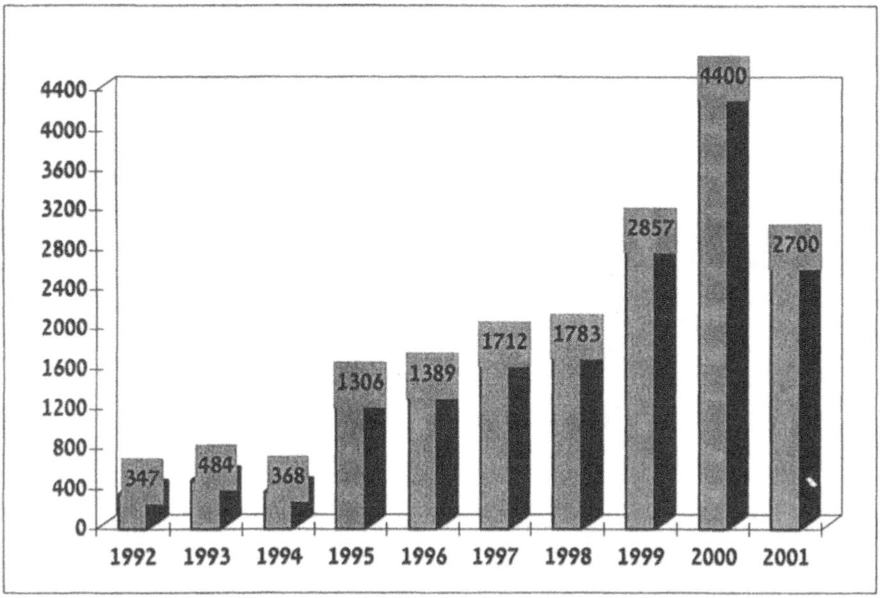

Figure 4.1 Foreign direct investment in Israel, 1990-1999

FDI-generated employment however, is of a smaller magnitude as much foreign interest is in small and new local research-based firms rather than in production-based branch plants. Thus, while the economies of countries such as Belgium, Scotland and Singapore look to FDI as an important employment generator (accounting for 33 percent, 34 percent and 51 percent of total employment in the respective economies), in Israel FDI presence probably accounts for less than 10-12 percent of all employment.

One particularly salient feature of the growth of foreign investment in Israel over the second half of the 1990's has been that related to the activities of high technology companies, The popular perception of FDI is that of foreign capital seeking out opportunities for investment in Israeli high technology. In terms of the number of FDI-based transactions, this image probably reflects reality. However in terms of the magnitude of the volume of investment, the limited data available shows that this perception is unrepresentative. Figure 4.2 shows a gross sectoral breakdown of FDI in Israel over the period 1995-7. This is the only time period for which sectoral data of foreign investment is available. Comparing high tech (electronics, software and telecommunications) with non-high tech (all other sectors) illustrates clearly that over this period, the majority of foreign investment was aimed at the non-high tech sectors. This aggregate picture is supported by evidence from individual transactions.

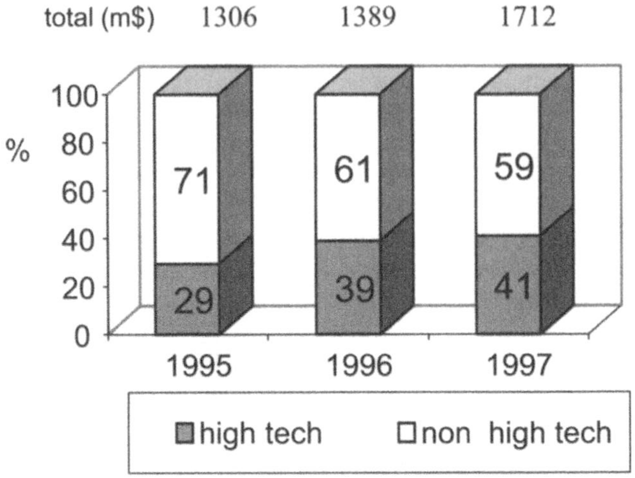

Figure 4.2 Percentage of foreign direct investment in high tech, 1995-1997

Much of the aggregate growth in FDI since the mid-1990's has been due to a few large transactions in the area of mergers and acquisitions (M&A). For example, in 1995 the majority of foreign investment in the local economy was due to foreign acquisitions of a 40 percent controlling interest in the Koor Industrial group, a 20 percent interest in Bezek telecommunications company, 15 percent in Israel Chemicals and the sale of the Lannet communications corporation (to Lucent Technologies). 1996 was characterized by just one large transaction that accounted for the majority of the volume of FDI that year: the Nestle corporation's acquisition of a part of the Osem food group. In 1997, the 2 major foreign investments were in the financial services sector with the sale of 25 percent of Bank Hapoalim to a US investor and 60 percent of the Migdal insurance company to Generali. In 1998, much of the pattern of FDI was further consolidation of foreign presence in corporations that already had some foreign control. Only 7 investments were above the $30m mark. However in the first half of 1999, a flurry of M&A activity saw nearly one dozen Israeli high tech companies being acquired by US firms culminating with Lucent Technologies paying an hitherto unprecedented sum of nearly $4.8bn for a small Israeli optical networking start-up called Chromatis Networks. This sum was equivalent in value to nearly 5 percent of gross national product.

The local acquisition of foreign high technology corporations is a relatively new phenomenon that started in the second half of the 1990s. Prior to the Lucent-Chromatics acquisition, a series of global US high technology corporations entered the local economy through buy-outs of small Israeli high tech firms. This activity has resulted in the arrival of corporations such as Johnson and Johnson (who acquired a local firm called Biosense), America-On-Line (Mirabeles), BMC (New Dimension), Lucent Technologies (Lannet), General Electric (Elscint MRI),

Platinum (Memko) Texas Instruments (Butterfly), Sunguard (Oshap Technologies), US Robotics (Scorpio) and so on. Aside from the symbolic significance of the presence of these global corporations in the local economy, much of the profile of this presence is due to the (unprecedented) magnitude of the sales that have accompanied this entry. Prior to the Chromatics buy-out, small, unknown and unproven local firms had been sold for much smaller sums (themselves of hitherto unknown proportions) such as the case of AOL's acquisition of Mirabeles for $400m the BMC acquisition of New Dimension for $675m.

In the light of these developments, it is easy to appreciate the source of the popular image of high-tech driven foreign investment in the local economy. A series of high-profile acquisitions of small local high tech firms has brought some large global high technology corporations to Israel. More importantly however, a second source is the increasing tendency of local high technology firms to raise capital abroad. Over the longer term, this is also probably a more significant trend as well.

Israeli companies that raise capital abroad, specifically on the NASDAQ stock market, comprise the second largest presence after Canadian firms with nearly 80 firms traded. This is a trend that can be traced to the beginning of the decade. Figure 4.3 illustrates that this aspect of globalization has been exclusively driven by high tech companies. They consistently account for over 60 percent of all capital raised abroad. The slowdown registered for 1998 simply reflects the lower level of stock market activity worldwide precipitated by the South East Asian crisis. As a result many planned stock issues were frozen by Israeli firms.

Research undertaken at the Bank of Israel (Blass and Yafeh, 2001) indicates that those local firms raising capital abroad are on average more technology and innovation oriented, younger and more innovative than firms raising capital locally. Yet, the tendency to raise funds on international markets has not been spurred by the price or availability of local capital. In many instances trading abroad can be a more expensive prospect than trading locally. In addition there has hardly been a shortage of local investment capital locally over the last few years. In 1996 the volume of capital raised abroad was only two-thirds of that raised locally and only one-third in 1997.

This tendency to trade abroad must be more than just a function of access to capital and its relative price. It could indicate a 'signaling' or 'positioning' strategy whereby small firms with little market credibility use the option of trading abroad in order to gain market visibility (Appold, 1991; Blass and Yafeh, 2001). This is very important for firms that are new and unknown. A mature market like that of the US is used as a testing ground for evaluating firms with few tangible assets and little track record. This suggests a very different rationale for foreign investment and for the entry of US firms into the local market, than generally suggested.

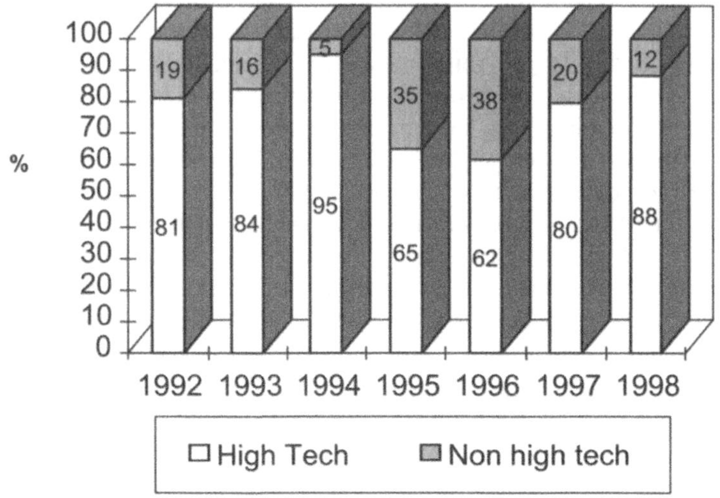

Figure 4.3 Percentage of capital raised abroad, 1992-1998

At this stage, this hypothesis remains purely speculative. It is tested below in Chapter 6 where an analysis of Israeli high tech firms is presented. This will contrast the characteristics of those high tech firms that trade locally with those that trade abroad. A significant difference between these two groups should shed some light on why Israeli firms are looking to global markets for investment and on the functioning of a (high tech) node economy in a global system. In turn this should also provide some support for the basic contention relating to the very different motivations for FDI with respect to a node economy.

Finally, foreign direct investment can also manifest itself in the form of venture capital activity. Again, in this area, the main developments have occurred since the second half of the 1990s and have been linked to the development of the local high tech economy. From a situation of zero venture capital presence in 1990, venture capital investment rose to $1.6bn in 1999 and to over 3.0bn in 2000, with 80 percent of this coming from foreign sources (Jerusalem Post, 2000). This volume of investment ranked Israel in 10th place worldwide with over 100 funds (both Israeli and foreign) operating in the local market. The worldwide recession that followed, saw this volume shrink to $1.25bn in 2001.

4.4 MODELING THE FOREIGN INVESTMENT AND LOCATION DECISIONS

Our basic framework sees the foreign investment decision process as three-staged (Figure 4.4). The first stage relates to the basic decision to invest in a foreign market. Once that decision has been executed, the magnitude of the foreign investment is considered. Many firms change this volume (upwards and downwards) over time after the initial strategic decision regarding foreign investment has been made. The third stage in the decision process relates to the actual place of investment in the target location.

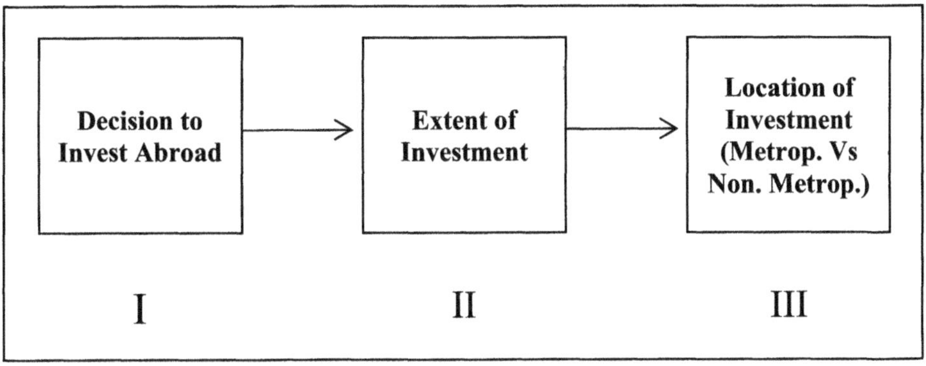

Figure 4.4 FDI and metropolitan location: the basic framework

These three stages can be linked in a causal framework. This suggests that each stage in the decision process is affected by the stage that preceded it. In addition, each stage is influenced directly and indirectly by a series of characteristics that describe firm age, size, sector and markets. The direct and indirect effect of these determinants can be estimated at each stage. This schema is presented as a simple path model in Figure 4.5. In this model, the system of equations has an underlying casual structure. Path modeling involves estimating path coefficients (standardized beta values) and on this basis calculating direct and indirect causal effects using the standard multiplication rule (Duncan, 1975).

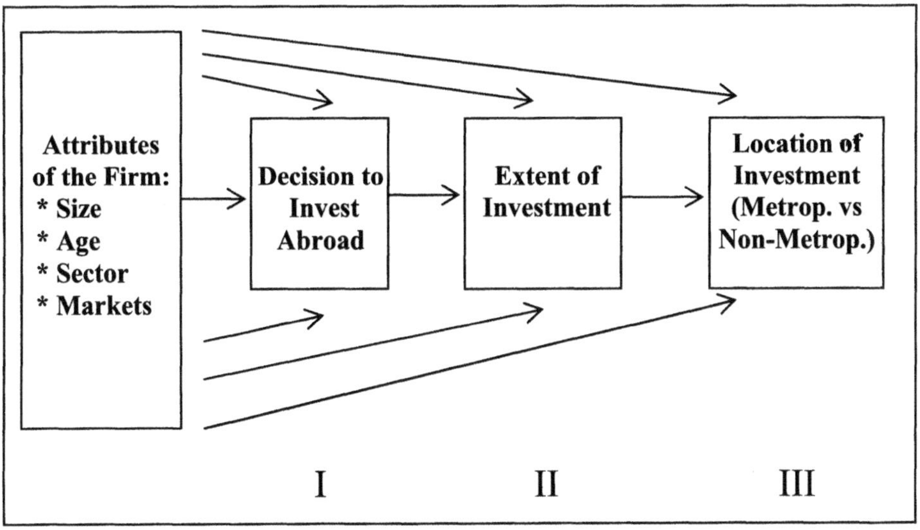

Figure 4.5 FDI and metropolitan location: a framework for analysis

More formally, the causal framework presented above can be estimated as a series of structural equations. We begin with the basic premise that a firm will attempt to maximize utility. This can be achieved through pure business decisions such as those relating to the decision to invest abroad or through spatial-business decisions such as those related to locational choice. For example, the utility function of the firm from a metropolitan location, m, will be;

$$U_m = f() + e_m \tag{4.1}$$

where $f()$ is the form of the utility function and e_m is a random error term. Assuming we know something about the form of f (e.g. location is contingent on firm size, sector, age and other firm characteristics), then our assumptions regarding the distribution of the error term become of prime importance. If we assume that the e_m's are independent of each other and Weibull-distributed, we are assuming a probability choice in which selection of location choice, m, out of the whole set of choices, n, is expressed by the general form;

$$P_{\mathrm{m}} = \exp \mathrm{f}_m\ () / \Sigma_l^n \exp\ \mathrm{f}_n\ () \tag{4.2}$$

This is of course a logit specification and is equally applicable to the basic decision to invest abroad or not. However, in the case of a hierarchy of choices in which the location choice is a lower-order choice that is taken after some more basic choice, in our case the decision to invest abroad or not, then a slightly different expression is needed. In this tree-like structure, the decision where to locate branches-out from the decision to invest abroad. In other words, the two decision choices are linked. In the first instance we have to estimate the probability of location for example in a metropolitan location, m, given the more basic decision to invest abroad, t, as follows;

$$P_{m|t} = \exp(\mathrm{k}_m + \mathrm{k}_{tm}) / \Sigma_l^{m^*} \exp\ (\mathrm{k}_m{}^* + \mathrm{k}_{tm}{}^*) \tag{4.3}$$

The terms k_m and k_t represent the components of the utility terms in the location and foreign investment decisions respectively, while the term k_{tm} denotes those components that are common to both levels in the decision hierarchy. For the foreign investment choice, the marginal probabilities are represented as;

$$P_{\mathrm{t}} = \exp(\mathrm{k}_t + \mathrm{b\ U'}_t) / \Sigma_l^{t^*} \exp\ (\mathrm{k}_t{}^* + \mathrm{b\ U'}_t{}^*) \tag{4.4}$$

where,

$$\mathrm{U'}_{\mathrm{t}} = \log \Sigma_l^{m^*} \exp\ (\mathrm{k}_m{}^* + \mathrm{k}_{tm}{}^*) \tag{4.5}$$

The assumption here is that at each stage of the decision process, the expected utility already accounts for the utility derived from earlier decisions. Thus the decision regarding the magnitude of foreign investment abroad accounts for the more basic binary choice of whether to invest abroad or not. Similarly, the decision to invest abroad and the volume of this investment is already accounted for in the expected utility from the location decision (e.g. metropolitan, small town, peripheral area etc). The size of the *b* parameter will affect the results. Assuming a value of $b \approx 1$ will allow us to estimate the above equations as a regular logit model.

The actual estimation method involves dealing with a 'mixed' system (Wrigley and Brouwer, 1986) where two dependent variables are categorical (the decision to invest abroad and the decision to choose a metropolitan location), while the other is continuous (volume of FDI). This necessitates the following stages of analysis:

Estimating the probability of investing abroad: the regression coefficients in this instance are logits and are thus not directly interpretable unless reported in probabilistic terms (ΔP). These probabilities can be interpreted as illustrating the probability of change in the dependent variable at the mean (i.e. in the likelihood of foreign ownership), due to one unit change in the independent variable[1]. Four our purposes however, these probabilities also represent some of the indirect effects on the decision to choose a metropolitan location.

Estimating the volume of the investment abroad: this is done by OLS regression with the standardized regression coefficients (β values) representing the indirect effects. These serve as inputs for calculating the indirect effects on location of foreign direction investment in the next stage. Indirect effects are derived by applying the standard multiplication rule to the regression coefficients (Duncan, 1975).

Estimating the probability of locating in metropolitan Tel Aviv: the effects of all the variables on this decision are then estimated. These represent the direct effects on the decision choice. As above, the probability changes (ΔP) represent the predicted changes in probability at the mean, given a unit change for continuous independent variables or a categorical change for nominal independent variables. These coefficients along with the indirect effects estimated at the previous stages allow for a comprehensive picture of both the direct and indirect effects on the probability of metropolitan locational choice given the prior decision to invest abroad.

This form of structural equation modeling based on path analysis estimation couched in probability terms has been used in the sociology and organization science literature (see for example Palmer *et al.*, 1987). It has been less utilized as a method for modeling industrial location and foreign investment decisions in economic geography despite the popularity of discrete choice modeling as an explanatory framework for both FDI and location studies (Ondrich and Wasyklenko, 1993; Felsenstein, 1996; Frenkel, 2001).

4.5 DATA SOURCES AND VARIABLES

The data source for this analysis is a composite file constructed from the Registrar of Companies (Ministry of Justice) data base and augmented by Dun and Bradstreet firm-level data. The former source gives a unique cross-sectional picture of the ownership structure of companies at one moment in time. The file includes details as to the form of ownership, e.g. regular shares, management shares, an identifier as to whether the shares are foreign owned but very little data on the company itself. In addition, records are compiled by foreign-owner. Thus a company with multiple foreign ownership will appear more than once. In principle, firms that have ceased operation are meant to report to the Registrar. In practice, they do not and thus many records are simply in active. Furthermore there is little way of distinguishing 'fictitious' companies (established for tax purposes), from real trading entities. The Dun and Bradstreet file augments the above source. While it does not include any details on foreign ownership it does provide general information at the establishment level such as year of foundation, activity, employees, sales, exports etc.

In principle, we analyze the data in four ways. The full data set (that is used for modeling the foreign investment and locational decisions) comprises 2595 observations. This is sub-divided into three further data sets that are used for the statistical descriptions below: data describing foreign owned firms only (819 observations), data describing metropolitan Tel Aviv firms only (1469 observations) and data relating to Tel Aviv foreign-owned firms (452 observations)

The main variables are as follows:

The Existence of Foreign Ownership (FOROWN); this is a binary variable whose source is the Registrar of Companies (Ministry of Justice).

Percentage Foreign Ownership (PERFO); a continuous (censored) variable: this comes from the Registrar of Companies (Ministry of Justice) and relates to the level of foreign ownership in March 1997.

AGE: this continuous variable relates to firm vintage in years. The source is as above, supplemented by data from DunsDisc 1997 (Dun and Bradstreet).

SALES: this continuous variable measures firm size and relates to sales in $m in 1996. The source is DunsDisc 1997.

EXPORTS: a continuous variable describing the company's market orientation and relating to exports ($m) in 1996. The source is DunsDisc 1997.

EMPLOYEES: this continuous variable also measures firm size and relates to the number of full-time employees in 1996. The source is DunsDisc 1997.

Location (MLOC): this binary variable relates to the firms' main location in metropolitan Tel Aviv (Tel Aviv and Central districts). The source is the Registrar of Companies data supplemented by DunsDisc.

Principal economic sector (HIGH TECH): this binary variable relates to whether the firm operates in a high-technology production, research or financial services sector. The source is the Registrar of Companies data supplemented by DunsDisc.

4.6 EMPIRICAL RESULTS

4.6.1 Frequency Distributions

The first task in the empirical analysis is simply to describe the distribution of the data set. To this end, we 'cut' the data according to a series of cross-sections as follows:

All Firms: description of all the firms for which we have information, irrespective of location or extent of foreign ownership

Foreign Owned Firms: this refers to all firms having some foreign ownership, irrespective of location.
Firms Located in Tel Aviv: this relates to all firms in the Tel Aviv metropolitan area, ignoring the presence of foreign ownership.
Tel Aviv Foreign Owned Firms: this is a small sub-set of firms that are both located in the Tel Aviv region and have foreign ownership.
Tel Aviv Non-Foreign Owned Firms: are located in Tel Aviv but without any foreign presence.

Table 4.1 shows the simple geography and the spatial pattern of the foreign ownership structure of the firms. As can be seen, the overwhelming majority of firms are located in the Tel Aviv region (65 percent) and within the city of Tel Aviv itself (53 percent). Foreign-owned establishments are slightly more pronounced, with 68 percent in the Tel Aviv metropolitan area and 54 percent in the city. It should be noted that the construction of this data set has resulted in an a priori over representation of the larger firms in the Israeli economy and thus the predominance of Tel Aviv and the Central region, is hardly surprising.

Table 4.1 Frequency distributions - all firms by location (district) and presence of foreign ownership

Ownership	*Jerusalem*	*North*	*Haifa*	*Center*	*Tel Aviv*	*South*
All Firms (n=2599)	173	202	215	288	1392	105
Foreign Owned (n=825)	81	78	63	105	452	45

Taking just the firms in the Tel Aviv metropolitan area (Tel Aviv and Central districts), we find that one third have some form of foreign presence. Proportionately, this presence is slightly greater in the Central area (37 percent) than in the Tel Aviv area (33 percent). However the absolute volume of firms in Tel Aviv dwarfs all the other areas combined.

Table 4.2 Frequency distributions - firms located in Tel Aviv and Central districts by presence of foreign ownership

	Tel Aviv	*Center*	*TOTAL*
Foreign Owned Firms	452	105	557
Non Foreign Owned Firms	940	174	1114
TOTAL	1392	279	1671

A sectoral breakdown of the data by the various cross-sections is presented in Table 4.3. In terms of absolute representation in the data, the commerce branch is the largest activity accounting for 26 percent of all firms and 29 percent of all the Tel Aviv firms. In this sector, overall 36 percent of establishments have some form of foreign presence although in Tel Aviv this proportion is somewhat lower (29 percent).

Financial services form one of the dominant activities of any large metropolitan area and Tel Aviv is no exception. In our data, financial services establishments account for 20 percent of all firms and for a similar proportion in the sub-set of Tel Aviv firms. Foreign presence in this industry is represented in 29 percent of all firms and in 25 percent of Tel Aviv establishments. It should be noted that these figures are based on establishment counts and still say nothing about numbers employed. It is reasonable to assume that in Tel Aviv this industry is a substantial employer (in the banking, insurance, finance and real estate industries) above the relative size of this sector when measured by the number of establishments.

For our purposes, the high tech sector is of particular importance in view of its' agglomerative and metropolitan locational tendencies the extent of foreign presence in this sector. While high tech establishments represent less than 7 percent of the firms in our data set (bearing in mind the bias toward large firms), 86 percent of these have some foreign ownership. In the Tel Aviv area, this proportion is hardly less pronounced and stands at over 80 percent. In total, 63 percent of the high tech firms are located in metropolitan Tel Aviv. These figures underscore both the role of FDI as a gateway to international networks and the limited spatial dispersal, characteristic of this industry.

As to be expected, both foreign presence and spatial agglomeration in Tel Aviv are much less prevalent in the low tech, transport and construction sectors. While Tel Aviv dominance in all these sectors is less pronounced, the sheer volume of population in the metropolitan area means that the proportion of firms in the Tel Aviv region is still large (for example in the private services and transportation sectors). Some of this concentration could also be due to the fact that in certain cases we have not been able to disengage the firm from its various establishments leading to an over-representation of Tel Aviv where many firms are head-quartered.

Table 4.3 Frequency distributions - all firms by economic activity, location in Tel Aviv and presence of foreign ownership

Economic Activity:	*All Firms (n=2599)*	*Foreign Owned (n=825)*	*Tel Aviv (n=1582)*	*Tel Aviv Foreign Owned (n=452)*	*Tel Aviv Non Foreign Owned (n=1130)*
Commerce	670	239	458	136	322
Construction	240	27	137	12	125
Financial Services	410	122	324	83	241
High Tech.	170	146	109	88	21
Low Tech	527	111	213	45	168
Private Services	232	58	160	29	131
Public services	158	35	57	17	40
Transport	134	34	95	17	78

Looking at the various cross-sections by age structure that differentiates new from old firms (Table 4.4), we see that foreign ownership is proportionately more prominent in newer firms than in older firms. For all the firms, roughly one quarter have been established post-1990. However for those with foreign ownership the share is 42 percent. These proportions are repeated when Tel Aviv is taken as the focus. For all Tel Aviv firms, the share of new firms stands at 23 percent. For those Tel Aviv firms with foreign ownership it stands at 38 percent.

Table 4.4 Frequency distributions - all firms by age structure, location in Tel Aviv and presence of foreign ownership

Firm Attributes	*All Firms (n=2599)*	*Foreign Owned (n=825)*	*Tel Aviv (n=1582)*	*Tel Aviv Foreign Owned (n=452)*	*Tel Aviv Non Foreign Owned (n=1130)*
Firm Age:					
Established Before 1990	1942	480	1210	281	929
Established After 1990	657	345	372	171	201
Firm Size (no. Employees):	1433	575	904	309	595
Less the 100 employees	1166	250	678	143	535
More than 100 employees					
Volume of Sales ($m1996):	2207	743	1286	395	891
Sales > $100m, 1996	392	82	296	57	239
Sales < $200m, 1996	2374	776	1407	416	991
Sales > $200m, 1996	225	49	175	36	139

The bias of the firm size distribution in the data set is immediately apparent (Table 4.4). Medium and large firms comprise nearly 45 percent of the surveyed firms, while their share of the total firms population in reality is rather smaller. While large firms are knowingly over-represented, when firm size is cross-tabulated with foreign ownership and location we can see that a disproportionately large number of small firms have some form of foreign presence (70 percent). This figure is repeated when we observe the Tel Aviv firms with foreign ownership. In this instance, their share reaches 68 percent while the share of small firms in all the Tel Aviv firms is somewhat lower (57 percent).

Sales volume is another measure of firm size. Here unfortunately our data is much more patchy, especially with respect to the firms with foreign ownership that are usually, smaller, newer and more high-tech oriented (see above). The distributions in Table 4.4 point to the fact that sales volumes are lower for firms with a foreign presence than for the others. While overall, only 15 percent of firms have sales in excess of $100m and 9 percent in excess of $200m, when firms with foreign ownership are separated out, this proportion drops to 10 percent and 6 percent respectively. When Tel Aviv firms are considered alone, the proportions are slightly higher than for all firms (19 percent and 11 percent respectively). Subsequently, when Tel Aviv firms with foreign ownership are extracted from the rest of the Tel Aviv establishments, the figures are correspondingly higher than for all firms with foreign presence (12 percent and 8 percent respectively). While Tel Aviv seems to be the repository for the newer, smaller and generally more high tech firms, when size is measured in terms of sales volume these firms would seem to be above average (see difference-of-means tests below, for statistical confirmation or rejection).

4.6.2 Descriptive Statistical Testing

We now focus on some descriptive statistics and some tests of univariate relationships between variables in order to lend some statistical weight to elementary hypothesis regarding firm attributes and their relationship to location and foreign ownership. Using the same cross-sections of the data set as above, the means and standard deviations of the continuous variables are presented in Table 4.5.

With respect to percentage foreign ownership, the average for all firms is 11 percent and for those firms with a foreign presence (one third of all firms) this figure stands at 36 percent. The corresponding figure for Tel Aviv firms with foreign ownership stands slightly lower at 33 percent. The data in Table 4.5 also serves to reiterate the fact that on average, firms with foreign ownership are smaller in employment terms and newer in age. However in this instance, even the average firm is quite large (300+ employees) due to the effect of the very large firms on the mean. The median might have been a better indicator in this case.

Table 4.5 Means and standard deviations (in parentheses) for firm attributes, by location in Tel Aviv and presence of foreign ownership

Firm Attributes	*All Firms (n=2595)*	*Foreign Owned (n=819)*	*Tel Aviv (n=1469)*	*Tel Aviv Foreign Owned (n=414)*	*Tel Aviv Non Foreign Owned (n=1130)*
Percentage Foreign Ownership, 1997	11.4 (25)	35.8 (32.9)	9.3 (22.7)	33.2 (32.2)	0 (0)
Sales (M $, 1996)	106.9 (523.6)	178.7 (108.5)	132.6 (612.2)	184.1 (80.5)	246.8 (1662)
Exports (M $, 1996)	17.4 (93)	40.3 (157)	14.4 (82)	37.3 (148)	5.8 (25)
Firm Age (yrs.)	21.4 (16.0)	14.5 (12.8)	21.3 (16.0)	13.8 (12.1)	20.2 (18.4)
No. Employees	351.5 (1215)	276 (1236)	374 (1330)	312 (1466)	515 (2423)

A major discrepancy should be noted with respect to firms' sales and exports. In this instance, missing values for many of the firms with foreign ownership that were identified through the Registrar of Companies but did not exist on the D&B database, has caused these rather unusual averages. While the export figures are plausible, there may be some bias in the sales figures.

The next logical step in the analysis is to run a series of difference-of-means tests in which the above continuous variables are the dependent variables and various categorical attributes of the firm (size, location, age structure, foreign ownership structure and type of economic activity), are the independent variables. Table 4.6 illustrates the results of this kind of statistical testing which is performed on the same cross-sections of the data that have served the analysis this far. The top panel in that table shows that however one cuts the data, the size categories of greater or less than 100 employees seems to represent a real breaking point in terms of firm performance. With very few exceptions, a statistically significant difference seems to consistently emerge between large and small firms across all the firm attributes (age, sales, export and percentage foreign holding). It should be noted that in the absence of the reporting of individual category means, will still cannot ascertain exactly where these differences lie: for example, just how different the average small and large firms are with respect to age. All we can say at this juncture is that they are statistically different.

The second panel in Table 4.6 looks at differences across the firm attributes with respect to location. In this case only two cross-sections of the data are considered (any separation of Tel Aviv from the rest of the data would be meaningless) and the categorical variable is location in the Tel Aviv metropolitan region or location elsewhere. With respect to all firms, we can say that across most attributes, significant differences do emerge between Tel Aviv and non-Tel Aviv firms. However, when taking only the firms with foreign ownership, none of these differences can be upheld. Foreign-owned firms in Tel Aviv do not seem to be significantly different to foreign owned firms elsewhere with respect to age, sales, exports and percentage foreign holdings.

The 'young' versus 'old' firm dichotomy is tested in the third panel of Table 4.6. The results however are not unequivocal. With respect to firm size, it would seem that there is a major difference between young and old firms, however the data is divided. With respect to the other attributes, the evidence is less consistent. Sales volume does seem to be related to firms' age, while export volume does not.

When foreign ownership structure is divided into three categories (less than 20 percent, 21-50 percent and more the 50 percent), a consistent and significant different emerges across these categories with respect to firm age and firm size (employees). This is reflected in the fourth panel of Table 4.6. However, this difference is not replicated when volume of sales and exports are considered (which are also indicators of firm size). The volatility of the latter variables has been noted above. Thus it is hard to determine whether this lack of significant difference across ownership categories is a substantive finding or one resulting from technical problems associated with these variables.

Table 4.6 Difference-of-means tests: attributes of firms by size, location, age structure and ownership structure (f-values)

	Dependent Variables			
	Firm Age (years)	*Sales ($m 1996)*	*Exports ($m 1996)*	*Percent Foreign Ownership*
Firm Size[1]				
Overall Mean	21.4	106.9	17.4	11.4
Foreign Owned (F.O.)	226.4**	24.9**	8.5*	19.3**
Tel Aviv	1.9	4.9*	4.0*	37.8**
Tel Aviv F.O.	106.7**	24.2**	6.5*	10.4**
Location[2]				
All Firms	8.5*	5.4*	1.4	19.8**
Foreign Owned	1.8	0.05	1.4	10.2**
Age Structure[3]				
Foreign Owned	–	3.3*	2.6	0.005
Tel Aviv	–	5.4*	0.9	28.4**
Tel Aviv F.O.	–	1.8	2.1	1.3
Foreign Ownership Structure[4]				
Foreign Owned	4.9**	2.1	1.1	–
Tel Aviv	2.4*	1.9	0.09	–
Tel Aviv F.O.	2.7*	1.2	1.3	–
Economic Activity[5]				
Foreign Owned	0.009	0.09	4.5*	3.0*
Tel Aviv	0.6	11.7**	5.9*	8.9*
Tel Aviv F.O.	0.6	0.01	3.4	1.1

* α significant at $p < .05$ ** α significant at $p < .001$

1. Firm Size categories: < 100 employees; > 100 employees
2. Location categories: Tel Aviv; elsewhere
3. Firm Age categories: Before 1990; After 1990
4. Foreign Ownership categories: 1-20 percent; 21-50 percent; >51 percent
5. Economic Activity categories: high tech and financial services; other activities

The high-tech and financial services firms are separated from all the others and comparisons are run between these two categories across the various firm attributes (Table 4.6, fifth panel). While significant differences do emerge with respect to exports and sales, we cannot state that there is any significant difference between the two groups with respect to firm age, size and percentage foreign ownership. Thus, the tentative image of the smaller, younger more high tech firm with a higher level of foreign ownership that seemed to emerge from the frequency distributions cannot be fully upheld on the basis of these results. The pattern is not as 'clean' and consistent as we had hypothesized.

4.6.3 Modeling the Investment and Location Decisions

The correlations amongst all the variables are presented in Table 4.7. These bivariate relations suggest a strong relationship between the extent of foreign investment and smaller, newer, firms with an orientation to exports, high tech and metropolitan location. Employees and sales are strongly related suggesting that only one of these should be used as an explanatory variable. Location in metropolitan Tel Aviv would seem to be significantly related to the extent of foreign control and the magnitude of sales and exports.

Table 4.7 Descriptive statistics and correlations amongst the variables

Variable	*Mean*	*SD*	*1*	*2*	*3*	*4*	*5*
1. PERFO.[a]	11.4	24.9	–				
2. AGE	21.4	16.0	-.241**	–			
3. EMPLOYEES	351	1215	-.103**	.215**	–		
4. SALES ($M)	107	523	-.082**	.043	.161**	–	
5. EXPORTS ($M)	17	93	.011*	.109**	.259**	.024	–
6. SECTOR[b]	–	–	.053*	-.129**	-.059*	-.015	-.169**
7. LOCATION[b]	–	–	.113**	-.002	-.016	.119*	.124**

* = Significant at $p < .05$ level ** = Significant at $p < .001$ level.
a All correlations are Pearson coefficients unless indicated otherwise.
b Spearman rank order correlation coefficients

Table 4.8 presents the series of structural models that comprise the analytical framework. Column 1 in the table shows the determinants of the decision to invest abroad (Model 1). At the outset, the large reduction in the number of observation (by two-thirds) should be noted. The model is thus run on a self-selecting sample with all the implications that this implies. As can be seen, this model correctly predicts over 70 percent of the cases. In interpreting the model's coefficients the important feature is their direction and significance. Foreign investment is likely to occur in younger and smaller companies that are oriented to high tech and advanced business services and that service export markets (although the latter is not significant). The probability changes (elasticities at the mean) suggest that a unit change in age and size reduces the average probability of foreign investment by 25 and 61 percent respectively. Similarly, an increase in export or high tech orientation is likely to increase the average probability of foreign presence by 6 and 12 percent.

At the next stage of the analysis (Model 2), the volume of foreign investment is predicted as a function of the firms' attributes plus the probability to invest abroad. In this instance, it is obvious that the prior strategic decision to invest abroad will have a large effect on the actual volume of that investment. However our interest here is in seeing the marginal effect of the other firm attributes after that strategic decision has been made. Does firm size age or market orientation impact on the magnitude of foreign investment once, the decision has been taken, and if so, to what extent? Because of the path-like structure of the model we can assume that decisions regarding the size of foreign investment already subsume the more basic decision to invest abroad and that factors such as firms age and size will have some independent influence. The standardized coefficients of the model (β's) are directly interpretable and are taken as representing the indirect effects on the decision to choose a metropolitan location, affected through the prior decisions to invest abroad.

Table 4.8 Estimating the determinants of foreign investment and locational choice

	Model 1		*Model 2*		*Model 3*	
	Logit	ΔP^2	b^3	β	*Logit*	ΔP
Constant	.271	–	-2.350	–	-.475	–
	(.451)[4]		(3.326)		(.685)	
AGE	-.017*	-.257	-.00022	-.015	-.013*	-.131
	(.006)		(.043)		(.004)	
LOGEMP.	-.449**	-.619	-1.031	-.028	-.150**	-.326
	(.144)		(1.065)		(.162)	
LOGEXP.	.019	.061	1.153	.040	.234**	.673
	(.114)		(.823)		(.118)	
HIGH TECH[1] (OTHER)	.636**	.126	3.336*	.038	.869*	.136
	(.205)		(2.453)		(.394)	
FOROWN[1] (NO FOROWN)	–	–	36.64**	.750	–	–
			(1.64)			
PERFO	–	–	–	–	.005	.040
					(.003)	
Means, Dep. Var.	.27		11.4		.58	
n	691		688		686	
R^2	–		.55		–	
-2x log likelihood	797.9		–		904.9	
χ^2 values for model / d.f.	38.8 / 5		–		25.1 / 5	
Percent correctly predicted	70.9		–		58.9	

* Significant at $p < .05$ level.
** Significant at $p < .001$ level.
1. Dummy Variables, reference group in parenthesis.
2. Change in probability, estimated at the mean from a unit change in the independent variable.
3. b = untransformed coefficients; β = standardized coefficients for continuous variables.
4. Standard Errors in parenthesis.

The results presented here validate the suggestion regarding the marginal impacts of firm attributes. These are all of the order of 1-4 (β values range from (-.02) to (+ 0.03) percent change in the mean level of foreign ownership with a unit change in firm characteristics (employees, sales etc). Overall the major effect is of course, the basic decision to invest abroad. A categorical change in this variable will account for some 75 percent of the probability of change in the level of foreign investment).

While Models 1 and 2 have estimated the indirect effect on metropolitan locational choice, Model 3 presents the direct coefficients through a further logit regression. This model correctly predicts just under 60 percent of all cases. The average likelihood of metropolitan location is 58 percent and it is against this yardstick that all changes need to be measured. The direction and significance of the logits and the size of the various ΔP's indicate that of all the direct effects, high tech and export specialization, increase the likelihood of a metropolitan location, at the mean by 13 and 67 percent respectively. Likewise, the size and age of the firm decrease this probability, by 32 and 13 percent. All these determinants are statistically significant.

Interestingly, the volume of foreign ownership while displaying the right sign, is not found to be a major determinant. Its' direct impact of the average probability is very small (a change in 1 percent foreign ownership increases the average probability of metropolitan location by 4 percent). This does not mean that the decision process outlined above cannot be upheld. Rather, it points to the fact the direct effect of foreign ownership on metropolitan location is of a smaller magnitude than the indirect effect.

The probability changes at the mean (ΔP's) indicate that increasing firm size by one year is likely to decrease the mean probability of metropolitan location by some 13 percent. Similarly, increasing firm size by 10 employees, is likely to decrease this probability by 3.2 percent. A categorical move from low to high tech, directly increases the likelihood of metropolitan location by 13 percent. The results also indicate that increasing exports by \$1m means a rise of over 60 percent in the average likelihood that the firm will be located in the Tel Aviv metropolitan region.

Combining direct and indirect effects (Table 4.9) leads to the conclusion that in all cases bar one, direct effects are of far larger magnitude than indirect effects. The indirect effects on the probability of choosing the metropolitan area are in most cases rather small. The one exception is, significantly, the effect of foreign ownership. In this case, the sum of the indirect effect outweighs the direct effect. The impact of foreign ownership directly is less than the case when foreign ownership subsumes firm attributes. This difference is in the order of 71 percent (75 percent minus 4 percent). In all other cases, indirect effects do not sum to a figure beyond 20 percent.

Table 4.9 The direct and indirect effects on the probability of choosing a metropolitan location

Variables	*Direct*[1]	*Indirect*
AGE[2]	-.131	.0056
LOGEMP.	-.326	.078
LOGEXP	.673	.199
HIGH TECH	.136	.012
FOROWN	–	.751
PERFO.	.040	–

1. ΔP values.
2. Probabilities for Continuous Variables based on standardized coefficients (β).

4.7 CONCLUSIONS

On the basis of the results presented above three salient points seem to emerge that shed light on the FDI process and the role of the high tech node. The first relates to the tendency of foreign investment to seek out the smaller, newer, more high tech and export oriented firms. This is not the 'classic' pattern of FDI behavior. It suggests very different motives to those that are standard in the literature. It would thus seem that foreign investment in a node economy takes place for reasons other than the incentive of local factors prices. The implications arising from these findings could suggest that local research capacity and the local innovations levels may be the key to understanding 'reverse' patterns of FDI and technology transfer (Mansfield and Romeo, 1984). This occurs when the foreign presence in an overseas location is initiated through investment in R&D and then reverses to production. This is the opposite direction to the classic FDI path which starts with production and local factor advantages and sometimes 'scales-up' to R&D. It should be noted however that this hypothesis has not been directly tested here.

The second finding is that the link between foreign investment and metropolitan location is indirect rather than direct. As seen above, firm attributes have a much larger effect on the probability of locating a metropolitan area, than does the amount of foreign investment in a company. This suggests that once firms have made the strategic decision to invest in an R&D node like Israel, the metropolitan location can serve to endogenize and augment that decision. This can best be accomplished in a metropolitan setting for the obvious advantages of scale economies and increasing returns that can be attained.

Finally, our findings show that all firm attributes display larger direct, than indirect effects in determining the choice of location. Again, this suggests the overwhelming importance of the Tel Aviv metropolitan economy in all that is to do with more advanced production and business services. In this respect, FDI in a research-oriented node economy is akin to 'classic' off-shore investment in developing countries where most economic activity is located in one 'primate' city or strictly follows the local urban hierarchy (Cantwell and Iammarino, 2000). It could be that in a small country like Israel, foreign investment is 'indifferent' to many locations, only because so many of them fall within the orbit of the Tel Aviv metropolitan (and to a lesser extent, the Haifa metropolitan) area.

NOTES

1 Following Petersen (1985), ΔP is calculated as follows:

$$\Delta P = exp(L1)/[1+exp[(L1)] - exp\ (L0)/[1+exp(L0)]$$

where:
$L0$ = the logit before the unit change in the dependent variable xy
$L1$ = the logit after the unit change in the independent xy (ie $L0+\beta_j$)

REFERENCES

Ahern, R. (1993). Implications of strategic alliance for small R&D intensive firms. *Environment and Planning A, 25*, 1511-1526.

Appold, S.J. (1991). The location process of industrial research laboratories. *Annals of Regional Science, 25*, 131-144.

Bank of Israel (2000). *Annual report of the controller of foreign currency*. Jerusalem: Bank of Israel (Hebrew).

Blass, A. & Yafeh, Y. (2001). Vagabond shoes longing to stray - Why foreign firms list in the United States. *Journal of Banking and Finance, 25*, 555-572.

Britton, J.H. (1996). High-tech Canada. In N.H. Britton (Ed.), *Canada and the global economy: The geography of structural and technological change* (255-272). Montreal, Canada: McGill-Queen's University Press.

Cantwell, J. & Iammarino, S. (2000). Multinational corporations and the location of technological innovation in the UK regions. *Regional Studies, 34 (4)*, 317-332.

Chapman, K. (1999). Merger/acquisition activity and regional cohesion in the EU. In N.A. Phelps & J. Alden (Eds.), *Foreign direct investment and the global economy* (121- 135). London: The Stationery Office.

Dicken, P. (2000). Places and flows: Situating international investment. In G. Glark, M.P. Feldman & M. Gertler (Eds.), *The Oxford handbook of economic geography*. Oxford: Oxford University Press.

Dicken, P. & Quevit, M. (Eds.) (1994). *Transnational corporations and European regional restructuring, Netherlands geographical studies,* 181. Utrecht: Royal Dutch Geographical Society.

Duncan, O.D. (1975). *Introduction to structural equation models*. N.Y.: Academic Press.

Dunning, J. (1993). *Multinational enterprises and the global economy*. NY: Addison Wesley.

Felsenstein, D. (1996). High technology firms and metropolitan locational choice in Israel: A look at the determinants. *Geografiska Annaler 78B*, 43-58.

Felsenstein, D. (1997). The making of a high technology node: Foreign-owned companies in Israeli high technology. *Regional Studies, 31 (4)*, 367-380.

Frenkel, A. (2001). Why high tech firms choose to locate in or near metropolitan areas. *Urban Studies, 38 (7)*, 1083-1101.

Glickman, N.J. & Woodward, D.P. (1989). *The new competitors: How foreign investors are changing the U.S. Economy*. NY: Basic Books.

Haaretz (2000). *The vast majority of Israeli high tech companies are registered in the US* (September 6th).

Haaretz (2001). *When being near to home is everything* (February 8th).

Jerusalem Post (2000). *Israel registers 10th highest investment in the world* (October 17th).

MacPherson, A.D. (1996). Shifts in Canadian direct investment abroad and foreign direct investment in Canada. In N.H. Britton (Ed.), *Canada and the global economy: The geography of structural and technological change* (69-83). Montreal, Canada: McGill-Queen's University Press.

Mansfield, E. & Romeo, A. (1984). 'Reverse' transfers of technology from overseas subsidiaries to American firms. *IEEE Transactions on Engineering Management*, EM-31, 121-127.

McNaughton, R.B. (1992). Patterns of foreign direct investment in Canada 1985-1989; Canadian-based versus foreign-controlled firms versus US and overseas investors. *The Canadian Geographer, 36 (1)*, 50-56.

Ondrich, J. & Wasylenko, M. (1993). *Foreign direct investment in the United States*. Kalamazoo, MI: W.E. Upjohn Institute for Employment Research.

Palmer, D., Friedland, R., Jennings, P.D. & Powers, M.E. (1987). The economics and politics of structure: The multidivisional form and the large US corporation. *Administrative Science Quarterly, 32*, 25-48.

Petersen, T. (1985). A comment on presenting results from logit and probit models. *American sociological review, 50 (1)*, 130-131.

Red Herring (2000). *Beyond the pale: Israel's VC's go global.* 298-319.

Thrall G.I. (1984). Geo-investment: The interdependence among space, market size and political turmoil in attracting foreign direct investment. *Conflict Management and Peace Science 8 (1)*, 17-47.

Wrigley, N. & Brouwer, F. (1986). Qualitative statistical models for regional economic analysis. In P. Nijkamp (Ed.), *Handbook of Regional and Urban Economics. Vol. 1.* (430-490). Amsterdam: Elsevier.

MICHAEL H. GROTE

5. FRANKFURT - AN EMERGING INTERNATIONAL FINANCIAL CENTER

5.1 INTRODUCTION

Characterized as "the mighty capital of the eurozone" (Sassen, 1999, p. 83), Frankfurt is regarded as a rising world city due primarily to its financial center. This is reflected in the use of such common nicknames as 'Bankfurt' and 'Mainhattan', as well as references made to the city in scientific publications. For example, Ronneberger and Keil (1995, p. 305) write: "A service economy [...] mastered by the finance sector forms the basis for the continuing integration of Frankfurt into the international market" (Author's translation). Frankfurt is not only the most important financial center in Germany, but throughout continental Europe as a whole. Thirteen of the thirty largest German banks are based in Frankfurt, as are approximately two-thirds of Germany's foreign banks. Its stock exchange (ranked 4th in the world) is by far the largest in Germany, with a turnover-share of more than 80 percent, and its derivative exchange (Eurex) has its sights set on becoming the largest in the world. As the host-city of the European Central Bank (ECB), it is also the headquarters of European monetary policy.

This chapter will investigate Frankfurt's functions as a major node within today's global financial network. Unlike most other national financial centers, Frankfurt has not held this position in Germany continuously since the Middle Ages; it only regained its predominance from Berlin after World War II. In contrast to the static 'phenomenon' of financial centers, which has been extensively discussed in the literature, the 'emergence and development' of financial centers is not as well understood. Examining the development of the Frankfurt financial center after World War II provides insight into the dynamics of the self-reinforcing mechanisms at work in financial centers, and this will constitute the second focus of this chapter.

The chapter will begin by examining the theory surrounding financial centers, with an emphasis on basic approaches to the emergence of financial centers and the method employed in this study. Next, we will ask whether or not Frankfurt meets the basic requirements for 'path dependence'; that is, whether it contains self-reinforcing mechanisms. After establishing that Frankfurt does meet these requirements, we will discuss the development of the city as both a financial center and a node in today's world financial system. Then we provide some speculative remarks regarding Frankfurt's future, and the concluding section will briefly summarize the overall findings of the chapter.

D. Felsenstein et al. (eds.),
Emerging Nodes in the Global Economy: Frankfurt and Tel Aviv Compared, 81–107.

5.2 FINANCIAL CENTERS IN THEORY

Financial centers are among the most visible agglomerations of companies. Due to the fact that they do not need natural resources for their production process, these concentrations of activity in specific locations are enigmas which need to be explained. Airports, train stations and other elements of infrastructure, which are often cited as key locational factors, seldom trigger the evolution of a financial center; rather, they themselves expand, along with the importance of the location. In general, economies of scale - both internal and external - are regarded as the major driving force behind the emergence and perpetuation of financial centers. 'Internal economies of scale' means that individual firms gain from concentrating their activities in one location, while 'external economies of scale' (introduced by Marshall as early as 1890) refers to the fact that it is profitable for financial firms to situate their activities in the same location as other banks. Most theoretical articles on financial centers examine the factors that favor the agglomeration of players within the financial industry, and some recent literature will be briefly reviewed below. While this literature explains the overall phenomenon and answers the question 'why do financial centers exist at all?', it leaves two questions unanswered: 1) why do financial centers emerge in specific locations?; and 2) how do certain financial centers become predominant over time? Very few articles have focused on the development of financial centers since the publication of Kindleberger's seminal paper in 1974. However, Porteous (1999) recently introduced the concept of 'path dependence' to the literature of financial centers, and this approach will be examined in more detail below.

Financial centers, like other agglomerations, are considered to be the result of both centripetal and centrifugal forces (Krugman, 1998). Based on examination of the ongoing centralization of financial activities (Sassen, 1999), however, centrifugal forces appear to be of minor importance. Gehrig (1995) actually asserts that financial literature should ask the reverse of the common question, why is economic activity concentrated in only a few places? It should ask, rather: why is *all* economic activity *not* concentrated in one single location? Localized knowledge about customers that is inaccessible from a financial center is considered to be the main centrifugal force at play in the financial sector. Ter Hart and Piersma (1990) focus on the determinants for physical, or spatial, proximity in financial sectors with respect to the requirements of financial transactions: the intensity of face-to-face-contact, the importance of contact rapidity and intensity, the scale of transaction, and acquaintance with the other party. They also provide a list of banking transactions, ranked according to their sensitivity to spatial proximity. The more complex and the closer the transaction is to the customer, the more the need for spatial proximity to customers, and the less concentrated financial activities will be.

Clark and O'Connor (1997) adopt a similar approach with more extensive terminology. They divide financial products into three categories - transparent, translucent and opaque, based primarily on the information type and specificity required in order to trade in each product. The more localized (or tacit) knowledge that is necessary for handling a product, the less concentrated financial activities will be. They suggest that opaque products tend to be traded in sub-national centers, translucent products mainly in national centers and transparent products in global financial centers. From a dynamic point of view, this leads to the conclusion that - *ceteris paribus* - the more products are independent of specific localized knowledge (or the more they are standardized), the more concentrated the financial activity surrounding them may be. These statements are based on the premise that the financial sector contains external economies of scale, which have constituted the subject of many studies of financial centers. By extending classical Marshallian externalities and adapting them to financial centers, Porteous (1999) provides a fairly exhaustive list of external economies. He cites labor market externalities, intermediate services, technological and informational spillovers, and socio-institutional and cultural factors as specific agglomeration economies within the financial sector.

The advent of new information and communication technology as a major force in the financial sector has had ambiguous effects on financial centers, by allowing for the concentration of activities and by increasing mobility (O'Brien, 1992; Grote, Lo and Harrschar-Ehrnborg, 2002). Standardized transactions requiring minimal interaction between financial actors (transaction processing, for example) can be concentrated in one place, and then shifted to any location. These activities often yield only small revenues, and therefore seek out peripheral locations (Walter, 1998; Lee and Schmidt-Marwede, 1993). One example of this type of activity, which will be examined in greater detail below, is stock trading. Thrift's comprehensive paper (1994) forcefully argues that, despite new communication technologies, physical proximity to other firms remains crucially important within the financial sector. The "need for information, for the expertise that allows that information to be interpreted and for the social contacts that generate trust, information, interpretive schemes - and business - is paramount." (Thrift, 1994, p. 334) Accordingly, social and cultural structures within the financial community ('social embeddedness') determine the economic success of financial centers.

The interplay between centrifugal and centripetal forces leads to a discernible hierarchy of financial centers on both the domestic and international levels (Gehrig, 1998; for a general discussion of this pattern, see Krugman, 1996). The above-mentioned literature, however, fails to explain this pattern's developmental path, as well as the evolution of respective predominant national financial centers.

An understanding of the dynamic interplay between external economies of scale and centrifugal forces is necessary in order to gain comprehensive understanding of the emergence and development of financial centers. Unfortunately, relatively little research has been done in this direction. Some studies - beginning with Reed (1981) - have isolated the macroeconomic factors that determine the country of origin of an international financial center. For instance, Goldberg, Helsley and Levi (1988, p. 86) found the following variables to be influential in the emergence of an international financial center: "1) the level of overall economic development; 2) the level of international trade; 3) the extent of financial intermediation; and 4) the stringency of financial regulation." However, while such studies have helped us understand which countries will develop financial centers of international importance, they have not told us very much about the dynamics of this development. Furthermore, the literature merely touches on the issue of how a specific city becomes a country's leading financial center, and this is also true of studies dealing with the development of a specific city over time, like those of Smith (1984) and the Economists Advisory Group (1984).

It was Kindleberger's (1974) frequently cited "The Formation of Financial Centers: A Study in Comparative Economic History" that addressed this question specifically. He describes the development of the leading financial centers in several countries and stresses the gradual movement of banks into these centers. This dynamic creates - in "an evolutionary and time-consuming process" (Kindleberger, 1974, p. 67) - economies of scale, that firmly bind banks and other financial institutions to a chosen location. External economies of scale are self-reinforcing: the more financial actors that are located in one place, the more attractive this place becomes for other financial actors. The literature regards diseconomies of scale, such as increased competition, higher wages and congestion, as of minor importance within the financial sector. So, increasing returns to scale plays a major role in the development of financial centers.

This dynamic process, which Davis (1990) terms 'cumulative causation', is widely accepted in financial center theory, but rarely analyzed with respect to competition between financial centers. First, Porteous introduced the notion of 'path dependence' in 1999 as a key concept for the process described by Kindleberger in his discussion of financial centers, to address increasing returns to scale. Porteous refers to the work of Paul David and Brian Arthur, who pioneered that concept and elaborated on it. "Processes that are [...] unable to shake free of their history, are said to yield path dependent outcomes." (David, 1997, p. 13).

Arthur (1994) offers a path dependence model that shows how a specific location can rise above others if external (or agglomeration) economies prevail. In terms of our discussion, it shows that a financial center with a small advantage for a specific type of financial business attracts more banks to do that specific type of business, and this, in turn, makes the location even more attractive for other banks. Such increasing returns to scale favor a geographic 'lock-in', or making one location superior to others. According to this model, new firms enter the center, but cannot move once they have chosen their location. With increasing returns, the point of departure of this process is of crucial importance. The location that 'naturally' best suits the needs of companies is not necessarily the one that will become the leading financial center. If agglomeration economies outweigh 'natural' location factors (clients, infrastructure, etc.), any location that just happens to initially attract more banks can end up as the predominant financial center. Small advantages at the beginning of the process are sometimes generated by 'small historical accidents', and are not necessarily recognizable as advantages at the time. In order to determine which circumstances actually triggered the emergence of a predominant financial center, it is necessary to closely examine the early history of its development.

This is one of the basic differences between the approach used in this chapter and the 'Krugman-style' approach to agglomerations (the 'New Economic Geography'). Instead of seeing small historical accidents as 'givens', this chapter stresses the circumstances in which Frankfurt emerged from World War II. To date, some features of New Economic Geography models make them unsuitable for application to the financial industry, unless they are first modified. These include general equilibrium models that are important tools for explaining urbanization effects, but too rough to explain low-scale localization effects (Ottaviano and Puga, 1998). Also, this approach in the literature relies heavily on the variation of transport costs to explain the emergence of agglomerations, and is highly formalized (see Fujita, Krugman and Venables, 1999 for an excellent overview). Formalization requires examining a very limited range of variables over time.

Yet, financial centers are extremely dynamic and difficult to define. First, it is not clear exactly what a financial center is. Most authors have their own definitions, which are often as basic as 'you know one when you see one'. Second, the definition of a financial center clearly changes over time. For instance, the importance of stock exchanges has increased dramatically in recent decades, derivative exchanges have come into being, and currencies have faded away. Third, it follows that the reasons why financial actors cluster together also change over time. This dynamic, which is not a common feature of New Economic Geography models, is the focus of this chapter. Nevertheless, this chapter will also employ a basic concept of New Economic Geography - positive feedback, or increasing returns to scale.

The dynamics of the low-scale localization that take place within a financial sector can only be discovered through case study. Only by analyzing the development and the respective competitive circumstances of a financial center over time is it possible to understand the changing agglomeration effects and their interactions. This may offer some insight into the mechanisms involved in financial center formation, as well as some clues concerning further developments in the financial sector. The Frankfurt financial center is a good focus of study for several reasons. It was not Germany's predominant financial center since the 'beginning of history', as is the case in other countries. Berlin held this position prior to World War II, and it was by no means clear afterwards which city would become its successor. Frankfurt is a rare opportunity to test theoretical predictions regarding the emergence and development of financial centers. While data availability regarding financial centers is anything but sufficient, some reliable Bundesbank data from recent decades does exist. Also, the post-World War II situation in Germany can be regarded as resembling the situation in Europe today; that is, the existence of different financial centers, different stock exchanges, a single currency, and unified regulations. By analyzing the development of Frankfurt within the German context and examining its functions as a node within today's global financial network, we can make some predictions regarding the future of the European system of financial centers.

5.3 METHOD

A survey of the post-World War II relocation to Frankfurt of financial institutions - primarily foreign and domestic banks - offers important insight into the development of the Frankfurt financial center. The 'nucleus' of Frankfurt's financial center consists of major German banks, and recently published literature on German financial institutions provides a good look at their motives for locating headquarters in Frankfurt during the 1950's. However, Frankfurt's international relevance is most accurately indicated by fluctuation in the number of foreign banks in the city. In addition, foreign banks are not restricted in their choice of location, as are some domestic banks (like savings banks), and they therefore also serve as an indicator of the relative importance of domestic financial centers. Bundesbank data (including 'Verzeichnis der Kreditinstitute', a register of banks that is published frequently) has been used to construct a database including the date of entry, location, moves, and exit of every foreign bank that has operated in Germany since World War II, according to country of origin and form of presence. The database lists representative offices, branches and subsidiaries of fully licensed foreign banks, as well as the location and number of offices for each year (when available). Financial institutions that are not fully licensed, such as mortgage banks, building and loan associations and investment trusts have been excluded. In spite of some of the data shortcomings, a portion of the institutions examined display somewhat different behavior regarding location, which is discussed below.

In the case of banks with more than one form of presence in Germany, each form is recorded in a separate entry. Each bank - regardless of form of presence - may have up to hundreds of offices. However, only head offices are recorded as separate entities, mainly due to lack of data. Multiple banks represented by one representative office in Germany are listed as separate banks, whereas 'umbrella' representative offices that cover many banks abroad (often cooperatives) are registered as one bank. Since the Bundesbank did not register foreign subsidiaries as foreign banks prior to 1996, a number of other sources had to be consulted as well. However, none of these surveys were conducted regularly, and this resulted in minor deviations in the number of foreign banks listed by different sources (as well as by different Bundesbank sources), most likely due to differing definitions of the term 'foreign bank'. These deviations, however, do not affect the overall trend.

Clearly, the simple recording the movement of banks to Frankfurt does not reveal the motivation behind these moves. Therefore, in-depth interviews with a number of board members of Frankfurt's foreign banks were conducted in order to investigate strategy as well, with an emphasis on the decision-making processes concerning foreign bank location. Thirty-seven interviews were conducted with representatives of foreign banks in Frankfurt during the spring of 1998. These officials represented 44 of the 242 banks operating in Frankfurt in 1998, as, on one hand, some foreign banks had several establishments, often in personal union (for example, one subsidiary and a representative office), while, on the other hand, it sometimes occurred that several banks were represented by one office. Respondents were top executives of their respective establishments in Frankfurt, mostly board members, and interviews were based on conversation guidelines. The sample of banks covered by the interviews provides as representative picture as possible of the totality of foreign financial institutions in Frankfurt, based on geographic origin, size, field of business and form of establishment.

At this juncture, some clarifications regarding different forms of banking establishment are in order. 'Subsidiaries', according to German law, are banks in which at least 50 percent of the capital belongs to foreign owners. 'Branches' of foreign banks are establishments that are legally dependant on foreign banks. Some foreign banks - both branches and subsidiaries - maintain several offices in

Germany. 'Representative offices' of foreign banks in Germany are not authorized to do any banking business. These predominantly small units (usually with a staff of between three and twenty) serve primarily to facilitate contact between German clients and other banks resident in Frankfurt on one hand, and their respective headquarters on the other. Representative offices focus on private customers, dealing, for example, with procuring funds or facilitating international transfers. The establishments that actually conduct business are foreign bank branches and subsidiaries. These different types of offices will not be handled separately here, as legal form hardly affects this type of business. In order to bypass the relatively strict German equity capital rules, some banks have branches parallel to their subsidiaries. Nevertheless, two establishments of the same bank are recorded as two entries, since they may be located in different cities. Following the literature, this chapter regards the business-conducting establishments of foreign banks as primary indicators of a financial center's importance.

5.4 FRANKFURT - A CASE FOR THEORY?

The emergence of Frankfurt as an international financial center may be effectively analyzed within the framework presented here only if the process was, in fact, a path-dependent process. Frankfurt could also have evolved as a major financial center due to other, simpler reasons: its central location in Germany (and in Europe), its large international airport, the presence of the Bundesbank (and now the ECB) and its surrounding industries and wealthy individuals. All this could have made Frankfurt attractive enough to draw a large number of financial firms. However, foreign banks explained their location in Frankfurt in very different terms.

The first three locational factors cited - not based on any default answers - were directly associated with the size of the financial center (Figure 5.1). Respondents were often astonished that such a question was being asked at all, answering: "Frankfurt is simply the financial center of Germany". The next factor - 'proximity to clients' - refers to production and commercial enterprises in the Rhein-Main area, as well to other banks. Five additional factors cited - 'interbank payments', 'image', 'qualified staff', 'specific financial services' and 'the stock exchange' - are also related to the size of the financial center. In short, banks are in Frankfurt because other banks are in Frankfurt, and this is exactly what a path dependent process with underlying increasing returns to scale is expected to reflect. This conclusion is also supported by the high degree of spatial proximity among banks in the Frankfurt financial district.

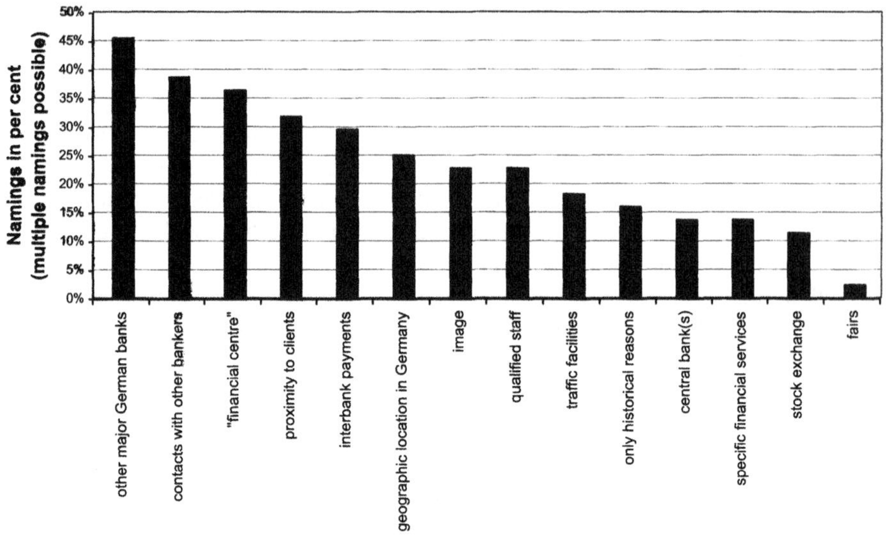

Source: Field survey and interviews

Figure 5.1 Locational factors in Frankfurt from the perspective of foreign banks in Frankfurt

Banks are not located next to the Bundesbank's office, rather close to one other (Figure 5.2). Their spatial proximity to the stock exchange does not hinder increasing returns to scale, as the stock exchange is not a gravitation point in and of itself. Rather, its attraction is based on the many people doing business on the exchange, which, in turn, attract more traders, and so on. In short, based on the premise of the existence of external economies of scale in the financial center, Frankfurt is a good starting point for further analysis.

5.5 FRANKFURT'S DEVELOPMENT

An understanding of Frankfurt's post-World War II evolution into Germany's predominant international financial center involves three components: 1) indicators of Frankfurt's national and international status and relevance; 2) the reasons for the clustering of financial actors; and 3) the nature and unique characteristics of Frankfurt's path dependent development. The task of identifying a group of indicators that reflect Frankfurt's importance over the decades is not an easy one. It is by no means clear exactly what elements constitute a financial center, and the use of different indicators may result in differing understandings of Frankfurt's development. It should also be noted that the international functions of financial centers have changed as well - not very much international business was carried out after World War II, and, in addition, some actors have become less relevant over time, while others have gained greater significance.

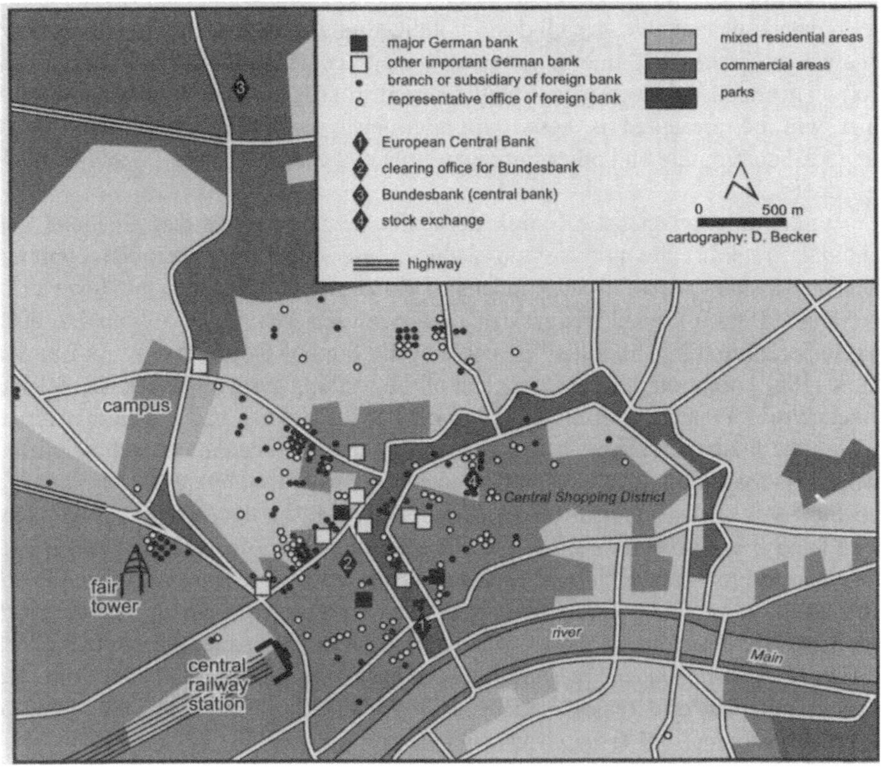

Source: Field survey.

Figure 5.2 The spatial pattern of financial institutions in Frankfurt

However, Porteous (1999) lists the following indicators: 1) finance sector employment; 2) finance sector employment in relation to the total labor force; 3) the number of head-offices located in the financial center; 4) the value of national assets controlled by banks in the financial center; 5) the amount of payments settled in the financial center; 6) stock exchange turnover (shares, bonds, currencies and derivatives); and 7) foreign bank presence. These indicators should be interpreted whenever possible in relative terms, with regards other financial centers. A number of other elements are also of interest. In the context of the internationalization of a financial center, strategies of domestic banks entering foreign markets from the financial center offer additional insight, as do the strategies motivating the entrance of foreign banks. The influx of investment trusts and other bank-substitutes must be considered as well. Companies providing services for the financial sector (such as specialized lawyers, consulting firms, and auditors) have been growing increasingly significant over the past decade, and, just as they were mentioned as a locational factor in interviews, they serve as indicators for the relevance of financial centers. Only a few studies have examined these companies, which comprise the supporting companies of the 'financial cluster' (for example, Lo, 2001). Since consistent long-term data is unavailable, not all desired indicators will be examined in the following analysis of Frankfurt's emergence as a financial center. Still, the literature provides some anecdotal evidence, which will be used in proxy. Other valuable information that will be presented is based on interviews conducted within the Frankfurt financial community and other European financial centers (Grote, Lo and Harrschar-Ehrnborg , 2002).

Based only on statistical indicators, the actual reasons that financial actors entered Frankfurt are not easy to deduce. Interviews with financial community decision-makers are a far better means of obtaining this information. However, this method suffers from the drawback that interviewees are usually only able to discuss agglomeration effects that they perceive at the time of the interview. As Chick and Dow (1988) point out, the development of the banking system has had several stages since World War II. In each stage, the capital market has had a different function within the financial system and the banking system has been integrated in a different way. This leads to the conclusion that each stage has different agglomeration effects on the level of the financial center. Combined with the development of (financial) technology, agglomeration effects are indeed very likely to change over time; it is therefore quite implausible that financial actors entering Frankfurt today are doing so based on the same factors as decades ago. Heterogeneous and changing actors (domestic banks, foreign banks, financial services, asset managers, etc.) all have different, time-dependent reasons for coming to Frankfurt. Present-day interviews cannot elucidate the reasons behind past moves into Frankfurt; therefore, only careful reasoning and research can help ascertain previous agglomeration effects. Specific historical circumstances regarding national and international regulation, economic development, and the banking sector have therefore been taken into account, always bearing in mind the danger of rationalizing locational decisions in retrospect. Historical and other sources have also been consulted, but, again, relevant sources of this type are hard to come by.

Path dependent processes play out in many small steps, but can only be presented in defined stages. Such stages, therefore, have to be constructed, and each one is an integral part of the process as a whole, which, in our case, is the growth of Frankfurt as a financial center. Such stages, however, are not easily defined; qualitative changes can be signaled by quantitative differences, while it is difficult to determine what level of quantitative change justifies advancing to another stage (Chick, 1988). This difficulty results in a degree of arbitrariness inherent in the act of defining the stages of any historic process, an arbitrariness of which we must always remain aware. We must also be cognizant of the danger of rationalizing past actions in retrospect. For the sake of our discussion, the criteria on which stage-definition has been based were either qualitative changes (such as the authorization to reunite the major German banks in 1958) or sharp changes in important indicators over a distinct time period. These stages may be similar to the stages identified by Chick and Dow (1988), but are not identical. Still, it should always be kept in mind that Frankfurt's emergence as an international financial center is a continuing process. It is perhaps especially interesting to consider whether Frankfurt's national predominance was crucial for the international importance it achieved. This question will be examined in more detail below.

The following section will present three roughly delineated stages of Frankfurt's development as a financial center. Due to a lack of available consistent data, the analysis relies to some extent on anecdotal evidence and description of the different stages. Indicators are discussed in the context of the stages during which they were most dynamic. As a location's development path is determined by 'small historical accidents' that are not reflected in indicators, this examination of the historical context of Frankfurt's development will add valuable insight to our analysis.

After World War II (1945-1958). Berlin served as Germany's chief financial center from the time it succeeded Frankfurt in this capacity until World War II. After the war, however, Berlin was unable to retain this role, due primarily to Soviet politics and the threat of Soviet invasion. In this context, the American and British governments decided to base the 'Bank deutscher Länder', which preceded the Bundesbank, in western Germany. Hamburg and Frankfurt were promising candidates, as were, to a lesser degree, Cologne and Düsseldorf. After the war, much was in favor of Hamburg: it had suffered less destruction than other cities during the war; it could provide the available office space necessary for banking; the largest non-Berlin offices of many banks were located in Hamburg (one major German bank - the Commerzbank - even had its head office in Hamburg); the turnover volume of its stock exchange was greater than that of all other German stock exchanges combined; and most foreign payments were cleared in Hamburg. Nevertheless, Frankfurt, with its central location in West Germany, its large airport and - most significantly - the headquarters of the American military government, was chosen as the location for the German Central Bank in 1948 (Holtfrerich, 1999). Other special state-owned banks moved to Frankfurt after 1948 as well, including banks for agricultural and housing financing. Of these, the most important was the Bank for Reconstruction and Development ('Kreditanstalt für Wiederaufbau'), which distributed the funds of the Marshall plan. These primarily political decisions were the 'historical accidents' that paved the way for Frankfurt's evolution as Germany's predominant financial center.

At the beginning of the 1950's, however, such a course of development was not at all clear. Hamburg was still the major center, while Düsseldorf, with its large industrial hinterland ('Ruhrgebiet'), controlled a major share in domestic credit activities (Wolf, 1998a). Furthermore, the three major German banks - Deutsche Bank, Dresdner Bank and Commerzbank - had in 1948 been split into ten separate banks, one in each state ('Land'). In 1950, for instance, the Düsseldorf division of Deutsche Bank controlled almost 40 percent of the balance-sheet total of all Deutsche Bank Group, in contrast to the mere 9 percent controlled by the Frankfurt division (Holtfrerich, 1995). In subsequent years, the parent organization of Germany's credit unions, and some other private banks from Berlin, relocated to Frankfurt, while the parent organization of Germany's savings banks based itself in Düsseldorf in 1950, only to relocate to Frankfurt in 1965 (Holtfrerich, 1999).

In 1952, the major banks were allowed to combine their ten divisions into three banks, and in 1957 a total recentralization was permitted. Dresdner and Deutsche Bank immediately located most of their headquarter functions in Frankfurt, while

Commerzbank - with its headquarters in Hamburg (!) - moved to Düsseldorf in 1958. Beginning in the 1970's, however, Commerzbank gradually shifted its headquarter functions to Frankfurt. The Union-Owned Bank ('Bank für Gemeinwirtschaft') also moved to Frankfurt in 1958 (Holtfrerich, 1999). The primary reason that banks moved to Frankfurt was the Central Bank. Banks that refunded themselves with funds from the money market had to be close to the institution with the power to alter market conditions and provide liquidity. Written messages from banks to the Central Bank - and vice versa - had to be transported by messenger, and the payment system relied heavily on paper exchange. These factors all made it inevitable that major German banks would headquarter themselves in Frankfurt (Holtfrerich, 1999). This explanation is supported by the fact that institutions that did not need daily contact with the money market (primarily mortgage banks) did not relocate to Frankfurt. In fact, only one of the 15 largest mortgage banks was located in Frankfurt in 1958 (Wolf, 1998b).

National Pre-Eminence (1958-1973). 1958 was a remarkable year in regulatory terms. The European Economic Community (the predecessor of the EU) was founded, the German Mark became fully convertible and a year had passed since the Bundesbank had replaced the Bank deutscher Länder (Wolf, 1998b). The late 1950's witnessed the beginning of the internationalization of the German capital market, with the first foreign bonds being traded in Frankfurt in 1956 and the first foreign shares in 1958. The first foreign currency bond was initially offered in Frankfurt in 1957, and the first foreign Deutsche Mark bond was placed in 1959 (Ambrosius, 1998; Holtfrerich, 1999). In quantitative terms, however, these activities were only of minor importance.

More important were the domestic shifts that took place within the banking system. Major banks began retail activities in the 1960's with small standardized loans and checking accounts; this expanded their available funds, and also strengthened Frankfurt's money market, where liquidity was balanced. During the same period, the importance of capital markets in Germany began to increase, exemplified by the fact that investment funds were made available to the public in 1957. As the head office functions of major banks were, for the most part, located in Frankfurt, it was the Frankfurt stock exchange that profited most from these shifts. An indicator of the onset of Frankfurt's predominance can be seen in the early decision of DWS (Deutsche Gesellschaft für Wertpapiersparen - currently Europe's largest investment company), which was founded in Hamburg in 1956, to move to Frankfurt in 1957 (Holtfrerich, 1999). Foreign exchange markets were established in Frankfurt and four other German financial centers (Berlin, Düsseldorf, Hamburg and Munich) in 1953. Because of the ongoing internationalization of the German economy and Bundesbank's strong focus on stability, the German Mark played an increasingly important role for international investors during the 1960's; and, in 1972, it was first classified as an international reserve currency. The Bretton Woods system, with its fixed exchange rates, experienced difficulties at the end of the 1960's due partly to the German Mark's consistently visible revaluation tendencies. Bundesbank undertook currency market interventions in Frankfurt only, and this too served to increase the city's attraction as a financial center (Holtfrerich, 1999).

Since the end of the 1960's, the majority of foreign banks entering Germany have based themselves in Frankfurt, after receiving treatment similar to domestic banks with the implementation of the Banking Law ('Kreditwesengesetz') in 1962 (Figure 5.3). Between 1960 and 1971, the market share of foreign banks in Germany rose fourfold, to about 4 percent, and, by the end of this period, the world's 15 largest banks (60 percent of which were American) had offices in Germany. In those days, the primary reason for establishing a presence in Germany was to advise different domestic firms as they went abroad (Pohl and Jachmich, 1998; Kindleberger, 1983; Schmidt, 1963). Locational choices of foreign banks serve as especially useful indicators when tracing the importance of a financial center. Legal restraints (in the case of savings banks) and comparatively high sunk costs often restrict the locational decisions of domestic banks in such a way that they are not likely to move. Also, many banks establish offices just to be present in a financial center, and such offices are not always recorded in Bundesbank records. In this way, the presence of foreign bank headquarters should be regarded as a reliable indicator as to the importance of a financial center.

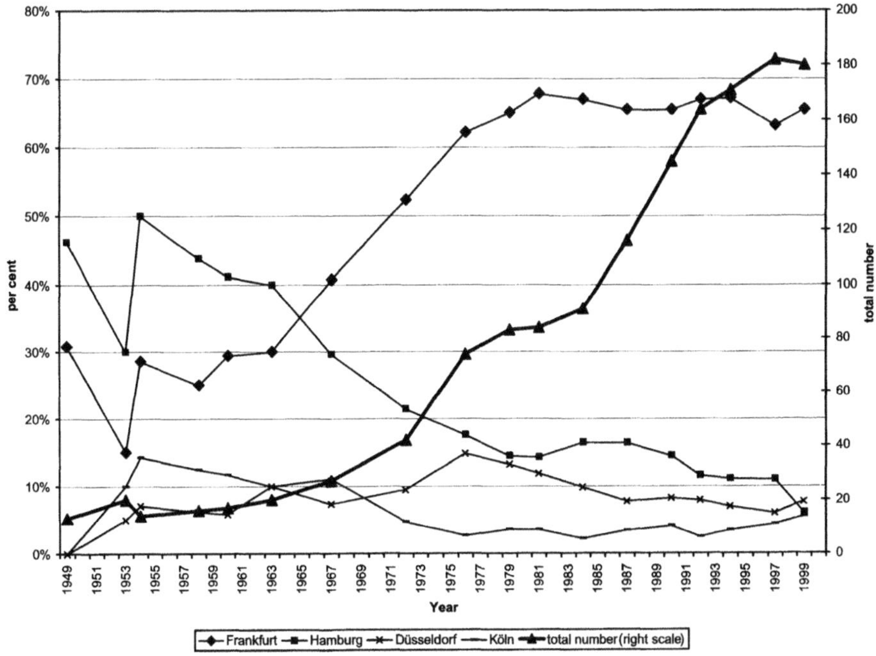

Source: Author's Database.

Figure 5.3 Branches and subsidiaries of foreign banks in Germany (share per financial center, and total number)

The break in recorded foreign banking presence in the largest German centers in 1953 resulted from the rise of 'other locations' at the time. Bank deutscher Länder's statistics from that year classify the numerous, dispersed special banks of the American military as foreign banks as well. In the early 1960's, many banks with headquarters throughout Germany either established offices in Frankfurt or acquired Frankfurt-based privately owned banks, primarily in order to do business with Frankfurt's stock exchange (Der Volkswirt, 1968). In this way, Frankfurt established itself as the most attractive financial center for domestic banks; subsequently, it also attracted the majority of foreign banks entering Germany.

Internationalization (1973-1998). After some turbulence, the Bretton Woods agreement collapsed in 1973, in the wake of the oil price crisis. The recycling of 'petrodollars' led to an unprecedented growth in internationally mobile money, which fostered the expansion of the international banking sector. German banks, which had relied on cooperating with foreign correspondence banks for quite a while, increased their foreign presence comparatively late (Stephan, 1998; Wolf, 1994). The recent increase in the foreign presence of Frankfurt's major banks (Figure 5.4) is primarily the result of an expansion of banking activity within Eastern Europe's emerging markets.

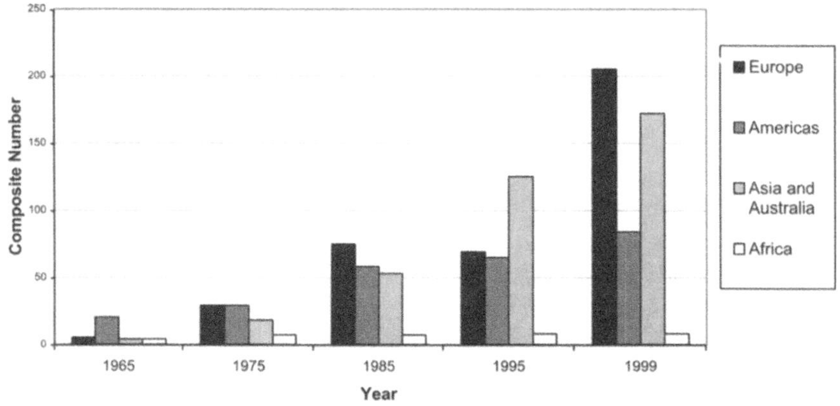

Source: Stephan, 1998; Petermann, 2000; Author's calculations.

Figure 5.4 Foreign presence of major Frankfurt-based banks

The graphs in Figure 5.4 reflect the foreign presence of the three major Frankfurt-based banks. In order to arrive at a single figure regarding foreign banking presence, branches and subsidiaries were assigned a value of '3' and representative offices, which do not facilitate banking business, a value of '1'. Different types of offices were considered separately, while multiple, same-type offices in Germany of the same bank were considered as one office.

As Frankfurt's banks went abroad, Frankfurt's economy increasingly specialized in the financial sector. While the financial sector has been characterized by a general trend that is becoming more important in all the cities mentioned above (Holtfrerich, 1999), financial sector employment in Frankfurt has increased more rapidly than in any other city in Germany, rising from a mere 2 percent in 1950 to 12 percent in 1999. Frankfurt's share of all German financial sector employment also rose significantly between 1950 and 1987, reflecting the city's growing importance in relation to other centers (Holtfrerich, 1999). Other sources (for example,

Landeszentralbank, 2000a) indicated that these trends were likely to continue after 1987. More recent, consistent data, however, is not yet available.

As capital markets gain significance within the German financial system, which until the 1980's had relied extensively on banking, the importance of stock exchanges in judging the relevance of financial centers has also increased (Schamp, 1999). Frankfurt's stock exchange possessed no advantage after World War II; rather, Frankfurt just happened to be chosen as the location of the Central Bank, and this attracted major private banks. The market share of Düsseldorf's stock exchange - Germany's second largest - plummeted from 35 percent in 1973 to 15 percent in 1988 (Rudolph, 1992), and to a mere 6 percent in 1997 (Schamp, 1999). In contrast, Frankfurt's stock exchange currently holds a market share of about 80 percent. This development was the result of the circumstances discussed above, as well as of a path dependence of stock exchange development: the more liquid a market is, the more advantageous it is to trade in that market. This, in turn, provides even more liquidity, and so on (Dietl, Pauli and Royer, 1999).

International liquidity began to rise sharply ('petrodollars') beginning in the 1970's. Many foreign banks came to Frankfurt in part because it had the best access to the German payment settlement system, but also in order to do business on Frankfurt's stock exchange. By the end of this period, Frankfurt had become the home of about two-thirds of all the foreign bank branches and subsidiaries in Germany. This pattern has been remarkably stable: while the number of business-conducting units of foreign banks rose from approximately 40 to 180 between 1973 and 2000, Frankfurt's market share has remained more or less unchanged (Figure 5.3). In contrast, Frankfurt's share of German representative offices, which had been concentrated in Frankfurt for quite a while, declined during the 1990's, primarily due to the new relevance of Berlin as the capital of a reunited Germany.

5.6 FRANKFURT TODAY: AN INTERNATIONAL FINANCIAL CENTER

5.6.1 German Banks

Today, 13 of the 30 largest German banks have their head offices in Frankfurt, and another two are headquartered in Mainz and Wiesbaden. The Rhein-Main-region, therefore, has by far the highest concentration of major banks in Germany, with a share of more than 50 percent of the 30 largest banks' balance sheet total (Die Bank, 1999; Author's calculations). In total, 211 business-conducting German and foreign credit institutions have their head offices in Frankfurt, while another 72 institutions based elsewhere in federal territory have offices in Frankfurt (Landeszentralbank, 2000b). Moreover, Frankfurt has the highest concentration of resident capital investment companies in Germany, with more than 60 percent of the reported companies.

The German banks of Frankfurt are also of international significance. Based on balance-sheet totals, Frankfurt is home to six of Europe's 50 largest banks and four of the world's 50 largest banks (the latest large mergers, however, have not been taken into account, The Banker 1999a; 1999b). In comparisons based on the number of top 500 banks in each European financial center, Frankfurt ranked second (107 banks) to London (201), but placed well ahead of Paris (90), Milan (77) and Madrid (75) (The Banker's Almanac, 1998; Institutional Investor, 1998; Grote, Lo and Harrschar-Ehrnborg, 2002). In general, German banks do not belong to the most internationalized group of banks. According to the '50 global banks' list issued by the journal 'The Banker', based on share of business volume abroad, the three major Frankfurt-based banks were ranked 10th (Deutsche Bank), 41st (Commerzbank) and 50th (Dresdner Bank) (The Banker, 2000a). The business volume of German banks abroad now stands at 30 percent of domestic business volume, up from 15 percent in 1984. The majority of this international activity, however, is concentrated in Luxembourg (Deutsche Bundesbank, multiple reports; Rudolph, 1998).

A survey of the German financial system provides added insight into the aforementioned patterns of internationalization within the Frankfurt financial center. There is no separation between commercial and investment banks in Germany, and most banks are permitted to engage in a wide range of financial activities, including insurance and securities ('universal banks'). Aside from mortgage banks and special purpose banks, Germany has three major banking groups: commercial banks, public savings banks and private cooperative banks. Both savings banks (the largest group, with a market share of 37 percent) and cooperative banks (15 percent market share) are regionally constricted in their ability to do business, in order to prevent competition within each group. Major banks control 10 percent of the market, while other more regionally oriented commercial banks control an additional 15 percent (Deutsche Bundesbank, 1998). Despite the distinctive roots of each of the three banking groups that are still discernible in their business biases, they are all similarly organized according to a three-tier structure (Deeg, 1996). The primary level includes offices dispersed more or less throughout the entire country. The secondary level, which is of minor importance in the case of commercial banks, consists of regional headquarters, with roughly one in each German state ('Land'). While the head offices, which constitute the third and final level, are all located in Frankfurt, some regional headquarters, primarily of savings organizations, belong to the largest banks in Germany.

Major banks once focused predominantly on financing large German companies, but, since the 1970's, they have been focusing on SME's ('Small and Medium Sized Enterprises' - the well known German 'Mittelstand', or middle-market) and private households as well, thereby competing with savings banks and cooperatives (Edwards and Fischer, 1994). The latter, in turn, have been attempting to get their share of wholesale financing through their regional and head offices. Nevertheless, the rise of international capital markets, most notably the Euromarket, has provided large firms with alternative financing possibilities, and in this way has had the greatest impact on major banks (Deeg, 1999).

Changes in international capital markets have also influenced the national German financial system. The dissolution of the Bretton Woods system of fixed exchange rates, and the subsequently high volatility of currency markets, led to an extended demand for international financial products. In parallel, the recycling of 'petrodollars' increased the liquidity of markets. The advent of information technology, along with the international tendency to deregulate financial markets, made it easier for industries and banks to finance their operations internationally. Due to heavy regulation in Germany, this process resulted in major German banks losing considerable business to competitors abroad. In a rare alliance, domestic banks, foreign banks (seeking entry into the German financial market) and the government (in search of financing for its own debt) worked together for the liberalization of financial markets. From the 1980's onward, Germany began its transformation from a bank-based financial system into a capital market based financial system, a process which is not yet complete. Since 1990, the stimulation of financial markets has been the explicit aim of the federal government, and this was reflected in the legislation of a series of 'financial market promotion laws' (Deeg, 1999).

The comparatively late internationalization of major German banks mentioned previously in this chapter can be partially explained by regulation in Germany. As long as the primary customers of major banks (large industrial firms) were unable to find less expensive financing in international markets, there was little need to internationalize. Only after a rise in international financial markets cut into their business did German banks follow their customers (or at least their customers' financing) abroad (Kindleberger, 1983). Nevertheless, German banks were less experienced in capital market transactions than their foreign competitors, particularly those from countries with a separation between commercial and investment banking (in either the past or present). In 1989, major German banks started acquiring British and American investment banks in order to close this knowledge gap (Deeg, 1999). Foreign investment banks however, still handle the majority of German investment banking.

5.6.2 Foreign Banks in Frankfurt

As was the case a decade ago, foreign banks still control only a small share of Germany's traditional bank activities, approximately 5 percent of the total balance sheet business (Verband, 2000). However, Frankfurt's foreign banks hold a 10.7 percent market share of all Frankfurt-based banks (Landeszentralbank, 2000a). Still, these figures do not take into account transactions like foreign exchange operations and numerous other investment bank activities, and therefore do not give a fair indication of the importance of foreign banks within the German banking system (Deutsche Bundesbank, 1998). German Mark bonds constitute another major sphere of activity. During the first half of 1999, foreign banks functioned as the syndicate manager for 63 percent of issued volume (not including government bonds or account issues). Foreign banks also led the market in terms of Germany-related M&A (mergers and acquisitions) deals, with a 78 percent market share of transaction volume and a 75 percent share of total mandates during the first half of 1999. Again, the only serious competitors are the investment bank subsidiaries of German banks (Verband, 2000).

In 2000, there were 337 foreign financial institution establishments in Germany, including foreign bank branches, German banks in foreign possession and representative offices. 60.5 percent are headquartered in Frankfurt, and the city therefore constitutes the most important location for foreign banks (Figure 5.5). In comparison, 429 foreign banking establishments were located in London (1997) and 237 in New York (1999) (Blanden and Charvet, 1997; Blanden, 2000). Of Frankfurt's foreign banking establishments, Japanese and American banks hold the largest share, followed by banks from various European states.

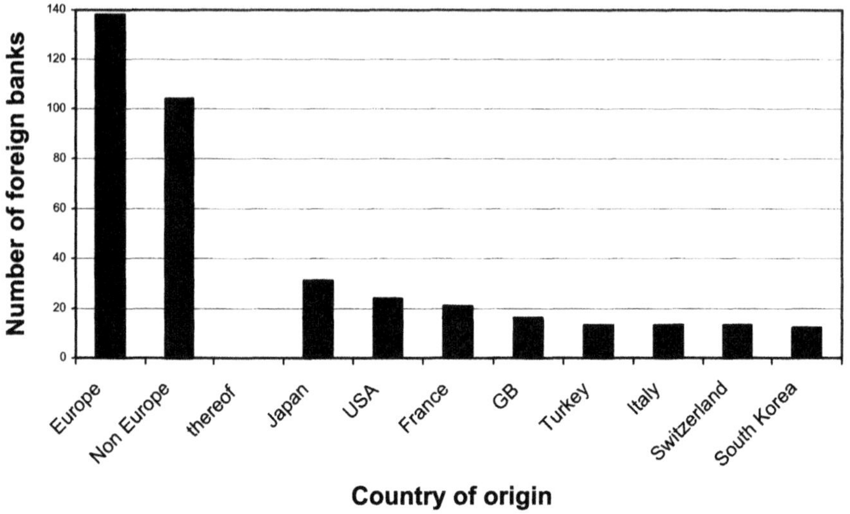

Source: Author's survey.

Figure 5.5 Origin of foreign banks in Frankfurt

The Frankfurt financial center, however, rarely serves as a starting point for the international operations of foreign banks. Rather, presence in Frankfurt is primarily related to the German market, and only Austria and, to a lesser degree, Switzerland are the other international markets covered from Frankfurt. Despite the expansion of German banks to Eastern Europe, foreign banks did not adopt a strategy of using Frankfurt as a gateway to Eastern European markets. These banks were either already represented, or their business was handled directly from main headquarters (European banks) or from London-based subsidiaries (Japanese and American banks). Such business is being covered from Frankfurt in only a few cases, primarily in connection with the entrance of German production enterprises into Eastern Europe.

As mentioned earlier in this chapter, foreign banks enjoyed a general advantage with respect to activities that had previously been heavily regulated in Germany, like investment banking (Verband, 2000; Tonomura, 1994). Foreign banks account for 18 percent of all parties making transactions on the Frankfurt Stock Exchange, and they make 18 percent of sales. Their share in the turnover of the Swiss-German Futures Stock Market (Eurex) totals 71 percent, and they account for 70 percent of all those making transactions. In this case, Eurex facilitates a unique feature that is especially effective, which will be discussed in more detail below - 'remote access'.

This feature enables people to perform market transactions from other countries via Eurex terminals established there. In 1996, the market had 47 remote members out of 93 foreign participants. By mid-1999, the figure had increased significantly, and 192 of 230 foreign market participants were 'remote members' (Verband, 2000).

5.6.3 Stock Exchange

Today, the Frankfurt stock exchange clearly dominates Germany's eight stock exchanges, with a market share of 80 percent of German security turnovers. This includes its share of Xetra, a screen-based trading system developed by the Frankfurt stock exchange, used widely to trade German blue-chip stocks. The stock exchange, as well as the foreign exchange (which trades in bonds and derivatives), focuses to a large extent on the national market. While the share of foreign products traded on German markets is small, a considerable portion of German financial products (such as German federal bonds) is traded abroad (Seifert, 1997).

The Frankfurt stock exchange has become more international over the past few years, with the rapid increase of foreign equities listings. This, however, has not increased the share of foreign equities traded in Germany in the same manner, since the turnover volume of these shares remains comparatively small (Deutsche Börse, 2000). More notably, the German stock exchange has undergone internationalization in two other ways. On one hand, the Frankfurt stock exchange cooperates with other stock exchanges. Two examples of this are its cooperation with the Vienna stock exchange, with each exchange enjoying full access to the other, and the Zurich stock exchange, where a joint derivative exchange (Eurex) was established. The proposed, but unsuccessful, merger of the Frankfurt and London stock exchanges in 2000 was the last in a series of attempts to establish a pan-European stock exchange. On the other hand, the German stock exchange provides 'remote access' for its derivative exchange, as well as for its spot share-trading system, Xetra. Many foreign participants use these systems (especially the older and better established Eurex system) from abroad. During the 1990's, the German stock exchange was transformed from a passive marketplace into an important actor in financial markets and centers. This change was facilitated by a 1992 modification of the exchange's legal structure, with the establishment of the 'Deutsche Börse AG' (German Stock Exchange Company), which now administers the Frankfurt stock and derivative exchanges, as well as some other related services. In 2001, the German stock exchange went public. The initial public offering enabled the Deutsche Börse to use stock in any future takeovers of other stock exchanges and with this prepared it to play a major role in the expected consolidation of European stock exchanges. The most important stockholders of the German stock exchange are still the major German banks, who pressure the exchange to become more efficient in order to be able to better compete internationally (Breuer, 1997).

A unique aspect of Frankfurt's stock exchange is 'remote access', which will continue to result in new types of competition between stock exchanges and to have significant impact on financial centers. A particularly good example of this dynamic is the 'battle for the Bund-future' between London's Liffe and Frankfurt's Eurex.

The Bund-future is the most widely traded derivative in the world. As the commodity is based on German federal bonds, it might have been expected to be traded in its 'home-country', Germany. However, as German regulation did not allow derivative trading until 1990, the market emerged at Liffe, and the relevant expertise was consolidated in London. The efforts of the German Derivative Exchange - after its formation in the early 1990's - to transfer Bund-future trading volume to Frankfurt were of little success, despite its comparatively low trading costs. Due to the prevailing lock-in effects (mostly relating to market liquidity), a large portion of trading continued to take place at London's Liffe. Only after Eurex terminals with remote-access facilities were installed in London, and German banks shifted all their trading volume to Eurex, London traders began using the Frankfurt-based system: in result, Eurex's turnover share of UK-based participants rose from 7 percent in 1997 to almost 30 percent in 2000 (Eurex, 2001). Eurex's market-share in Bund-future trading now stands at 99 percent. Figure 5.6 shows that Eurex's gain in Bund-future trading volume coincides with an increase in the number of traders from abroad (Grote, Lo and Harrschar-Ehrnborg and Lo, 2002).

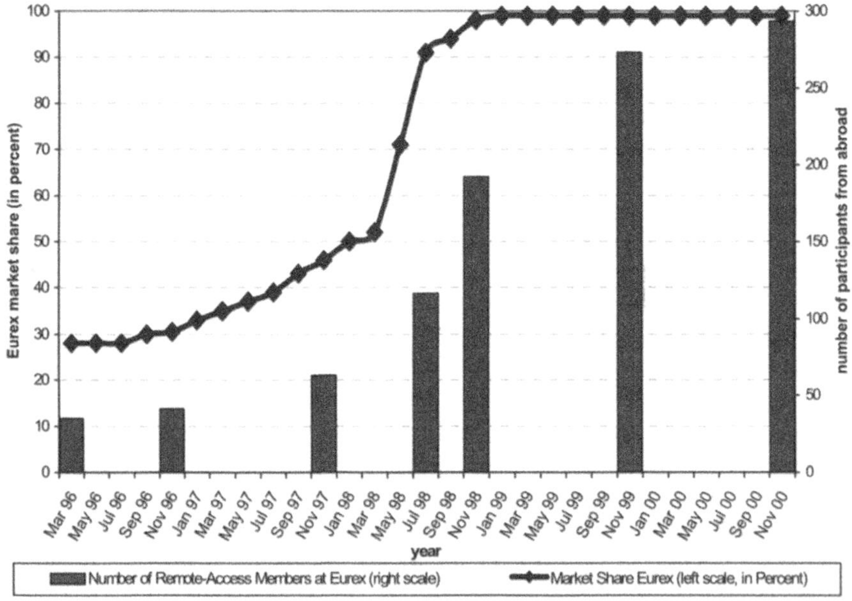

Source: Grote, Lo and Harrschar-Ehrnborg, 2002; Eurex, 2001.

Figure 5.6 Market share in Bund-Future Trading and remote access members of Eurex

The Frankfurt trading system is therefore now the central marketplace for Bund futures, despite the fact that most traders access the system from foreign financial centers, primarily London. Any future merger among European stock exchanges that would form a common trading system for all major European shares could have similar consequences. Most likely, more trading will take place on the joint stock exchange, while fewer traders will be located in Frankfurt.

5.7 FRANKFURT'S FUTURE: SOME SPECULATIONS

The situation in Germany following World War II resembles the situation in Europe today in many ways, including the existence of various financial centers and stock exchanges, a single currency and unified regulations. Banking regulation has become almost completely standardized in Europe (Rudolph, 1998). For instance, the introduction of the European common market in late 1992 allowed banks to do business throughout the European Union with a single license ('euro-passport'). The introduction of the Euro in 1999 initiated a new dimension of the integration of European capital markets. Still, inferences regarding the development of the German financial system cannot be applied on the European level without taking into consideration other, more divisive aspects of Europe; national languages, tax systems and legal systems remain important barriers to the full integration of Europe's financial system.

The concept of path dependence so applicable to Germany suggests that the largest European financial center will, over time, attract the lion's share of banks in Europe. By far, the largest financial center in Europe today is London, and our analysis is complicated by the fact that Great Britain has yet to introduce the Euro. In order to gain perspective on the possible nature of the future system of European financial centers, we will now examine the agglomerative forces that fostered Frankfurt's emergence as Germany's leading financial center in Germany, with respect to their applicability today. This will also facilitate a more detailed discussion of the crucial impact of new financial technologies on 'traditional' agglomeration forces.

5.7.1 The Traditional Forces of Attraction

The European Central Bank: Having been a main agglomeration force in Germany in the 1950's, the location of the ECB was also the subject of long political disputes between European governments. Once Frankfurt was chosen, the people of the city were quite enthusiastic about its potential as a European financial center. One headline read: 'An additional 10,000 bankers are expected to come to Frankfurt.' (Frankfurter Allgemeine Zeitung, 1998) So far, however, they have been disappointed; the ECB has attracted neither additional banks nor bankers to Frankfurt. In contrast to the past, decisions of the Central Bank are instantly spread all over the world. In addition, a small department is often sufficient for gaining an understanding of the goings-on inside the ECB.

The Money Settlement System: With the introduction of the Euro and the emergence of new technology, low-cost settlement of Euro payments is possible all over Europe by means of electronically linked national payment systems (for example, 'Target'). Since very few currencies remain in use in Europe, the need for on-site presence in different states within the foreign exchange business has diminished dramatically.

Stock Exchange: A common European stock exchange has yet to be established, so not much has changed in this area. However, since economies of scale (or liquidity) play an important role in stock exchange competition, it is very likely that one predominant stock exchange will prevail. In fact, the proposed London-Frankfurt stock exchange merger was the latest in a series of attempts to achieve such an outcome. Any future pan-European stock exchange will feature remote accessibility, and there will no longer be any technical necessity for spatial proximity to stock exchanges at all.
The Labor Market and Spillover Effects: When asked why they are located in Frankfurt, 'other banks' and 'the labor market' where the most important responses of bank officials interviewed (see Figure 5.1 above). Clearly, this centralizing force in the European system of financial centers remains important. For instance, traders like to be where other traders are - especially in order to get the news before it is officially announced. In fact, the removal of many other barriers could result in additional concentration of traders in one city - London, which boasts the largest agglomeration of traders today.
'Other Banks' and Specialized Service Firms: Investment banks that entered Frankfurt in the 1990's sought easy access to other capital market actors and highly specialized lawyers and accountants. These professional service providers, in turn, were already present in Frankfurt because of the banking activities taking place there. This can also be interpreted as a positive response, pointing to further agglomeration of the European banking business into one single financial center.

5.7.2 The Case for a Local Presence

Some of the agglomeration effects that brought banks to Frankfurt after World War II are virtually irrelevant today, while others point to the conclusion that banks will move to the location of most other banks (or London, in the European context). But the question of local financial centers remains valid. Why are not all foreign banks in Germany located in Frankfurt? Or, on the European level, why are all banking activities not concentrated in London?

Among the reasons for coming to Germany, the factor cited most often by foreign banks in Frankfurt was their clients' desire for a contact person physically present in Germany (Author's survey; Pulm, 1993). 'Face-to-face' contact is crucial in banking, and knowledge regarding changing regulatory frameworks (laws, for example) and the changing needs of potential clients necessitate a presence in the country as well. Some bankers, however, held that maintaining a presence in Germany is no longer necessary, and others were still concerned with German Mark payments until the final introduction of the Euro. Still, the majority of responses related to close contact with clients. Language is still an important issue, but not as significant as might have been expected; in most cases, it has not been possible to serve German clients from a 'German bureau' located abroad, even if staffed by Germans (some banks attempted to use this approach a few years ago). As one respondent explained, "The connection to the domestic cultural milieu gets lost once you are located abroad" (Author's interviews; see Gehrig, 1998 for a similar statement). Knowledge of the nation-specific customs of business ('usances'), the ability to assess the state of a firm and its loans and the ability to gain access to clients all demand a permanent presence in the country where business originates. Additional factors cited were face-to-face contacts with other bankers and the need to demonstrate commitment to German clients by means of a German address and telephone number (Author's survey). The order of importance of these statements, however, may vary according to the financial products in question (Grote, Lo and Harrschar-Ehrnborg, 2002).

5.7.3 The Re-bundling of Functions

It is still very unlikely that all banks will relocate to London, even if Great Britain were to introduce the Euro. However, bankers' deviating responses to the question of why they are operating in Germany indicate that the European system of financial centers is likely to experience some changes in the coming years. These changes will be difficult to quantify by means of indicators like number of banks and a headcount of respective financial centers. Instead, a qualitative shift in the local presence of banks is likely. Financial businesses are unique in their need for proximity to clients, other banks, and bank headquarters, and predictions regarding the future of the European system of financial centers must take this into consideration (Grote, Lo and Harrschar-Ehrnborg, 2002). In general, the less client-contact needed, the more likely a business will be mobile. Some examples of the tendency of banking establishments to relocate are outlined below.

Back-office functions are becoming increasingly mobile through technology advancements and harmonization within the EU. A similar centralization of back-office functions on the firm level is likely, in order to exploit economies of scale (Breuer, 1998). If a financial center provides an infrastructure that is favorable for these specific functions, businesses can easily concentrate there. This will occur when the external economies of close proximity to other specialists outweigh the economies of close proximity to other back-office departments of the same firm. For instance, Frankfurt has developed one of the most sophisticated settlement systems for the clearing of German Marks (EAF - 'Elektronische Abrechnung Frankfurt'), which is now being widely used by foreign banks as a Euro clearing system (referred to as EAF-2, or 'Euro Access Frankfurt'). In fact, non-European banks have actually started concentrating their Euro-clearing in Frankfurt (Author's interviews). While back-office functions are clearly the most mobile due to the little if any contact with clients they entail, M&A consulting is an example of an extremely immobile business. 'Thick communication' is an essential element of the deal, and requires spending extensive time with the different actors, as well as a thorough knowledge of the respective markets of the firms involved (Lo, 2001). Even in the case of international transactions, firms are advised almost exclusively by investment bankers from the home and target markets. Bankers involved with M&A tend to move to the country of origin of the business in question.

Stock trading will be the final example discussed here. Liquidity is crucial to stock exchange competition, as stock market liquidity attracts traders. In the past, this has led to numerous attempts to achieve mergers and alliances between European stock exchanges. Liquidity alone, however, does not impact the location of traders, since new stock exchange technology has introduced remote accessibility, thereby facilitating trading from any stock exchange. After the failure of the merger between Frankfurt and London in 2000, many potential alliances and mergers are again possible; if a pan-European stock exchange will, in fact, be established, different forces will be at work influencing the location of traders. Headquarters prefer that their trading departments be within close range, as: trading departments profit from the presence of other related departments; this facilitates more personal control over the traders; and this serves to avoid future catastrophic losses. Also, having local knowledge of the firms whose shares are being traded helps traders stay one step ahead of the game and make profits (Hau, 1999). On the other hand, traders like to be where other traders are, in order to get a feeling for the tacit 'mood' of the market, and this dynamic would lead to an agglomeration of traders in a single location. Altogether, the future result of these tendencies is far from being clear - even regarding banks that frequently shift most of their traders from their headquarters to London and back - and demands further research (Grote, Lo and Harrschar-Ehrnborg, 2002, Lo and Grote, 2002).

5.8 CONCLUSION

The previous section demonstrated that external economies of scale will play a major role in shaping any future system of financial centers. National financial centers will continue to exist based on labor markets, infrastructure, face-to-face contact with other bankers, and other 'low-range' centralizing forces. Specialized staff remains the decisive factor in the settling down of the 'footloose' finance industry, even in the advent of new communication technologies. Financial centers will be *national* due to the necessary 'cultural proximity' between banks and clients, as long as language, customs and laws remain within the bounds of the nation. This conclusion confirms the findings by Ter Hart and Piersma (1990) and Clark and O'Connor (1997) on the product level. The closer the client is to the business, the less concentration will occur. However, classifying financial centers on the product level is no longer sufficient, as developments in technology and deregulation, which allow the unbundling of business processes, mean that economies of scale can be exploited on a scale smaller than the product.

What does this mean for Frankfurt as a financial node in the global system? Analysis of a node's functions within the global financial network has to take into account the various stages of the value chain of the business conducted there. Overall, not much business from abroad is done in Frankfurt; rather, the business opportunities provided by the German economy attract foreign banks. Still, Frankfurt has provided an increasing range of functions for other European financial centers. Besides the monetary politics carried out through the ECB, Frankfurt also exports the less visible Euro-clearing and stock exchange technology to other financial centers. Frankfurt is also losing to London and other financial centers, as back offices of foreign banks migrate back to their respective head offices, and stock exchange trading in German shares takes place increasingly in London and elsewhere. The nature of competition between financial centers is changing, from a situation in which each center provides every service, towards a greater division of labor and cooperation between the centers themselves. We can thus refer to a sort of 'co-opetition' evolving within the European financial center system. Sassen (1999) predicts that Frankfurt will stand at the top of a 'secondary network', behind London and New York.

Our analysis of Frankfurt's development into Germany's leading financial center, and its application to today's European financial center system, allow us to make three important generalizations. First, we observe that the agglomeration effects themselves differ depending on the exact point in time they are examined. Even if they remain constant in size, the underlying business of the agglomeration may be changing, and, in this context, technology can have a crucial impact. Second, it is not particularly useful to take into consideration the non-shifting agglomeration forces at play over a long period of time. In the finance industry, *different* and *changing* forces lead to agglomeration. Third, we can conclude that path dependence and related concepts are useful tools for describing trajectories of agglomerations that display economies of scale. However, as our first two conclusions suggest, while "each successive stage reflects forces that are obvious in retrospect, attempts at prediction nearly always get it completely wrong" (Krugman, 1999, p. 4).

REFERENCES

Ambrosius, G. (1998). Intensives Wachstum (1958-1965). In H. Pohl (Ed.), *Geschichte der deutschen Kreditwirtschaft seit 1945* (149-202). Frankfurt: Knapp.

Arthur, W.B. (1994). *Increasing returns and path dependence in the economy*. Ann Arbor: University of Michigan Press.

Blanden, M. (2000). Shrinking in the big apple. *The Banker 150*, March, 66-67.

Blanden, M. & Charvet, E. (1997). Making tracks for London - Foreign banks in London. *The Banker 147*, No. 861, 27-29.

Breuer, R.E. (1997). Die Zukunft der Börse: Technologieplattform oder Dienstleistungsunternehmen? In D. Hummel (Ed.), *Banken in globalen und regionalen Umbruchsituationen, Festschrift für Johann Heinrich von Stein* (65-79). Stuttgart: Schäffer-Poeschel.

Breuer, R.E. (1998). Der Finanzplatz Deutschland im Wettbewerb. In H.E. Büschgen (Ed.), *Finanzplatz Deutschland an der Schwelle zum 21. Jahrhundert* (145-157). Frankfurt: Knapp.

Chick, V. (1988). *The evolution of the banking system and the theory of monetary policy*. In Johann Wolfgang Goethe-Universität Frankfurt am Main, Geld und Währung Working Papers, Nr. 8.

Chick, V. & Dow, S.C. (1988). A post-Keynesian perspective on the relation between banking and regional development. In P. Arestis (Ed.), *Post-Keynesian monetary economics* (219-250). Aldershot: Elgar.

Clark, G. & O'Connor, K. (1997). The informational content of financial products and the spatial structure of the global finance industry. In K.R. Cox (Ed.), *Spaces of globalization* (89-114). London, New York: Guilford Press.

David, P.A. (1997). *Path dependence and the quest for historical economics: One more chorus of the ballad of QWERTY*. University of Oxford, Discussion Papers in Economic and Social History, Number 20, November.

Davis, E.P. (1990). International financial centers - An industrial analysis, Bank of England Discussion Paper, No. 51, September, 1-23. Reprinted in R. Roberts (Ed.) (1994), *International Financial Centers, I* (3-27). Aldershot: Elgar.

Deeg, R. (1996). German banks and industrial finance in the 1990s, *WZB Discussion Paper* FS I 96-323, Berlin.

Deeg, R. (1999). *Finance capitalism unveiled - banks and the German political economy*. Ann Arbor: The University of Michigan Press.
Der Volkswirt (1968). Der Zug nach Frankfurt. *Der Volkswirt* Nr. 11, 15.3.1968, 34-35.
Deutsche Börse (2000). *Historical statistics: Cash market*. Frankfurt.
Deutsche Bundesbank (1998). Entwicklung des Bankensektors und Marktstellung der Kreditinstitutsgruppen seit Anfang der neunziger Jahre. *Monatsbericht März 1998*, Frankfurt.
Deutsche Bundesbank (several years). *Monatsberichte*, several volumes.
Die Bank (1999). Die 100 grössten deutschen Kreditinstitute. *Die Bank 8/99*, 566-567.
Dietl, H., Pauli, M. & Royer, S. (1999). *Frankfurts Position im internationalen Finanzplatzwettbewerb: Eine ressourcenorientierte Analyse*, Working Paper No. 1999/10. Frankfurt/M.: Center for financial studies.
Economists Advisory Group (1984). Regulation, competition and technology in the supply of financial services, chapter 4 of city 2000: The future of London as an international financial center. London: Lafferty Publications (37-55). Reprinted in R. Roberts (Ed.) (1994), *International Financial Centers, I* (387-405). Aldershot: Elgar.
Edwards, J. & Fischer, K. (1994). *Banks, finance and investment in Germany*. Cambridge: Cambridge University Press.
Eurex (2001). *Eurex monthly statistics*. Derivatives Market, April.
Frankfurter Allgemeine Zeitung (1998). Frankfurt profitiert von der neuen Zentralbank. *Frankfurter Allgemeine Zeitung, No. 123*, May 29.
Fujita, M., Krugman, P. & Venables, A.J. (1999). *The spatial economy*. Cambridge, MA: MIT Press.
Gehrig, T. (1995). Koreferat zum Referat Nobert Schulz. In B. Gahlen, H. Hesse & H.J. Ramser (Eds.), *Standort und Region* (79-82). Tübingen: Mohr.
Gehrig, T. (1998). *Cities and the geography of financial centers*. Center for Economic Policy Research, London, Discussion Paper No. 1894.
Goldberg, M.A., Helsley, R. & Levi, M.D. (1988). On the development of international financial centers. *Annals of Regional Science*, XXII, February (81-94). Reprinted in R. Roberts (Ed.) (1994), *International Financial Centers, I* (81-94). Aldershot: Elgar.
Grote, M.H., Lo, V. & Harrschar-Ehrnborg, S. (2002). A value chain approach to financial centers - The case of Frankfurt. *Tijdschrift voor Economische en Sociale Geografie* (forthcoming).
Hau, H. (1999). Evidence on the information geography of a stock market, speech at the *CFS research lecture*, Center for Financial Studies Frankfurt, 3. November 1999.
Holtfrerich, C.L. (1995). Die Deutsche Bank vom Zweiten Weltkrieg über die Besatzungsherrschaft zur Rekonstruktion 1945-1957. In L. Gall *et al.*, *Die Deutsche Bank 1870-1995* (409-578). München: Beck.
Holtfrerich, C.L. (1999). *Finanzplatz Frankfurt*. München: Beck.
Institutional Investor (1998). The world's largest banks. *Institutional Investor, August,* 41-74.
Kindleberger, C.P. (1974). *The formation of financial centers: A study in comparative economic history*. Princeton: Princeton University.
Kindleberger, C.P. (1983). International banks as leaders or followers of international business. *Journal of Banking and Finance 7*, 583-595.
Krugman, P. (1996). *The self-organizing economy*. Malden, MA: Blackwell.
Krugman, P. (1998). The role of geography in development. Paper prepared for the *Annual World Bank Conference on Development Economics*, Washington, D.C., April 20-21, 1998.
Krugman, P. (1999). *Some chaotic thoughts on regional dynamics*. Available: http://web.mit.edu/krugman/www/temin.html
Landeszentralbank in Hessen (2000a). Zwei Jahre bis zur Einführung des Euro-Bargelds. *Frankfurter Finanzmarkt-Bericht,* Nr. 35.
Landeszentralbank in Hessen (2000b). *Vierteljahreszahlen*, 4. Quartal 1999, Frankfurt.
Lee, R. & Schmidt-Marwede, U. (1993). Interurban competition? Financial centers and the geography of financial production. *International Journal of Urban and Regional Research 17 (4)*, 492-515.
Lo, V. (2001). Zwischen regionalen und globalen Beziehungen: Wissensbasierte Netzwerke im Finanzsektor. In J. Esser & E.W. Schamp (Eds.), *Metropolitane Region in der Vernetzung*. Frankfurt/M.: Campus.
Lo, V. & Grote, M. (2002). Where traders go when stock exchanges go virtual - concentration, dissemination or persistence. In A. Mullineux & D. Llewellyn (Eds.), *Technology & Finance:*

Challenges for Financial Markets, Business Strategies and Policy Makers. London: Routledge (forthcoming).

Marshall, A. (1890). *Principles of economics*. London: MacMillan.

O'Brien, R. (1992). *Global financial integration - The end of geography*. London: Pinter.

Ottaviano, G. & Puga, D. (1998). Agglomeration in the global economy: A survey of the 'new economic geography'. *The World Economy, 21(6)*, 707-731.

Petermann, A. (2000). *Niederlassungspolitik deutscher Grossbanken im Spiegel der Internationalisierung der Kapitalmärkte*. master thesis, Goethe-University Frankfurt, Institute for Economics.

Pohl, H. & Jachmich, G. (1998). Verschärfung des Wettbewerbs (1966-1973). In H. Pohl (Ed.), *Geschichte der deutschen Kreditwirtschaft seit 1945* (203-248). Frankfurt: Knapp.

Porteous, D. (1999). The development of financial centers: Location, information externalities and path dependence. In R. Martin (Ed.), *Money and the space economy* (95-114). Chichester *et al.*: John Wiley & Sons.

Pulm, J. (1993). *Die Wettbewerbsfähigkeit des Finanzplatzes Frankfurt im internationalen Vergleich*. Frankfurt: Lang.

Reed, H.C. (1981). *The preeminence of international financial centers*. New York: Praeger.

Ronneberger, K. & Keil, R. (1995). Ausser Atem - Frankfurt nach der Postmoderne. In Hitz *et al.* (Eds.), *Capitales Fatales. Urbanisierung und Politik in den Finanzmetropolen Frankfurt und Zürich*. Zürich: Rotpunktverlag.

Rudolph, B. (1992). Effekten- und Wertpapierbörsen, Finanztermin- und Devisenbörsen seit 1945. In H. Pohl (Ed.), *Deutsche Börsengeschichte* (293-375). Frankfurt: Knapp.

Rudolph, B. (1998). Die Deutsche Kreditwirtschaft im Europäischen Markt. In H. Pohl (Ed.), *Geschichte der deutschen Kreditwirtschaft seit 1945* (463-492). Frankfurt: Knapp.

Sassen, S. (1999). Global financial centers. *Foreign Affairs, 78(1)*, January/February, 75-87.

Schamp, E. (1999). The financial sector and urban competition in Germany, 1970 to 1995. In E. Wever (Ed.), *Cities in perspectives I: Economy, planning and the environment* (83-98). Assen: Van Gorcum.

Schmidt, K.G. (1963). Niederlassungen ausländischer Banken in der Bundesrepublik. *Bank-Betrieb, Nr. 11*, 219-222.

Seifert, W. (1997). *Finanzplatz Frankfurt - Dynamics for Europe*. Lecture for Representatives of Foreign Banks in Germany, Frankfurt, May 20.

Smith, W.D. (1984). The function of commercial centers in the modernization of European capitalism: Amsterdam as an information exchange in the seventeenth century. *Journal of Economic History*, XLIV (4), December, 985-1005. Reprinted in R. Roberts (Ed.) (1994). *International Financial Centers, I* (269-289). Aldershot: Elgar.

Stephan, C.W. (1998). *Die Grundlagen der strategischen Standortpolitik im Kreditwesen*. Köln: Eul.

Ter Hart, H. & Piersma, J. (1990). Direct representation in international financial markets: The case of foreign banks in Amsterdam. *Tijdschrift voor Economische en Sociale Geografie 81 (2)*, 82-92.

The Banker's Almanac (1998). East Grinstead: Reed Business Information.

The Banker (1999a). *Top 1000 banks*, July.

The Banker (1999b). *Top 500 European banks*, September.

The Banker (2000a). *Top 50 global banks*, February.

Thrift, N. (1994). On the social and cultural determinants of international financial centers: The case of the city of London. In S. Corbridge, R.L. Martin & N. Thrift (Eds.), *Money, power and space* (327-355). Oxford: Blackwell.

Tonomura, H. (1994). On the role of foreign banks in the internationalization of Frankfurt as a financial center: A view from Japan. In Landesbank Hessen-Thüringen (Ed.), *Finanzplatz Frankfurt* (169-182). Frankfurt: Knapp.

Verband der Auslandsbanken in Deutschland e.V. (2000). *Foreign banks in Germany 2000*. Frankfurt.

Walter, I. (1998). *Globalization of markets and financial-center competition*. Unpublished Paper presented at the symposium 'Challenges for Highly Developed Countries in the Global Economy' at the Institut für Weltwirtschaft (March), Kiel.

Wolf, H. (1994). Als Deutschlands Banken wieder in die Ferne gingen. *Die Bank*, 3/94, 185-189.

Wolf, H. (1998a). Von der Währungsreform bis zum Grossbankengesetz (1948-1952). In H. Pohl (Ed.), *Geschichte der deutschen Kreditwirtschaft seit 1945* (59-110). Frankfurt: Knapp.

Wolf, H. (1998b). Vom Grossbankengesetz bis zur 'Normalisierung' (1953-1958). In H. Pohl (Ed.), *Geschichte der deutschen Kreditwirtschaft seit 1945* (111-148). Frankfurt: Knapp

DANIEL FELSENSTEIN AND YARON ERGAS

6. TEL AVIV AS A GLOBAL HIGH TECH 'HOT SPOT' - SEEDBED OR ENCLAVE?

6.1 INTRODUCTION

One of the most salient features of technological development and progress is its tendency to agglomeration in space. Popular accounts glorify the emergence of these new global high tech 'hot-spots' (Business Week, 1998; Newsweek, 1998) and academic studies debate their uniqueness (Bania, Eberts and Fogarty, 1993; Castells and Hall, 1994, Pouder and St. John, 1996). However, one feature that seems to have been over-looked relates to the extent to which these agglomerations are concretely linked into their regional and national economies. If they act as integral components in their regional contexts, then we would expect some form of unique linkages to exist between them and their environs, linkages which could not exist if the concentration was located elsewhere. On the other hand, if they function purely as nodes in global networks, then the local context within which they perform will act purely as a back-drop. In this kind of abstract environment, little uniqueness is related to a specific location. The external economies of the agglomeration could have developed in similar fashion somewhere else. As Krugman notes with respect to the Los Angeles economy:

> (the people of L.A.) are there because of each other: if one could uproot the whole city and move it 500 miles, the economic base would hardly be affected (Krugman 1996, p. 209).

This chapter investigates the validity of this claim with respect to the emerging global high tech 'hot-spots'. In the context of these new nodes, we can posit two divergent roles that a high tech concentration might assume in the national economy. On the one hand, it can be characterized as playing a 'seedbed' function generating technological spillovers and externality effects that percolate throughout the whole economy. In this instance there is an active interdependence of the agglomeration with the surrounding milieu, its institutions and markets. On the other hand, the high tech concentration can be perceived as an 'enclave' with all major flows (of capital, information etc) taking place with other nodes and leap-frogging the local economy. In this case, spillovers are contained within the agglomeration itself. The agglomeration is a node in a wider network with no unique ties to the surrounding area. Aside from the standard input-output linkages and regional expenditure-induced patterns of development that are likely to occur in the immediate vicinity, other major transfers (of knowledge, skills and information) will take place non-locally.

D. Felsenstein et al. (eds.),
Emerging Nodes in the Global Economy: Frankfurt and Tel Aviv Compared, 109–130.

While the regional embeddedness and local synergies of the celebrated agglomerations such as Silicon Valley, Boston MA, Cambridge UK, Emilia Romagna etc. cannot be denied, can we attribute these same effects to the new global high tech hot-spots? Is it reasonable to expect similar outcomes in Hsinchu, Banagalore or Tel Aviv? Using the latter as a case study, we advance the claim that many of the emerging high tech locations function as nodes in wider networks. As such, their immediate environment is not as important an issue as the quality of linkages with more distant peer nodes.

The chapter proceeds in the following manner. After examining the reasons why technological activity is associated with spatial concentration and why this concentration is increasingly selective, we present Tel Aviv as an emerging node location for detailed examination. We use the notion 'Tel Aviv high technology' to refer to high tech activity within the Tel Aviv metropolitan area. While this in not uniformly distributed and exists either in planned clusters (science parks) or at a few select business locations in the northern sections of the metropolitan, we consciously avoid the micro-geography of this activity. Rather, we prefer to emphasize the processes at work in the formation of new, high tech agglomerations and the way in which this high tech hot-spot is uniquely linked to, or by-passes, the local economy. We adopt a similarly catholic approach to defining 'high technology'. While the definitional issue is a thorny one, all the firms and sectors surveyed here meet the criteria outlined in other recent studies (for example, Acs and Ndikumwami, 1998).

Empirical evidence of the enclave-nature of this concentration is assembled using three distinctive features of Tel Aviv high tech to highlight the argument: network formation amongst Tel Aviv firms, the decision to offer stock options abroad rather than locally and the introvert nature of Tel Aviv science parks. We conclude by outlining some of the regional policy implications of these results.

6.2 SPATIAL AGGLOMERATIONS; SEEDBEDS OR ENCLAVES?

The recent resurgence of interest in spatial agglomeration of technological activity has yielded a copious new body of work. The main contours of this literature can be drawn loosely around two approaches; the new economic geography school and the institutionalist school. The former, associated with the work of Blanchard and Katz (1992), David and Rosenbloom (1990), Krugman (1995) Porter (1998), and others, places spatial agglomeration squarely in the realm of externalities and increasing returns. The geographic concentration of technological activity, skilled labor and inter-related industries confers advantages that can be translated into economic growth and competitiveness. While the roots of this interest are diverse (endogenous growth theory, international trade and competitive advantage), the broad message is relatively uniform: territorial proximity is an important element in economic growth and regions (or places) matter.

In attempting to translate the above dynamics into the realities of real-world, technology-based agglomerations, stress has been placed on technological spillovers, supplier networks and labor-force pooling as the main areas in which these processes operate. A wealth of evidence is available on the existence of spillover effects, the critical mass needed for them to occur, the spatial extent of their diffusion, the central role of the university in their creation and the types of economic base likely to spawn them (Anselin *et al.*, 1997; Audretsch, 1998; Feldman and Audretsch, 1999; Jaffe *et al.*, 1993; Varga, 2000). The role of localized supplier networks in creating and sustaining agglomerations and clusters of sophisticated activity has been exemplified in studies of Indiana (Rosentraub and Przybylski, 1996) and New York State (Held, 1996). Finally, labor market processes that reinforce initial concentration have been shown to exist in expanding labor markets. In high velocity markets, firms can reduce recruiting costs and acquire local human capital at low costs (Herzog and Schlottmann, 1991).

In contrast, the institutionalist school plays down the role of externalities, specialization, spillovers and transaction costs economies in the formation of agglomerations. These "fail to capture the importance of the socio-institutional context and embeddedness of regional economic development" (Martin and Sunley 1998, p. 220). As a place or a region is also a repository of local social, cultural and institutional ties, these need to be incorporated into any analysis of regional concentration (Amin, 1999). This 'social capital' and the 'untraded interdependencies' that it promotes are said to be the glue that sticks economic development to certain places and not to others (Storper, 1995). Thus the institutionalist lexicon is very different to that of the new economic geography, stressing the roles of local trust, norms and conventions, relational assets, institutional thickness, tacit knowledge and face-to face relations in contributing to the emergence of local innovative concentrations.

In applying these concepts to explaining localized agglomerations of technological activity, the stress has been on unraveling the networks that lie at the base of successful examples of fast-growth locations and illustrating how these structures are grounded in local social and institutional conventions. These processes are claimed to underpin much of the success of Silicon Valley (Saxenian, 1994) and a host of industrial districts in disparate locations such as Emilia Romagna, Baden-Wurttemburg, (Cooke, 1996) and Texas (Hansen and Echeverri-Carroll, 1997). They also lead to very clear policy prescriptions that call for public support for 'clusters' of associated industries rooted in local capabilities, intervention to assist regions to become more responsive to global trends (i.e. 'learning regions') and steps towards diversifying and 'thickening' the local institutional base.

This approach however is accepted uncritically. Its obvious policy thrust has been interpreted as a smokescreen for a "neo-mercantalist platform for special interests" (Lovering, 1999, p. 391). Other commentators point out that the emphasis and glorification of a few choice agglomerations is perceived as a form of local boosterism. In addition, there is a tendency to over-endogenize the growth of the agglomeration and the stress on the simultaneous collaboration and co-operation in these locations is the product of 'fuzzy thinking' (Markusen, 1999). Institutionalist analysis also infers regional characteristics (such as competitiveness, adaptability) on the basis of attributes of leading firms (Lovering, 1999). This is a debatable form of inductive method (for an alternative opinion, see Markusen, 1996).

It is not surprising therefore, that attempts have been made to reconcile or augment each of the perspectives. The usual approach has been through confronting the issue of spatial agglomeration from the vantage point of the new economic geography and augmenting some of its more reductionist excesses through adding insights from institutional and evolutionary economics. Recent attempts include Pinch and Henry's (1999) account of the development of the British motor sport industry and Glaeser's (1999) work on incorporating non-market interactions (flows of ideas, peer effects, social capital flows etc) in the study of urban economies.

One issue that seems to have been overlooked relates to the position of the agglomeration of technological activity within the regional or national economy. This might seem unusual, as a *sine qua non* of most of the above explanatory accounts is the territoriality of the agglomeration and the way it is grounded into a certain place.

Our interest however is not in the external economies shared by all firms and households in the agglomeration. Rather, it is concerned with just how anchored the agglomeration is to its present environment. Could a similar concentration have developed at an alternative location? How dependent are the economic functions of the agglomeration on the unique physical setting? Krugman (1996) claims that a lack of rootedness stems from the "abstractness of the modern city's economy" (p. 208). If the agglomeration could be transplanted to another site and function in the same manner we can claim that it is purely an 'enclave' in the regional or national economy. This could be the case when the concentration functions as a node in a wider network with much stronger non-local flows than local linkages. In this case, the economic functions of the agglomeration are 'abstract' and indifferent to a particular location.

On the other hand, if the agglomeration cannot function as efficiently at an alternative site, we can posit that it is playing some form of regional seedbed function. In this instance, local flows are more important than non-local links. The functions of the agglomeration are much more 'concrete' and the success of the concentration as a whole is linked in with a particular place.

One avenue for investigating this issue arises from the recent work of Ellison and Glaeser (1997, 1999). They have suggested three factors contributing to spatial agglomeration: natural resource endowment, industry spillovers and random chance. Following this approach, we can suggest that agglomerations grounded in 'concrete' functions will be those that develop initially on the basis of some form of natural physical advantage. They cannot be easily transplanted to another location and therefore serve a regional or national 'seedbed' function. In a sample of US agglomerations, Ellison and Glaeser (1999) estimate that this factor explains 20 percent of concentration.

At the other end of the spectrum are the agglomerations that develop on the basis of chance or historical accident. This hysteresis-type approach is also based on the fact that once an activity (such as high tech research or development) is 'locked-in' to one location, it also simultaneously 'locks-out' all other locations. In this random chance story, the agglomeration is based on 'abstract' economic functions, that could be equally performed anywhere. Finally, the case of technological spillovers as promoting agglomeration, occupies an intermediate position. This kind of agglomeration can give rise to both abstract economic functions which will result in an 'enclave'-type concentration or equally to concrete economic functions that would promote the emergence of a 'seedbed'-type agglomeration. Of the three possibilities, high technology agglomerations are most likely to be derived from either technological spillovers or random choice. This would seem to indicate a higher probability of their developing as enclaves rather than as anchors.

6.3 TEL AVIV AS A GLOBAL HIGH TECH 'HOT-SPOT'

In its quest for 'the next Silicon Valley', the popular press often engages in identifying the 'new global hot spots' (Business Week, 1998; Newsweek, 1998). While some of the locations that turn up on these listings are hardly surprising (Boston MA, Cambridge UK), less obvious locations such as Bangalore, Hsinchu and Tel Aviv also appear consistently. These are all emerging node locations linked in one way or another to global networks. Following the argument presented above, we contend that they function as high tech enclaves within their regional economies. Most of their qualitative and information-rich flows are with distant peer locations. Their immediate environment is of little consequence; they could easily have cultivated their node function at an alternative location. That is why the high tech agglomeration in Bangalore for example, operates despite severe infrastructure constraints and bureaucratic bottlenecks (Fromhold-Eisebith, 1999) in a local physical environment that is hardly commensurate with a high tech 'image' (viz. cows on the street, telecommunications breakdowns, power outages and excessive transportation shortcomings). Similarly, this might explain why the Hsinchu concentration is based on imported skilled labor who function as 'weekday migrants' living in spartan accommodation during the week and returning home to Taipei at weekends. This enclave is largely removed from the environment in which it is located (Castells and Hall, 1994). In both instances, the agglomeration functions as a node economy tied into global networks. Most important linkages are with distant peer nodes and the immediate physical environment is of secondary consequence. Due to the 'abstractness' of the economic function of the agglomeration, the context or setting is not crucial. As suggested earlier, if the agglomeration could be preserved and 'replanted' elsewhere, it would probably function in a very similar manner.

A similar argument is advanced for Tel Aviv. The abstractness of the Tel Aviv concentration to the regional economy is manifest in other ways and will be examined below. With over 1,000 firms employing 50,000 workers, the Tel Aviv metropolitan concentration is Israel's premier center of high technology. Much of this development is relatively recent. It has been fuelled throughout the 1990's by synergetic relationships between the military establishment (especially the Israeli Army's Central Unit for Data Processing), local industry and the presence of research and design centers of the major US multinationals. The demonstration effect of highly visible fast-growth start-ups, foreign currency and trade liberalization, growing exposure to global business practice and the availability of US and local venture capital funds have together created the infrastructure for innovation. Much of the aforementioned interaction has been Tel Aviv-based: the location of the fast growth start-ups, the army computer center, most of the venture capital funds and much of the US multinational presence. It should also be noted that the country's two other satellite high tech centers (in Haifa and Jerusalem) are less than one hour's drive from Tel Aviv. So for all intents and purposes, a sizeable part of Israel's high technology activity is contained within one spatial labor market. Israel's high tech economy is largely synonymous with the Tel Aviv economy.

The Israeli high tech economy is firmly grounded in the Silicon Valley mold. Start-ups, venture capital funds and the globalization of capital and assets markets are the motors behind this model of high tech development and these have combined with local institutions (universities, defense establishment) in order to fuel this growth. In addition, much of this activity is double-pronged: much Israeli high tech has a parallel presence in the US. A popular route involves setting up a company in the US (invariably Silicon Valley) in order to understand market demand. Following that, a design and production team is assembled in Israel (invariably in Tel Aviv). Thus much of the Tel Aviv high tech boom of the 1990's relates to companies that may not officially be classified as Israeli companies. They are registered in the US in order to give local clients the perception of dealing with a local company, to beat high tax rates and arcane merger laws in Israel and to avoid capital gains problems related to distributing stock options to Israeli employees (Haaretz, 2000).

One indication of the 'gold rush' character of Israel's high tech development over the last decade is the magnitude of capital raised abroad by Israeli high tech firms. In 1993, private Israeli firms raised capital (shares and debentures) to the order of $4.3b. Of this, 87 percent ($3.76b) was raised as offerings on the local Tel Aviv stock exchange and 13 percent ($.54b) as IPO's abroad. By 1999, these volumes had been reversed. Of the $4.97b raised through public offerings, $3.34b (67 percent) was raised on foreign exchanges (about $ 2.5b in stock issues) and only $1.63 b (33 percent) was raised locally (Bank of Israel, 2000). Most of this reversal was led by high tech firms in the electronics, communications and software sectors. Over the period 1992-1998 they accounted annually for between 62 percent and 95 percent of all capital raised abroad. In view of the fact that some Israeli high tech companies are registered abroad (as noted above), these figures are likely to be an under-estimate by a further $1.4b. Local financial conditions and the local stock exchange would thus seem to be marginal to the high tech boom.

Further underscoring this point is the structure of venture capital investments in Israel. Prior to 1990 there was no venture capital industry in Israel. In 1991, venture capital investments in Israel summed to $58m. By 1999, there were 80 funds operating locally, of which 75 percent were local Israeli companies while the other 25 percent were foreign funds active in Israel. These funds raised close to $1.5b for private firms in 1999 and an accumulated sum of close to $4b since 1991.This figure doubled in 2000 but the worldwide recession saw it half again in 2001. Forty three percent of the capital raised in 1999 was raised by the Israeli-managed funds. The remainder came from foreign-managed operations and an estimated 85-95 percent of all venture capital investments in Israel are from foreign sources (Bank of Israel, 2000).

These facts serve to further highlight the way local high technology by-passes the local economy. First, local companies choose to register abroad with all the distortionary effects that this implies. Foreign investments in these companies are not registered as part of the Israeli economy, Israeli venture capital investments in these companies are registered as 'capital exports' and the operations of these companies in the local economy is registered as 'foreign activity'. This also has implications for national accounts causing biases in macro indicators of growth, employment and tax revenues. Second, local high technology firms tend to go public abroad rather than locally. Third, local venture capital funds are heavily capitalized by sources from abroad. Thus, the high tech 'gold rush' of the 1990's has developed in a bubble, parallel and sometimes incidental, to developments in the local economy.

The question now arises whether the development of Tel Aviv as a high tech hot-spot has also resulted in the development of an 'enclave' economy with all major flows taking place outside the local economy? If the high technology agglomeration functions as a node in a network, then the chances of it being embedded in the region are considerably diminished. High tech enclaves may be 'locked-in' to a few select locations but their markets, business horizons and aspirations are often elsewhere. While they feed off local labor markets and perhaps local information channels, we argue that their effect on regional or national economies should not be over-stated. High tech 'hot spots' may be highly visible image-builders for the region or even the nation, but their local effect might be simply to stress the gap between them and the rest of the economy.

We illustrate this argument by looking at the Tel Aviv high tech agglomeration. To embellish our argument that the Tel Aviv high tech economy is simply a node in a wider network with terms of reference much wider than the regional or national economy (see Chapter 4), we draw on both qualitative and quantitative evidence. The former refers to the process of network formation between firms in Tel Aviv and Silicon Valley. This stresses the growing importance of network interactivity and the concomitant decreasing importance of spatial proximity in network formation. The latter is investigated via two issues. The first relates to the decision of local Israeli high tech firms to go public abroad rather than on the Tel Aviv stock exchange. The second addresses the introvert nature of Tel Aviv science parks. The desire of new, small high tech firms to go public abroad and to agglomerate on high cost, high profile science parks is interpreted as the result of a conscious 'signaling' strategy that again has increasingly less to do with local conditions.

6.4 NETWORK FORMATION IN TEL AVIV HIGH TECH FIRMS

In this section we outline some theoretic insights relating to network formation and the role of distance in this process. We then illustrate these ideas on the basis of qualitative interview evidence culled from both our own interviews with senior executives of high tech firms in the Tel Aviv metropolitan area and secondary evidence from other studies.

At the outset we should note that hierarchies have been the mainstay of models in economic geography. Central place theory, location theory, the theory of the firm, core/periphery relationships etc. all assume the underlying existence of a structured hierarchy. However, when faced with network forms of organization this pattern often breaks down (Powell, 1990). Networks do not operate according to the simple principles of proximity and distance-decay. They can tie disparate nodes (places and firms) together despite barriers of distance. Some studies even show that certain types of networks are most efficient when linking distant rather than proximate neighbors (Kilkenny, 2000). Peer-to-peer contact across distances can be more important than local interactions. These benefits to distance are noted below.

While high tech concentrations may act as enclaves within their own regions, they may have wide ranging contacts and accessibility to other distant, yet similar, concentrations. Starting with some general insights of spatial interaction analysis we may assume that the contact between two nodes in a network (C_{ij}) is subject to some distance decay effect such that:

$$C_{ij} = K^{\alpha}_{j} \exp(- \beta d_{ij}) \tag{6.1}$$

where, K^{α}_{j} represents the attractiveness of j as measured by its information or knowledge stock, α and β are parameters and the negative exponential represents an impedance factor.

The contact patterns of node i with the whole network (C_i) would be the sum of the above across all nodes j and in addition would be contingent on i's level of high tech or research activity (R_i), as follows:

$$C_i = \Sigma_j K^{\alpha}_{j} \exp(- \beta d_{ij}) + R_i \tag{6.2}$$

The above does not go much further than standard spatial interaction analysis. However, as Batten and Tornqvist (1990) have pointed out, a singular feature of networks is their contact frequency or 'interactivity'. There are increasing returns to network size: networks can add members and become more efficient. This contact potential needs to be included. Batten and Tornqvist (1990) suggest adding a measure (F_{in}) that would express all frequency contacts of node i with all other networks n for Z agents (firms, individuals) in node i, such that:

$$F_{in} = Z_i \exp(C_{in}) \tag{6.3}$$

On this basis, a measure of node interactivity (M_i) can be formulated which would simply be the average of all frequency contacts, as follows:

$$M_i = (\Sigma_n F_{in}) / Z_i \tag{6.4}$$

Thus while distance may cause some fall-off in connection between nodes in a network, this is more than compensated by the interactivity and accessibility that being a member of the network provides. While face-to-face contact cannot be sustained over great physical distances, membership of a network opens up other opportunities for contact and information flows. Distance may even have a 'cushioning' effect allowing nodes to screen and mediate demands coming from other nodes. In network formations, disparate nodes are connected across space in both formal and informal modes of interaction. In contrast to the standard central place model, there is no hierarchical distance decay pattern here. Interactivity is essentially between enclaves distributed across the globe.

Applying this analytical framework to essentially qualitative interview-based data we can examine the case of network formation between Tel Aviv and Silicon Valley firms. Recent work has noted the pivotal role played by transnational flows of skilled workers between key global cities (Beaverstock, 2001). Saxenian (2002) has illustrated the importance of the international links established by Chinese and Indian entrepreneurs based in Silicon Valley, in nurturing long-distance networks linking Silicon valley into the new global high tech 'hot spots' such as Hsinchu and Bangalore. The entrepreneurs are uniquely placed for creating transnational communities and allowing local high tech nodes in their home countries to link into the global networks.

The case of Israeli entrepreneurs in Silicon Valley is very similar. A recent study has attempted to chart some of the formal and informal networks that have developed between these two economies (Autler, 2000). Overcoming distance-decay impediments, Israel's high technology sector has become increasingly integrated with that of Silicon Valley. In sectors such as semiconductor design and internet security, the presence of Silicon Valley has pervaded the development of a local indigenous capacity from the start. On a formal level, large Silicon Valley multinationals (such as National Semiconductor, Intel, 3Com, Applied Materials and Cisco Systems) have seeded the Tel Aviv cluster and the Israeli industry through setting up foreign design and fabrication centers and training local personnel in California. Silicon Valley-based venture capital funds, have been greasing the wheels of much of the internet and network security boom (although the origin of this phenomenon lies in expertise in data and network security developed in the Israeli military). Cisco for example recently decided to relocate its premises within the Tel Aviv metropolitan area, signing what the local press has labeled the 'largest rental deal ever' involving office facilities of over 40,000 sq. m. (Haaretz, 2001), equivalent to the size of a large out-of-town shopping center.

Tel Aviv-Silicon Valley networks are equally sustained by informal channels. Many Israeli entrepreneurs have a Silicon Valley chapter in their work biographies. Frequently, Israeli entrepreneurs traverse the Tel Aviv-Silicon Valley high technology route, in both directions. Some have multifarious family and social networks in Silicon Valley, comprising fellow entrepreneurs, colleagues from military units (military service is compulsory in Israel) and business associates. Others have spent long periods of employment in California culminating in their persuading US employers to open a plant or design center in Israel thereby facilitating their own return. While the establishment of US semiconductor design centers in Israel can be seen as a form of 'reverse' transfer of technology (Felsenstein, 1997), it can also serve to open up additional two-way flows of technical and market knowledge. In many cases firms with connections in both places and an established presence in either Israel (invariably Tel Aviv) or Silicon Valley, invariably end up with operations in both locations (often R&D and design in Tel Aviv, marketing and product service in the US). This demands constant email and phone exchanges and the other disadvantages that go with physical distance such as shipping delays, communications breakdowns etc. Thus part of this structure is subject to distance decay.

However, this network organization also confers certain advantages that do not decay with distance. In line with the model outlined above, we can suggest that a major benefit of network structure lies in the accessibility it affords. For Israeli companies it means exposure to markets, management practices and entrepreneurial demonstration effects that simply do not exist locally. For Silicon Valley firms, it means access to specific technological expertise, the ability to assemble relatively stable research teams, and the ability to tap into one of the last available reservoirs of R&D, to be found in small firms.

Aside from greater interactivity and accessibility we can note the cushioning effect of distance that frees designers and engineers in Israel from the daily supervision of US management and allows them to improvise and solve solutions away from the immediate pressure of the market. The 10-hour time difference between Tel Aviv and Silicon Valley also means an added benefit. Clients' problems in California can be downloaded in Tel Aviv and solved before the start of the next working day in the US.

The spatial agglomeration that characterizes the development of the high technology node serves to mediate some of the excesses of distance decay. Those firms that are part of the agglomeration benefit from the external economies that it affords. However, as we have seen above, this is only one part of the network story. The fact that networks are not spatially-bound means that accessibility and interactivity are more important features of network formation than spatial proximity. Formal and informal linkages transcend the confines of distance. This implies that high technology concentrations grounded in network formation may be irrelevant to the needs of regional development. Aside from the standard employment and expenditure induced impacts that they generate locally, all other spillover effects that they might create (flows of information, technology and the like) may be realized in places other than the local economy. In fact, the conspicuous nature of these enclaves and the lifestyles and living standards of those linked into them, may simply serve to highlight the gap they are creating with the rest of the economy.

6.5 TEL AVIV HIGH TECH AND GLOBAL CAPITAL MARKETS: THE DECISION TO TRADE ABROAD

The hypothesis advanced here relates to 'signaling' behavior of firms located in the new high tech, hot-spots and the secondary importance of location when trying to break into global networks. One way of breaking into global networks is through foreign investment. For high technology firms in Israel two options exist. The first is the more traditional route of mergers and acquisitions with global corporations which were valued as approximately $2bn in 1999 (Bank of Israel, 2000). A second point of entry is via initial public offerings (IPO's) abroad. This is a strategy that Israeli high tech firms have increasingly adopted, using stock issues on the NASDAQ market as a route to global networks (see Chapter 4).

The NASDAQ market is market popular with non-US firms looking to go public in the US. Due to it's electronic, floor-less structure, it has lower listing fees than the other stock exchanges and is also the main market for small high technology companies looking to raise capital in sectors such as information technology, telecommunications, biotechnology, pharmaceuticals, finance and insurance. As such, it is the main source of stock-market capital for Israeli high tech firms. In mid 1998 it had more foreign-based firms listed (453) than either the NYSE (364) and AMEX (65) markets. The market value of these companies ($4481 bn) however, was less than that of NYSE ($5776 bn) but way ahead of other international financial centers such as London ($1989 bn), Paris ($ 1414 bn) and Frankfurt ($1067 bn) (NASDAQ, 1998).

Of the 307 foreign companies with shares actually traded on NASDAQ (the other 150 companies raise capital through ADR's - American Depository Receipts), more than half (165) are Canadian. The second largest presence after the Canadian firms are the Israeli high tech companies with a further 20 percent (66 companies). All but two of these are Tel Aviv-based and all the Tel Aviv companies are engaged in high tech activities. The total number of Tel Aviv firms is more than the sum total of all other foreign firms combined; the Netherlands for example, has 17 companies and the United Kingdom, 13.

The approach adopted here is to estimate the determinants of Tel Aviv firms being traded abroad. Ostensibly, this is an inherently spatial question that poses a choice between different locational alternatives: Tel Aviv versus New York (or no IPO issues at all). Tel Aviv is the location of the local stock exchange and New York is the location of the target exchange (NASDAQ) for Israeli firms seeking to raise capital abroad. However, for two reasons, this is less of a spatial choice issue than might be imagined at first glance. First, due to the floor-less nature of the trading in New York, the question is not really a choice between two distinct alternatives but rather relates to the choice of trading in Tel Aviv versus 'somewhere else'. In this particular case, the preferred 'somewhere else' for high tech firms happens to be New York but it could quite easily be some other alternative.

Second, while Israeli high technology activity is increasingly agglomerated in the Tel Aviv metropolitan area, the importance of this location in the present story is solely as context. While nearly all the firms trading abroad are Tel Aviv-based, the presence of a Tel Aviv high tech agglomeration is not treated as an active factor in the decision-making process. The characteristics of the metropolitan area, its labor force etc. are not taken as influencing the behavior of the high tech firm. Rather they are back-drop in which the scene is set. Had the context been some other spatial agglomeration (Haifa, for example), we would expect the same behavioral forces to be present. In both these instances breaking into global networks through IPO's has very little to do with both the location of the place of offering and with the location of the firm wanting to go public.

Instead, trading abroad is interpreted here as an active strategy consciously pursed by firms in high-risk sectors where market visibility is paramount. New high technology companies that are largely unknown in the market will issue offerings abroad as a 'signaling' strategy (Blass and Yafeh, 2001). This way they indicate to markets and investors that they should be taken seriously. The main focus of interest here is the motive for investing abroad, rather than the performance-based measures resulting from this decision. We are looking to provide some support for the hypothesis relating to the 'enclave' nature of the Tel Aviv high tech economy and the way in which global capital markets and global networks serve to further bolster this image.

6.5.1 Data and Analysis

The main sources of data for this analysis are company prospecti submitted to the Tel Aviv stock exchange, Dun and Bradstreet data from the 1997 Duns Disc, company data that is available on-line at the NASDAQ website, the Tel Aviv Stock exchange directory and the Standard and Poor's directory for publicly traded firms (1998). Together, these sources yielded cross-sectional information on the following firm characteristics: sales, number of employees, industry description, ownership structure, location of main markets, exports as a percentage of revenues and percentage equity being offered.

In total, we managed to assemble data on over 60 Tel Aviv high tech companies traded abroad and another 20 that are traded locally. The former also includes a small number who are traded both locally and abroad. We matched this population with a further sample of high tech firms that are not publicly traded. This control group comprises a further 70 firms matched on the basis of size and revenue with very large (over 2000 employees and / or over $350m sales) and very small firms (less than 50 employees and $10m) excluded. The final data set therefore contains over 140 observations (high technology firms of similar size and sales volume), roughly half of which are traded (mainly in New York).

Due to data limitations, this empirical analysis is based on a limited selection of indicators. In terms of the characteristics of the high technology firm, size is measured by the number of employees and the volume of sales. The firm's experience and level of establishment is measured by age in years. Market characteristics are characterized by volume of exports and their geographic destination and by the firms leading SIC area. This was divided into the following high technology sub-areas: software, communications, electronics, biotechnology, and robotics.

In order to answer the basic question, just how different are firms that issue stock from those that do not?, we run a series of difference of mean tests on the main explanatory variables. The firms are stratified into three categories: non traded, traded locally and traded abroad (Table 6.1). The results would imply that in terms of firm size (employees and sales) and vintage, those firms traded abroad would seem to be younger but also larger than those not traded abroad. It would also seem that firms trading abroad have more sales than those traded locally, although a question of causality here remains unanswered: do they have a higher sales volume and therefore seek capital abroad, or is it because they have raised capital abroad that their sales volume is larger? While the differences of means for exports, also seem to indicate a clear distinction between those traded abroad and the others, it should be noted that the many missing values on this variable, could lead to misleading conclusions.

Table 6.1 Difference of means test: Tel Aviv high tech firms, non-traded, traded locally and traded abroad

	Means			
Variable	*Non-Traded*	*Traded Locally*	*Traded Abroad*	*F-statistic*
Employees	197	272	399	3.1*
Age (Yrs.)	12.1	24.1	14.3	15.5**
Sales ($m)	23.1	11.1	83.0	7.2**
Exports ($m)	34.1	5.0	96.9	2.0

* Significant at the p<.05 level.
** Significant at the p<.001 level.

An examination of the markets of the high technology firms is revealing (Table 6.2). These data refers to only the high tech firms that are traded either locally or abroad. The average exports for all firms shows a much 'smoother' picture than in reality. As noted above, the average sales volume for a firm traded abroad in $83 m and this is significantly larger than the sales volume of either firms traded locally or firms not traded at all.

For our purposes however, it is more instructive to examine the geographic pattern of sales. Total sales volume in 1998 summed to nearly $5 billion. While on average, the market seems to be divided equally across North America and Europe, the sector distribution shows that this is not the case. Software exports are dominated by the US (internet and multi-media firms) while communications firms seem to be more oriented to the European market. This pattern also describes the relative advantages of the US and Europe in the global markets for these different sectors. Other electronics (such as medical devices), biotechnology and robotics are much more marginally represented amongst the high tech firms that issue stock and this of course is also represented in sales patterns.

As anticipated, the size of the local market, seems to be irrelevant to the global markets of these high technology companies. Across all sub-sectors, local sales are way below those to foreign markets and would seem on average, to be marginal to the stock-issuers product sales patterns. Of course, some of the local competitive advantage in software and electronics may have initially stemmed from locally-driven demand (e.g. from the defense sector and from public procurement contracts) but this is not reflected in the present pattern of sales and their destinations.

Table 6.2 Product sales by geographic destination (traded firms only)

	Total Sales (1998) (M $)	Destination							
		N. America		Europe		Far East		Local	
		Tot.	Avg.	Tot.	Avg.	Tot.	Avg.	Tot.	Avg.
All High Tech Firms	4,970	1,068	13.7	1,117	14.3	274	3.5	175	2.2
Software	1,760	464	11.5	316	7.8	130	3.2	72	1.7
Communications	1,448	260	16.2	340	21.2	68	4.4	34	2.6
Electronics	275	55	4.2	14	1.1	23	1.7	21	1.6

6.5.2 Method and Results

The estimation procedure involves analytic testing of a statistical model that will predict the probability of trading abroad as a function of firm characteristics, especially size, age and market structure (leading high tech product, destination of sales).We look at the behavioral determinants of this choice rather than the economic outcomes (share performances at the two locations etc.). The binary nature of the dependent variables (traded / non-traded and traded abroad / traded locally) necessitates a logit estimation as follows:

The probability that firm (*i*) will trade abroad is expressed as:

$$(i) = 1/1 + \exp\,(B_0 + B_1X_1 + \ldots B_n\,X_n) \qquad (6.5)$$

This is a non-linear model parallel to the general utility model:

$$P_{(i)} = [exp\ V_i] \,/\, [\sum_{i=1}^{n} \exp\,(V_i)] \qquad (6.6)$$

where:
$P_{(i)}$ = the probability of firm *i* being traded abroad
V_i = vector of characteristics of the firm and it's market
N = the number of options available

To estimate the model, we assume that V_i is a linear function of the independent variables such that $Vi = B'X_i$, where X_i represents that characteristics of the firm and its market. These can be decomposed into firms attributes (essentially age and size, x_{ik}) and market attributes (product and product destination, y_{im}). Taking the natural log of (6.1) we get the equation in a form operative for estimation;

$$ln\{[P_{(i)}] \,/\, [1\text{-}P_{(i)}]\} = \Sigma_k\alpha_k\,(x_{ik}) + \Sigma_m\delta_m\,(y_{im}) \qquad (6.7)$$

In order to analyze trading abroad as a form of strategic behavior, we define three basic decisions that face the high tech firm:

1. At the outset, there is the basic decision to issue a public offering. We can estimate the probability of being traded as a function of the two sets of characteristics outlined above.
2. A variant on this decision is the issue of whether to go abroad to seek funds or to do something else (i.e. not to issue stock or to issue stock locally).
3. Once one of the above two decisions has been made, a further decision is necessary, provided the outcome is the decision to trade abroad. This involves the decision regarding the location of the stock issue: on a local exchange (Tel Aviv) or a foreign exchange (New York - NASDAQ).

These decisions are all binary choices and call for estimations based on logit-modeling. To fully appreciate the decision processes involved, decision 1 (above) needs to be contrasted with decision 3 and similarly, decision 2 needs to be compared with decision 3. The analytical results presented below (Table 6.3) are structured according to this sequence. Model 1 presents the determinants of decision 1 and similarly for Models 2 and 3.

Table 6.3 Estimates of the probability of Tel Aviv high tech firms (1) being traded, (2) being traded abroad and (3) being traded in New York

Variable	*Model 1*	*Model 2*	*Model 3*
Constant	-1.329**	-.835	2.046*
	(.437)[2]	(.495)	(1.012)
AGE (yrs)	.070**	-.059*	-.195**
	(.026)	(.035)	(.067)
	[.055][3]	[.042]	[.059]
SALES ($m)	.00008*	.0002**	.0005*
	(.00004)	(.0006)	(.0002)
	[.001]	[.004]	[.004]
SOFTWARE & COMMS.	.707	.373**	1.622
(OTHER)[1]	(.470)	(.555)	(1.242)
	[.114]	[.054]	[.100]
n	114	114	53
Means, Dep. Var.	.55	.47	.73
-2x log likelihood	157.4	138.9	69.1
χ^2 values for model/d.f.	20.1 / 3**	28.7/3**	33.9/3**
Percentage correctly predicted	70.2	77.2	84.9

* Logit coefficient significant at p<.05 level
** Logit coefficient significant at p<.001 level
1. Dummy Variable; reference group in parenthesis
2. Standard Errors in parenthesis.
3. *ΔP*; probability change estimated at the mean, for a unit change in the independent variable. For derivation, see Chapter 4 (Note 1).

As can be seen from Table 6.3, the probability of a high tech firm being traded (versus the alternative option of not being traded, (Model 1), is positively related to firm age and size (both factors are statistically significant). In terms of market characteristics, data constraints allowed us only the use of a dummy variable indicating whether the firm's main SIC was software or communications. This dummy has the expected sign but is not significant. Thus it would seem that larger and older firms are more likely to be traded. The *ΔP* values (elasticities at the mean) enable us to interpret the logit coefficients in probabalistic terms. From Table 6.3 we can see that a unit change in age, increases the average probability of being trading by over 5 percent. Similarly a unit change in sales (a $10m increase in sales) means that the average probability of being traded rises by 1 percent.

Once the firm decides to trade publicly the next decision is where to issue the public offering (New York versus Tel Aviv, Model 3). Comparing the results of Model 1 with Model 3, reveals that in this decision, the probability of issuing in New York is this time *negatively* related to firm age and positively related to firm size (both coefficients are significant). Thus the newer the firm and the higher its sales volume the more likely it will be to raise capital on the New York Stock exchange. Again, type of market displays the 'correct' sign but the result is not statistically significant. The elasticities at the mean are also slightly higher than in Model 1 and the model correctly predicts a higher proportion of cases than the previous model.

As noted above, another way of looking at the decision making process involves estimating the probability of trading abroad (versus being traded locally or not being traded altogether), in the first instance (Model 2), and then comparing these results with the decision relating to New York versus Tel Aviv. As can be seen from Table 6.3, the younger the firm, the greater its sales volume and the more it is oriented to software/communications the greater the probability it will decide to raise capital abroad. All three independent variables are statistically significant and all display the 'correct' signs. The *ΔP* values for the logit coefficients indicate that an unit increase in age decreases the average probability of being traded abroad by over 4 percent. An increase in sales of $10m increases the chances at the mean by 1 percentage point and a categorical change in product specialization from some 'other' category to software/communications, increases the probability at the average by over 5 percent.

Once the probabilities of the firm raising capital abroad (versus the alternatives of being traded locally or not being traded abroad at all) have been established, the firm then has to decide where to be traded. In this decision choice, the alternative to being traded abroad is raising capital locally (Model 3) Therefore, it is instructive to compare these estimations of Model 2 with the narrower decision-choice facing the firm as estimated in Model 3. The results show that the coefficients are consistent across both models, although the sector coefficient is insignificant in the model predicting raising capital in New York (Model 3).

The results show smaller firms with higher sales volumes and an orientation to software and communications are more likely to undertake public offerings abroad, than other firms. On the other hand, larger and older high tech firms, are more likely to go public. By implication, the results presented here therefore seem to suggest that smaller firms that go public abroad are looking for more than just raising capital. Otherwise they would go public locally.

The hypothesis presented in this section is that the utility gained from a public offering abroad, results in improved positioning and signaling. This generates a public profile for a high tech firm with little proven track record and acts as a point of entry into global networks. This further underscores the irrelevance of the local context faced with global capital and assets markets. The local economy acts as a spring-board or setting, but no more than that. Despite a flourishing local stock exchange and a plethora of local venture capital funds, Tel Aviv's small high tech firms would seem to look a NASDAQ offering as more than an instrument for raising capital.

6.6 THE INTROVERT NATURE OF TEL AVIV'S SCIENCE PARKS

The case of Science Parks adds a further example to our hypothesis as to the enclave nature of the spatial agglomerations. As planned concentrations of technological activity, their role is open to various interpretations. They can be viewed as purely real estate initiatives, as vehicles for promoting and diffusing innovation and as instruments for regional growth. Public policy rhetoric has widely espoused them as fostering innovation and promoting interaction with local universities However, the empirical evidence supporting these conjectures is rather thin. Studies of innovation levels and linkages to universities have found little difference between on and off-park firms (Westhead and Storey, 1995; Westhead, 1997) and have failed to establish conclusive evidence of park-induced local employment growth (Shearmur and Doloreux, 2000).

Our hypothesis is that the real estate role of the science park over-shadows that of fostering innovation or promoting local economic growth. Firms are prepared to pay a premium in the form of high rents for science park location, but that it not due to the information flows or technological spillovers that they promote. Rather, we have a further case of location acting as a 'signal', akin to the case of issuing stock abroad. Being located on a prestigious science park may be of symbolic importance for new firms that want to be taken seriously but have no proven track record or market presence.

To test this proposition we undertake a two-stage analysis. First, we observe whether the 'classic' profile of a firm founded by an academic entrepreneur and with intensive links to a local university, in fact leads to greater innovation levels. Then, we analyze whether the archetypal high tech firms (firm with high levels of innovation, entrepreneur with R&D background) have any greater propensity to agglomerate on science parks than off them. We report evidence resulting from an empirical survey of 162 high technology firms in Israel (Felsenstein, 2000), 110 firms located on one of Israel's three major science parks in either Tel Aviv or Jerusalem and a further 50 firms serving as a control group of similar ,off-park, high tech companies. The survey responses provide categorical data on (a) firm characteristics (location on/off science park, innovation level (high/low), intensity of connection to a local university (high/low) and (b) entrepreneur/manager characteristics educational level (PhD/below PhD) and work experience (R&D/production and sales). To analyze the data and test multi-dimensional contingency relationships we use log-linear modeling (multi-dimensional χ^2). This involves predicting the log of the frequencies in each cell as a function of the values of the various combinations of categorical variables and the interactive affects between them.

A reduced form (main effects) model is fitted for the two sets of relationships outlined above. The first (Table 6.4), tests the relationship between the firm innovation level (*I*), interaction with a university (*U*) and the educational background of the entrepreneur/manager (*E*). The second (Table 6.5), tests the relationship was between the innovation level of the firm (*I*), location on the science park (*L*) and the prior work experience of the entrepreneur/manager (W).

Table 6.4 presents the results of a three-way cross tabulation of the variables in a log-linear equation. Taking the natural log of all the terms makes the equation linear and the table shows the various combinations of factors that lead to innovation. While education and university linkage are significant in their own rights, for our purposes the interaction effects are of more interest. Although the second-order interaction effect between university interaction and education level is significant this combination does not necessarily lead to more innovative activity. The E*I relationship is not significant, but was forced into the model. The third-order interaction (E*I*U) is also not significant. All this would seem to indicate that that successful commercial innovation is not necessarily tied to academic education or university linkage.

Table 6.4 Inter-relationships between education, university interaction and innovation

$$\ln(M_{ijk}) = \ln(\alpha) + \underset{(30.09/1)}{\ln(\gamma E_i)} + \underset{(7.51/1)}{\ln(\gamma U_j)} + \underset{(9.39/1)}{\ln(\gamma I_k)} + \underset{(1.96/1)}{\ln(\gamma EI_{ik})} + \underset{(5.44/1)}{\ln(\gamma EU_{ij})}$$

$(i,j,k = 1,0)$

likelihood ratio χ^2 value for model = 4.64 (p=.0106/2)

where:

(M_{ijk}) = the expected cell frequency, α = overall mean of the log of the expected cell frequencies, γE_i = effect attributable to the *i*th category of education, γU_j = effect attributable to the *j*th category of university interaction, γI_k = effect attributable to the *k*th category of innovation level, γEI_{ik} = effect attributable to the interaction between the *i*th category of education and the *k*th category of innovation level and γEU_{ij} = effect attributable to the interaction between the *i*th category of education and the *j*th category of university interaction. Figures in parentheses are chi-square statistics and degrees of freedom, all significant at the $p<0.05$ level except for the γEI_{ik} term that was forced into the model.

We next test for 'seedbed' effects of a science park location (Table 6.5). If physical proximity is really important for creating linkages, interactions and information flows, then we would expect to find more innovative firms founded by entrepreneurs with research backgrounds, opting to locate in these planned agglomerations. We therefore test for the inter-relationships between science park location (*L*), innovation level (*I*) and work background of the entrepreneur/manager (*W*).

Table 6.5 Inter-relationships between, work experience, innovation level and science park location

$$\ln(M_{ijk}) = \ln\alpha + \underset{(18.18/1)}{\ln(\gamma W_i)} + \underset{(8.53/1)}{\ln(\gamma I_j)} + \underset{(4.54/1)}{\ln(\gamma WI_{ij})} + \underset{(8.14/1)}{\ln(\gamma WIL_{ijk})}$$

$(i,j,k = 1,0)$

likelihood ratio χ^2 value for model = 5.76 (p=.0461/3)

where:

$\ln(M_{ijk})$ = the expected cell frequency, $\ln\alpha$ = overall mean of the log of the expected cell frequencies, γW_i = effect attributable to the *i*th category of work background, γI_j = effect attributable to the *j*th category of innovation level, γWI_{ij} = effect attributable to the interaction between the *i*th category of work experience and the *j*th category of innovation and γWIL_{ijk} = effect attributable to the third-order interaction between the *i*th category of work background, the *j*th category of innovation and the *k*th category of location. Figures in parentheses are chi-square statistics and degrees of freedom, all significant at the $p<0.05$ level.

The results show that only one second-order and one third-order interaction term are significant. Both these terms express the interaction effects of work background with innovation (W*I). The effect of location (L) only shows up in one three-way interaction. All the two-way interactions including location are not significant and even the direct effect of science park location by itself is not included in the model.

These results do not provide any support for the science park agglomeration acting as a seedbed. They seem to suggest that innovation is not contingent on the agglomerative conditions offered by the science park. The attractiveness of the science park location (as evidenced by the rents it collects) must therefore be due to something else rather than technological spillovers and information flows. If it does not promote any more innovative activity than an off-park location, it is hardly fulfilling an anchoring function. Our (untested) hypothesis is that the popularity of science park 'enclaves' is as much due to the prestige effects that they confer as to any innovative edge. In this respect, science parks revert to more life-like proportions as planned, real estate-driven concentrations whose success is often driven by the image-creating skills of property developers.

6.7 CONCLUSIONS

We have presented both qualitative and quantitative evidence to buttress the case that some of the new global high tech hot spots are functioning as high tech 'enclaves'. Arguably, the Tel Aviv story could represent a particularly idiosyncratic case: a highly skilled entrepreneurial society, with social and business connections worldwide, a developed scientific and military research infrastructure, liberal public support for technological activity and a miniscule local and regional market. All this would seem to work in favor of the emergence of a node-type economy linked into other similar and distant locations. However, many of these conditions patently do not exist with respect to other new high technology agglomerations, such as Bangalore and Hsinchu, that seem to be developing in a similar fashion.

The evidence therefore seems to suggest that emerging node locations may not foster unique linkages with their surrounding environment. In some ways they will be detached from what is going on around them. The economies of scale and spillovers afforded by spatial concentration are internalized within the agglomeration itself and do not percolate to the wider economy. This is not to say that the standard inter-sectoral (input-output) linkages are not generated by these agglomerations or that they have no impact in generating expenditure-induced growth. As major regional employment concentrations they cannot fail to create an aggregate local and regional income impact. However, the argument advanced here relates to the development of *unique* linkages locally that cannot be replicated elsewhere. On this count, we have not found much supporting evidence.

Bearing in mind the existence of these standard economic impacts, the regional development implications of the enclave economy may not be as bleak, as they might appear at first sight. Some economic impact will always 'trickle down' to the region or national economy, if only through the multiplier process, the tax system and the expenditure patterns of local workers. However, perhaps the least-encouraging aspect of the enclave economy relates to the distributional and equity impacts of this growth. In Israel, inequality in income distribution rose consistently over the 1990's, coinciding with the high tech boom. The Gini coefficient rose nationally from .46 in 1985 to .53 in 1997. Even after discounting direct taxes and government transfers there was still a rise from .32 to .36 over this period (Ben Shachar and Helpman, 2000). Furthermore, these figures are very likely to under-estimate the true inequalities as they are based on salaried workers only (excluding the self-employed) and do not include income from capital such as savings, stocks and inheritances.

It would evidently seem that large segments of the national population are not enjoying the fruits of the digital dividend. In fact, the high visibility of the Tel Aviv technological enclave may just serve to underscore the differences between it and the rest of the economy. High tech agglomerations that are not uniquely linked to their regional and national economies, that are comprised of firms qualitatively linked with other nodes and that coalesce around local firms registered and traded abroad, are visible symbols of the locational abstractness of the high tech economy. Juxtaposing them with the rest of the economy highlights the existence of a digital divide. In this instance, the physical agglomeration of the technology 'haves', serves to reiterate that this divide is not just social and technological, but spatial as well.

REFERENCES

Acs, Z. & Ndikumwami, A. (1998). High technology employment growth in major U.S. metropolitan areas. *Small Business Economics, 10*, 47-59.

Amin, A. (1999). An institutionalist perspective on regional economic development. *International Journal of Urban and Regional Studies, 23 (2)*, 365-378.

Anselin, L., Varga, A. & Acs, Z. (1997). Local geographic spillovers between university research and high technology innovations. *Journal of Urban Economics. 42 (3)*, 422-448.

Audretsch, D.B. (1998), Agglomeration and the location of innovative activity. *Oxford Review of Economic Policy, 14 (2)*, 18-29.

Autler, G.H. (2000). *Global networks in high technology: The Silicon Valley-Israel connection.* MA Thesis, Department of City and Regional Planning, University of California, Berkeley.

Bania, N., Eberts, R.W. & Fogarty, M.S. (1993). Universities and the startup of new companies: Can we generalize from Route 128 and Silicon Valley? *Review of Economics and Statistics, 75 (4)*, 761-766.

Bank of Israel (2000). *Annual report of the controller of foreign currency.* Jerusalem: Bank of Israel (Hebrew).

Batten, D. & Tornqvist, G. (1990). Multilevel network barriers: The methodological challenge. *Annals of Regional Science, 24*, 271-287.

Beaverstock, J.V. (2001). *Transnational elite communities in global cities: Connectivities, flows and networks*. GaWC Research Bulletin 63. Available: http://www.lboro.ac.uk/gawc/rb/rb63.html

Ben Shachar, H. & Helpman, E. (2000). *The main socio-economic problems.* Available: http://econ.tau.ac.il/research/projects/priorities/article1-probs.htm

Blanchard O.J. & Katz L.F. (1992). Regional evolutions. *Brookings Papers on Economic Activity, 1*, 1-75.

Blass, A. & Yafeh, Y. (2001). Vagabond shoes longing to stray - Why foreign firms list in the United States. *Journal of Banking and Finance, 25*, 555-572.

Business Week (1998). *Global hot spots*, August 31st, 72-77.

Castells, M. & Hall, P. (1994). *Technopoles of the world: The making of 21st century industrial complexes*. London: Routledge.

Cooke, P. (1996). Building a twenty-first century regional economy in Emilia Romagna. *European Planning Studies, 4 (1)*, 53-62.

David, P. & Rosenbloom, J. (1990). Marshallian factor externalities and the dynamics of industrial localization. *Journal of Urban Economics, 28 (3)*, 349-370.

Ellison, G. & Glaeser, E.L. (1997). Geographic concentration in US manufacturing industry: A dartboard approach. *Journal of Political Economy, 105 (5)*, 889-927.

Ellison, G. & Glaeser, E.L. (1999). The geographic concentration of industry: Does natural advantage explain agglomeration? *American Economic Review, 89 (2)*, 311-316.

Feldman, M.P. & Audretsch, D.B. (1999). Innovation in cities: Science-based diversity, specialization and localized competition. *European Economic Review, 43*, 409-429.

Felsenstein, D. (1997). The making of a high technology node: Foreign-owned companies in Israeli high technology. *Regional Studies, 31 (4)*, 367-380.

Felsenstein, D. (2000). University-related science parks - 'seedbeds' or 'enclaves' of innovation? In P. Westhead & M. Wright (Eds.), *Advances in entrepreneurship*. UK: Edward Elgar.

Fromhold-Eisebith, M. (1999). Bangalore: A network model for innovation-oriented regional development in NICs? In E.J. Malecki & P. Oinas (Eds.), *Making connections: Technological learning and regional economic change* (231-260). Aldershot: Ashgate.

Glaeser, E.L. (1999). *The future of urban research: Non-market interactions*. (unpublished).

Haaretz (2000). *The vast majority of Israeli high tech companies are registered in the US.* September 6th.

Haaretz (2001). *When being near to home is everything*. February 8th.

Hansen, N. & Echeverri-Carroll, E. (1997). The nature and significance of network interactions for business performance and exporting to Mexico: An analysis of high technology firms in Texas. *Review of Regional Studies, 27 (1)*, 85-99.

Held, J.R. (1996). Clusters as an economic development tool: Beyond the pitfalls. *Economic Development Quarterly, 10 (3)*, 249-261.

Herzog, H.W. & Schlottmann, A.W. (1991). Metropolitan dimensions of high technology location in the U.S.: Worker mobility and residential choice. In H.W. Herzog & A.M. Schlottmann (Eds.), *Industry location and public policy* (169-189). Knoxville TN: University of Tennessee Press.

Jaffe, A.B., Trajtenberg, M. & Henderson, R. (1993). Geographic localization of knowledge spillovers as evidenced by patent citations. *Quarterly Journal of Economics, 108 (3)*, 577-598.
Kilkenny, M. (2000). *Community networks for industrial recruiting.* Presented at conference on 'Entrepreneurship, ICT and Local Policy Initiatives: Comparative Analyses and Lessons', May 22-23, 2000, Amsterdam.
Krugman, P. (1995). *Development, geography and economic theory.* Cambridge, MA: MIT Press.
Krugman, P. (1996). *Pop internationalism.* Cambridge, MA: MIT Press.
Lovering, J. (1999). Theory led by policy: The inadequacies of the 'new regionalism' (illustrated from the case of Wales). *International Journal of Urban and Regional Research, 23 (2)*, 379-395.
Markusen, A. (1996). Studying regions by studying firms. *Professional Geographer, 46 (4)*, 477-490.
Markusen, A. (1999). Fuzzy concepts, scanty evidence, policy distance: The case for rigor and policy relevance in critical regional studies. *Regional Studies, 33 (9)*, 869-994.
Martin, R. & Sunley, P. (1998). Slow convergence? The new endogenous growth theory and regional development. *Economic Geography, 74 (3)*, 201-227.
NASDAQ (1998). *NASDAQ 1998 fact book.* Available: http://www.nasdaq.com
Newsweek (1998). *The hot new tech cities.* Nov 9th, 44-55.
Pinch, S. & Henry, N. (1999). Paul Krugman's geographical economics, industrial clustering and the British motor sport industry. *Regional Studies, 33 (9)*, 815-829.
Porter, M.E. (1998). Clusters and competition: New agendas for governments and institutions. In M.E. Porter (Ed.), *On competition* (155-196). Boston MA: Harvard Business School Press.
Pouder, R. & St. John, C.H. (1996). Hot spots and blind spots: Geographical clusters of firms and innovation. *Academy of Management Review, 21 (4)*, 1192-1225.
Powell, W.W. (1990). Neither market nor hierarchy. In B. Straw & L.L. Cummings (Eds.), *Research in organizational behavior* (295-336). Greenwich, Connecticut: JAI Press.
Rosentraub, M. & Przybylski, M. (1996). Competitive advantage, economic development and the effective use of local public dollars. *Economic Development Quarterly, 10 (4)*, 315-330.
Saxenian, A. (1994). *Regional advantage; culture and competition in Silicon Valley and Route 128*, Boston: Harvard University Press.
Saxenian, A. (2002). Silicon Valley's new immigrant high-growth entrepreneurs. *Economic Development Quarterly, 16 (1)*, 20-31.
Shearmur, R. & Doloreux, D. (2000). Science parks: actors or reactors? Canadian Science parks in their urban context. *Environment and Planning A, 32*, 1065-1082.
Storper, M. (1995). The resurgence of regional economies, ten years later: The region as a nexus of untraded interdependencies. *European Urban and Regional Studies, 2 (3)*, 191-221.
Varga, A. (2000). Local academic knowledge transfers and the concentration of economic activity. *Journal of Regional Science, 40 (2)*, 289-309.
Westhead, P. (1997). R&D 'inputs' and 'outputs' of technology-based firms located on and off science parks. *R&D Management, 27 (1)*, 45-62.
Westhead, P. & Storey, D.J. (1995). Links between higher education institutions and high technology firms. *Omega; International Journal of Management Science, 23 (4)*, 345-360.

EIKE W. SCHAMP

7. FROM A TRANSPORT NODE TO A GLOBAL PLAYER: THE CHANGING CHARACTER OF THE FRANKFURT AIRPORT

Frankfurt's airport is well known; it is the largest intercontinental airport in Germany and, measured by number of passengers, the second largest in Europe. Although the European global cities of London and Paris have more airports (Frankfurt has only one), the importance of Frankfurt as a transportation node in the pattern of global connections is reflected in this extent. Airports belong to the transportation infrastructure of every modern economy. As cities becoming increasingly embedded in international relationships they need the appropriate infrastructure for the transportation of people, goods, and information. The integration of the modern global system also touches upon the enormous possibilities available for frequent and distant travel, for either business or pleasure. These reasons highlight not only the importance of international and intercontinental air traffic, but also the importance attached to airports as transportation nodes. On a world-wide scale, air traffic has grown at an unbelievable rate over the past decades and many experts predict a continuation of this growth in the future.

The idea that an airport functions as public infrastructure leads us to consider two salient points. First, the indivisibility of physical infrastructure with increased use causes significant economies of scale. Second, the responsibility of 'government' for the provision of that infrastructure. Government controls the location, size, and growth of physical infrastructure and the rules governing its use as well. In Germany, the State has three levels of political organization. The federal government is interested in the functions of an airport as a transportation node to the international and intercontinental world. The regional level (the state of Hessen) and the local level (the city of Frankfurt and its neighboring communities) see the airport as a motor for economic growth in the region. The federal government owns part of the most important international airports in Germany. At the beginning of 2001, it held 25.9 percent of the Frankfurt Airport Company (FAG), the state of Hessen owned the majority with 45.2 percent and the city of Frankfurt owned 28.9 percent.

The idea of an airport being an important part of public infrastructure originates from the ongoing significance of the national government as regulator of its use. In addition, national territory still seems to be a more or less closed market for air transport. Air traffic rights are subject to government sovereignty. National carriers carry out transportation duties in air traffic while national and regional airports provide the infrastructure. Domestic customers, private as well as business, use domestic airports in order to fly with domestic flag carriers. In fact, even today, at least in scheduled air traffic, domestic customers show loyalty to national carriers

D. Felsenstein et al. (eds.),
Emerging Nodes in the Global Economy: Frankfurt and Tel Aviv Compared, 131–145.

such as Lufthansa in Germany. This promotes those airports that act as a central hub for domestic carriers. So far, no carrier has ever had had its central hub outside of its own country.

Deregulation, commercialization, and privatization have over in the past decade thrown doubt on the role of the airport as a purely public infrastructure in a government controlled air traffic system made up of several national territories in Europe. Since the 1980's, the entire sector of European air transport has gone through considerable restructuring due to air traffic deregulation by European governments. National governments have implemented deregulation at a slow pace, and this process was only completed in Germany in 1997. The consequences are now becoming noticeable. Airlines in Europe are still to a great extent nationally bound, the allocation of landing rights and the rights to fly over a country en-route to another are still regulated by the government. Airports still have the character of public infrastructure. However, the persistent process of deregulation, commercialization, and privatization in Europe, first in Great Britain (Humphreys, 1999) and then step by step on the continent, have lead privatized airlines to new anticipative strategies. Their customers' strategies have also changed the market for services at the airport. A small number of larger and more powerful airlines have developed with new demands on infrastructure design. One force behind the transformation of airports from an infrastructure commodity to an active strategic player lies therefore in the changes made within the air traffic market. Airports now compete with other airports in order to become hubs for international and intercontinental air traffic of the larger carriers. One can differentiate between the air traffic markets such as the market for business travel, the private travel market, the market for mass tourism in charter traffic, the market for air freight and the market for mail and courier post and so on. Although there is already a tendency for airports to specialize in these markets, most of them are still interrelated because they often make use of the same aircraft.

A consequence of this increasing competition is the steady pressure for airports to become privatized and the diversification of the airport companies' strategies. This chapter will focus on how airports are changing from being a local infrastructure commodity to a diversified holding with a broader, more global perspective. This will be illustrated in the case of Frankfurt airport. The airport can no longer be considered 'passive' infrastructure, but rather acts in its own interests within a system of actors. This system is marked by competition and collaboration between a few larger actors: the few intercontinental airports in Western Europe, the national carriers, and the government in the form of the EU Commission, the federal government, and the state of Hessen.

The perspective adopted here is rather different to that normally taken when considering global and globalizing cities and the city system. Quite often, the existence of a large airport is simply taken for granted; city and airport are often synonymous, as air traffic is a metaphor for the importance of the city as an international node. For example, Cattan (1995) and Smith and Timberlake (2001) use air traffic volume as an indicator of the position of the city in an urban system. The relationship between the size and importance of a city and its airports is nowhere as plausible as in London or Paris. However, the metropolitan region of

Frankfurt/Rhein-Main is, by European standards, quite small with only 4 million inhabitants. Additionally, it is located in a highly urbanized section of Europe which stretches from the mouth of the Rhein River to Switzerland and has a number of international airports. Nevertheless, the Frankfurt airport is still the second largest in Europe.

This chapter proceeds as follows: First, the growth and size of the Frankfurt airport over the past decades are examined. Then deregulation of the European air traffic market, and the emergence of powerful new actors are discussed. Following that we introduce the force driving the Frankfurt airport company, namely the national carrier Lufthansa. The reorganization of the airport, its new diversification strategy and the partial privatization into the new Fraport AG is then examined and is followed by a section that uses examples to portray the airport company's efforts to improve its competitive position with other airports. This will make clear the extent to which the airport company has already become an actor of national and international importance. In the final section, we discuss the question of what the changed strategies of the Fraport AG mean for the metropolitan region.

7.1 SIZE AND GROWTH OF THE FRANKFURT AIRPORT

The Frankfurt airport is without a doubt a leading node of air traffic in Europe. When its importance is measured in transport capabilities, Frankfurt airport takes second place after Heathrow London and before Charles de Gaulle airport in Paris, in number of passengers (including transit). When air freight is considered, it takes first place, followed by Schiphol, Amsterdam. The number of passengers served has continued to climb considerably, while the amount of air freight has grown at a much slower rate (Table 7.1).

Table 7.1 Development of the Frankfurt airport 1994-2000

	1994	*95*	*96*	*97*	*98*	*99*	*2000*
Passengers (including transit) in million	–	–	38.8	40.3	42.7	45.9	49.4
Freight in million tons	–	–	1.4	1.4	1.4	1.4	1.6
Turnover in billion Euro	1,1	1,2	1,2	1,2	1,3	1,3	–

Source: www.fraport.de.

The growth of the Frankfurt airport and its importance in relation to other international airports in Germany is the result of a developmental process in which Frankfurt gained an advantage from the outset. The years after WWII were of special importance to the development of the Frankfurt airport as Germany was forbidden to partake in air traffic. Frankfurt was the most important American airport in Germany and American military headquarters in Germany were located there up until 1991. The start of commercial air traffic soon after the end of the war made Frankfurt into Germany's new air traffic center in international air traffic. In 1946, American Overseas Airlines, which would later become Pan American World Airways, started flying between Germany and the USA. A little later, the Scandinavians followed with a European connection from Copenhagen via Frankfurt to Marseilles (FAG, 1996). In 1951 the US Airforce returned to the neighboring military airbase and made room for more civil air traffic. In 1952, 19 foreign airlines were using the Frankfurt airport on a regular basis. As western Germany regained sovereignty over its airspace in 1955, Lufthansa, which had restarted operations in Cologne two years earlier, started taking off out of Frankfurt. This made Frankfurt, from the very beginning, the central airport of Germany.

The splitting of Germany into east and west changed the flow of both rail- and highway traffic: instead of the traditional east-west connection (Ruhr area to Berlin), a north-south connection (Hamburg-Frankfurt-Munich) was started. Frankfurt became the central node of this national land traffic, allowing the airport's scope of influence to grow considerably. Already in the 1950s, Frankfurt had become one of West Germany's most important international airports with double the amount of outgoing foreign flights of competing airports such as Düsseldorf and Hamburg. Even more evident was the comparison in international air freight (Schamp, 1957). The growth of the Frankfurt airport has not been driven by the economic growth of the metropolitan region Frankfurt/Rhein-Main alone, but from that of West Germany as a whole.

Recent attempts to measure the importance of cities based on their share of air traffic have made it clear that, even on a European scale, Frankfurt airport has continued to gain importance over the past decades. Smith and Timberlake (2001) introduce a new perspective in measuring the importance of airports by evaluating the role of a node in the airline network by considering its connections to other nodes. On the basis of this approach, Frankfurt moved from third place to second in Europe during the 90s (Table 7.2). The reunification of Germany, which meant the enlargement of the domestic market for air traffic services as well as the building of a European Single Market, has contributed to this high growth trajectory.

Table 7.2 Network prominence ranking for the top 5 cities

Rank	*1980*	*1985*	*1991*	*1994*	*1997*
1	London	London	London	London	London
2	Paris	Paris	Frankfurt	Frankfurt	Frankfurt
3	Frankfurt	Frankfurt	Paris	Paris	Paris
4	New York	New York	New York	New York	New York
5	Amsterdam	Amsterdam	Tokyo	Amsterdam	Amsterdam

Source: Smith and Timberlake 2001, pp. 1666f.

Other German airports could not catch up after the Frankfurt airport's head start. Neither the functions of the national capitol (Cologne-Bonn) nor those of the business center of the Ruhr region (Düsseldorf) were able to incorporate increased transportation services with their airports. Quite on the contrary, Frankfurt's share of German air traffic grew steadily. Only with the completion of the Munich II airport in 1992, which took approximately 23 years to build, was a new and important competitive force brought onto the scene (Haas, 1994). Munich is the second most important airport in Germany today, far ahead of Düsseldorf, Berlin and Hamburg (Table 7.3). Recently, however, there has been much discussion concerning the extension of the Berlin-Brandenburg airport. However, the expectation that a new hub comparable to Frankfurt can be constructed hardly seems a realistic prospect for the next decade.

Table 7.3 International airports in Germany according to their share in total local air transport markets (1998)

	Passengers %	*Air freight* %	*Air mail* %
Frankfurt/Main	34.1	67.0	51.3
Munich	15.8	5.8	8.9
Düsseldorf	11.8	2.9	-
Berlin*	9.2	1.3	6.3
Hamburg	7.0	1.7	6.6
Cologne/Bonn	4.5	18.5	7.5

* 3 Airports

Source: FAG 2000, p. 21.

The growth and the size of the Frankfurt airport have made it into one of the most important economic factors of the Frankfurt/Rhein-Main region. The FAG (Flughafen Frankfurt/Main AG), with its 13,000 employees, is one of the largest employers in the region. On airport property are more than 460 additional companies who employ approximately 50,000 employees. When considering direct and indirect employment, the airport has a position comparable to the financial sector in the city of Frankfurt.

Recently, several studies have examined the effect of the airport on regional business in order to prove the necessity of its expansion (Bulwien *et al.*, 1999; Baum *et al.*, 1999). The direct effect of the airport, including all business on its property, on regional business has been calculated with 2.76 billion Euro in economic value in 1998. The combined gross income of the employees was, at that time, approximately 2 billion Euro. Based on those numbers and using an input-output model Bulwien *et al.* (1999) came up with an employment multiplier of 1.3 and an income multiplier of 1.26 for the entire region. This was enough to compensate the negative influences on the unemployment caused by de-industrialization within the airport's region (see Chapter 2). It should be noted, that economic effects are traded off with high social costs such as excessive land consumption and increasing noise pollution. This has been the basis for ongoing political resistance towards the unbridled growth of the Frankfurt airport.

7.2 EUROPEAN LIBERALIZATION OF THE AIR TRAFFIC MARKET

The current importance of the Frankfurt airport and the strategy of the airport company can only be understood as the result of a political-economic process in which the government increasingly loses power over the market. A place like Frankfurt is on the one hand an important national node and on the other hand a global node particularly perceptible to non-local forces. Air traffic in Europe, and especially Germany, is known for the continuous national government resistance to deregulation and liberalization both of which are encouraged by the USA and the EU. The result is an extraordinary development path in air traffic which gives existing 'big players' a head start in the new wave of competition.

In the world order that resulted after WWII, international air traffic was governed by bi-national contracts. These generally called for strict limitations on market access, prices, and the capacity of international air traffic (Nuhn, 1998). Countries encouraged the development of national flagship carriers and Germany had Lufthansa, which was owned by the federal government. Government agencies organized the flight routes of foreign airlines so as to force them to concentrate at the main nodes of national carriers. Frankfurt airport profited from this system as Lufthansa had its central route node located there (Boss *et al.*, 1996). Cooperation between the Lufthansa and the airports continues to deter competition, for example through making 'preferred contracts' concerning the use of specific terminals. Terminal 1 at Frankfurt for example, is reserved for Lufthansa. One result of such policies is that Frankfurt airport constantly operates at the limits of its capacity.

The federal government, however, did not just make and oversee the rules of air traffic. It also was part owner of the airports that were considered of international importance. Up into the mid 1990's, the federal government still owned 26 percent of the airport in Frankfurt, Munich and Hamburg, 31 percent of the airport in Cologne/Bonn, and 48 percent of the Berlin-Brandenburg airport (Boss *et al.*, 1996). The highly regulated world air traffic system was already under pressure in the 1970s due to, among other issues, over-capacity and the undermining of tariff systems. At the end of the 1970s, air traffic in the USA was deregulated. The new positioning of American airlines increased their competitiveness and therefore exported the pressure to deregulate to Europe. While Great Britain deregulated during the 1980s, the European Single Market was the vehicle the EU used to facilitate their deregulation policy (Graham, 1998). While the EU released its first liberalization guidelines in 1987, only the third guideline package, released in 1993, can be considered a radical step towards liberalization calling for a single air traffic market within the European Union (Graham, 1998; Reynolds-Feighan and Berechman, 1998; Hakfoort, 1999). This guideline package removed barriers between scheduled and non-scheduled operations in Europe, lifted bilateral agreements between countries, released the pricing, developed cabotage rights and gave the European Commission control over competition on the European air traffic market. This move was designed to break up national monopolies as well as to lower barriers for market entry.

However, four more years were necessary until this deregulation was made law in Germany. In the meantime, the competition had been increased through the charter companies. Around 45 percent of people in 1993 who were traveling by plane from Germany to other EU countries flew on charter flights (Boss *et al.*, 1996). Also, more and more people were opting to use nearby foreign airports in order to take advantage of lower prices. This caused pressure both on national flag carriers and on German airports.

A result of the increasing competition among European airlines also led to their demand to liberalize the ground-transportation services of the airports and to oppose a coalition of national government and the airport company. The EU Commission obligated this in 1998, despite the federal government request for an exception to be made in the case of Frankfurt airport (Kunz, 1999b). This resulted in splitting the traditional vertically integrated activities of the airport. As ground-transportation services in Frankfurt contribute approximately 35 percent of airport's profits, this liberalization made it necessary for the airport to look for new fields of activity.

These factors together result in extreme policy changes for the airport management. Although airports have a natural monopoly due to their position in regional markets, liberalization of the air traffic market has long term effects on competition among airports. As illustrated in the case of Lufthansa in Frankfurt, national carriers are the driving force in competition between airports. The liberalization of air traffic has resulted in increased competition and a new strategic orientation among the larger carriers in Europe. Their demands have, in turn, put the airports under competitive pressure. However, the cooperation between national carriers and the larger airports that has been going on for decades will most likely continue in negotiations for new strategies.

7.3 A DRIVING FORCE: LUFTHANSA AND ITS NEW POLICIES

Beginning in the 1980s, deregulation in the USA and Great Britain set the European carriers in competition among themselves, especially for the vital North Atlantic routes. Deregulation of the European air traffic market in the 1990s intensified this situation. In contrast to the US, step by step deregulation over a nine year period (completed in 1997), allowed European airlines to learn new strategies and to adopt to a new business environment. Recent studies show that the effects of deregulation on Europe were different to those in the USA (Schnell, 2000; Wiezorek, 1998). These conditions worked to Lufthansa's advantage. A privatization process lasting close to ten years allowed the airline to implement new growth strategies which secured its position as the second ranking European passenger airline and the leading operator in air freight, catering and technical services.

Most European flag carriers are still either entirely or partly nationally owned. One exception is BAA, which became the first leading private carrier in the early deregulation process in Great Britain. While Lufthansa was partly privatized in 1966, the federal government still remained the majority share-holder in the 1990's when growing competition with American airlines and the BAA brought Lufthansa into a crisis. In 1994, the federal share was reduced to 35 percent due to a capital increase and was later transferred to the Federal Bank KfW in 1996, who in turn sold it on the stock market a year later. This period of time also marked the end of Lufthansa's financial crisis.

Overcoming its financial crisis brought a considerable change of strategy in the 1990s. As an integrated company comprising many activities, Lufthansa could fall back on both economies of scope and economies of scale. To make external growth of business fields possible, many of these activities were transformed to subsidiary companies. Today the Lufthansa group comprises subsidiaries in the following seven business areas: German Lufthansa in passenger transportation with 47 million passengers in the year 2000; Lufthansa Cargo; Lufthansa Technik; LSG, which makes up approximately 34 percent of the world market for catering services; C&N Touristik and Condor Charters, which together are in second place in the German market; Lufthansa Systems Group which is an important global player in IT and GlobeGround, a ground transportation service provider at 131 airports in 31 countries.

Considerable steps towards securing the company's growth in all fields have only recently been made. In this process, Lufthansa prefers cooperating and making alliances with both large and small companies. Code sharing in passenger transport is generally a first step towards building up a cooperative relationship between airlines. It can eventually end in an extensive strategic alliance in passenger transport. Lufthansa, in comparison with other European carriers, began to build cooperative relationships very slowly. The strategic alliance with United Airlines in 1994 developed successfully and was transformed in 1997 into the Star Alliance - a growing global alliance originally composed of 15 airlines from Europe, North American, South America, Asia, and New Zealand (Wiezorek, 1998; Schnell, 2000). This has lead to a considerable network effect. After Mexicana and British Midlands joined, the Star Alliance covered 815 destinations in 130 countries (Lufthansa, 2000). A powerful union was formed in which Lufthansa not only saved money, but also gained an increased marked share and reduced both competitive pressure and risk.

Lufthansa Cargo has only recently entered into important cooperative air freight industry relationships. Today, Lufthansa is the second largest freight airline in the world, after the express integrator Federal Express. In 1999, Lufthansa entered a joint venture on express business with the largest postal company in the world - Deutsche Post (German Postal Service). In 2000, it arranged cooperation with 11 haulage contractors specializing in the transport of larger goods and united with SAS Cargo and Singapore Airlines in order to form a global freight system. Lufthansa therefore is pursuing a strategy that aims at transforming a freight airline into an integrated operator in all air freight market segments, thereby re-fashioning a national company into a global one.

In response to the financial crisis of the 1990s Lufthansa took the United States as an example and strengthened the hub and spoke system. The Frankfurt Airport, traditionally Lufthansa's central location, was made into Lufthansa's central hub for both passenger and freight transport. Here, Lufthansa took advantage of its starting and landing slots assigned during an era of regulation and persisting due to a 'grandfather' clause. This situation hinders other airlines from entering Frankfurt Airport, as capacity is almost at its limit. Additionally, due to strategic alliances, the hub of the national carrier is also used as a node for foreign partners.

For this reason, Lufthansa's strategies are of utmost importance for the further development of the Frankfurt airport. Airports are competing with one another for the role as primary or secondary hubs. Lufthansa Cargo owns, for example, a secondary hub in Cologne/Bonn; the new joint venture with DHL strengthens this airport with the later using it as its central German hub. When the new airport opened in Munich, Lufthansa saw this as an opportunity to enter into a joint venture with the local airport company and have the second terminal set up for the exclusive use of Star Alliance airlines (Kunz, 1999a). This caused Munich to become the second hub for Lufthansa and the Star Alliance for intercontinental flights in Germany, which of course increased FAG's competitive edge.

7.4 THE RISE OF AN INTERNATIONAL CORPORATION IN THE AIRPORT INDUSTRY: FROM THE FAG TO THE FRAPORT AG

The German federal government's Aviation Concept 2000 (1994) perceives international airports as contributing towards national economic goals such as performance improvement and increased competitiveness (Jakubowski, 1999). Germany's international airports are run by the government, but managed like private corporations. Flughafen Frankfurt AG (FAG, today known as the Fraport AG) is the only German airport company working as a joint stock corporation. This enables the realization of two objectives: future privatization as well as raising capital via the stock market.

The EU's various steps towards deregulation which effect airport activities have changed all the rules of the game, and therefore have also changed the strategies of the airport companies. The term 'airport industry' reflects the change in perspective from the airport as infrastructure commodity to the airport companies` strategic dealings within their own market. Traditional economic research that treats the airport as a 'natural monopoly' and as indivisible good subject to increasing returns, seems increasingly irrelevant to the experience of the modern airport as a competitive global corporation (Jakubowski, 1999).

In this new environment, the airport is no longer seen as a single integrated system, but rather as a collection of various business areas for which differing strategies can be used (Humphrey, 1999). Self perception and models become quite important. Manfred Schoelch, the vice chairman of the FAG has described the changes at the Frankfurt airport with the help of 'role models' which develop in a cumulative and complimentary fashion. In the 1960's, the airport was considered an 'air train station'. In the 1970's it became an interface between air and rail traffic as well as a shopping center, in the 1980's it stressed its role as a business center and in the 1990's leisure time and entertainment have been prioritized (FAG, 1996).

The FAG is presently pursuing three strategies. First, the diversification into new business fields. Second extending their capacity in traditional business fields, and third internationalizing their business activities. This diversification considerably expands the spectrum of services offered. FAG's traditional main competence is the ground handling of airplanes, passengers and freight. This includes airside management (services for aircraft for starting and landing procedure) as well as land side management (services for handling passenger and air freight transport). Two thirds of FAG revenues are in these areas. Since the beginning of 1999 parts of the land side services are now offered through external competitors. The FAG has reacted to deregulation by strengthening its traditional services and offering new services, often in the form of joint ventures in the areas of terminal and security services.

With the privatization and growth of the passenger traffic comes the increasing importance of the property management business area. Real estate activity already contributes around 24 percent of the FAG's revenues. In total there are 400,000 square meters of office space and 12,500 square meters of retail space available at the airport. The space for both business types is currently being expanded through the roofing of the ICE train station. However, the FAG is still far from making the profits that other airports make in property management already. BAA and Schipol report 66 and 56 percent of their total profits respectively from property management (Nick, 1998).

The supporting services in the air freight field are of special importance for the FAG. This is very closely bound to passenger transport because 51 percent of air freight is still transported using passenger planes and only 49 percent is actually sent via freight planes. Frankfurt is Europe's leading air freight location. More than 50 percent of the air freight traffic is global with Asia the largest market followed by North America. Air freight activities demand extensive space from an airport for the handling and shipping of goods. This creates, however, new value-added activities and therefore contributes to the regional economical impact of the airport.

Permanent capacity shortages make a strategy of expanding the airport's capacity a necessity. The FAG justifies this with the demands of its most important clients, Lufthansa and the Star Alliance, which together have approximately 70 percent of all flight activities. In this strategic field, consensus and cooperation with the federal government is essential. On the air side are long-term plans for building another runway. On the land side, capacity can be expanded at a much faster rate. Terminal 1 is already being expanded to accommodate passenger transport needs. The federal government also has strongly supported the intermodal connection of the airport as it is located on Germany's most frequently used highway intersection. In 1999 the Deutsche Bahn AG (German Rail company), owned by the federal government, opened a high speed train station at the Frankfurt airport. This makes it the only airport in Germany with a direct connection to the nation's high speed railway.

New facilities for air freight have also been expanded extensively. The US Air Force partially moved from airport property in the mid 1990's handing it over to the

FAG. This made it possible to build the new south Cargo City. The FAG felt this was an important step in keeping its competitive edge versus other airports, especially Schiphol and defending its position as number one in the air freight business. The agreement between the US and German government to re-locate the US Air Force operations from Frankfurt Airport property to Rheinland-Pfalz, offered the FAG an opportunity to further strengthen its role in global air freight as well as its ties to the second largest air freight carrier in the world, Lufthansa.

The third strategic dimension involves the internationalization of business activities. On the one hand, the airport uses its own competencies to influence the growing global market of the airport industry. On the other, the FAG connects with foreign airports in the form of partnerships and strategic alliances in order to improve their own business areas through market expansion and cost reduction.

Airport company internationalization means some large airport companies become global players in various air traffic markets. The FAG has founded German AeroConsult incorporated as a subsidiary company for worldwide consulting. In addition, it acquires partnerships in other airports facilities and services. At the end of 1999, FAG had nearly 40 contracts with other airports, partly for the building and managing of facilities, and partly for managing specific services. At present, FAG is pursuing two terminal projects in Anatolia, Turkey and in Manila, Philippines. Ground transport services have been acquired at the Portuguese airports in Lisbon, Porto, and Faro, as well as in German airports such as Cologne-Bonn and air freight services have been acquired in Nairobi.

The first cooperative relationship between international airports in the world was made in 2000 between the FAG and the Schiphol Group/Amsterdam. Under the name Pantares, global services are offered concerning the management of terminals, airplane and freight preparation, IT technologies, and retail sales.

The wide range of policies relating to diversification, expansion, and internationalization strategies all make for a change in the management culture of the FAG as it transforms from a infrastructure provider to a diversified corporation acting on various markets facing a number of competitors. In combination with the transition from a bureaucratic into an entrepreneurial culture these policies are a costly undertaking for the FAG. Airport companies at leading European airports are indeed highly profitable ventures. The British management company BAA had a revenue of approximately 571 million Euro in 1998, Schiphol's profit reached 135 million Euro and the Paris airports earned 80 million Euro. The profit of FAG (53 million Euro in 1998) was relatively small however considering that Frankfurt airport is the second largest in Europe. The leverage of additional capital therefore became paramount, even though the company showed constant profit increases during the 1990s.

With the agreement of its governmental shareholders the FAG became partly privatized in June 2001 and raised 2.5Billion Euro by selling new shares to private investors on the stock market. In preparation for this, the airport company was given a new name: Fraport AG. Originally, the federal ministry of finance had planned to privatize the federal share but not the city and the state, which were determined to stay involved in the future development of the airport. The Fraport AG has already outlined new strategic goals which are designed to improve the competitiveness of the company on the international airport services market. One way of achieving this is the idea recently proposed by the CEO of the Fraport AG: the creation of a German airport company composing the most important airports in Germany led by the Fraport AG.

7.5 STRENGTHENING RESOURCES IN EUROPEAN COMPETITION

The 'classical' way for an airport company to overcome capacity problems is to expand its own infrastructure. This includes building new runways as well as developing new software for the tower to optimize start operations and increase the number of starts. The densely populated Frankfurt area and the highly regulated German planning system make quick capacity expansion via runway building impossible. The last expansion of the western runway was completed in 1984 - after 19 years of planning and the sometimes heavy political resistance throughout Germany. Due to this experience, the further expansion of the airport by one extra runway (suggested by the local chamber of commerce in the mid 1990's) was never seriously discussed promoted. It took a public request from the CEO of Lufthansa, in 1997 for these plans to gain any momentum.

Unsure if public opinion would be as vehement as in the 1970s, the state government of Hessen, as majority share holder and planning authority, suggested an information and consulting (mediation) process as used in the US since the 1970's (Troost, 2001). During mediation, stakeholders who would profit from expansion would debate with those who fear its costs in order to reach a compromise that would finally be decided upon by politicians. The mediation group presented their ideas on the expansion of the airport at the beginning of 2000. They recommended expansion along with strict adherence to suspending 'night flights' between 11:00 p.m. and 5:00 a.m. Both the mediation group and the results of their work were controversial. Important groups against airport expansion were not included in the mediation process, and it seemed a decision for expansion had been reached by the state government. The results of the mediation process are still not concluded. However, it does seem that the expansion of the runway will occur although this is unlikely to start before 2010.

The debate on whether or not to expand the runway has however, opened a new issue. A former military airport Frankfurt-Hahn in Rheinland-Pfalz has become available as an ersatz airport as American troops left Germany after its reunification. This is located in the Hunsrück, a mountainous area approximately 120 km west of Frankfurt. Civilian air traffic started operating there in 1993 and an operating license for accommodating low noise level aircraft was given by the federal government in 1997. While the state of Rheinland-Pfalz holds a blocking minority share of 25.1 percent of airport ownership, the FAG has been acquiring shares in the facility.

The FAG already uses the Frankfurt-Hahan airport as an overflow facility for price sensitive types of air traffic. That includes charter flights, especially those to Turkey and to Germany's most popular vacation spot Mallorca, as well as to attract the Irish low cost carrier Ryanair. Starting in 2002, Ryanair would like to make

Frankfurt Hahn its second hub on the continent after Belgium's Charleroi, operating 30 flights a day to 10 European destinations.

Air freight at the airport is also expanding. Three freight and logistics corporations already use the Frankfurt Hahn airport which is Germany's 4th ranking airport. Since 1999, Danzas/German Post has been regularly flying to the USA and Aeroflot and Air France are using Hahn as a freight airport. There is however, fierce competition with the cheaper nearby Benelux airports in Luxembourg, Liège and Amsterdam, fierce enough that one airline already has left.

Various interests coalesce in the case of Frankfurt-Hahn. Fraport considers expansion of its capacity at the Frankfurt-Hahn airport, almost as good as expansion in Frankfurt itself. The state of Rheinland-Pfalz sees the Hahn airport as an integral motor for economic development in a region that has suffered severely since the re-location of the military. The state of Hessen hopes that with the help of the Frankfurt-Hahn airport, several of the disadvantages of Frankfurt can be by-passed. For example, night flight postal operations have been slated to move from Frankfurt to Frankfurt-Hahn. This would allow Frankfurt to expand its northern runway while still forbidding night flights. Negotiations between the neighboring states have already started. The state government of Hessen has demanded the government of Rheinland Pfalz to improve the highway infrastructure between the two airports in order to reduce the travel time between the two locations, which currently takes over an hour.

7.6 CONCLUSIONS: REGIONAL DISEMBEDDING OF THE FRAPORT AG?

Due to deregulation and partial privatization, the Fraport AG has lost its character as an infrastructure department and is in transition to developing into a diversified international corporation. This chapter has shown that on the one hand, both federal and state government still have considerable influence. On the other hand, deregulation has produced a powerful customer for the Fraport AG in the form of Lufthansa and Star Alliance. In this triangle of government, carrier, and airport company, the Fraport AG has begun to develop from the role of a facility and service provider to a global corporation.

The partial privatization of the Fraport AG has revealed a new type of market logic. A process has been set in motion that is likely to culminate in total privatization of the Fraport. As Doganis (1999) confirms: "Privatization will inevitably lead to cross-border airport ownership and the creation of multinational airport companies. No one has begun to consider what the long-term implications of this might be" (p. 108). As the largest airport company in Germany, Fraport AG, through its head start in the airport market, has opened up the chance to grow into a global player. However, this development path is not problem-free. First, the influence of the government is as large now as before. Second, the market in this area is not clearly defined and third, this opening allows the influx of other competitors, for example foreign airport companies, domestic construction companies such as Hoch-Tief or property management companies. This makes Fraport's route to becoming a global player in no way secure.

At the dawn of the new millennium it seemed that the air traffic sector was booming. The Fraport AG expected 80 million passengers (50 million in 2001) in the future as well as a doubling of freight air traffic from 1.5 million tons per year to 2.8 million tons. The aftermath of the terror attacks in September 2001 has led to a considerable downward revision in growth expectations. The effect has been to intensify the existing threat of recession on world markets and at the same time to bring on an over-capacity crisis among European carriers. Within only a few weeks, Swissair and Sabena went bankrupt, which affected their hub airports in Zurich and Brussels. These reverberations affected the German charter airline LTU with its hub in Düsseldorf. Alitalia can also be called an endangered airline. Even though Lufthansa is also suffering, it seems that its sheer size and strong global alliance are aiding it in overcoming this crisis.

The present crisis in the European airline industry is likely to effect European airports as well. Airports that serve as hubs for successful airlines will emerge, on one hand, as winners. On the other hand, they will probably be more vulnerable in negotiations with those airlines, as the crisis gives the latter a chance of opening second hubs at other airports. The successful airport companies will react by becoming more and more international, a strategy that was unthinkable before their privatization. The interest of management must therefore not be focused on domestic airports alone, but rather must be globally-based. The consequences of the changing strategy of becoming transnational can be seen in other respects. Companies that tend to re-locate from their home region in order to strengthen their global position, create negative effects in their home region. The former FAG for example, was also a patron of the region and supported regional developments. Recent developments make the prospect of regional co-operation seem dim. Full privatization of the Frankfurt airport would most likely curtail any local Frankfurt influence on any future airport development.

REFERENCES

Baum, H., Esser, K., Kurte, J. & Probst, K.M. (1999). *Der Flughafen Frankfurt/Main als Standortfaktor für die regionale Wirtschaft*. Koeln: Universität Köln.

Boss, A., Laaser, C.F., Schatz, K.W. *et al.* (1996). *Deregulierung in Deutschland. Eine empirische Analyse*. (Kieler Studien 275).Tübingen: Mohr.

Bulwien, H., Hujer, R., Kokot, St., Mehlinger, Ch., Rürup, B. & Vosskamp, Th. (1999). *Einkommens- und Beschäftigungseffekte des Flughafens Frankfurt/Main - Status-quo Analysen und Prognosen*. München u.a.: Bulwien und Partner GmbH.

Cattan, N. (1995). Attractivity and internationalisation of major European cities: The example of air traffic. *Urban Studies 31*, 303-312.

Doganis, R. (1999). The future shape of the airline and airport industries. In W. Pfaehler, H.M. Niemeier & O.G. Mayer (Eds.), *Airports and air traffic* (103-113). Frankfurt am Main: Peter Lang.

FAG, Flughafen Frankfurt Main AG (1996). *1936-1996. 60 Jahre Flughafen Frankfurt. Geschichte eines europäischen Verkehrsflughafens*. Frankfurt/M.: FAG.

FAG, Flughafen Frankfurt Main AG (2000). Geschäftsbericht 1999. www.flughafen-frankfurt.com

Graham, B. (1995). *Geography and air transport*. Chichester: John Wiley.

Graham, B. (1998). Liberalization, regional economic development and the geography of demand for air transport in the European Union. *Journal of Transport Geography 6*, 87-104.

Haas, H.D. (1994). Europäischer Luftverkehr und der neue Flughafen Münchens. *Geographische Rundschau 46*, 274-281.

Hakfoort, J.R. (1999). The deregulation of Europan air transport: A dream come true? *TESG 90*, 226-233.

Humphreys, I. (1999). Privatisation and commercialisation. Changes in UK airport ownership patterns. *Journal of Transport Geography 7*, 121-134.

Jakubowski, P. (1999). Flughafenpolitik im liberalisierten EU-Luftverkehrsmarkt. In *Neuere Ansätze zu einer effizienten Infrastrukturpolitik*. (Beiträge aus dem Institut fuer Verkehrswissenschaft an der Universitaet Münster 148) (209-256). Göttingen: Vandenhoeck & Ruprecht.

Kunz, M. (1999a). Airport regulation: The policy framework. In W. Pfaehler, H.M.Niemeier & O.G. Mayer (Eds.), *Airports and air traffic. regulation, privatisation and competition* (11-55). Frankfurt/Main: Peter Lang.

Kunz, M. (1999b). Entbündelter Zugang zu Flughaefen: Zur Liberalisierung der Bodenverkehrsdienste euf europäischen Flughäfen. *Zeitschrift fuer Verkehrswissenschaft 70*, 206-232.

Lufthansa (2000). *Geschäftsbericht 1999*. Köln: Lufthansa.

Lufthansa (2001). *Geschäftsbericht 2000*. Köln: Lufthansa.

Nick, A. (1998). Flughafengesellschaften auf dem Weg zu einer internationalen Branche. In Credit Suisse/First Boston (Ed.), *Flughafenprivatisierung in Europa* (9-12). Frankfurt am Main: Boersen-Zeitung.

Nuhn, H. (1998). Deregulierung der Verkehrsmaerkte in Westeuropa und räumliche Konsequenzen. In H. Gebhardt, G. Heinritz & R. Wiesner (Eds.), *Europa im Globalisierungsprozess von Wirtschaft und Gesellschaft* (158-170). Stuttgart: Franz Steiner.

Reynolds-Feighan, A.J. & Berechman, J. (1998). Network impacts of changes in the European aviation industry. In K. Butten, P. Nijkamp & H. Priemus (Eds.), *Transport networks in Europe - concepts, analysis and policies* (265-290). Cheltenham, Northampton.

Schamp, H. (1957). *Luftverkehrsgeographie. Deutschlands Lage im Weltluftverkehr (Erdkundliches Wissen 4)*. Wiesbaden: Franz Steiner.

Schnell, M. (2000). Zur Effektivitaet möglicher Kooperationsformen im liberalisierten europäischen Luftverkehr - eine empirische Analyse. *Zeitschrift für Verkehrswissenschaften 71*, 242-270.

Schoelch, M. (1996). Der Flughafen als Kommunikationszentrum, Marktplatz und interkulturelle Begegnungsstaette. In Arbeitskreis Luftverkehr der Technischen Hochschule Darmstadt (Ed.), *Drittes Kolloquium Luftverkehr: Grossflughäfen auf dem Weg zu urbanen Zentren* (1-30). Darmstadt: Technische Universitaet.

Smith, D.A. & Timberlake, M.F. (2001). World city networks and hierarchies, 1977-1997. *American Behavioral Scientist 44*, 1656-1678.

Troost, H.J. (2001). Neue Vernetzungsstrategien in der metropolitanen Region Rhein-Main: Das Beispiel des Mediationsverfahrens Flughafen Frankfurt. In J. Esser & E.W. Schamp (Eds.), *Metropolitane Region in der Vernetzung. Der Fall Frankfurt/Rhein-Main* (245-279). Frankfurt/Main: Campus.

Wiezorek, B. (1998). *Strategien europäischer Fluggesellschaften in einem liberalisierten Weltluftverkehr*. Frankfurt am Main: Peter Lang.

SECTION III:

PRODUCER-DRIVEN ACTIVITIES

AMIR MOSSEK

8. THE TEL-AVIV PRODUCER SERVICES SECTOR: CHANGE IN AN ERA OF GLOBALIZATION

8.1 INTRODUCTION

This chapter examines advanced producer services and the processes of globalization in Tel-Aviv. More precisely, it focuses on the impact of two major sub-sectors of advanced producer services - advertising and accountancy - on the global processes and changes at play in the emerging node metropolis of Tel-Aviv. 'Globalization' is a general term used to refer to the social, political, environmental and, perhaps most significantly, economic phenomena that picked up speed around the globe at the end of the twentieth century. It denotes a situation in which decisions and activities taking place in one part of the world have rapid effect elsewhere by virtue of the diminishing influence of distance and borders..

By definition, producer services differ from other services in that they are not intended for final consumption, rather as intermediate components in the production of other goods or services. This may appear to be a simple definition, but attempting to classify different sectors based on this definition can be confusing. The ultimate result of such classification is a system of numerous sub-divisions and categories within the producer services sector. While most manufacturing services sectors are regarded as sectors that manufacture tangible products, others, such as software companies, manufacture actual products. Furthermore, some sectors, like consulting and data processing, use sophisticated work methods and instruments while others, like supply and maintenance, provide far more basic services. Some researchers regard the insurance sector as belonging to producer services, while others include it in the finance sector.

The sub-sectors that constitute the focus of this chapter, advertising and accountancy, belong to a category for which a definitive consensus exists: advanced producer services. These are generally identified with 'traditional' producer services, such as legal services, engineering and computer services (Wernerheim and Sharpe, 1999).

Over the last decade, Tel-Aviv has undergone, and continues to undergo, significant economic changes that are directly linked to transformations taking place within the global economic system. Similar changes took place in developed cities and countries ten and twenty years earlier. However, for a number of reasons, these changes began later in Tel-Aviv; and the speed and intensity at which they are progressing appears to have compensated for this late start.

The changes in question were brought about by a number of factors. Structural change over the last decade (such as monetary stability, and the removal of marginal

D. Felsenstein et al. (eds.),
Emerging Nodes in the Global Economy: Frankfurt and Tel Aviv Compared, 149–172.

trade and currency exchange barriers) eased Israel's entry into the global economy. Political processes, peace agreements and the easing of the Arab boycott were followed by a rise in Israel's credit rating, and this, in turn, sparked the entry of large international firms into the local market, foreign direct investment by investors and international companies in the Israeli economy, and massive growth within the Israeli high-tech sector. In addition, the arrival of approximately one million immigrants from the former Soviet Union during the 1990's served to considerably expand Israel's domestic consumer market.

Many Israeli companies, particularly those in the high-tech sector, issued shares on the international stock market, most notably in the United States, where over one hundred Israeli companies are members of the New York Stock Exchange and NASDAQ. Israel has the second largest number of foreign companies on these exchanges after Canada (see Chapter 6). Government-led deregulation in the spheres of communication and information exchange also contributed to the entry of global factors to Israel.

One of the major effects of globalization has been an ever-increasing need for companies with international distribution that provide advanced, internationally-oriented producer services. This trend has resulted from a growing demand for experts who can provide assistance regarding all aspects of international investments, contracts, transactions (accountants) and global mergers, as well as experts in marketing, public relations and market analysis (advertising experts). Thus, Israeli and other accounting and advertising firms have had to adapt to providing global services to both international and local companies.

Tel-Aviv is the financial capital of Israel. It is the location of the head offices of all major local and international producer companies, as well as of all the country's financial facilities and institutions: the stock exchange, head offices of banks, insurance companies, brokers, etc. Consequently, large offices within the advanced producer services sector as a whole, and accountancy and advertising firms in particular, are based in Tel-Aviv, with smaller branches in Jerusalem and Haifa. For this reason, this chapter focuses on those producer services uniquely associated with Tel-Aviv.

Similar to global trends, these two sub-sectors in Tel-Aviv have joined international networks and alliances in order to provide ongoing services to their international clients, both locally and abroad. The past few years, have also seen signs of global connections in other service sectors, most importantly the banking sector. Banking giants such as Citibank, HSBC and Bank of America have initiated a process of breaking the monopoly of Israeli banks in Israel. Representatives of a number of international insurance companies, such as A.I.G., have integrated themselves into the insurance sector, although not as markedly as has been the case in accountancy and advertising. Law firms have also been showing signs of joining international networks, and mergers among local firms in different areas of specialization are underway. This phenomenon, however, has not yet reached a critical mass of research.

This chapter will review the changes that have taken place within the advertising and accountancy sub-sectors in the context of global trends, and examine the factors that have resulted in the entry of international networks into Israel and their collaboration with local firms. Until now, these sub-sectors have not been examined in any systematic fashion, despite their high propensity to globalize. We will address the following questions:

- How has globalization progressed in these sectors?
- How have these processes affected Tel-Aviv, its advanced producer services sector and this sector's structure?
- What changes have occurred within firms themselves?
- How have these changes been expressed in spatial terms?
- What are the potential trends for the future?
- What can other cities learn from Tel Aviv's experience?

8.2 GLOBALIZATION AND ADVANCED PRODUCER SERVICES

Advanced producer services are not located everywhere. Rather, they tend to be distributed unequally among a limited number of cities that play key roles in the current global processes of the world economy. Sassen's (1991) study of the development of global cities suggests two main reasons for their growth: the globalization of economic activity and the organizational structure of producer and financial services. These factors are expressed by producer and financial services' assumption of global dimensions and concentration in cities, as centers vital to management. They result in the coordination of economic power within the global economy. The most prominent examples of this dynamic are Tokyo, London and New York. Sassen (1994) also maintains that the rapid growth and agglomeration of advanced producer services within cities has determined the formation of global cities. Examining the location of advertising and accountancy firms facilitates a better understanding of the agglomeration and concentration of management functions in global cities.

The globalization and internationalization of the producer services sector has attracted considerable attention in recent years (Roberts, 1999; Bagchi-Sen, 1997; Lesley, 1997; West, 1996; Daniels, 1995; Kim, 1995; Perry, 1990; Beaverstock, 1991, 1996). Most researchers, however, have examined only first tier global cities, and not much has been written about the influence of globalization on producer services in smaller, emerging, centers.

The internationalization of producer services is not a new phenomenon. It can be traced back to the end of the 19th century, when many large scale British and American producers were expanding their international businesses and establishing presences in foreign countries. As the advertising and accountancy firms that had provided these companies with producer services in their home countries followed them abroad, they began to establish connections and representatives in various parts of the world, with the aim of providing the same services internationally.

Subsequently, and especially over the last 30 years, many changes have taken place in the importance of producer services and their variety and scope of activity, as well as the sector's international organization and number of employees. For the past three decades, the presence of producer services has been an important condition for economic growth, most significantly in the economies of developed countries. In all such countries, we observe a clear drop in the demand for labor in manufacturing sectors, along with a considerable growth in the labor needs of the producer services sectors. One component of the global economy has been the transfer of production sites to developing countries such as South America, South East Asia and Eastern Europe.

The new structure of international production is based on the organization of vast multinational companies with significant turnover and income, each controlling production and marketing centers in a large number of countries and each employing tens of thousands of workers. The more global, widespread and complex markets become, the greater the need for extremely efficient professional, managerial and organizational frameworks capable of supervising and controlling production and marketing networks (Coffey and Bailly, 1992).

A number of factors are often cited as resulting in major changes in the scope and importance of producer services in developed countries. These include differentiation, range and distribution in production processes and the supply of services; changing aspects of government regulation and intervention; the transition to 'flexible' production that adapts easily to demand fluctuations; the rapid, critical development of telecommunication, information and computer systems; and the ability of advanced producer services to find business opportunities and to serve the changing needs of their clients.

The growth and internationalization of the producer services sector can also be explained by the sub-contracting of producer services departments, which until relatively recently constituted an integral part of international producer companies. A number of factors have contributed to these structural changes: the desire of producer companies to lower overhead costs; the increasing use of expert services, particularly those requiring expensive skilled human resources; and the need for flexibility in periods of economic slowdown (it is easier for a company to reduce or cut its ties with an external company than to dismiss its own producer services employees).

Indeed, increased control is facilitated by new telecommunication and information systems technology. However, professional, skilled employees are still irreplaceable when providing advanced services to international manufacturing or service companies. This need is what has fueled the development of international networks of advanced producer services over the past few decades, such as legal services, information systems, insurance, advertising and accountancy.

It is generally accepted that a major portion of the huge increase in advanced producer services has been due to the global activity of large producer firms outside of their own countries. These firms' extensive export to, and foreign direct investment in so many countries has necessitated the support of advanced producer services, thereby encouraging the development of global networks. This relationship, however, is not unidirectional. Advanced producer services networks also search out new markets and clientele independently, taking advantage of their size, experience, technology and capabilities in order to increase their business volume.

Some empirical research suggests that a major factor of past growth of the producer services sector was the producer companies' sale of services to primary producers. In recent years however, the main income of producer services has been increasingly generated by services and contacts sold to other service providers. Sources show that over half of all advanced producer services are sold to other service providers, like insurance companies and banks (Juleff-Tranter, 1996). These networks, spread throughout world, are connected and coordinated in such a way as to offer significant advantages to their clients for entering and establishing new markets. Thus, international producer clients often follow, rather than lead, their global producer services provider into new markets. In this way, the various nodes of producer services networks serve as a vanguard, locating potential markets for multinational companies.

8.3 STRATEGIES AND STAGES IN THE ENTRANCE OF GLOBAL NETWORKS INTO LOCAL MARKETS

International service networks adopt different strategies in order to enter new markets or countries. Bagchi-Sen (1997) and Roberts (1999) describe the main strategies as follows:

Export of Producer Services: An agency or network supplies services to clients in a foreign country directly, without establishing representation or an infrastructure in that country.

Foreign Direct Investment: This refers to the establishment of a network branch in a new market. The branch is set-up and run by expert labor sent by an agency or a global network, and supported by local personnel. It is owned solely by the network. Both options are likely to be preferred when entering a developing market in which the professional level of local personnel is not high enough to run a firm according to global standards.

The Stages Approach: Entering the market of a developed country is undertaken in stages and at varying speeds. Well-established local firms serve as globalization agents for a number of reasons. First, despite the great advancements in telecommunication and information systems that facilitate the export of advanced services, there is still no substitute for personal, discreet relations between clients and service providers. This is particularly true of accountancy, a sub-branch entrusted with the client's most sensitive information. Second, in a sector where great attention is paid to the quality of service, first-hand knowledge of local culture and the client's particular taste (in advertising) is a must, as is a chemistry between the client and the services firm. Experience, accumulated knowledge of the local market and expert employees are extremely important factors, and provide some firms with competitive advantages over others.

Strict regulations are often enforced in the case of a global network's direct entry into a country. Accountancy is a field with even more stringent government regulation than others, and this is the case in Israel, as well as most advanced countries. Foreign accountants cannot work on or sign reports without first receiving local training and qualification.

The process that has evolved in Tel-Aviv corresponds to processes in other developed countries, where producer service firms with professional labor exist on the international level. Initially, the network explores the quality and suitability of local firms with respect to its own standards. At this early stage, the global network is not usually interested in establishing a binding tie, and strives to minimize both risk and expense. After a suitable firm is found, an affiliation or joint venture agreement is signed. Rather than being legally contractual and binding, the extent of commitment in the first agreement is determined by the mutual interests of the two parties. For the local firm, this is a matter of prestige and of cementing international ties; for the network, it is an initial foothold in a new country which it will use to become better acquainted with the local market. Leading local firms often enter into several agreements simultaneously, despite the possible conflict of interests involved. Most large accountancy and advertising firms in Tel-Aviv were in this stage until 1993.

The next stage involves deeper commitment, and is based on exclusive contracts between the two parties that provide the network with the option of acquiring some, or all, of the local firm in the future. Another option is a merger between the global network and another network that has branches in several countries (economies of scale). Entering a new market through a merger or the acquisition of an existing firm offers many advantages. One is operative, increasing the speed at which the international network can enter into ongoing activity in the new market. Another is the ability to acquire contacts and clients together with the local firm, as well as the accumulated experience and local market knowledge that local staff bring with them.

Mergers are a common strategy in both the local and global market particularly in accountancy, as regulations in this sub-sector are especially stringent. For this reason, market structure is becoming increasingly centralized. Mergers and takeovers are also becoming increasingly fashionable in the field of advertising.

8.4 THE GLOBALIZATION AND INTERNATIONALIZATION OF ACCOUNTANCY AND ADVERTISING IN TEL-AVIV

A marked transformation of Tel-Aviv's advertising and accountancy sectors took place during the 1990's. Some new major firms appeared, and mergers between firms increased; the names of foreign networks were added to existing firms; employment numbers in some firms skyrocketed; budgets increased significantly; and locations changed, with some firms moving to large, prestigious offices. As a result, work methods and client-lists have, in many cases, changed completely.

Israeli advertising and accountancy firms have been affiliated with international firms and networks for decades. These affiliations, however, were flexible, as local firms could represent more than one network, despite possible conflicts of interest. Paradoxically, when the globalization of the advertising and accountancy networks started to slow down and efforts were made to increase efficiency, Israeli firms embarked on a process of growth and expansion.

Official statistical data for these two sub-sectors cannot be accurately isolated from the all-encompassing data that exists for finance and business services in general, and it is therefore impossible to quantify the changes that have taken place in terms of personnel and turnover. However, data for the general category of finance and business services (to which advertising and accountancy belongs) reflects the structural change in division of labor that the Tel-Aviv economy has experienced over the past twenty years (Table 8.1). Like most developed economies, the Tel-Aviv local economy has witnessed a relative increase in employment within the services sector and a relative decrease in employment in the manufacturing sector.

Table 8.1 Number of employees in Tel Aviv according to economic sector, 1979-1999

Year	*1979*	*1984*	*1989*	*1994*	*1999*
Total Number (thousands)	241.3	253.8	259.6	320.5	325.4
Economic Branch (Percentage)					
Manufacturing	21.4	19.5	17.2	15.6	11.2
Construction	4.7	3.3	2.9	5.1	4.2
Trade, Accommodation, Restaurants	16.4	18	20.5	19.1	18.6
Transport, Storage and Communication	7.6	7.2	7.1	7	7.1
Finance and Business Services	18.6	23	24.2	23.7	28.4
Public Services	22.7	20.8	20.5	20.5	19.8
Personal Services	6.6	6.3	6.5	7.7	8.7
Other	2	1.9	1.1	1.3	2
Total	100	100	100	100	100

Source: Municipality of Tel-Aviv - Yafo. Statistical Yearbook, 1999.

The advertising and accountancy sub-sectors of the Tel Aviv economy have expanded since 1993. Since the mid-1990's, the global connection between local firms in these two sub-sectors and international networks has increased tremendously. On the global level, however, it should again be noted that this process had already gained speed prior to its appearance in Israel.

A number of factors were responsible for these changes. First, structural change in the local economy resulted in price stability at the macro level, the liberalization of capital markets, the deregulation of leading sectors of the economy and the removal of trade barriers. Second, the Arab boycott was eased, enabling international firms to establish contacts and invest in Israel. This process intensified as the peace process progressed and diplomatic initiatives to end the Israeli-Palestinian conflict continued. Large foreign corporations entered the local market, in search of local representatives of accountancy and advertising networks to provide them with services on the global level. Foreign investors began to display interest in investing in the Israeli economy and sought the support of advanced producer services.

Israel's high-tech sector, with its inherently global nature, began to issue shares on foreign stock markets, and was therefore in need of contacts and professional advice. In addition, the growth of the Israeli electronic media and its technological competency, along with the global homogenization of tastes, styles and fashion, enabled local advertising talents to be catapulted into the global arena. The local economy was thus exposed to global shifts, and the local producer services sector responded to this new reality.

8.5 GLOBALIZATION IN TEL-AVIV'S ACCOUNTANCY SECTOR

The processes taking place in Israel must be seen within a global context. The accountancy sector has experienced a period of key mergers that changed its internal balance of power. Significant global mergers began to take place in the mid 1980's, when the American company Peat Marwick Mitchell merged with KMG's (which had been widespread and successful in Europe, particularly in Germany and Holland) network of companies. In 1989, the two smaller companies within the 'Big Six' merged. Not all such mergers succeeded, however. In some cases, opposition within a network based on local interests halted its expansion. Some claim that this was proof that these mergers did not create true global firms, rather international networks operating in the same way as franchise businesses (Mednick, 1999).

Globalization and the need for maximum control and efficiency resulted in mega-mergers between large accountancy networks in 1997. Price Waterhouse and Coopers Lybrand merged, becoming the world's largest accountancy network. Other networks followed suit, announcing additional mergers (not all of which materialized), and an overall dynamic of mergers took hold. It was this global dynamic that resulted in a series of local shifts and mergers in 1998.

Arthur Andersen was the only 'Big Six' company that did not take part in global merging, but instead increased its number of offices outside of the United States in a different way. In the 1950's Arthur Andersen began establishing branches in selected locations outside of the United States. This was not an easy task, considering the regulatory restrictions in foreign locations and the stiff competition of experienced local companies, which required the partners in the US to fund losses (Mednick, 1999).

Until the late 1980's, Israel's accountancy sector dealt mainly with the technical side of the profession, focusing on auditing. In 1980, there were approximately 1,500 practicing accountants in Israel. This small number was due to both low demand and the especially rigorous qualifying exams supervised by the National Association of Accountants. The sector was structured in large (at the time, 100-200 employees), medium (20-40 employees) and small firms. Larger firms acquired many of their clients through the partners' business and personal connections with institutions and public figures within the business 'establishment'. One such institution was the *Histadrut* (General Federation of Labor), which then constituted one of the most dominant forces in the Israeli economy. An example of a partner using his connections for business purposes was the decision of a long-time Labor

Party Comptroller to move into the private sector. Predictably, the firm that he established rapidly evolved into a large, successful company.

During the 1970's and 1980's, the local market witnessed some mergers on a small scale, but this did not change the sector's structure in any significant manner. Limited international connections with global accountancy networks or producers were maintained primarily for business resume reasons, and not as real business contacts. The hierarchy within the accountancy sector, therefore, did not reflect an international structure. It was the process of mergers between the international accountancy networks themselves, in combination with accelerated local economic growth, that triggered the local race for affiliation with international networks. Mergers between networks limited possibilities, and the race became more and more pressured.

Mergers within Tel-Aviv's accountancy sector began with larger companies. These mergers affected the medium sized firms that merged with them and, in the long run, smaller firms, which sought to expand and specialize in order to survive in the new world of giant firms. Of the ten largest firms in Tel-Aviv, four merged with one another, and four others merged with medium sized firms. Naturally, the mergers increased the centralization of the accountancy sector. In 2000, the sector was structured within six large firms (with a combined total of more than 4,200 employees), a small number of medium sized firms and a large number of small firms.

Of the 6,000 active accountants in Israel today, half are practicing professionals, while the rest hold positions in management and finance. Israel as a whole has approximately 1,000 accountancy firms, the largest six of which employ a combined total of approximately 1,300 accountants (Globes, 2000). In other words, approximately 40 percent of Israel's practicing accountants are employed by less than 1 percent of the country's firms. And, out of approximately 750 Israeli public companies located in Israel and abroad, 600 are handled by the country's six largest accountancy firms. By all measures, then, this sector is highly centralized, and, as time passes, it simply reflects the trend towards mega-organization that has been prevalent worldwide. As a result of the global mergers of the last decade, five dominant global networks remain, together controlling over 90 percent of world accountancy (see Table 8.2).

As Tel Aviv is the country's business center, the centralization of Israel's producer services sector has been a Tel-Aviv-centered phenomenon. The restructuring and merger-mania of Tel-Aviv firms over the last few years can be explained by three major factors. The first is the fact that the minimum critical-mass needed for entering global markets has led to an active merger strategy. Scale economies mean that a minimum staff and capital base are needed in order to finance expensive computer and communication systems, and to adapt local standards to the global requirements of networks. Second, the dictates of specialization have led to global mergers. Large and medium sized firms merge with other firms in order to cover areas in which they do not specialize (insurance, real estate, agricultural settlements, etc.) or to expand into new geographical regions. Third, scale economies have also caused medium sized firms to seek out global partners, as demand for their services wanes; large firms compete with the medium sized market with identical prices, and medium sized firms, with the exception of specialists, simply cannot survive the competition. The merger of two large firms, or a large firm and a medium sized firm, inevitably results in redundancies and personnel cut-backs aimed at increasing efficiency. Mergers between large firms and small specialist firms, however, seldom require cuts in personnel.

Table 8.2 'Big Five' accounting firms - financial information, 1999

Firm	*Total Employees*	*Total Worldwide Sales ($US millions)*	*Total Worldwide Partners*	*Forbes Ranking of Private Companies*
Andersen Worldwide	140,000	16,200	2,788	8
Deloitte and Touche	97,500	10,800	5,680	14
Ernst and Young	97,800	12,500	6,200	12
KPMG	102,000	12,200	6,800	11
PricewaterhouseCoopers	150,000	17,300	9,196	6
Total	587,300	69,000	30,664	

Source: http://www.ibig5.com

Global integration of this degree also imposes costs, standards and constraints on local accounting firms. They must begin operating according to the standards of global network as a whole, including, among other things, working methods and uniform computer systems. The network provides a local firm with professional assistance and necessary databases. In general, the local firm then begins representing the local agencies of international corporations that are represented worldwide by the global network. Today, however, most large local firms still provide services to the same local agencies of international corporations that they did before the era of globalization, albeit at a decreasing rate. This is the case, despite the fact that the local firm is not always affiliated with the international network that has been contracted to provide services to the international corporation in question. This is due primarily to the level of trust established over the years between the local accountancy firm and its local clients and the convenience of these relationships. Senior personnel, however, claim that the pressure of international corporations will bring to a halt the provision of services by accountancy firms not connected to their international accountancy networks.

Current legal restrictions in Israel prohibit international networks from establishing local branches in Israel and acquiring shares of local accountancy firms. Affiliation, therefore, can be defined as membership in an international network, which is secured by agreements and totally binding. It is no longer possible to represent more than one network, and a local firm adds the name of the global network to its own name, despite Israeli legal restrictions.

Formerly medium sized firms claim that their mergers with international networks have meant a significant leap forward, with some undoubtedly benefiting considerably from sector globalization. A number of firms have tripled their turnover and number of employees during the past decade (Table 8.3). In fact, three local formerly medium sized firms have overtaken formerly 'large' firms, and today are among the six largest firms in Israel. In contrast, other medium sized firms have been swallowed up by global corporations and have virtually disappeared. It should be noted that, at the outset, it was larger firms that opposed change in the nature of affiliation between local and global firms. They preferred to maintain the status quo, in which each local firm represented several networks simultaneously. Initially, it was the medium sized firms that joined the largest international networks, and for this reason, the two largest accountancy firms in Israel are affiliated with only the fourth and fifth largest global networks.

On the personnel level, the integration of local firms into global networks has meant the addition of Israeli representation to various committees of international networks. In addition, Israeli personnel represent their firms (generally larger firms) to a limited extent in network offices in the United States and Europe. International accountancy networks, however, maintain no permanent representatives in Israel.

Israel's booming hi-tech industry has attracted foreign and local investment alike. Large conservative accountancy firms served to identify promising start-up companies, and dealt with mobilizing capital and with its issue abroad; in this context, these firms became the spearhead of Israel's new economy. In fact, a situation evolved in which hi-tech entrepreneurs supplied the technology, and accountancy firms provided the business know-how. In this way, large accountancy firms now have a strong foothold in all aspects of hi-tech.

Table 8.3 Global mergers among Tel-Aviv accounting firms, 2000

Local Firm	*International Network*	*Number of Employees*		*Number of Accountants*	*Number of Public Companies Represented*	
Year		*1994*	*2000*	*2000*	*1994*	*2000*
Cost Fuhrer	Ernst & Young	190	1020	290	71	195
Kesselman & Kesselman	Price Waterhouse	360	750	NA	48	78
Somekh Chaikin	KPMG	320	780	263	65	105
Breitman Almagor	Deloitte Touche	190	670	203	30	127
Shlomo Ziv	BDO	100	600	180	22	70
Luboschitz Ksirer	Arthur Anderson	160	425	160	36	90

Source: Globes 1994; 2000.

With these changes, local firms began to adapt themselves to the new economy. New departments were set up, new employees were hired, and existing personnel were retrained to provide services to hi-tech firms, particularly to inexperienced start-up companies. These new services differed quite a bit from traditional, conservative auditing practices, and transformed local firms into a one-stop station for hi-tech entrepreneurs. New services included: supervision and financial reports; tax services to firms, entrepreneurs and investors at the time of 'exit'; strategic consulting during the establishment of a company; capital mobilization assistance; business plan preparation; setting up meetings with investors; and assisting with the opening of branches abroad. When competing for hi-tech clients, accountancy firms with global connections enjoyed a distinct advantage over their competitors, who did not benefit from such connections.

Hi-tech activity now accounts for up to one-third of the total activity of large accountancy firms. Many firms strive to increase their high-tech oriented activity, based on the large potential returns involved. As is becoming increasingly common in the new economy, payment has been in shares and options. Services have also assumed more of an advisory form rather than one of accounting proper, as legal restrictions prevent a firm's accountant from receiving shares or options.

8.6 GLOBALIZATION IN TEL-AVIV'S ADVERTISING SECTOR

Parallel to developments within the accountancy sector, Israel's advertising sector underwent a dynamic process of mergers, acquisitions, takeovers and partnership splits. Israel's large advertising agencies have become powerful media groups, also specializing in areas like strategic and political consulting, sales promotion and the internet. They have increasingly established new operations as a means of expanding business volume in an era when specialization is a key word. Terms from the world of high-tech such as options, shares, CEO and Deputy CEO, startups and dividends have entered the jargon of the Israeli advertising sector, as a result of the process of globalization that has enveloped the sector. Like the accountancy sub-sector, the Israeli advertising sector is completely Tel-Aviv centric, with over 90 percent of its firms and employees located in the Tel-Aviv metropolitan area.

In the 'Pre global' era (i.e. between 1960 and 1990), Israel's advertising sector was compatible with elements that then characterized the Israeli economy: a virtually closed market with minimum imports, as well as limited representation of multi-national firms and international brands. Advertising was unsophisticated and geared primarily towards local products. Commercial television did not yet exist in Israel, and advertisements either appeared in newspapers or cinemas, or were heard on the radio. While Israel had a relatively large number of advertising firms, most were small. A 'large' firm in those days, meant a maximum of 100 employees.

Similar to the accountancy sector, most affiliations with international networks during this period were for public image, and were not expressed in turnover. Global affiliation was therefore not an indicator of a local advertising firm's size or standing. Moreover, the sector had fewer employees and a smaller overall budget than in the mid 1990's and onwards, and the skill and specialization of firms was less developed than during later years. A 'creative' department and a budgeting department were typically regarded as sufficient for establishing a successful, competitive advertising firm. Salaries and turnover were also much lower than during the global era, but so were expenditures. For this reason, today's owners of large firms claim that, despite sharp increases in business turnover during the global era, profits are much smaller due to high expenses and stiff competition.

The structure of the global advertising sector is more complex than the structure of accountancy networks. At the top of the pyramid are holding groups, each of which is composed of several global advertising networks, as well as a number of groups specializing in media acquisition, public relations, communications, the internet and other areas. Each such group employs tens of thousands of workers, and the budgets of the larger groups can reach tens of billions of dollars.

Since each holding group has several advertising networks, it can serve global clients simultaneously, despite the fact that they may have conflicting interests. The advantage of size to advertising networks becomes even more significant in the context of major holding groups, as they provide comprehensive solutions for their sophisticated, demanding global clients. The new millennium, however, has been characterized by major holding group mergers, and the creation of new, larger entities with wider deployment and even greater influence. These trends are already affecting the local market, most visibly by the pre-merger maneuvering of local firms representing advertising networks that have been placed together under the umbrella of the same holding group.

Data published by the Israeli Advertisers Association in 2000 reflects the existence of 142 advertising agencies in the Tel-Aviv metropolitan area, employing an approximate combined total of 2,500 personnel. Nineteen of these agencies have affiliation agreements with international advertising networks. Shares of seven agencies have been acquired by international networks and three others are currently in advanced stages of negotiation for acquisition of some of their shares (see Table 8.4). With the signing of an affiliation agreement, a local agency adopts the name of the international network (although this does not necessarily ensure long-term cooperation between the parties). Some claim that an affiliation agreement that does not lead to the international network's acquisition of the local agency is not worth much, and that in the long run, the network will inevitably purchase one agency in Israel or another.

The local sector's first affiliation agreement was signed in the early 1980's, when the Grey Group affiliated with a local agency. Still, most agreements have been concluded during the last decade. The BBDO Group was the first to purchase 49 percent of a local agency's shares (Gitam). Today, Israel's ten largest agencies are linked to international networks, although only some of them have actually sold shares to the networks. The scope of a local agency's activity is the decisive factor considered by international networks interested in purchasing its shares. Paradoxically, an agency's scope of activity is to a large extent dependent on its international ties and the budget it receives as a result of these ties. Share acquisition is carried out in several stages that are defined by both parties through negotiation. Most international networks strive to gain 100 percent control over a local agency, while some networks insist on receiving full control (at least 51 percent of shares) from the outset.

Table 8.4 Profile of a communication group - WWP Group Plc

Employees: 39,000; Offices: 950; Countries: 92

Category	*Number of Firms*	*Tel-Aviv Branch*
Advertising	11 networks or firms, including:	
	Young & Rubicam,	Shalmor Avnun
	Walter J. Thompson	Tamir Cohen
	Ogilvy & Mather	Fogel Levin
Branding & Identity	15	
Demographic Marketing	5	
Direct Promotion & Relationship Marketing	20	
Food Services	1	
Healthcare	4	
Information & Consultancy	9	
Investor Relations	1	
Media & Technology Services	6	
Media Investment Management	18	
Public Relations & Public Affairs	1	
Real Estate	1	
Strategic Marketing Consulting	7	
Technology	2	

Source: http://www.wpp.com

The entrance of international advertising networks into Israel must be regarded as part of a process that has been occurring all over the world for the past two decades. As noted earlier, this process has impacted not only the advertising sector, but other producer services sectors such as accountancy, law and banking as well. Networks join, merge with and acquire local firms based on their commitment to providing important international clients with services. In addition to the global factor, a number of local, more immediate factors have brought the Israeli economy increasingly into the international arena. The Middle East's changing geopolitical situation and the relaxation of the Arab boycott caused large international companies to invest, trade, and market their products in Israel. With their entry into Israel, the entire advertising 'pie' expanded, increasing budgets, the number of agencies and overall employment.

The accelerated growth of the advertising sector was bolstered by the 1994 establishment of Channel 2, Israel's first commercial television station. In 1994, television-advertising accounted for 17 percent of total advertising expenditures in Israel, while today, it represents some 25 percent. In real financial terms, this constituted an increase of almost 100 percent - from $122 million in 1994 to $237 million in 1998 (Globes, January 1999).

The growth of the advertising sector, along with its evolving international ties, has resulted in structural changes within the local sector. The entry of international networks into Israel has been the main cause of polarization; huge agencies offer a full basket of marketing services on one hand, and small agencies specialize in specific areas on the other. In contrast, medium sized agencies find it increasingly difficult to specialize and to gain significant advantages. This dynamic is similar to current dynamics impacting the accountancy sector, which were described previously in this chapter.

Local agency expansion is achieved in two primary ways: 1) the acquisition of smaller advertising agencies, and 2) entering into associated fields. Large agencies expand and gain strength by acquiring small and medium sized advertising agencies, setting up branches and establishing or purchasing companies that provide services to the advertising sector. The enormous budgets of multinational advertisers are fully focused on the leading advertising networks, as only they can uphold a standard level of service throughout the world and provide an overall market response to the needs of global advertisers. This trend makes advertising networks all the more attractive, and in this way the process is also self-stimulating.

In Israel as well, large local agencies have either affiliated with or become part of global networks. In 1993, Israel's seven largest agencies controlled only one-third of all advertising budgets. The figures for six years later, however, reflect a marked change. By 1999, Israel's seven largest agencies had come to control 50 percent of the total advertising market, with an estimated value of approximately $900 million. It should be noted that this figure includes the budget of the state's Publications Bureau (Globes, January 1999).

As mentioned earlier, the long-term strategy of many international networks is to acquire 100 percent control of a local agency, while others aim for 51 percent to 75 percent. In some countries, networks purchase local agencies outright. Others employ a phased approach consisting of an initial acquisition of shares, a second round of acquisition between three and five years later, and a third round after another three to five years. When deciding which local agency to acquire, global networks consider both quantitative and qualitative factors. Quantitative factors include the agency's total budget, the commission that it is able to raise from the local media, and net profit; the actual equity of the agency is not of major significance. Qualitative factors include the agency's creative quality, agency-client relations and management culture. The most important factor is the absence of conflict of interests between the international network's clients and the clients of the local agency. When such a problem arises, it is settled by the global network acquiring shares in two local agencies. The commission that the local agency is to pay the international network is determined during negotiations.

Israel's advertising sector has witnessed primarily two-stage acquisitions. The first reason for this has been fact that local agency owners are also often active directors; global corporations prefer to leave shares in their hands in order to give them an incentive to continue developing the agency. Second, a two-stage buy-out minimizes economic risk. Furthermore, the relationship between a local agency and an international network regarding representation of clients in the local market is not always clear-cut. It sometimes happens that a local agency refuses to accept a budget from its international network due to a conflict of interest with an important client.

8.7 WHAT DO LOCAL AGENCIES GAIN BY ENTERING GLOBAL NETWORKS?

In cases of acquisition, Israeli shareholders earn hundreds of thousands, and sometimes millions of dollars, without forfeiting management of the agency (at least not for 10-15 years). The network only intervenes in agency management regarding major issues, such as the establishment of subsidiary companies or the acquisition of small companies. On the other hand, the network is committed to the local agency, providing it with cumulative experience and knowledge, research resources and the budgets of international clients. Every network has an international information center that offers assistance, such as data and work methods, to all members of the network.

The personnel of local agencies also appear to benefit from forging ties with international networks. New professional advancement opportunities arise within the network, and salaries increase as the professional level of the agency increases. It should also be noted that an improved global image results from participating in international events, presenting international advertising material to local clients, and the general cosmopolitan atmosphere brought about by the new relationship. Finally, some agencies adopt models used by their networks, for distributing shares and options to their employees.

Local agencies also participate in the global tenders of the network's clientele (Table 8.5). Recently, the Tel Aviv partner of Young & Rubicam won the global tender for management of the creative side of Citibank's world-campaign, budgeted at $100 million. While the network will receive most of this budget, and not the local agency, this achievement constitutes an important step in the recognition of the abilities of Israel's advertising sector within global advertising. This success could never have been achieved without the agency's membership in the global network.

Global connections also result in extra work and bureaucracy. Local agencies must report on major issues to network management and present annual financial reports, and new clients must be approved by the network in order to avoid conflicts of interest with network clients. Despite the massive expansion of the sector, the profitability of local agencies has declined considerably in recent years due to strong competition between local agencies. This competition, in combination with the draw of large advertising budgets, means that local agencies are prepared to invest huge amounts of money in a single presentation in order to obtain an advertising budget. Current average profit margins stand at 2-3 percent, so that a budget of $4 million is required in order to earn $50,000. Specialization has also raised salary levels, and this has created a financial burden for agencies.

For these reasons, the tendency among advertising agencies to expand into peripheral areas is much more than a strategic plan for turning into a media group. The aim of this approach, rather, is to establish a subsidiary company that will serve as an independent source of profit on one hand, and facilitate cooperation with clients who are not among the clientele of the advertising agency on the other, regardless of any conflict of interest that may exist between the clients of the subsidiary company and those of the agency.

Table 8.5 Global patterns of mergers and acquisitions in the Tel Aviv advertising sector, 2000

Local Agency	*International Network*	*Connection Type*	*Holding group*	*Head-quarters*
Kesher Barel	McCann Erickson	50%	INTERPUBLIC	New York
Shalmor Avnun	Young & Rubicam	25%	WPP	London
Baumann Behr	Saatchi & Saatchi	Affiliation	PUBLICIS	New York
Gitam	BBDO	49%	OMNICOM	New York
Tamir Cohen	Walter J. Thompson	50%	WPP	London
Fogel Levin	Ogilvy & Mather	Affiliation	WPP	London
Dachaf	Bozell	Affiliation	INTERPUBLIC	New York
Adler Chomsky	Grey	Affiliation	GREY	New York
Arieli	Publicis	60% + 19% by American public	PUBLICIS	Paris
Lineal	DDB	Affiliation	OMNICOM	New York
Geller Nassis	D'Arcy	Affiliation	BCOM3	St. Louis
Reuveni Pridan	Leo Burnet	25%	DENTSU	Tokyo
Yehoshua	TBWA	25%	OMNICOM	Los Angeles
Zarfati	RSCG Euro	Affiliation	HAVAS	France
Raban Golani	McCann Erickson	60%	INTERPUBLIC	New York
Armoni	Bates	Affiliation	CORDINAT	London
Weinberg	Ammirati Puris	Affiliation	INTERPUBLIC	New York
Carasso	Lintas			
Shimoni	FCB	Affiliation	TRUE NORTH	Chicago
Drori	BBDO	30%	OMNICOM	New York

8.8 THE IMPACT OF THE GLOBALIZATION OF THE PRODUCER SERVICES SECTOR ON METROPOLITAN DEVELOPMENT IN TEL AVIV

The Tel-Aviv metropolitan area's office market reflects, to a large degree, the economic changes that have characterized Israel over the last decade, as well as the city's planning policy response to these changes. This response has lacked a long-term strategic view of metropolitan development. Tel-Aviv has become the business capital of Israel within a relatively short period, and this has meant dealing simultaneously with issues of growth, urban management, rapid population increase and demographic change, and structural changes within the city's economic base. Tel-Aviv has also had to enter into competition for economic development with the contiguous cities and towns that make up the metropolitan area.

Advanced producer services, particularly advertising and accountancy, have played an important role in determining the spatial lay-out of the Tel-Aviv office market during the last decade. Data published by the Israeli Advertisers Association and the Institute of Certified Public Accountants in Israel, provides a good impression of Tel-Aviv's spatial centrality with regard to the location of producer services in Israel. In 1997, there were 6,600 accountants in Israel (with over 60 percent working in the Tel-Aviv metropolitan area. In 1999, 110 advertising agencies were located in the city of Tel-Aviv, 22 agencies in the inner ring of the Tel-Aviv metropolitan area and 10 agencies in the metropolitan area's outer ring. Furthermore, all of Israel's 10 largest firms are located in Tel-Aviv.

Until the 1980's, Tel Aviv's largest offices employed a maximum of 200 people, and most offices had staffs of less than 30. Medium sized and large accountancy firms were for the most part located in the city's Central Business District (CBD), near the stock exchange and the head offices of banks and insurance companies (see chapter 3). Larger offices were located in office buildings, while smaller ones were situated in apartment blocks, which had been converted into offices. Although this area was, considered to be an exclusive, high-rent location for offices, in many cases the buildings are old and not suited for new computer and communications technologies. City accessibility has also become increasingly complicated with a chronic shortage of parking facilities and stalled plans for a Tel-Aviv light railway.

Tel-Aviv's larger advertising firms were also concentrated within the city's traditional CBD until the 1990's. Many large manufacturing companies maintained head offices in this area, and the need for close proximity was seen as obvious. In general, the tendency of advertising firms to cluster in certain cities and to be concentrated in certain areas within these cities (such as New York's Madison Avenue) is evident around the globe (Leslie, 1997). Advertising is a dynamic and glamorous field closely bound to national culture, street culture, changing fashions, designer labels, national mood, shopping and leisure. Advertisers must therefore be open to change, innovation and new creation and design in each of these areas. They must also be ready to transform the city in which they work into a state-of- the-art city. Tel-Aviv is Israel's culture and fashion center, and in this capacity is a natural magnet for advertising activity, as well as the supporting services that accompany creative activity: entertainment, restaurants, shopping centers and diverse cultural institutions. These services are located within the city and the surrounding area in considerable numbers. The city is a place for advertising professionals to meet and exchange experiences and ideas, both during and after working hours. Until the 1990's, many advertising professionals also lived in the renovated areas close to the city, and, while some offices were located in dour buildings on old streets, this did not negate the advertising offices' distinct interior design.

The process of globalization that integrated local companies into global networks also resulted in structural change with a spatial expression. Large advertising and accountancy companies experienced significant expansion, either through mergers or self-expansion. This resulted in the addition of hundreds of new employees in new, specialty departments and as extra support within existing departments, and more floor space was necessary in order to accommodate for this growth. In addition, offices had to be restructured in order to conform to architecture and design standards, as well as the global requirements for computer and telecommunication infrastructures.

The city's real-estate market had to contend with this new office space demand, which continued to increase with the entry of representatives of international companies, as well as the growth of the financial services sector and the local hi-tech industry. Increased demand was accompanied by increases in rental costs. At this point, head offices of producer companies and finance and producer services began to look for more modern alternatives with more space and better accessibility, all at a lower cost.

The mass relocation of service firms is a standard phenomenon in global cities. In New York, London and Paris, alternative specializing areas developed in new or renewed areas where it was cheaper and more convenient to construct modern, high-end office blocks in multi-storey buildings. While it is true that New York advertising firms moved into Midtown for reasons of slowdown and the need for increased efficiency, and not because of expansion, it should not be overlooked that they were also seeking an alternative location with similar characteristics (Leslie, 1997). Relocation in the service sector also generally involves the physical transfer of accompanying services to the new location. This is particularly true within the advertising sub-sector, with its accompanying services of printing, messengers, catering, graphics, photography, and film and sound editing.

In addition to the CBD, in which a considerable number of accountancy and advertising firms still remain, another three concentrations of advertising and accountancy offices have developed in the Tel-Aviv area. The first concentration is located in the vicinity of the Diamond Exchange in Ramat-Gan, just across Tel-Aviv's municipal border. Inter-city competition for economic development within the metropolitan area has resulted in the efforts of local authorities to encourage the development of offices and hi-tech facilities. This is achieved by allocating large expanses of land and considerable tax-reductions, and by expediting the planning process. The Diamond Exchange area is perhaps the largest and most densely occupied office area in Israel, and should be regarded as a market-stimulated response to the demand for an alternative Tel-Aviv CBD (see Chapter 3). The area experienced accelerated development over the last decade, and this resulted in a highly visible collection of modern multi-storey buildings. It is easily accessible by car, from the Ayalon freeway, and by rail, via the nearby North Tel-Aviv train station. The area has become an important business center, with head offices of large firms, hi-tech and start up companies, and financial and producer service firms. As is also true of locations throughout the world, there is a tremendous difference in this area between business activity during the day and night. The Diamond Exchange office area has no residential buildings, and it therefore becomes an arena for sex clubs, prostitution and illicit gambling after nightfall.

Two additional office areas have evolved on both sides of the Ayalon freeway, which is the major means of access to various parts of Tel Aviv (Figure 8.1). The eastern area is long and narrow, and does not contain a large concentration of office space; still, the offices of a large number of advertising firms and supporting services are located there, as are some accountancy firms. It is interesting to note that some large global advertising firms are located far from both the CBD and other concentrations of supporting services, probably due to the fact that these large firms are able to provide their own in-house graphics and printing. They are also well enough established that they do not feel obligated to locate themselves in close proximity to their clients. The office area to the west of the Ayalon is large and has experienced rapid development during the past five years. It is close to the 'city' and has been the destination of many firms that have moved out of the traditional CBD, particularly those that still feel a need to be close to the heart of the financial center, like financial advisory firms, insurance companies and head offices of banks, accountancy firms and advertising firms.

Figure 8.1 The location of (a) large accounting firms and (b) large advertising firms in Tel Aviv, 1985 and 2000

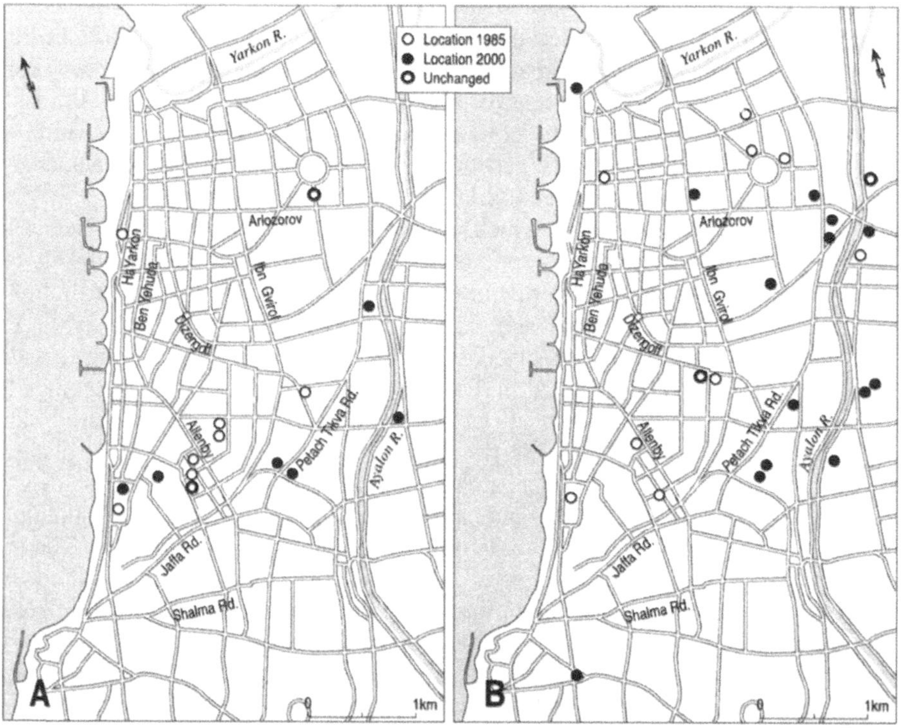

8.9 TEL AVIV AND THE WORLD CITY HIERARCHY

Researchers have made several attempts to identify major cities and their relative ranking according to different criteria. Some base their studies on cities' cosmopolitan characteristics, others consider the concentration of multi-national and trans-national companies headquartered and still others use international financial centers to define world cities. This chapter finds special interest in rankings that focus on the internationalization, concentration and intensity of producer services in world cities.

Exemplary of this approach is the work by Beaverstock, Smith and Taylor (1999). They present an inventory of world cities "in terms of the provision of advanced producer services" and assess the presence of major corporate service firms in each city. By examining several firms within many cities, they offer an understanding of the relative importance of each city within the context of a particular service. By repeating this exercise for several services, they evaluate the overall 'world cityness' of each city. Their research examined the sectors of advertising, accountancy, legal services and banking, and their basic unit of analysis was the service firm.

Using indicators that provided information for cities in which firms with global networks existed, cities were assigned separate rankings for each of the four advanced producer services sectors examined. The results were organized according to prime global service centers, major global service centers and minor global service centers. Tel-Aviv was classified as a minor global service center for both the advertising and accountancy sectors.

The minimum conditions for receiving a grade in the accountancy ranking was either 20 partners (within several networks), or the presence of at least two representative firms of one network in a given city. Tel-Aviv was ranked in the third group of 27 cities (all minor global accountancy service centers) along with cities such as Miami, Singapore, the Hague and Geneva. The ranking of world cities in the advertising sector was based on representation of the world's fifty largest advertising networks (according to turnover). In this category as well, Tel-Aviv was classified as a minor global advertising service center, together with another 30 cities including Montreal, Bangkok, Rio de Janeiro and Buenos Aires.

Based on all four sectors of advanced producer services examined, Tel-Aviv was included in a group regarded as displaying "relatively strong evidence of world city formation". It is likely that, if data were updated to reflect the global connections within the accountancy, advertising, banking and legal services sectors to the end of 2000, Tel-Aviv would receive a higher ranking, since globalization accelerated significantly between 1997 and 2000.

8.10 CONCLUSIONS

Assessing the extent to which a city is 'global' is not a simple task. Globality is a relative term that is difficult to quantify, partially due to the fact that the parameters for its measurement are not necessarily agreed upon. Nevertheless, it is clear that certain cities serve as important nodes within the global network, while others do not. If we base ourselves on Sassen (1991) and Beaverstock, Taylor and Smith (1999), who regard the development of global, advanced business services as determining the potential of a global city, then Tel-Aviv undoubtedly has such potential. Shifts in the Israeli economy during the 1990's resulted in dramatic changes within the country's business services sector and within Tel-Aviv, its business capital. A flourishing hi-tech sector attracting large-scale foreign investment; hopes for a 'new Middle East' in which Tel-Aviv would constitute the regional business center; the arrival of one million immigrants from the former Soviet Union and the resulting expansion of the consumer market; significant technological advancements facilitating increased information transfer - all these factors contributed to the economic momentum of Tel-Aviv, whose need for the support of an efficient, varied business services sector continued to grow.

Based solely on their number of global contacts, advertising and accountancy firms stand out as global spearheads within the sector. Many firms joined international networks, and many clients joined these firms because of their international contacts. A phase of mergers and acquisitions then began, which enabled firms to reach the dimensions necessary to satisfy the demands of global networks. The advertising sector went one step further, as some firms not only joined networks, but were actually acquired by networks at high prices. Local firms adopted international standards, and also proved that they were capable of participating in tenders, assuming advisory roles and competing as equals with the large, well-established firms from countries with greatly advanced business services.

Israel's local advertising and accountancy sectors quickly assumed the characteristics of their respective global sectors. Sector structure became increasingly polarized and centralized, with fewer firms controlling a greater share of clients and budgets. As in the rest of the world, the large firms of Tel-Aviv expanded their 'traditional' spheres of activity into more varied areas, to the clients' advantage. Mergers between global networks led immediately to agitation and structural changes on the local market and to an increase in competition and turnover. The latter did not, however, mean consistently higher profits.

It is difficult to determine the exact overall contribution of these sectors to the city. However, it is clear that the growth of the advanced business services sector served as an impetus for economic development in terms of new employment, intensive, exclusive office construction, attraction of foreign capital (especially in the advertising sector), and the bolstering of supporting services within the accountancy and advertising sectors.

When comparing these two sectors of the Tel-Aviv economy, it should be noted that, despite a marked increase in the international contacts of accountancy firms, each of which employs hundreds of staff, it is the advertising sector that has developed more significant international ties and has been influenced by global factors and processes to a greater extent. A number of identical features can be identified within both sub-sectors. In both cases, global networks had similar motives and timing considerations when entering the Israeli market; they sought to strengthen the interests of their international clients and to expand into the growing, promising markets of the 1990's. Their methods for entering the local market was also similar in both sectors, establishing contacts with leading, existing firms rather than setting up new branches of existing networks. This kept risk to a minimum, preserved time and resources, and utilized the professional, highly qualified human resources of Tel-Aviv. In addition, both sectors are now characterized by a new polarized structure, with large firms providing comprehensive services on one end of the spectrum, small, specialist firms at the other end, and the gradually disappearing medium sized firms in between.

However, the two sub-sectors differ in several respects as well. A number of advertising firms have already sold a considerable number of shares to international networks, and their commitment is therefore greater than that of firms within the accountancy sector. And, while both sectors represent Israeli clients abroad and foreign clients in Israel, local advertising firms take an active part in advertising campaigns of international network clients all over the world. This reflects a greater correlation between the global advertising network's international representation of international manufacturers on one hand, and the representation of those clients on the local level on the other, than exists in the accountancy sector. It appears that the relatively dynamic nature of the advertising sector and the more uniform language it employs has made it easier for it to become global.

The two sectors have yet to form stable and permanent structures, and their internal balances of power still have the potential to change significantly. The global and local economies have recently slowed due to both macro economic trends and local geopolitical instability, and the flourishing of large accountancy and advertising firms has slowed with it. The NASDAQ technology-share crisis resulted in reduced business activity, especially in the field of hi-tech, and both start-up and large established technology firms have found themselves in difficult positions, and have started to make cuts in activity and personnel. The effect of this dynamic on accountancy firms, particularly those oriented to high-tech, has been immediate and severe. Within months, firms that until recently had been competing with one another for human resources in order to reach 'top ten' ratings began to dismiss tens of employees, and to transfer others to departments dealing with auditing and with the actual companies hurt by the crisis. Salaries have been cut, functions combined and office space reduced. Some claim cynically that the real growth areas are in the departments dealing with liquidation and bankruptcy in accountancy and legal service firms.

The advertising sector and its budgets have also been affected, albeit to a lesser extent. Evidence of this impact exists in the recession that followed the dot.com crisis, the unstable political situation that caused redundancies and reductions throughout all large local firms, and changes in the status of mergers and acquisitions between large advertising networks.

At any rate, it appears that the changes that have taken place within Tel-Aviv's advanced producer services sector over the past decade have had decisive structural impact. So decisive, in fact, that despite recent recession and decline, they will continue to serve as global indicators of a developing Tel-Aviv - a city that will most likely continue to develop global ties with other service sectors in the near future.

REFERENCES

Bagchi-Sen, S. & Sen, J. (1997). The current state of knowledge in international business in producer services. *Environment and Planning A, 29*, 1153-1174.

Beaverstock, J.V., Smith, R.G. & Taylor, P.J. (1999). A roster of world cities. *Cities, 16 (6)*, 445-458.

Beaverstock, J.V. (1991). Skilled international migration: An analysis of the geography of international secondments within large accountancy firms. *Environment and Planning A, 23*, 1133-1148.

Beaverstock, J.V. (1996). Subcontracting the accountant! Professional labor markets, migration, and organizational networks in the global accountancy industry. *Environment and Planning A, 28*, 303-326.

Coffey, W. & Bailly, A. (1992). Producer services and system of flexible production. *Urban Studies, 29*, 857-868.

Daniels, P.W. (1995). Services in a shrinking world. *Geography, 80 (2)*, 97-110.

Globes Daily Newspaper. Various daily editions (Hebrew).

Ha'aretz Daily Newspaper. Various daily editions (Hebrew).

Juleff-Tranter, L.E. (1996). Advanced producer services: Just service to manufacturing? *The Service Industries Journal, 16*, 389-403.

Kim, K.K. (1995). Spreading the Net: the consolidation process of large transnational advertising agencies in the 1980s and early 1990s. *International Journal of Advertising, 14*, 195-217.

Leslie, D. (1997). Abandoning Madison Avenue: The relocation of advertising service in New York City. *Urban Geography, 18*, 568-590.

Leslie, D.A. (1995). Global scan: The globalization of advertising agencies, concepts, and campaigns. *Economic Geography, 71*, 402-426.

Municipality of Tel-Aviv-Yafo (1999). *Statistical Yearbook*. Tel Aviv.

Mednick, R. (1999). Dynamic changes in liberal professions in a global market. *The Accountant, 48*, 293-298 (Hebrew).

Perry, M. (1990). The internationalization of advertising. *Geoforum 21(1)*, 35-50.

Roberts, J. (1999). The internationalization of business service firms: A stages approach. *The Service Industries Journal, 19*, 68-88.

Sassen, S. (1994). *Cities in world economy*. London: Pine Forge Press.

Sassen, S. (1991). *The Global City*. Princeton: Princeton University Press.

Wernerheim, M. & Sharpe, C. (1999). Producer services and the mixed-market problem: Some empirical evidence. *Area 31 (2)*, 123-140.

West, C.D. (1996). The determinants and consequences of multinational advertising agencies. *International Journal of Advertising, 15*, 128-139.

EIKE W. SCHAMP, URSULA RACHOR-HAGELUEKEN AND ALEXANDER GRIMM

9. THE FRANKFURT METROPOLITAN REGION AS A MARKET HUB

9.1 MARKETS AND MARKETPLACES IN EUROPEAN INTEGRATION

Urban marketplaces and their market regions seem to have become topics of the past. The traditional symbiosis of the urban marketplace and its 'own' market area has been challenged by many factors, including the following three. First, modern information and communication technologies appear to have made the urban marketplace obsolete, most notably through the new distribution path of e-commerce. The internet serves as a virtual marketplace not only for consumer goods, but increasingly for intermediary products as well (business-to-business, or B2B, solutions). Second, traditional regional markets are being undermined by the integration of national business areas into larger business regions, as well as by the growing interrelation of global business flows. A new business region was created in 1993 with the establishment of the European domestic market, which is the largest in the world in terms of population and economic power. Third, the global division of labor continues to develop, and this results not only in the extension of many value chains through new intermediary production phases, but also in a disproportionate increase in intermediary products and services that can be traded on markets. Virtually all publications on the subject of globalization note that worldwide trade has increased more over the past decades than world production (Dicken, 1998), and that it continues to grow.

The thesis of this chapter is the contrary - that markets have and will continue to retain their territoriality and that marketplaces will remain necessary elements of territorial markets. The expansion of markets and the changes that they undergo will most likely result in an immense change in the set-up and functioning of the urban marketplace. We will argue that the role of a marketplace like Frankfurt/Rhein-Main, within the context of the current trend of Europeanization, is changing due to specialization. This process of specialization includes elements of competition and cooperation that are interconnected with other regions of Europe.

With the growing global exchange of goods and services, market territories do not simply disappear in a chaotic pattern of linkages. Rather, they either continue to exist or are redefined. Markets in national territories continue to exist, even within the European domestic market. 'Real' markets (Boyer, 1997) are historically grown institutions composed of several factors: a national legal system, with its contract law, property rights and liability; national sales structures, which deal with, among

D. Felsenstein et al. (eds.),
Emerging Nodes in the Global Economy: Frankfurt and Tel Aviv Compared, 173–191.

other things, the type and standing of trade intermediaries; and national or sub-national customer preferences (Sayer and Walker, 1992). This last factor includes different 'cultures' - of work organization, for example - that are critical for the trading of investment goods (Gertler, 1997). Regulating forces on the "spatial scale of the nation-state" (Gertler, 1997) also possess great influence here. Finally, it must be noted that markets are untenable without the exchange of information concerning the expectations of buyers and sellers and that many market exchanges necessitate forms of systemic, and even personal trust. As a result, the critical element of language constitutes a barrier that both limits and structures communication, and in this way serves to define market limits.

Thus, national markets for most consumer goods and intermediary products do indeed exist in Europe. The domestic market of the EU has overcome tariff based and non-tariff based trade barriers between EU nations, but differences in legal systems and customer preferences still remain intact. Germany is undoubtedly the largest national market in Europe. With a GDP of US$2.134 billion (in 1998), it is the most important country in the EU in terms of trade, and it is also the largest exporter and importer. 57 percent of Germany's exports are bound for other EU countries, and 53 percent of its imports come from within the EU. One might think that the establishment of the EU domestic market has transformed Germany into merely one region within the greater European market. But, with EU217 billion in exports and EU203.5 billion in imports outside the EU, Germany is at the same time one of the largest production and market territories within the world market.

When markets retain their territoriality despite new developments, urban marketplaces are also most likely to retain their importance, or to even gain additional importance. It may sound trivial to state that international trade between production areas and market areas is "channeled along a specific route" (Dicken, 1998), but our thesis is that these routes are organized differently today than they were in the past. With the emergence of transnational companies (TNC's), international trade is being increasingly carried out from within the hierarchical organization of the company. TNC's are increasingly pursuing global strategies instead of the multi-domestic strategies (as defined by organizational theory) of the past (Ruigrok and Van Tulder, 1995). Therefore, it is often the case that TNC's no longer produce and sell in individual national market territories, but develop a complex network of production, logistic, and distribution locations with a presence in many national territories. The organizational and territorial separation between information and goods flows is made easier by modern information and communications technology. As a result, an ever-increasing number and variety of company functions for the same market territory can be performed in different locations. For example, sales organization and other related services can be based in one place, while logistics and transportation and storage of goods can be based in another. This facilitates another spatial division of labor between regions and, in the context of domestic market, between nations. In turn, this results in the metropolitan region specializing in expanded flows of goods and information.

A real market with a real market territory demands a physical infrastructure, which traditionally has been provided by the city as a marketplace. Frankfurt's long history as a central trading and trade-fair location in Europe actually reached its prime prior to the construction of the modern nation state. The beginning of the 21st century witnessed the changing role of the traditional marketplace, as the primacy of the nation state was challenged not only by globalization but by the integration of domestic markets in Europe as well. Some authors predict a spatial decentralization of market access activities, as flexible logistical systems and the use of information and communication technologies for the marketing process produce 'virtual marketplaces' that no longer have to be anchored in specific cities. Others, however, foresee a growing concentration of market activities in a small number of cities, which would serve as points of crystallization for new ideas, images and product presentation. In such markets, which are characterized by fierce competition and high risk, spatial proximity and social relationships lower information costs, and, in turn, transaction costs. Besides the flow of goods, the amount of attainable information present is also considerable. The marketplace is transformed into a center of information on customers and their demand, serving to inform foreign suppliers about local customers as well as local suppliers about foreign customers. The city therefore becomes a hub within a broad system of streaming goods and information - the spaces of flows, as they are termed by Castells (1996).

Individual cities on their own, however, have long been unable to play this role, and the locational demands of companies, which have transformed the marketplace into an interface of global streams, have remained unfulfilled by individual cities for quite some time. Instead, companies now seek out their locations on the outskirts of the city's region (Hessen, 2000). Trade and logistical activities in particular are more likely to be found today in areas surrounding the city, where land prices are lower and the infrastructure available for transporting goods more developed (see Chapter 2). The urban marketplace must therefore be understood as an urban (or metropolitan) region, which, in turn, can develop into an interface between local and global markets for the flow of services, goods, and information. This chapter will address this new role, as assumed by the city region Frankfurt/Rhein-Main.

9.2 THE VARYING ROLES OF THE MARKETPLACE

Cities and city regions still possess importance in real markets. This importance, however, assumes a new form, as cities and city regions serve as hubs along logistic chains through which suppliers reach customers. This is especially true for manufacturers whose production plants are located far from their customers, the best examples of which are foreign companies. TNC's are capable of maintaining quite complex distribution systems, which are dependent on company strategies, while at the same time providing solutions to market uncertainties. One of these uncertainties is whether the development of a European domestic market will result in the full integration of national market territories into a single market territory for specific goods, or, alternatively, whether the strategy of multi-domestic supply should be retained. TNC's from European cities, as well as from overseas, have varying answers to this question. The importance of a city region as a marketplace depends on the value of the function allotted to the location by the multi-national company within its organizational structure.

Four basic dimensions of the market process can be identified in the functioning of a city region as a geographic marketplace. The downstream and upstream functions of marketing constitute the first two dimensions (Cornish, 1995; 1997a,b). The third dimension is the degree to which the service infrastructure is prepared for strategic decisions, and the fourth is the positioning of the transportation infrastructure for logistical and informational processes. While the importance of an urban region as a location for the last two functions is undisputed, it cannot be said that downstream and upstream functions are still bound to urban regions today. 'Downstream' functions refer to all activities connected to distribution, including all trade activities and services (maintenance and repair services, as well as logistic services). Even though these activities are traditional elements of marketing, the significance of their reorganization is underestimated today. Nowhere is this as obvious as in the case of electronic products. In modern consumer products (such as televisions and computers) and investment products alike, software and hardware are inextricably bound together, and this results in new demands for an extended value chain in the area of distribution.

Increasing global competition and shorter product cycles had made it more important for suppliers to place the 'right' product on the market at the 'right' time. Innovative competition is competition between companies regarding future products for future customers, and for this reason, knowledge about customer expectations concerning the products in demand is absolutely necessary. Companies must be able to anticipate future customer needs and desires, while at the same time making their customers aware of new products. The activities involved with this task can be referred to as 'upstream' activities, and include, among other things, market research, research and development, and product presentation.Cornish refers to such work, aimed at discovering information on the *future* market of a *future* product, as 'market intelligence' (MI).

> MI may be defined broadly as the process of acquiring and analyzing information in order to understand the market (for both existing and potential customers); to determine the current and future needs and preferences, attitudes and behavior of the market; and to assess changes in the business environment that may affect the size and nature of the market in the future (Cornish, 1997b: 147).

Much is in favor of the urban marketplace remaining the key realm of market intelligence, as well as the source of new types of information on future products.

In terms of the third dimension, a marketplace can achieve advantageous conditions for strategic handling of market participants by making use of related service providers such as business consultants, auditors and financial services. As far as these advanced services are concerned, the city of Frankfurt and its surrounding region is one of the leading locations in Germany. In terms of the fourth dimension, transportation factors that affect accessibility - are central to the functionality of a marketplace. The Frankfurt/Rhein-Main region is located on primary channels of mobility between northern and southern Europe: Germany's Autobahn intersections experience the highest frequency of vehicle travel in Germany, several inter-city railway lines merge in the city, and Frankfurt has the largest airport on the European continent (see Chapter 7).

The context of the prevailing city system also plays a role in building a marketplace. It should be noted that Germany has developed a fully functional decentralized city system over the centuries and, unlike other neighboring countries, has no dominant metropolis. Market access for foreign companies is therefore possible in several cities. The Japanese companies that initially settled in the vicinity of Hamburg's harbor, where Japanese products were imported to the country, serve as good examples of the multiple possibilities. With the increasing integration of the European union, Japanese companies relocated to Düsseldorf, the 'office center' of the Ruhr area and the strategic center of the largest urban market territory in Germany. Today, Japanese companies have diffused all over Germany, and have reached Frankfurt on the Main (Schlunze, 1997). These 'mobile' companies cause fierce competition between German cities. Such competition is on one hand indirect, assuming the form of infrastructure politics concerning the location and accessibility of the city's marketplace (for example, the airport; see Chapter 7). On the other hand, more direct competition is exemplified by more city-based endeavors, such as the trade-fair, which has an impact on market intelligence.

The following sections will first address downstream market functions within the Frankfurt/Rhein-Main region, using electronic products as an example. Through analysis of importers of intermediary electronic products, we will argue that increased concentration of market activities in the Frankfurt/Rhein-Main region may be anticipated. We also believe that the role of the metropolitan region as a gateway to the German market will increase in comparison to competing German cities. Next, we will focus on the role of the Frankfurt trade-fair corporation within a discussion of upstream marketing functions in the Frankfurt marketplace. The chapter will conclude with some thoughts on the complimentary and competitive elements of the Frankfurt/Rhein-Main marketplace in relation to other European regions.

9.3 FRANKFURT/RHEIN-MAIN AS A POINT OF MARKET ACCESS: THE CASE OF THE ELECTRONICS SECTOR

Electronic products account, to a large degree, for the technological backbone of modern economic development. Furthermore, electronic products as intermediary products are indispensable for a number of sectors. For example, Germany's electronic component market is valued at an estimated EU17 billion. Twenty-six percent of this market is accounted for by the automotive industry, the leading export sector in Germany, another 25 percent by telecommunications, which has been growing quickly in Germany since deregulation, and 21 percent by data technology (ZVEI, 2000).

Germany is not yet a leading manufacturer of electronic products and is therefore dependent on imports (see Figure 9.1). In this way, Germany is similar to most other large industrial European nations.

The reunification boom of the early 1990's, as well as the subsequent recession and the dampened economic recovery that followed, had virtually no impact on electronic and electro-technical imports. On the contrary, import growth throughout the sector as a whole has been steady, both in terms of absolute value and as a percentage of total imports. Despite the fact that statistics do not address electronic products as an entity in and of itself, it is probable that they account for a large portion of the sector's increasing imports. The Frankfurt/Rhein-Main region is obviously not the sole gateway to the German market in this sector. But what role does the region play for the market entry of foreign companies? Does a regional course of development exist that intensifies the growing importance of the metropolitan region as an up-and-coming hub in the European or global network of flows? In order to answer these questions, we conducted a survey of foreign companies in the Frankfurt/Rhein-Main electronics sector.

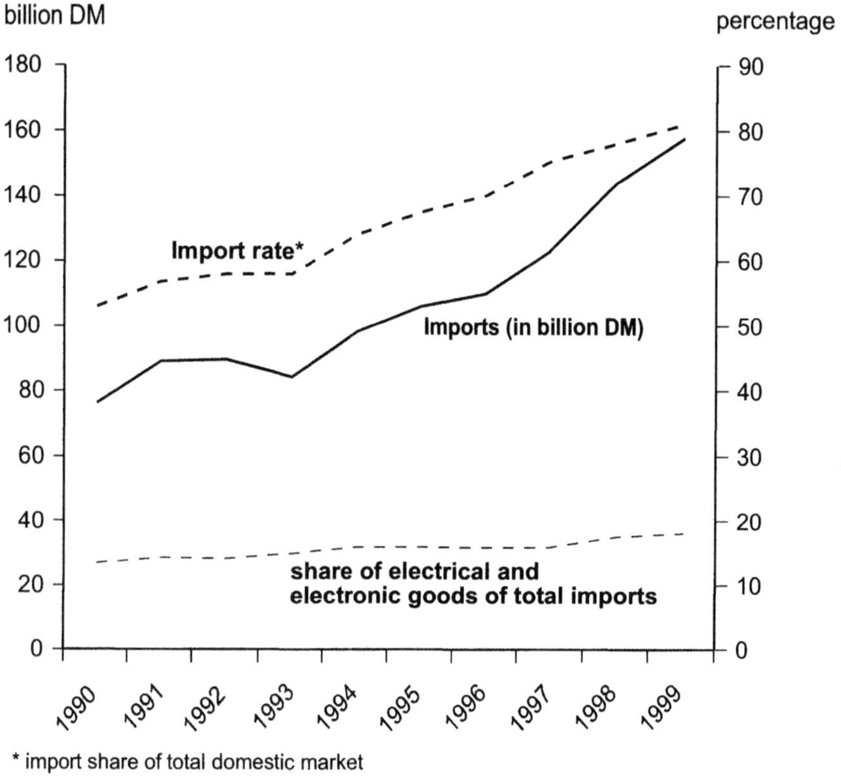

Figure 9.1 Growth of electro-technical and electronic goods imports to Germany, 1990-1999

9.3.1 Methods and Data

Every survey concerning foreign companies in general, and electronics companies in particular, is confronted with the problem of imprecise terms and the absence of a dependable and accessible address list. We therefore tapped a variety of sources in order to compile a databank of approximately 2,500 foreign companies operating in the Rhein/Main area (representatives of foreign countries, international chambers of commerce and consulates, and company listings like the Commerzbank and the

Hoppenstedt directories were especially helpful in this task). This list includes only a portion of the foreign companies in the region, and may suffer from bias towards larger companies. The distribution of countries, however, is representative of FDI in Hessen (see Chapter 2). Our databank identified 168 foreign companies with some connection to the electronics sector. But what exactly is the electronics sector? Electronics today is a multifaceted technology that is used everywhere. It links hardware and software, as well as the value-added services provided by both. The companies identified were selected from our databank based on the fact that they produce or trade in electronic goods, develop software or provide services (Table 9.1).

A subsequent telephone survey reduced the number of companies to 131, and additional questioning further reduced the number to 108. Of these 108 companies, 51 were willing to take part in a written questionnaire in April 2000. Questionnaire results were supplemented and sharpened through a series of telephone interviews. Not surprisingly, the resulting sample demonstrates the great heterogeneity of the electronics sector in the Frankfurt/Rhein-Main region. The overwhelming majority of companies, however, turned out to be distributors and service providers. For this reason, we will focus our attention on these companies and refrain from addressing the companies involved with production in this study.

Table 9.1 Primary branches of the electronics sector

Manufacturing	
30	Manufacture of office machines
31	Manufacture of various electro-technical components
32	Manufacture of electronic components and devices for telecommunication and mass communication
Trade	
51	Commerce mediation and large scale trade of electro-technical and electronic goods
52	Retail trade
Services	
64	Telecommunications services
71	Rental of electronic devices
72	Software development and servicing

Source: according to NACE, or Nomenclature of Activities in the European Community (Nomenclature des Activités dans la Communauté Européenne).

9.3.2 The Frankfurt Marketplace and the Electronics Sector

A fundamental drawback of single-date regional company questionnaires is that they provide information only about companies operating at that time. They also provide only a cross-section of the regional course of development, as is the case in this study. Without the possibility of comparison, questionnaire results serve as additional evidence supporting assumptions regarding the role of the Frankfurt/Rhein-Main region as a marketplace. Within this context, country of origin and date of arrival of foreign electronics companies allow us to discern a specific developmental course in the Frankfurt/Rhein-Main region, which over the past four decades has come to represent a gateway to international networking and cooperation. The significant number of American companies that came to the region after the Second World War was not surprising, considering the presence of American military headquarters in Frankfurt. Japanese companies only became global players in the 1970's, and therefore arrived in Europe much later than American companies. Despite its beginnings with the Roman Contracts of 1957, the European Union only started developing a domestic market in the 1990's. Thus, at the beginning of its course of development, the national market was primarily an objective of foreign companies. Approximately a quarter of the companies participating in our questionnaire arrived in the Frankfurt/Rhein-Main region during the 1960's and 1970's, and most of these were American and Japanese companies aiming to enter the German market with intermediary goods. For some of the American companies in question, the American military constituted the primary intended customer. Still, it is interesting to note that a number of Japanese companies chose Frankfurt as their German location very early on, in contrast to what was then a general trend of locating in Düsseldorf (Schickhoff, 1990; Schlunze, 1997). The exceptional case of one Japanese company, which has been doing business in the realm of nautical electronic equipment with the domestic shipping industry of the Rhein-Main area since 1972, indicates an early stage of marketplace development towards a larger market territory.

Table 9.2 Origin of electronics companies and year of arrival in region (distribution and service firms only) (n = 47)

	North America	*Japan*	*EU*	*Other*	*Other Europe World*
Until 1980	4	5	1	–	1
1981-90	8	5	5	2	1
1991-99	3	4	8	–	–

Source: Authors survey.

Most companies that participated in our questionnaire arrived in Frankfurt during the 1980's, while some arrived later, in the 1990s. Two aspects of the immigration of foreign companies must be considered: one that is sector related and one that is regional. Sectoral change is demonstrated first and foremost by the current predominance of new technologies. While companies during the 1980's were primarily involved in electronic components and software, companies dealing in telecommunications began arriving at an increasing rate during the 1990s. In addition, Frankfurt represented the only city on the continent in which several suppliers of local city-based networks were present. These suppliers regarded banks as their primary customers. Today, Frankfurt has 13 city networks and virtually leads Europe in this area, second only to London. City administrators made efforts to improve Frankfurt's ability to function as a primary financial center, offering public space for the laying of fiber optic cables (see Chapter 5). Finally in 1985, Frankfurt became the location of Germany's central internet hub (DE-CIX, Deutscher Commercial Internet Exchange). This, in turn, attracted internet service providers, telecommunications companies, and 'next-generation carriers'. In addition to the 15 internet service providers active in Germany, 13 global internet providers and next generation carriers appeared in Frankfurt during 2001, 11 of which have their main offices in Frankfurt. As a result, 85 percent of Germany's internet traffic is transmitted through Frankfurt, making the city second only to London as Europe's largest telecommunications hub. It is therefore no surprise that foreign telecommunications and carrier companies like Colt Telecom, MCI WorldCom and Level 3 Communication have moved to Frankfurt (LZB, 2001).

On the regional level, the immigration of foreign companies has meant that the Frankfurt/Rhein-Main region is finally assuming the role of a new European market place. Since the beginning of the 1980's, and even more discernibly in the 1990's, European companies have been setting up their German business centers in the Frankfurt/Rhein-Main region (15 of 48 participating companies). Will this result in a redefinition of Frankfurt's role as a regional marketplace within the larger European domestic market? It helps to keep in mind that the more recent foreign arrivals insist on having their German operations based in the Frankfurt/Rhein-Main region, or at least locating their German company headquarters there (20 of 48 participating companies). In contrast, it is more the exception than the rule that the Frankfurt/Rhein-Main region acts as a gateway to the entire European market. Only several Japanese electronics companies in specialized market niches, and one American firm, have positioned their European headquarters in Frankfurt, in addition to their German headquarters (9 of 48 participating companies).

While eight Japanese companies chose to locate their European headquarters in Frankfurt/Rhein-Main, the majority of American companies preferred London or elsewhere in Great Britain. Some Japanese companies have located their European headquarters in Amsterdam. However, not all foreign companies are structured with a European headquarters presiding over multiple national headquarters, and five companies had no European headquarters at all.

It is virtually impossible today to acquire accurate information on responsibilities for certain market territories due to the unknown hierarchical positioning of subsidiaries within TNC's. In addition, strategies of multinational companies are extremely diverse, ranging from centralized hierarchy to total decentralization. While few of the multinationals examined deviated from the traditional model, those with a German national headquarters that also serves as a European headquarters, or even a world headquarters, reflect that some strategies in use today are more competence-oriented than market-oriented. For the majority of participating companies, the Frankfurt/Rhein-Main marketplace covered a market territory including Germany and its neighboring countries (Austria, Switzerland, the Netherlands, Poland, Hungary and the Czech Republic) (Table 9.3).

Due to the small size of these neighboring countries and their markets, choosing a location with the largest market share makes good sense. Still, the question remains: why do companies choose the Frankfurt/Rhein-Main region above other cities within the decentralized city system of Germany? The reasons that these companies provided are not surprising. Three-quarters of the companies that responded to questions on this topic cited either the location of the airport, Germany's central location within Europe, or both. For some companies, like those in telecommunications, Frankfurt's standing as a financial center was also an initial deciding factor.

The rate of locational fluctuation within the Frankfurt/Rhein-Main region is high: 42 percent of participating companies had already moved once, generally due to rental costs and standard reasons connected with company growth, but also in order to relocate closer to the airport. This high rate of locational mobility is not difficult to explain. The participating companies are distribution and service-oriented and are therefore in need of office space, which is usually rented. Fluctuation rates are traditionally higher in such contexts. Also, due to the fact that most of the businesses in question are relatively small, moves are generally not difficult; approximately 85 percent of participating companies have less than 100 employees, and many have less than 10.

Table 9.3 Position of operations in the company's hierarchical structure and market territory (n=48)

	Market Territory				
Position in the Organization	*Regional*	*National*	*Central Europe*	*Europe as a Whole*	*Global*
European Headquarters	–	1	–	7	1
German Headquarters	2	17	13	2	1
Regional	3	–	–	1	–

Source: Authors survey.

As the European Union's unified domestic market continues to develop, foreign companies are now not only able to choose one of several German locations for their point of entry to the national market, but they also have an increasing number of choices among other European nations. One indicator of the importance of the Frankfurt/Rhein-Main region in this competitive arena is the degree of interregional mobility of the foreign companies. This assertion, however, could not be proven by our survey. Only two companies made such a move to the region: one from Düsseldorf and one from London. As reflected by the distribution of European headquarters, it appears that many Japanese companies prefer Germany, particularly the Frankfurt/Rhein-main region, as their location, while others prefer London and locations in Great Britain. As previously noted, the more the Japanese companies become familiar with the German market, the more they tend towards decentralized locations in Germany (Schlunze, 1997). Still, anecdotal evidence has repeatedly indicated that Frankfurt/Rhein-Main is an important point of market entry. One example is the recent joint venture between Fujitsu and Siemens in the computer sector; while the European headquarters will be located in the Netherlands, sales and marketing operations will be based in Frankfurt. Service providers in the electronics industry have yet another locational motive: demands of powerful customers in the financial, transportation (air traffic) and telecommunications sectors, which are concentrated in the Frankfurt/Rhein-Main region.

9.3.3 Frankfurt/Rhein-Main as a Logistic Hub

In addition to its growing significance as a distribution center, the metropolitan region's role as a logistic hub has expanded as well. In comparison to other city agglomerations in Germany, the Frankfurt/Rhein-Main region has become the leading logistics center over the past two decades (Table 9.4). While German seaports like Hamburg are loosing their importance, inland urban agglomerations, most notably that of Frankfurt/Rhein-Main, are on the rise. Frankfurt today is the urban agglomeration with the highest employment rate in the logistics sector, despite the fact that it is smaller than the Rhein-Ruhr region in both area and population (Läpple and Decke, 1999). One likely explanation for this is the airport, which serves as Europe's leading airfreight center. Other likely explanations are ground transportation, such as the rail system, and the city's heavy trucking industry. A logistic hub is a central trading post for goods in the logistics process, and space, therefore, is a necessary element. The highest concentration of storage facilities in Germany is located in the urban agglomeration regions of Düsseldorf, Frankfurt, Berlin and Hamburg. Among these, Frankfurt/Rhein-Main had the highest rate of renter fluctuation in 1999, and this indicates both instability and uncertainty. So, even though Frankfurt is an important hub for many companies, its future role in logistics is questionable.

The modern organizational structure of many multinational companies facilitates the assigning of dedicated functions to various locations. Obviously, there is no fail-proof model for companies to determine the optimal location for a sales structure or how to best organize a logistical stream of goods. Differing strategies and partially contradictory company reorganization reflect what appears to be a high degree of uncertainty among foreign companies as they attempt to assess future domestic market development. In a survey of the 36 participating electro-technical companies, the majority (approximately 60 percent) had moved their logistical activities to the region as well, despite the fact that the sales office was sometimes located elsewhere in the region. However, one-third of these companies chose to locate their logistic hubs in areas completely remote from their actual points of market access. In some cases these hubs were located in German locations such as Hamburg, Mönchen-Gladbach or even Bebra and Hersfeld (the latter two being located in central Germany), while in others they were located in places like Ireland, Great Britain, or Rotterdam.

Table 9.4 Logistics sector employment development in Germany's leading urban agglomerations, 1987 and 1997 (in thousands)

Agglomeration Region	*1987*	*1997*	*Growth/Loss in %*
Hamburg	66.4	56.4	- 15
Rhein-Ruhr	50.2	65.2	+ 30
Munich	23.7	29.8	+ 26
Frankfurt/Rhein-Main	60.6	71.5	+ 18

Source: Läpple and Decke, 1999.

One example of this phenomenon is a Japanese manufacturer of CDR's (recordable CD's). This firm has a factory in Ireland, and its sales office for the Eastern Europe and German speaking market (Germany, Austria, and Switzerland) has been located in Frankfurt/Rhein-Main since 1984. Just recently, this company transferred its logistic hub from Ireland to Frankfurt/Rhein-Main. Therefore, goods now flow from the company's east-Asian and Irish production locations, over Rotterdam, to Frankfurt/Rhein-Main, and from here onward to the markets of central and Eastern Europe. Other foreign companies, including many American and Korean firms, have their main European storage facilities near Rotterdam. While their information and service flows run over European headquarters in London, as well as over national headquarters (some in Frankfurt/Rhein-Main), goods are delivered from central storage facilities directly to customers. This, in turn, provides a basis for the development of a division of labor among city regions: Rotterdam and Randstad serve as the logistic hubs of Europe, and Frankfurt/Rhein-Main serves as the logistic hub and sales office for central Europe. As a result of rising land prices in the Frankfurt/Rhein-Main region and the ability of companies to react quickly (due to relatively short-term storage facility rental agreements of five to eight years), several companies are currently moving their logistics operations out of the region itself and into the periphery, which also provides the advantage of a central location within the market itself. Bad Hersfeld, located approximately 120 km north of the Frankfurt/Rhein-Main region, is currently developing into a central hub for logistics companies and operations in Germany, and the development of a quickly growing British distribution company for electronic components serves as a good example of this phenomenon. In 1991, a German subsidiary was established in close vicinity of the Frankfurt airport. Ten years later, Bad Hersfeld witnessed the construction of a new main storage facility with 80,000 square meters of space and 80 employees, capable of delivering 80,000 products to customers at short notice. The company's sales office, with 350 employees, remains in the Frankfurt/Rhein-Main region.

In addition, foreign electronics manufacturers traditionally based in the Frankfurt/Rhein-Main region have reorganized their locations in a manner that reflects an increased importance of logistics and service operations and a decreased importance of manufacturing. A unique, well-documented case of such company reorganization is that of IBM in Europe (Kelly and Keeble, 1990; Savary, 1991). IBM developed its locational patterns in Europe at a time when the public sector and a small number of large firms constituted the primary customers for the company's mainframes. This necessitated a multi-domestic strategy, as governments conditioned access to their respective national markets on investment in manufacturing plants. This type of politics was not characteristic only of centralized government systems in countries like France or Italy. In Germany as well, IBM opened another plant in 1967 in Mainz, a city near Frankfurt, in addition to its headquarters in Sindelfingen near Stuttgart. However, privatization of markets and the expansion of IBM's service activities, in addition to the formation of a common market, have made these structures obsolete.

IBM responded to the new market conditions with various phases of reorganization. As part of the phase of orienting themselves to the German national market, they established a central logistic hub in Niederrodgau (near Frankfurt) in 1975. The hub was charged with receiving components from several European plants, assembling them, delivering them to the West German market, and possibly providing services. Frankfurt's central location along the predominantly north-south transport and traffic flows of West Germany was one major factor in its designation as the hub's location, as was the international accessibility provided by the city's airport.

This step also provided IBM with a location useful for new global strategies aimed at the European market as a whole. Within the context of company reorganization in 1995, the logistic hub was charged with new tasks. It now became responsible for controlling logistic streams between all IBM plants in Europe, in order to facilitate new internal streams of goods between European plants, like those in France, Italy, Germany, and Hungary. Several plants in Germany were then turned into service centers; the Hanover plant was completely transformed, while plants in Berlin and Mainz only partially. The resulting Europe-wide specialization of manufacturing plants and transport logistics placed Frankfurt in a central position within the production process on the continent. In addition, Frankfurt's logistical responsibility for market regions such as Austria, Switzerland, and Eastern Europe was expanded. The city's central location - not only for Germany, but also for Europe as a whole - and its airport were both integral factors in its choice as a hub. Still, it should be noted that was not the only possibility; for example, IBM's air freight can be controlled just as easily from 'neighboring' airports such as Luxembourg and Schiphol/Amsterdam.

9.4 FRANKFURT/RHEIN-MAIN AS A POINT OF MARKET INTELLIGENCE

So far, this chapter has been primarily concerned with downstream marketplace functions, as discussed by Cornish (1997). As the integration of market areas generates an increasingly competitive atmosphere between companies, upstream marketplace functions in particular will become increasingly significant. Frankfurt is not known as a fashion or design city and is therefore not competitive in this field with European metropolises like Paris and Milan. In addition, the region's stock of available industrial research space is shrinking, and with it opportunities in the region for designing new products for global markets (see Chapter 2). In contrast, Frankfurt/Rhein-Main is contending to become a switchboard for the exchange of ideas and information regarding new products for a global, or at least European, market.

The exchange of codified information is less important for this aspiration. Far more important is the exchange of non-codified information, which is bound to individuals and not public, and which provides firms with competitive advantages. In order to facilitate the exchange of such knowledge between companies and customers, meetings are critical yet possible at only a few locations. In this context, trade-fairs and conferences play both a traditional, as well as one of increasing new importance, as intermediaries of market intelligence. The number of trade-fairs around the world grew by almost 50 percent during the five years leading up to 2000, reaching a total of 9,600 (Messe Frankfurt, 2001). The total number of visitors to trade-fairs and conferences has also grown. There is thus a current need to expand the infrastructure of trade-fair facilities and conference-centers, as well as the hotel and transportation infrastructures that improve the accessibility of trade-fairs and conferences from an ever-expanding area (see Chapter 11). This will enhance the ability of trade-fairs and conferences to raise the international profile of a given city and to assist in its image building (Cuadrado-Roura and Rubalcaba-Bermejo, 1998).

In fact, trade-fairs are increasingly being linked with conferences, as this allows domestic producers to disseminate product information to international customers and international producers to disseminate information to domestic customers. In addition to this exchange, linking conferences and trade-fairs also enables international manufacturers to learn more about customer demands regarding future products. Both of these functions are important for consumer goods and intermediary goods alike. Europe's trade-fairs are oriented more towards presenting goods and products than actually selling them on site, and their informational nature is the essence of the trade-fair's contribution to market intelligence.

As in the past, Germany is a crucial area for trade-fairs. It has an impressive number of fair grounds, in all larger urban agglomerations as well as in several mid sized cities. It should also be noted that Frankfurt leads the German market in terms of absolute size, number of exhibitors, number of foreign exhibitors and number of visitors (Table 9.5). Only Düsseldorf and Cologne draw more foreign visitors. Still, while this makes these cities on the Rhein more likely trade-fair grounds for visitors coming from an expanded western European area (especially from the Netherlands and Belgium), Frankfurt appears to carry greater import in the eyes of suppliers in terms of upstream marketing.

Table 9.5 The five leading trade-fair locations in Germany (1999)

City	*Exhibitors*	*Foreign Exhibitors*	*Visitors*	*Foreign Visitors*
Frankfurt	31,441	17,510	1,856,622	205,598
Düsseldorf	25,034	12,784	1,443,421	377,542
Cologne	23,119	15,084	915,556	307,384
Hannover	20,363	8,812	1,376,142	281,163
Munich	16,637	5,855	848,551	121,038

Source: Statistisches Bundesamt (2000), Statistisches Jahrbuch für die Bundesrepublik Deutschland. Wiesbaden, pp. 260.

A clear hierarchy of trade-fair locations in Germany and Europe is by no means simple to construct. Cuadrado-Roura and Rucalbaba-Bermejo (1998) identify Paris, London, Milan and Birmingham, as well as Frankfurt, Cologne, Düsseldorf, Munich and Hanover, as European cities in competition with one other on the global market. However, our discussion focuses less on the quantitative calculation of Frankfurt's trade-fairs in comparison to other European cities and more on the deviation of trade-fair companies from the role of an infrastructure provider to that of a global player in upstream marketing.

The 'market' for trade-fair events is still composed predominantly of public institutions owned by respective cities. City based trade-fair companies, in competition with other German and European cities, strive to maximize the use of their infrastructure by organizing their own trade-fairs in addition to attracting 'guest' trade-fairs; for, if they restrict themselves to 'guest' fairs, they become little more than specialized real estate companies. They have long been regarded as providers of public infrastructure, but not as entrepreneurial actors themselves. Due to the force of globalization, however, trade-fair companies today are transforming into strategically oriented actors, cooperating and competing among themselves. By functioning as vital intermediaries for the exchange of non-codified knowledge for international clientele, they influence the economy of the region as a whole, and at times even that of the nation. The large number of city based trade-fair companies operating today obligates each individual company to adopt strategies based on specialization, which they employ to their advantage while competing and cooperating with other trade-fair companies.

The market intelligence of trade-fairs is primarily determined by the strategy of a central body - the city trade-fair company. Due to their increasing dependence on European and global competition, larger city trade-fair companies are adopting strategies resembling those of privately owned internationalized companies. Privatization in practice, however, has not taken place. In the following discussion, the strategies of a given city trade-fair company should be regarded as an indicator of the internationalization of the market intelligence functions of the city in question.

The Frankfurt trade-fair company (MFA) is owned by both the city of Frankfurt (60 percent) and the state of Hessen (40 percent). Its first task is to attract trade-fair events and conferences for the city of Frankfurt. A trade fairground is a real estate site that must be marketed accordingly, taking into consideration its location within an urban agglomeration, the amount of available space and additional service establishments available (for example, a congress hall). The Frankfurt trade-fair, which is centrally located in the city, has profited from a recent change in city infrastructure - the closing of the nearby central freight depot, which makes fairgrounds expansion possible. The recent construction of a congress center, a luxury hotel and a new train station are all investments that aim to increase the competitiveness of both the trade-fair company and the fair grounds.

Large, important trade-fairs are organized not by the trade-fair company alone, but in conjunction with business associations. Frankfurt benefits from the fact that a number of business associations that organize major fairs are based in the city. These associations include "Verband der Automobilindustrie" (VDA, or Automobile Industry Association), the German Society for Chemical Devices, Chemical Technology and Biotechnology (DECHEMA) and the German Publishers and Booksellers Association. Their trade-fairs include, respectively: the International Automobile Exhibition (IAA), the International Meeting for Chemical Technology and Biotechnology, and the Frankfurt Book Trade-fair. Still, the trade-fair company must do its part to guarantee that its site is attractive, in order to avoid client migration to other trade-fair locations. This was the case a number of years ago when the IAA threatened to move to Berlin. Trade-fair companies also 'invent' and organize a number of their own trade-fairs, which results in a degree of pressure to continually specialize in their competition with other trade-fair locations. For this reason, Frankfurt failed to become an important European trade-fair location for art, as the "Art Frankfurt" trade-fair unsuccessfully competed against the current leaders in art trade-fairs, Basel and Cologne. In 1999, the MFA trade-fair company organized 49 trade-fairs and exhibitions, 25 of which were international.

During such trade-fairs, the city becomes a showcase for the world. Company adaptability to changing market conditions is particularly important in markets for high-grade consumer goods in the Triad (i.e. Europe, the United States and Japan). Powerful luxury goods customers have emerged with the emergence of the 'life style' group in Triad retail trade, and similar developments are discernible in Gereffi and Korzeniewicz's 1994 analysis of global commodity chains with mass consumer goods. German leather goods producers, who had traditionally used the annual leather goods trade-fair in nearby Offenbach to make foreign contacts, were faced with the fact that foreign exhibitors and visitors came to find their trade-fair increasingly unattractive. In response, the Offenbach leather goods trade-fair was eventually tacked on to the successful Ambiente trade-fair for lifestyle products, held in Frankfurt, which succeeds in drawing many Asian (especially Japanese) customers. These customers are now able to conveniently inform themselves about leather goods as well. Luxury goods companies in Offenbach also have their own showrooms open during the trade-fair, in order to enhance their access to the growing Asian market.

The demands posed by urban trade-fair companies' policies of active acquisition and organization has increasingly transformed these companies into a new strategic hub within the global context. As in the case of the global economy, the Frankfurt trade-fair company has adopted a strategy of branding. This means that special trade-fairs are designed as brand name products, and subsequently exported to where the customers are. For this purpose, the trade-fair company founded subsidiaries in Tokyo, Hong Kong, Singapore and Atlanta, and in 1998, in Milan, Mumbai and Sao Paulo. For example, the brand name 'Heimtextil', which is a trade-fair for home textiles, is organized from these locations for the respective region of each. In the year 2000, Heimtextil was held in three locations in Europe (Frankfurt, Vilnius and Moscow), four locations in Asia (Tokyo, Hong Kong, Shanghai and New Delhi) and six locations in the Americas (Atlanta, Boston, Miami, Las Vegas, Chicago and Sao Paulo) (Messe Frankfurt, 2000).

Such strategies, however, mark only the beginning of the trade-fair company's strategy of internationalization. Furthermore, it is not yet clear which of the competing German city trade-fair companies will become the first global player. Even though strategic efforts point clearly towards increasing internationalization, their success rate is still relatively small. Trade-fairs in Germany, including Frankfurt, are still largely aimed at a European market, with only 15 precent of all exhibitors and 4 percent of all visitors at German trade-fairs hailing from non-European countries (Frankfurter Allgemeine Zeitung, 2001).

It goes without saying that other branches of the service sector, like the advertising and communications branches, play a role in supporting Frankfurt as a center of market intelligence. With more than 200 advertising agencies, including the headquarters of many American agencies, Frankfurt, along with Hamburg, is one of the most important advertising cities in Germany and in Europe as a whole. Frankfurt also has internationally oriented companies in the fields of market research, corporate consulting, legal associations and business associations (Noller, 1999) that contribute to the city's role as an integral center for market intelligence. The majority of these companies, however, tend to serve only the German and/or central European markets.

9.5 CONCLUSIONS

This chapter presented a number of examples of how the real marketplace is still important for real markets. It also illustrated that the importance of some marketplaces may even grow as their market region expands and becomes increasingly specialized. The metropolitan region of Frankfurt/ Rhein-Main constitutes a marketplace in all four dimensions (see section 9.2). While two of the four dimensions - the location of Frankfurt's services and the city's transportation infrastructure- have already been discussed (see Chapters 2 and 7), this chapter sheds additional light on downstream and upstream functions. The conclusions of this discussion are mixed. On one hand, the Frankfurt/Rhein-Main region is becoming increasingly important as a marketplace for international streams of goods and information; on the other hand, we have discovered that the position of the metropolitan region within the city system of Europe as a whole is still uncertain. As far as policy is concerned, we can conclude that securing the functions of Frankfurt/Rhein-Main as a marketplace will continue to demand additional effort.

By using one specific type of product (electronic goods) as an example, it was shown that European markets are still bound to territories and that they are expanding territorially into smaller neighboring countries. The range of Frankfurt/Rhein-Main's marketplace has extended beyond the limits of its national territory, and the region has become an interface for a larger European area. As noted above, however, its future importance is uncertain, as significant foreign players obviously have differing perceptions of the Frankfurt/Rhein-Main marketplace. American companies operate differently to Japanese companies in their choice of sales and logistics locations in Europe. In the realm of downstream marketing functions, their strategies are heterogeneous as well: European headquarters may be located in either London or Amsterdam, and only occasionally in Frankfurt. Logistic hubs may be located in Frankfurt/Rhein-Main, Rotterdam or other German locations with good transportation infrastructures. The present storage tendencies of logistic functions may endanger the role of the Frankfurt/Rhein-Main region as a logistic hub in the future.

We also identify an increasing importance of the Frankfurt/Rhein-Main region in Europe in terms of upstream marketing functions. There is, however, fierce competition among individual German trade-fair locations, as well as cooperation between other city based trade-fair companies.

These empirical findings lead to two conclusions. Firstly, the process of specialization among the metropolitan regions of Germany and Europe is currently intensifying. It appears safe to say that Frankfurt/Rhein-Main will continue to specialize in the downstream functions of sales and the upstream functions of information, with the long-term possibility of the emergence of a new hierarchy of European metropolitan regions. Secondly, this process is characterized by competition and cooperation among metropolitan regions, as well as other types of regions, within the European community. For this reason, the emergence of a single uniform marketplace for any specific market territory is improbable. We can also expect growing heterogeneity of urban marketplaces, as well as an increasingly unstable situation of competition among them, as Europe continues to grow together.

REFERENCES

Boyer, R. (1997). The variety and unequal performance of really existing markets: Farewell to Doctor Pangloss? In R.S. Hollingsworth & R. Boyer (Eds.), *Contemporary capitalism. The embeddedness of institutions* (55-93). Cambridge: Cambridge University Press.

Castells, M. (1996). *The information age* (Vol.1): *The rise of the network society*. Cambridge, Mass: Blackwell.

Cornish, S. (1995). Marketing matters: The function of markets and marketing in the growth of firms and industries. *Progress in Human Geography, 19*, 317-337.

Cornish, S. (1997a). Strategies for the acquisition of market intelligence and implications for the transferability of information inputs. *Annals of the Association of American Geographers, 87*, 451-470.

Cornish, S. (1997b). Product innovation and the spatial dynamics of market intelligence: Does proximity to markets matter? *Economic Geography, 73*, 143-165.

Cuadrado-Roura, J.R. & Rubalcaba-Bermejo, L. (1998). Specialization and competition amongst European cities: A new approach through fair and exhibition activities. *Regional Studies, 32(2)*, 133-147.

Dicken, P. (1998). *Global shift. Transforming the world economy* (3rd. ed.). London: Paul Chapman.

Frankfurter Allgemeine Zeitung (2001). Deutsche Messen suchen Wege zur schnellen Globalisierung. *Frankfurter Allgemeine Zeitung, 109,* 11 May 2001, 23.

Gereffi, G. & Korzeniewicz, M. (Eds.) (1994). *Commodity chains and global competition.* Westport, Conn: Praeger.

Gertler, M.S. (1997). The invention of regional culture. In R. Lee & J. Wills (Eds.), *Geographies of economies* (47-58). London: Arnold.

Hesse, M. (2000). Städte im Binnenland - Vom Marktplatz und Zentrum des Warenumschlags zum logistischen Satelliten? In H.H. Blotevogel *et al.* (Eds.), *Lokal verankert - Weltweit vernetzt, 52.* Deutscher Geographentag Hamburg 1999. Stuttgart: Franz Steiner, 212-220.

Kelly, T. & Keeble, D. (1990). IBM: The corporate chameleon. In M. de Smidt & E. Wever (Eds.), *The corporate firm in a changing world economy. Case studies in the geography of enterprise* (21-54). London: Routledge.

Läpple, D. & Decke, H. (1999). *Strukturwandel der Weltwirtschaft und seine Auswirkungen auf Seehäfen.* Paper presented at the 52. Deutscher Geographentag Hamburg.

LZB, Landeszentralbank in Hessen (2001). New economy in Rhein-Main. *Frankfurter Finanzmarkt-Bericht 39.* Frankfurt/M: Deutsche Bundesbank.

Messe Frankfurt (2000). *Geschäftsbericht 1999.* Frankfurt: Messe Frankfurt GmbH.

Messe Frankfurt (2001). *Geschäftsbericht 2000.* Frankfurt: Messe Frankfurt GmbH.

Noller, P. (1999). Globalisierung, Stadträume und Lebensstile. *Kulturelle und lokale Repräsentationen des globalen Raums.* Opladen: Leske+Budrich.

Ruigrok, W. & van Tulder, R. (1995). *The logic of international restructuring.* London: Routledge.

Savary, J. (1991). Une multinationale globale: Le modèle IBM. In C. Dupuis, Ch. Mirelli & J. Savary (Eds.), *Atlas mondial des multinationales II, Stratégies des multinationales* (154-181). Montpellier: Reclus.

Sayer, A. & Walker R. (1992). *The new social economy. Reworking the division of labor.* Oxford: Blackwell.

Schickhoff, I. (1990). Japanische Direktinvestitionen in der Bundesrepublik Deutschland, insbesondere Nordrhein-Westfalen. *Berichte zur deutschen Landeskunde. 64*, 49-66.

Schlunze, R.D. (1997). *Japanese investment in Germany: A spatial perspective.* Münster: Lit.

ZVEI (2000). *Jahresbericht des Fachverbandes Bauelemente der Elektronik 2000.* Available: http://www.zvei-be.zvei.org/aktuell/Jahres2000.html

SECTION IV:

CONSUMER-DRIVEN ACTIVITIES

NOAM SHOVAL

10. GLOBAL TRENDS IN THE TEL-AVIV TOURISM SECTOR

10.1 INTRODUCTION

Globalization has come to serve as a general term referring to a number of political, sociological, environmental and economic trends. In its purely economic sense, 'globalization' refers to the growing interdependence of markets and production in different countries, through trade in goods and services, cross-border capital flows, international technology exchange, strategic alliances, co-operative ventures and mergers. The tourism sector has traditionally served as a catalyst for globalization, as tourism is inherently concerned with international interaction. An early example of the role of tourism as a globalizing agent can be seen in the worldwide activities of Thomas Cook & Son Ltd. during the mid-19th century (Brendon, 1991).

Due to tourism's growing importance in large cities towards the end of the 20th century, research on urban tourism has received increased attention (Ashworth and Tunbridge, 1990; Law, 1993; Page, 1995; van den Berg *et al.*, 1995; Law, 1996; Mazanec, 1997; Judd and Fainstein, 1999). Despite this heightened interest, researchers have on the whole neglected globalization of the tourism industry and its impact on cities; Swarbrooke's (2001) study on the impact of globalization on destination management must be regarded as an exception to this general trend. On the other hand, globalization's impact on the tourist industry itself has received more comprehensive treatment (see, for example: Shaw and Williams, 1994; Wahab and Cooper, 2001). Tourism as a significant globalizing agent and catalyst has also been overlooked by the rich literature focusing on the globalization of cities and economies. Such neglect is also evident in studies of cultural globalization in cities and of cultural globalization in general, a phenomenon that has been coined alternately 'McDonaldization' (Ritzer, 1996), 'McDisneyfication' (Ritzer and Liska, 1997) and even 'McGuggenisation' (McNeill, 2000). Short and Yeong-Hyun (1999) describe the global metropolitan cultures that emerge as the result of economic and cultural globalization in the following manner:

> The rise of transnational cultural flows has enabled large cities to taste diverse cultural samplings from all over the world. Such samplings include art exhibitions, opera events and sports competitions. Similar cultural traits such as the minimalist modernist look of many coffeehouses are found in cities around the world. The formations of global metropolitan cultures is a significant aspect of urban change. Global metropolitan cultures can be generalized as increasing commonalties between large metropolises around the world including built environments, specific lifestyles, policy instruments and dynamic business atmospheres (Short and Yeong-Hyun, 1999, p. 11).

D. Felsenstein et al. (eds.),
Emerging Nodes in the Global Economy: Frankfurt and Tel Aviv Compared, 195–212.

Tourism acts as a central force in shaping city areas due to its focus on and concentration in central parts of cities. In this and other cases, however, researchers have failed to address the major role of tourism as an agent of the cultural and economic forces behind this process.

The aim of this chapter is to investigate the nature and extent of the relationship between tourism and globalization in the Tel-Aviv metropolitan area. The chapter will focus on four primary areas of investigation related directly to the impact of globalization on Tel-Aviv's tourist industry. The findings from these areas will serve to support the basic hypothesis that the globalization that has taken place in Israel since the beginning of the 1990's has had two decisive effects on the Tel-Aviv tourism sector. One effect has been an increasing number of tourists, most significantly those visiting the city on business. This trend has resulted from growing international involvement in the Israeli economy, the most important financial center of which is Tel-Aviv. Another effect has been the restructuring of the accommodation sector, which has yielded a greater number of hotel rooms managed by international hotel chains.

The first issue addressed in this chapter will be the development of Tel-Aviv as a tourist destination, and whether or not tourism in Tel-Aviv increased in importance during the 1990's (in either relative or absolute terms). Results are compared with those of other leading urban tourist destinations in Israel, such as Jerusalem and Haifa. The second issue addressed will be the change in ownership of tourist services in Tel-Aviv, for which the accommodation sector will serve as a case study. This section will investigate the different ways in which international hotel chains have entered the Israeli market, and Tel-Aviv will then be compared in this respect to other tourism destinations in Israel, such as Jerusalem, Eilat, the Dead Sea and Tiberias. The chapter will then turn to the issue of business tourism in Tel-Aviv, drawing primarily on the annual tourist survey carried out by the Israeli Ministry of Tourism. This section will be augmented by original empirical research based on a survey completed by tourists just prior to leaving the country. The fourth and final issue addressed by this chapter will be the relationship between tourism and culture in Tel-Aviv (see also Chapter 12). Tel-Aviv claims to be an important cultural center and is undoubtedly the cultural capital of Israel's population. The city does not, however, enjoy this status among tourists from abroad. This section will assess the extent to which tourists in Tel-Aviv consume the 'cultural product' that the city offers. It should be noted that this chapter's focus on Tel-Aviv, along with the empirical data regarding the city's tourism sector that is being published here for the first time, represents a contribution to the relatively scarce academic literature on urban tourism in Israel. Up to the present, research in this field has been limited (Shachar and Shoval, 1999; Shoval and Hattab, 2001).

10.2 GLOBALIZATION IN THE TOURISM SECTOR OF TEL-AVIV: THE PRIMARY ISSUES

10.2.1 The Development of Tel-Aviv as a Tourist Destination

Tourist destinations are dynamic and constantly developing. The nature of their evolution is determined by a number of factors, such as changing demands in origin countries and changing tourist products at the destinations themselves. Small seaside resorts are more vulnerable to such changes than other destinations, as they usually depended solely on one tourist sector. Butler (1980) conceptualized the evolution of such small resorts in a model that described and analyzed the concept of a 'tourist area cycle of evolution'. While the concept of a tourist destination's life cycle may not appear to be particularly relevant to large urban destinations characterized by a variety of visit-motivations (leisure and sightseeing, business and conventions, friends and relatives, etc.), we hold that it accurately depicts the perpetual change typical of such locations. Like any other tourist destination, cities must constantly modify their image and tourist product, in order to maintain their tourist status in the face of growing competition among cities on both the local and global levels (Judd and Fainstein, 1999).

The city of Tel-Aviv, established in 1909, is a relatively young city in comparison to other tourist destinations in Israel, such as Jerusalem, Tiberias, Nazareth, Bethlehem and Acre. Still, its importance as a financial center from the 1920's onward sparked the evolution of a flourishing tourist industry very early on. In addition, the development of Tel-Aviv's shoreline during the 1930's added another important element to the city's tourist product. From then on, the city's sandy beach and role as Israel's financial capital served to position Tel-Aviv as a major tourist center. Based on recent tourism indicators, however, it is clear that the city has not been successful in improving its national and global position. This lack of success must be contrasted to recent rapid growth in urban tourism in general, and the region's improved image over the 1990's following the onset of the peace process on one hand, and the economic restructuring and globalization of the Israeli economy on the other.

10.2.2 Indicators of Tel-Aviv's Tourism Industry

Inbound tourism to Israel has seen ups and downs during recent decades due to ongoing political conflicts between Israel and its neighbors (see Figure 10.1). This instability results from tourism's nature as an 'image-driven' industry that is highly sensitive to political change (Pizam and Mansfeld, 1996). The peace negotiations that began with the local Palestinian leadership at the Madrid Convention (1991) and continued with the Palestinian Authority after the Oslo Agreements (1993) led to a sharp increase in tourism to the region. This growth trend, however, gave way to decline during the second half of the 1990's, due to the security problems caused by terrorist attacks carried out by Palestinian Muslim fundamentalists and the slowdown in normalization between Israel and the Arab world. More significantly, the outbreak of the 'Al-Aqsa Intifada' in September 2000 and the terrorist attacks carried out in America by Islamic fundamentalists in September 2001 caused a severe decline in tourism to the region. In fact, the present decline in global tourism in general, and tourism to Israel in particular, has been more serious than even the impact of Iraq's invasion of Kuwait and the Gulf War that followed.

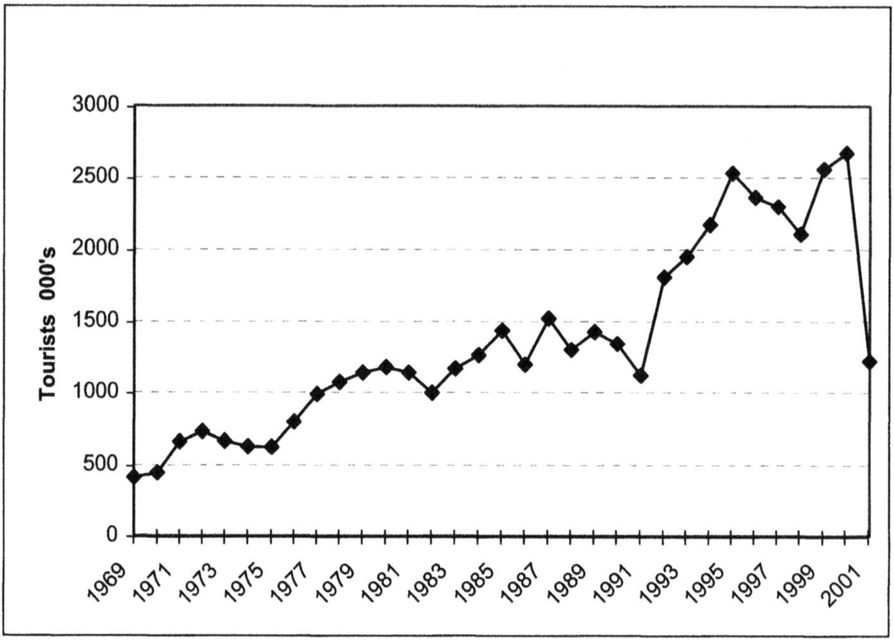

Source: Central Bureau of Statistics and Ministry of Tourism, 2001.

Figure 10.1 Inbound tourism to Israel, 1968-2001

In recent decades, tourism to Tel-Aviv has not increased proportionally to overall tourism to Israel. Rather, Tel-Aviv has experienced a constant decline relative to all other tourist sights in Israel. This has been partially due to stagnation in new hotel construction in the city, but more significantly due to the rapid growth of relatively new tourist areas in Israel, like the Dead Sea region and the resort-city of Eilat.

Stagnation in total hotel room stock also characterized Jerusalem during the late 1980's and early 1990's, due to the unexpected arrival of thousands of immigrants from Ethiopia over a very short time period. In order to accommodate this influx, the Israeli government rented all available accommodation. Many hotel proprietors preferred to turn their hotels into temporary absorption centers for several years, in return for lucrative government contracts instead of investing funds in renovating aging properties. The government, in turn, sought quick solutions for accommodation for thousands. The increase in inbound tourism of the first half of the 1990's caused some hotel owners in Jerusalem, Tel-Aviv and other locations to return to the tourism sector and convert their properties back into hotels for tourism proper. The result of this trend was that no new hotels were built in Jerusalem between 1986 and 1996. In Tel-Aviv during the same period, the number of total hotel rooms available for tourists continued to decline. Prior to the completion of the David Intercontinental Hotel in 1999, the last large hotel with more than one hundred rooms that had been constructed in the city was the Ritz Carlton, completed in 1979. The data in Table 10.1 regarding the city's total hotel room stock reveals that less than one hundred rooms were added in the city during the fifteen years under examination.

Table 10.1 Indicators of Tel-Aviv's tourist industry

	1985	*1990*	*1995*	*2000*
Tourist person-nights in Tel-Aviv (in thousands)	2154	1725	2002	2000
Tourist person-nights in Tel-Aviv as a percentage of total tourist person-nights in Israel	23.8%	21.5%	17.3%	20.6%
Number of participants from abroad in international conferences in Tel-Aviv	7585	1070	5400	na
Number of hotel rooms in Tel-Aviv	5788	5141	4846	5855
Number of hotel rooms in Israel	31345	29831	34801	45504

1. In 1996, there were 12,351 international conference participants from abroad in Tel-Aviv. In 1997, there were only 1,252 participants from abroad. 1998 witnessed only a slight increase in this number, bringing the figure to 1,947.

Sources: Central Bureau of Statistics and Ministry of Tourism, 2001; Center for Economic and Social Research, 2000.

Another indicator of the performance of the tourism industry in a given destination is its absolute number of person-nights, and its percentage as part of the total number of person-nights in the country. The data presented in Table 10.1 reveals that Tel-Aviv saw fewer person-nights during the year 2000 than during 1985 (in absolute terms). The data also reflects a decline in Tel-Aviv's position relative to other tourist centers in Israel in terms of total person-nights. In 1985, one-quarter of all person-nights in Israel were spent in Tel-Aviv, while the city's share fell to just one-fifth of all person-nights in the country by the year 2000.

A possible explanation for the current state of Tel-Aviv's hotel industry relates to the role of recent historical events. Until 1967, Tel-Aviv enjoyed the largest share of tourist-nights in Israel; Jerusalem was still a divided city whose main attractions were located under Jordanian rule, and Eilat and the Dead Sea region had not yet developed into major resort areas. In result, it was decided in the 1960's to develop Tel-Aviv's northern shoreline with a row of luxury hotels, which would contain more than 2,500 rooms. The first hotel completed was the Hilton (1965) and the last was the Ritz Carlton (1979). The 1967 war and the subsequent unification of

Jerusalem resulted in the rapid construction of hotel rooms in Israel's capital, as well as a major shift from Tel-Aviv to Jerusalem as Israel's major tourist center. It appears that the tourist peak of the mid 1990's proved that Tel-Aviv was capable of filling more hotel rooms, and this conclusion on the part of both the public and private sectors led to the planning of several large hotels. In reality, however, only one hotel was built. The 1999 opening of the 600-room David Intercontinental Hotel on Tel Aviv's southern shoreline represented the first significant addition to the city's hotel stock in twenty years.

10.2.3 International Conventions and Trade Fairs in Tel-Aviv

Globalization of the world economy has resulted in a dramatic increase in conferences and trade fairs in developed countries (Law, 1993). In order to attract conferences and trade fairs, many cities have made major investments in either expanding existing convention and trade centers or building new facilities (Braun, 1992; Fenich, 1994). Despite the economic globalization of the 1990's, however, Tel-Aviv's convention and trade fair industries have not expanded significantly in terms of convention volume or numbers of participants. Data collected by Israel's Central Bureau of Statistics (1999) reflects the importance of Jerusalem as a conference location, capturing two-thirds of all international conferences despite the economic primacy of Tel-Aviv (an approximate annual average of 50,000 participants from abroad in Israel). This is most likely due to three key factors. The first is Jerusalem's religious and historic attraction. The second is the fact that Tel-Aviv's convention center and fair grounds are located at a site that is unattractive for participants from abroad, with no accommodations in reasonable proximity. As a result, most international meetings are held in several of Tel-Aviv's shoreline hotels. The third factor relates to the nature of conventions held in Israel, the majority of which are not purely scientific, academic or what has been termed 'professional conventions'. Rather, they are usually either religious (pilgrimage groups that naturally prefer Jerusalem) or organized by large Jewish organizations, and therefore 'Jerusalem-oriented' by definition.

These findings are surprising, as one would naturally expect an economic center as important as Tel-Aviv to attract more international conventions and trade fairs, especially in light of the globalization process that Israel experienced during the 1990's.

10.2.4 Changes in Ownership of Tourist Services in Tel-Aviv: The Accommodation Sector as a Case Study

The organization of the worldwide tourism industry has changed rapidly over the past two decades, as the sector has become increasingly centralized and integrated on the global level. Transnational companies have come to dominate the hotel, airline, travel agency, tour operator and restaurant sectors (Clancy, 1998). These global organizations with worldwide distribution systems, scale economies and vertically integrated operations have increased the pressure of globalization on small and medium sized operators (Smeral, 1998; Vanhove, 2001). In many countries in which tourism has become a major export industry, the hospitality sector is the focal point at which globalization takes root. It is at the center of the transfer of ideas and cross-fertilization of cultures, and it plays an important role in physically bringing people together in a global community. Indeed, tourism has become the worlds largest export industry, involving enormous cross-border flows of people and capital.

The accommodation sector has witnessed worldwide rapid growth among international hotel chains during the past decade, and has also undergone significant overall restructuring. During this period, the share of the world's largest 200 hotel groups increased from 26 percent to 36 percent of the global market (Johnson, 1997; Bailey, 1998). This process has also been characterized by geographical differentiation, with Europe on one end of the spectrum, with a great number of small, family-run businesses, and the United States on the other end, with its America-based global hotel chains. A major reason for this process of restructuring has been technical changes that have taken place within the tourism industry in general and the hotel industry in particular, like the development of 'Computerized Reservations Systems', or 'CRS' ('Galileo', 'Sabre', 'Amadeus', etc.). The cost of developing and maintaining such systems is high, but hotels that are connected to these networks enjoy significant marketing advantages (Milne and Pohlmann, 1998; Vanhove, 2001). Technical developments of this kind have resulted in changes in the overall marketing approaches within the tourism industry and created the need for economic and geographic restructuring. This, in turn, has resulted in the integration and globalization of the tourism industry (Milne and Gill, 1998).

Additional explanations of increasing globalization are that:

- The different advantages of economies of scale to hotel chains have spurred further acquisitions and mergers within the industry (Shaw and Williams, 1994).
- The development of international hotel chains has been partly determined by the requirements of international business travelers. In addition, the ongoing integration of the world economy, which serves to generate more business travel, has resulted in a greater worldwide demand for internationally managed hotels (Shaw and Williams, 1994).
- The brand name recognition demanded by tourists is an important benefit of being part of an international hotel chain. This concept is becoming increasingly important in terms of everyday consumption (Gottdiener, 1997).
- Growth in international travel creates a need for intensive hotel construction. The new globalization of large construction-project funding and financing encourages affiliation with international chains as a way of raising funds, as investors tend to trust the experience and efficiency of such chains.

10.2.5 The Globalization of Tel-Aviv's Accommodation Sector

The global trends affecting the accommodation sector, as discussed above, have also impacted Israel's leading tourist destinations over the past decade. This is especially true of Tel-Aviv, which serves a large segment of Israel's business tourism. Prior to the 1990's, Hilton, Sheraton and Hyatt were the only international hotel chains active in Israel's hotel industry. The political instability in the region, most notably the Arab boycott, delayed the intensive restructuring of this sector in Israel until the 1990's.

Three factors created an increased interest on the part of international hotel chains in entering the Israeli market: the growing inbound tourism to Israel that characterized the past decade, the informal end of the Arab boycott in the mid-1990's and expectations of significant Millennium-based tourism in the year 2000. During a very short period, chains such as Holiday Inn, Days Inn, Howard Johnson, Accor, and Park Inn began to establish footholds in Israel, choosing Tel-Aviv's central tourist district along the city's shoreline as their national headquarters for operations. Simultaneously, hotel chains such as Hyatt, Hilton, and Sheraton, which had been active in Israel prior to these developments, decided to broaden their investments in Israel.

These developments led to a rapid, significant change in hotel management in Tel-Aviv. Figure 10.2 shows how, in less than a decade, the accommodation sector was transformed from being dominated by owner operated hotels in the early 1990's to hotels managed by local and international chains in the late 1990's. This dramatic restructuring took place without a significant increase in the number of hotel rooms in the city, and this reflects the fact that the transformation was caused by changes within the management of existing hotels, and not by new construction.

This shift in ownership and management took place in all of Israel's major tourist destinations, as reflected in Table 10.2. A shift from predominantly owner-operated establishments to either local or international hotel chains is discernible across the board. However, such shifts in places like Eilat and the Dead Sea region were caused mainly by the rapid construction of new large hotels, managed primarily by international chains.

The shift towards international chains in Tel-Aviv and elsewhere primarily impacted large hotels, as smaller, usually older hotels were less attractive for chains due to size and physical condition. However, growing competition and the increasing importance of 'branding' left independent hotel proprietors no choice but to seek affiliation. The outcome was the consolidation and expansion of local hotel chains. For example, the 'Atlas' chain in Tel-Aviv is based on a local company that has been providing individual hotels with management services since the early 1970's. During the second half of the 1990's, three additional Tel-Aviv hotels joined this management company in response to the forces described above. Another strategy open for the smaller and older hotels overlooked by international chains was to join different international hotel consortia. Companies such as 'Best Western International', 'Leading Hotels of the World' and 'Relais and Chateaux' offer independent hotel proprietors membership affiliation in a centralized organization, which enables them both to remain independent and to benefit from the marketing, financial and educational services provided by the company.

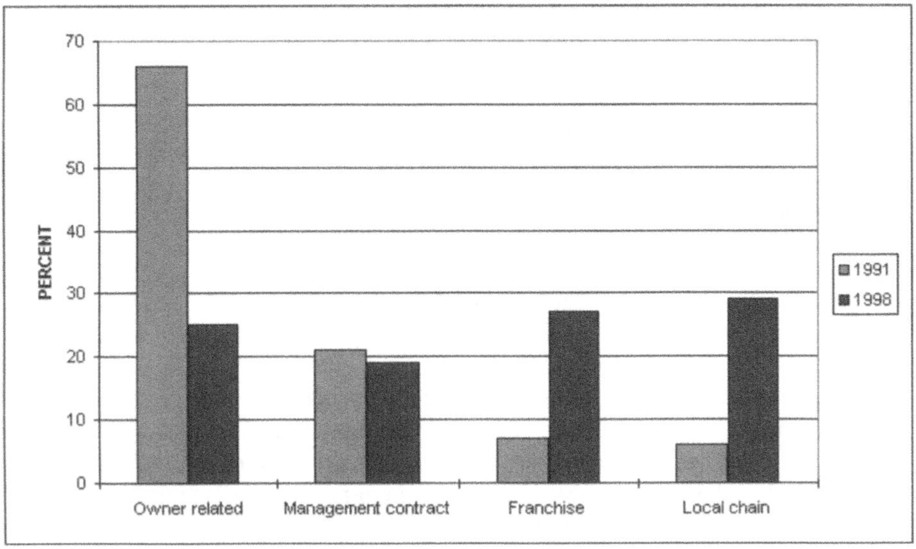

Figure 10.2 Hotel room management-type in Tel-Aviv

Table 10.2 Percentage of rooms managed by international hotel chains in tourist locations in Israel

Location	*1992*	*1993*	*1994*	*1995*	*1996*	*1997*	*1998*	*1999*
Tel-Aviv	36.3	38.6	32.5	32.9	39.8	38.7	42.1	46.6
Jerusalem	29	26.6	21.7	26.1	32.1	41.9	47.5	50.3
Tiberias	0	0	7	6.3	16.4	22.2	33.7	30.2
Dead Sea	0	0	0	28.5	48.2	58.7	45	53.2
Eilat	0	0	5	3.5	12.4	17.6	29.3	29.9

10.2.6 Business Tourism in Tel-Aviv

Cities are centers of economic activity, and the business tourism segment is an important element of urban tourism. Thus, growth in business tourism is one of the most visible manifestations of economic globalization (Rowe, 1994; Shachar, 1995). The business segment is constantly expanding due to the globalization of the world economy, and increasing telecommunications efficiency only serves to entrench this trend (Rowe, 1994). Still, relatively little attention has been paid to this area in the academic literature. Tourism segment spending is extremely significant for cities, as business tourists spend an estimated average of three times more than other types of urban tourists (Rowe, 1994). However, empirical data from Israel suggests that this segment spends only about 20 percent more than other types of tourists (Taskir, 1995; Midgam, 1996; Midgam, 1997). The following section will highlight the role of Tel-Aviv's business tourism segment. Emphasis will be placed on tracing changes in this segment's size over time and on analyzing the consumption patterns of business tourists in terms of attractions visited and spatial behavior.

10.3 SURVEY-BASED FINDINGS

10.3.1 Data Sources

This study has employed two data sources in its analysis of the Tel-Aviv business tourism segment. The first source is the Ministry of Tourism's annual survey of inbound tourists to Israel (see, for example, Midgam, 1997), which is based on a sample of 14,000 questionnaires representing close to 40,000 tourists (both individuals and organized groups). This source's major drawback is its lack of geographic detail and the inability to identify the activities of tourists within a given city. The survey provides data on the expenditure patterns of different tourist segments in Israel, such as people visiting the country for business purposes.

The second source is a representative survey of over 1,700 tourists sampled by the author prior to their departure from Israel at Ben-Gurion International Airport, between September 1998 and March 1999 (Shoval, 2000). This survey resulted in the identification of 307 'business tourists' (including those arriving for conventions and official missions) that had visited Tel-Aviv.

10.3.2 Analysis of Business Tourism Patterns in Tel-Aviv

The growth of Tel-Aviv's business tourism segment during the 1990's appears to reflect the impact of globalization on the surrounding metropolitan region. The Ministry of Tourism surveys conducted in 1994 (Taskir, 1995) and 1996 (Midgam, 1996) identify three main categories of tourist-visits to Tel-Aviv (Figure 10.3):

- *Tel-Aviv Centric* - Tourists that do not stay anywhere in Israel aside from Tel-Aviv.
- *Transient* - Tourists that stay 1-2 nights in Tel-Aviv, usually on the first or last night of their visit to Israel.
- *Mixed-Location* - Tourists that stay in Tel-Aviv for at least three nights. For these tourists, Tel-Aviv is an attraction in and of itself, and not just a place to spend the night.

This data suggests a growing tendency for shorter visits to the city, as well as an increasing number of tourists that are 'Tel-Aviv-centric' and who do not leave the city at any point during their stay. This may be indicative of increasing international business activity in Tel-Aviv, as the pattern of a short stay in Tel-Aviv without visiting any other location is characteristic of business-tourists.

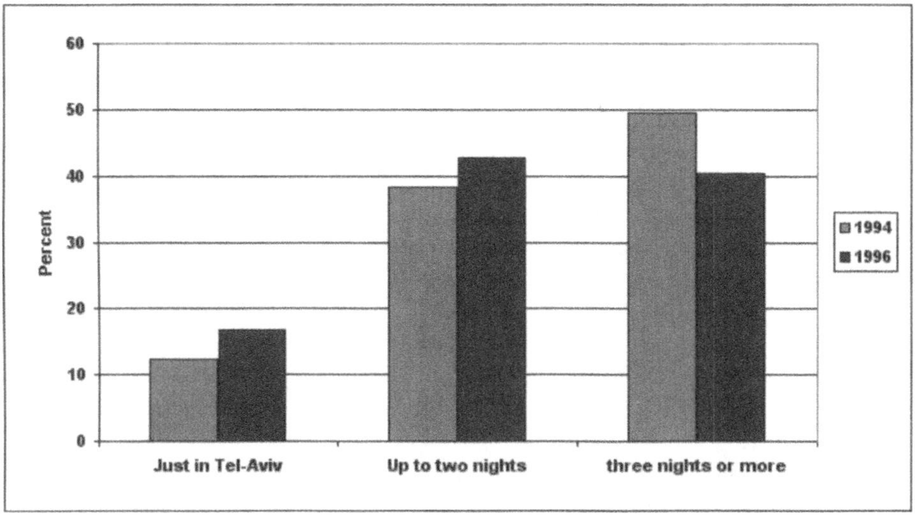

Figure 10.3 The length of visits in Tel-Aviv, 1994 and 1996

Figure 10.4 illustrates trends in business tourism over time. Between 1994 and 1996, the proportion of business visitors out of total visitors increased more than any other visitor category. Based on previous evidence, it can be tentatively suggested that these increases reflect a coalescence of disparate economic trends that have been taking place in the Tel-Aviv economy, all of which impact the volume of business tourism activity. Foremost among these trends has been the emergence of the Tel-Aviv high-tech industry as the primary motor of national economic growth (Chapter 6). In addition, increasingly globalizing tendencies can be observed in other fast-growth and Tel-Aviv-oriented sectors that have begun to integrate into global networks during this period (for example, business services; see Chapter 8). These structural changes have resulted in a host of secondary effects in other tertiary activities, and this has been reflected in the growing volume of Tel Aviv-bound business tourism.

The previously mentioned survey of visitors undertaken at Ben-Gurion Airport facilitates the incorporation of issues of geographic relevance that have generally been excluded from Ministry of Tourism surveys. This data suggests that the main purpose of more than 25 percent of all visits to Tel-Aviv is business (See Figure 10.5). Among the reasons given for visiting the city, 'visiting friends or relatives' was the most popularly cited reason. This can be explained by the fact that Tel-Aviv lies at the center of the largest metropolitan area in Israel, which is home to close to 40 percent of the country's total population.

Data regarding the primary economic activities of business tourists visiting Tel-Aviv shows, not surprisingly, that the high-tech sector represents the single largest area of economic activity among business tourists (35 percent). Hi-tech has been the driving force of economic growth in Israel for the past decade. In contrast, other traditional Israeli export industries, including diamonds, agriculture and tourism, represented only a combined 12 percent of the sample.

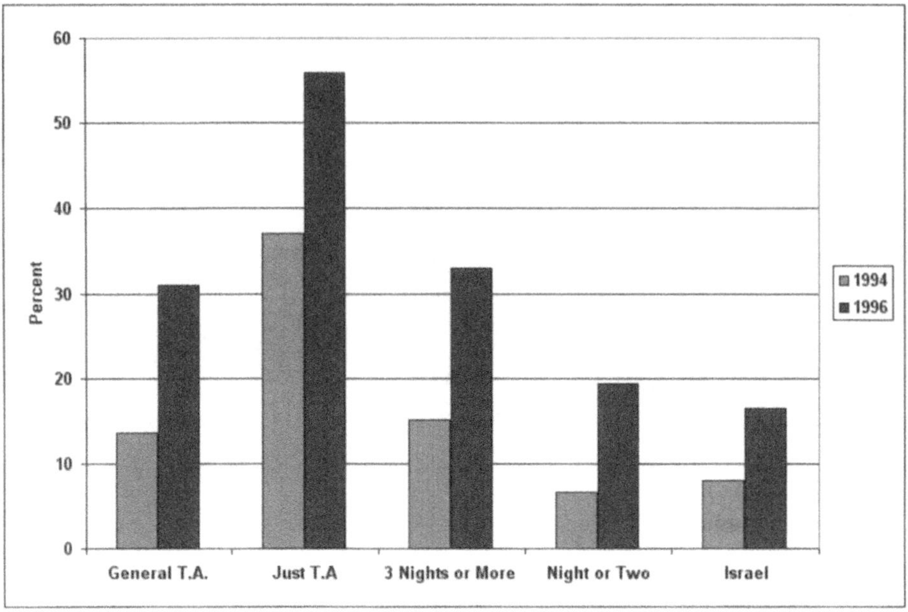

Figure 10.4 Business tourism to Tel-Aviv according to 'type of visit'

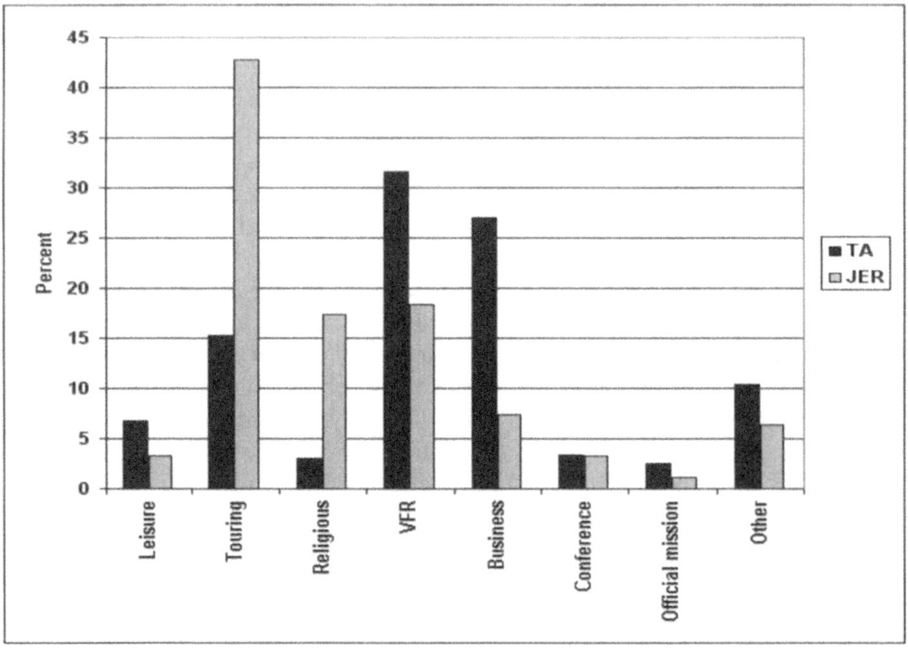

Figure 10.5 Purposes of visits to Tel-Aviv and Jerusalem, as cited by individual tourists

10.3.3 Time-Space Patterns of Business Tourists in Tel-Aviv

Time-space patterns of business tourists in a given metropolitan area enable us to assess the extent to which different parts of the metropolitan area display different levels of 'globalized' activity. In this way, mapping the activity patterns of business visitors reveals patterns of globalization within the Tel Aviv metropolitan area. Such mapping reveals a clearly discernible pattern of business visitors leaving the core of the metropolitan area to its outlying parts during the day and returning to Tel-Aviv during the evening. In practice, this phenomenon is the reverse of the local population's commute to Tel-Aviv in the morning and return home to outlying parts of the metropolitan area in the evening. The intensive activity of business visitors outside the city of Tel-Aviv and in the contiguous towns and suburbs that comprise the metropolitan area illustrates a significant spatial shift in the economic geography of the Tel-Aviv metropolitan area. It appears that, for business visitors, the traditional central business district (CBD) has been replaced by a new CBD located just off the Ayalon freeway, as well as by the outer-metropolitan high-tech nodes of locations such as Herzliya and Ra'anana in the north, Rosh Ha'ayin in the east, and Kiriat-Gat in the south (Felsenstein, 1996). These nodes of high-tech industries are inherently characterized by intense international activity, due to the international nature of high-tech manufacturing and marketing processes. Another factor has been the presence of international companies like Intel, whose plant in Kiriat-Gat currently manufactures the company's newest products, and many other companies, which are considered 'local companies' but are listed on stock exchanges in the United States or Europe.

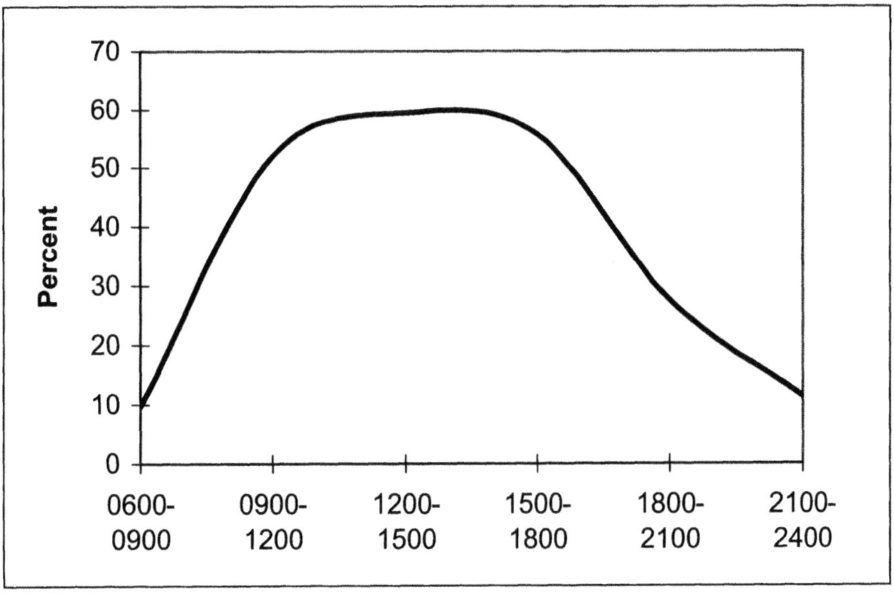

Figure 10.6 The percentage of business tourists outside city limits during different periods of the day (based in Tel-Aviv hotels)

This bipolar spatial pattern of business tourist activity suggests the relative weakness of Tel-Aviv compared to its metropolitan region as a 'day' location for business visitors due to economic globalization. At the same time, however, it also suggests a relative strength in comparison to the outer areas of the metropolitan region as a 'night' location, emphasizing the attraction of Tel-Aviv as a center of entertainment and nightlife.

10.3.4 Tourism and Culture in Tel-Aviv

The increasing importance of culture in contemporary society, together with the increasing importance of tourism as a facet of the economic base of post-industrial cities, has led many cities to adopt strategies of promoting cultural institutions and heritage in an effort to attract tourism (Whitt, 1987). Newman and Smith (2000, p. 5) assert that:

> Cities have been the places where cultural institutions and facilities are located but also where our notions of cultural expression have been forged. However in the past twenty years, the relationship between cultural expression and the city has been turned on its head as cultural expression is thought of less as a socioeconomic practice that follows in the wake of urban life, but is regarded instead as the motor of the urban economy (see Bianchini and Parkinson, 1993). As such a motor, modes of cultural expression have been identified as a quality of a city that allows it to compete within the global economy.

European cities have adopted a culture-based urban tourism strategy, following the example of American cities like Baltimore and Boston in the 1970's (Law 1992, 1993). In this way, urban cultural policy has become increasingly important.

Evidence of globalization in some of Tel-Aviv's main cultural institutions is addressed in Chapter 12. This study, however, focuses on ascertaining the extent to which cultural attractions can be used to augment business tourism. Based on the important status of culture as an economic resource and as a major component of the urban tourism product in post-industrial cities, one would expect culture to account for a significant share of tourist consumption in Tel-Aviv. Empirical evidence based on the survey of in-bound visitors (Shoval, 2000), however, indicates that culture consumption is not a significant element of tourism in Tel-Aviv in general, and that this is especially true of business tourism.

Using visits to major museums as an indicator of consumption of local culture, the findings of this study suggest that business tourists consume less culture than all other major tourist segments in Tel-Aviv. For example, only approximately 4 percent of business tourists visited the Diaspora Museum (see Table 10.3), despite the fact that it is considered to be the most important museum in the city. Still, Table 10.3 indicates that other tourist segments did not visit the museum in high numbers either, and that only slightly more 10 percent of all tourists that visited Tel-Aviv visited the Diaspora Museum as well. Similarly, only 3 percent of business tourists visited the Tel-Aviv Museum of Art, the city's largest art museum that displays important collections of well-known Israeli artists. Again, figures for other tourist segments were not significantly higher.

Contrary to what might have been expected based on the experience of other urban destinations throughout the world, Tel-Aviv's three large museums do not attract significant numbers of visitors. Elsewhere, large museums are considered 'must-see' attractions (Law, 1993). For example, the British Museum in London, the Metropolitan Museum of Art in New York and the Louvre in Paris are among the most visited tourist attractions in each of these cities city (Trew, 1999; Citrinot, 1999a; Citrinot, 1999b). Museums are central components of the urban tourism experience for several reasons. First of all, highly celebrated museums usually become attractions that visitors feel they cannot afford to miss and serve to extend the tourists average stay. This, in turn, results in more money being spent in the city. Second, a museum with constantly changing exhibits attracts repeat visitors, unlike monuments, which tourists tend to visit only once. Galleries also attract repeat visitors, as 'blockbuster' exhibits create constant attraction. Third, in addition to the cultural importance of museum collections, spectacular museums in terms of their architecture have become an attraction in and of themselves, often serving as icons for the cities in which they are located (Hamnett and Shoval, forthcoming).

Table 10.3 Visitors to Tel Aviv museums by main purpose of visit (percentages)

	Business or Conference	*Visiting Friends or Relatives*	*Touring or Sightseeing*	*Leisure*	*Total (n=1000)*
Diaspora Museum	3.7	14.1	15.4	9	10.6
Tel-Aviv Museum of Art	3.1	10.5	5.1	2.6	5.2
'Eretz-Israel' Museum	1	2.5	3.3	0.6	1.8
Helena Rubinstein Pavilion	0.3	1.1	2.2	0.6	1

Source: Shoval, 2000.

The overall findings discussed above point to the conclusion that tourists, overall, come to Tel-Aviv to 'play', and not in search of cultural attractions. This city-based division of activity was succinctly formulated by the Fodor's tourist guidebook: "Tel-Aviv plays, Haifa works, Jerusalem prays" (Fodor's, 1996). A possible explanation is that tourists come to Tel-Aviv in search of either work or leisure - not 'culture'. Tel-Aviv's relative proximity to major cultural and historical attractions such as Jerusalem, and even Nazareth, enables tourists to enjoy both worlds: the cultural heritage of the 'Holyland' by day, and the entertainment and leisure of the modern metropolis by night.

10.4 CONCLUSIONS AND POLICY IMPLICATIONS

From the evidence presented in this chapter, it is clear that Tel-Aviv's tourism industry has undergone a major reorientation, brought on by increased globalization of the local economy during the 1990's. It is interesting to note that these changes have taken place while the overall volume of tourists, person-nights and new hotel construction in the city has remained relatively static. Local policy makers have not adopted strategies of intensive tourist development since the construction of the 'hotel row' along the Tel-Aviv shoreline during the 1960's and 1970's. As an emerging node in global networks, Tel-Aviv is clearly in need of a tourism infrastructure in order to maintain this status. This calls for a well-articulated development strategy similar to those being pursued by other cities worldwide. On this basis, it would seem that an expected policy geared towards promoting business tourism in Tel-Aviv should focus on three key issues.

The first relates to hotel construction. Due to its hotels' relatively high occupancy rate throughout the year, Tel-Aviv is in need of several thousand new hotel rooms, in addition to the 6,000 rooms that already exist. Such an addition to Tel-Aviv's hotel room stock would enable the city to compete nationally and internationally for conventions and trade fairs and for hosting the growing business segment. The CBD's geographical shift from its traditional location to a new location alongside the Ayalon highway also needs to be augmented by additional hotel construction. Presently, only one hotel (part of the Sheraton chain) exists in the area, which is rapidly emerging as the main business node of both the city and the country (see Chapter 3).

The second issue on which new policy should focus is relocation of the city's convention center. Today's convention center is spatially disconnected from the city's business and tourism areas, and a more suitable location might enable Tel-Aviv to compete seriously on the national, regional and global levels of this growing market. For this reason, the appropriate step appears to be relocation, not expansion and upgrading of the existing center. Industry analysts and academic literature suggest that venue location is of critical importance to the success of convention centers (Law, 1993), as event organizers and participants expect proximity to restaurants, shopping areas and tourist attractions, as well as accessibility to accommodation. Even a planned expansion of the present center is unlikely to succeed in providing the external economies so vital for successful centers.

The third and final issue relates to strengthening the city's cultural attractions. The growing importance of culture in contemporary society, together with the increasing significance of tourism within the economic base of post-industrial cities, has resulted in the construction of new urban cultural attractions around the world. A good example of this phenomenon is the construction of 'flagship museums' in various cities (Hamnett and Shoval, forthcoming). Such museums are typically characterized by spectacular urban architecture, as in the cases of the Guggenheim Museum in Bilbao, the Getty Museum in Los Angeles, the Musee d'Orsay in Paris and the New Modern Tate in London. These museums have given rise to a new form of urban cultural consumption that incorporates architecture, art and spectacle. Based on their radical and dramatic design, it can be argued that these buildings function as tourist attractions in and of themselves, in addition to the attraction of the art they contain. As previously noted, Tel-Aviv's three leading museums hardly fill this role. A hallmark cultural institution can give an emerging urban center an enormous boost, raising its global visibility and augmenting its role as a center of economic activity.

REFERENCES

Ashworth, G.J. & Tunbridge, J.E. (1990). *The tourist-historic city*. London and New York: Belhaven.

Bailey, M. (1998). *The international hotel industry: Corporate strategies and global opportunities*. London: Travel & Tourism Intelligence.

Bianchini, F. & Parkinson, M. (1993). *Cultural policy and urban regeneration: The West European experience*. Manchester: Manchester University Press.

Braun, B.M. (1992). The economic contribution of conventions: The case of Orlando, Florida. *Journal of Travel Research, 30 (3)*, 32-37.

Brendon, P. (1991). *Thomas Cook: 150 years of popular tourism*. London: Secker & Warburg.

Center for Economic and Social Research (2000). *Tel-Aviv-Yafo statistical yearbook 1999*, 39.

Central Bureau of Statistics (1998). *Tourism 1997*. Jerusalem.

Central Bureau of Statistics (1999). *Tourism 1998*. Jerusalem.

Central Bureau of Statistics and Ministry of Tourism (2001). *Tourism and hotel services statistics quarterly, 29*.

Citrinot, L. (1999a). *Paris. Travel and tourism intelligence city reports, 1 (1)*, 53-75.

Citrinot, L. (1999b). New York. *Travel and tourism intelligence city reports, 1 (3)*, 53-73.

Clancy, M. (1998). Commodity, chains, services and development: Theory and preliminary evidence from the tourism industry. *Review of International Political Economy, 5 (1)*, 122-148.

Felsenstein, D. (1996). High technology firms and locational choice in Israel, a look at the determinants. *Geografiska Annaler, 78B (1)*, 43-55.

Fenich, G.G. (1994). An assessment of whether the Convention Center in New York is successful as a tool for economic development. *Economic Development Quarterly, 8 (3)*, 245-255.

Fodor's (1996). *Exploring Israel*. New York: Fodor's Travel Publications.

Go, F.M. & Pine, R. (1995). *Globalisation strategy in the hotel industry*. London and New York: Routledge.

Gottdiener, M. (1997). *The theming of America: Dreams, visions and commercial spaces*. Boulder (Colorado): Westview Press.

Ha'aretz Daily Newspaper. Various daily editions.

Hamnett, C. & Shoval N. (Forthcoming). Museums as 'flagships' of urban development. In L.M. Hoffman, D. Judd & S.S. Fainstein (Eds.), *Tourism and regulation in the millennial city: The intersection of culture, politics and economy in the 21st century*. Oxford: Blackwell.

Johnson, M. (1997). Hungary's hotel industry in transition, 1960-1996. *Tourism Management, 18 (7)*, 441-452.

Judd, D.R. & Fainstein, S.S. (Eds.) (1999). *The tourist city*. New Haven and London: Yale University Press.

Law, C.M. (1992). Urban tourism and its contribution to economic regeneration *Urban Studies, 29 (3-4)*, 599-618.

Law, C.M. (1993). *Urban tourism: Attracting visitors to large cities*. London and New York: Mansell.

Law, C.M. (1996). *Tourism in major cities*. London: Routledge.

Mazanec, J.A. (Ed.) (1997). *International city tourism: Analysis and strategy*. London and Washington: Pinter.

McNeill, D. (2000). McGuggenisation? National identity and globalisation in the Basque country. *Political Geography, 19 (4)*, 473-494.

Midgam - Consulting and Research Ltd. (1996). *Tourist's survey: March 1995 - February 1996*. Jerusalem: Ministry of Tourism.

Midgam - Consulting and Research Ltd. (1997). *Tourist's survey: January - December 1996*. Jerusalem: Ministry of Tourism.

Milne, S. & Pohlmann, C. (1998). Continuity and change in the hotel sector: Some evidence from Montreal. In D. Ioannides & K.G. Debbage (Eds.), *The economic geography of the tourist industry: A supply-side analysis*. London and New York: Routledge.
Milne, S. & Gill, K. (1998). Distribution technologies and destination development: Myths and realities. In D. Ioannides & K.G. Debbage (eds.), *The economic geography of the tourist industry: A supply-side analysis*. London and New York: Routledge.
Newman, P. & Smith, I. (2000). Cultural production, place and politics on the South Bank of the Thames. *International Journal of Urban and Regional Research, 24 (1)*, 9-24.
Page, S.J. (1995). *Urban tourism*. London and New York: Routledge.
Pizam, A. & Mansfeld, Y. (Eds.) (1996). *Tourism, crime and international security issues*. Chichester: Wiley.
Ritzer, G. (1996). *The McDonaldization of society*. Thousands Oaks, CA: Pine Forge Press.
Ritzer, G. & Liska, A. (1997). McDisneyization and 'post-tourism': Complementary perspectives on contemporary tourism. In C. Rojek & J. Urry (Eds.), *Touring cultures: Transformation of travel and theory*. London and New York: Routledge.
Rowe, I.V. (1994). *International business travel: A changing profile*. London: The Economist Intelligence Unit.
Shachar, A. (1995). Metropolitan areas: Economic globalisation and urban tourism. In A. Montanari & A.M. Williams (Eds.), *European tourism: Regions, spaces and restructuring*. Chichester: John Wiley & Sons.
Shachar, A. & Shoval, N. (1999). Tourism in Jerusalem: A place to pray. In D. Judd & S.S. Fainstein (Eds.), *The tourist city*. New Haven: Yale University Press.
Shaw, G. & Williams, A.M. (1994). *Critical issues in tourism: A geographical perspective*. Oxford: Blackwell.
Short, J.R. & Yeong-Hyun, K. (1999). *Globalisation and the city*. Harlow (UK): Longman.
Shoval, N. (2000). *Segmented and overlapping tourist spaces: Jerusalem and Tel-Aviv case studies*. Unpublished Ph.D. dissertation, Department of Geography, The Hebrew University of Jerusalem.
Shoval, N. & Cohen-Hattab, K. (2001). Urban hotel development patterns in the face of political shifts. *Annals of Tourism Research, 28 (4)*, 908-925.
Smeral, E. (1998). The impact of globalisation on small and medium enterprises: New challenges for tourism policies in European countries. *Tourism Management, 19 (4)*, 371-380.
Swarbrooke, J. (2001). Organization of tourism at the destination. In S. Wahab & C. Cooper (Eds.), *Tourism in the age of globalisation*. London and New York: Routledge.
Taskir - Survey and Research Ltd. (1995). *Survey of tourists departing from Israel 1994*. Jerusalem: Ministry of Tourism.
Trew, J. (1999). London. *Travel and tourism intelligence city reports, 1 (2)*, 37-63.
van den Berg, L., van der Borg, J. & van der Meer, J. (1995). *Urban tourism: Performance and strategies in eight European cities*. Aldershot: Avebury.
Vanhove, N. (2001). Globalisation of tourism demand, global distribution systems and marketing. In S. Wahab & C. Cooper (Eds.), *Tourism in the age of globalisation*. London and New York: Routledge.
Wahab, S. & Cooper, C. (Eds.) (2001). *Tourism in the age of globalisation*. London and New York: Routledge.
Whitt, A.J. (1987). Mozart in the metropolis: The arts coalition and the urban growth machine. *Urban Affairs Quarterly, 23 (1)*, 15-36.

HOLGER RUDOLPH AND RALPH STEINERT

11. INTERNATIONAL TOURISM IN THE FRANKFURT/RHEIN-MAIN REGION

11.1 INTRODUCTION

> I'm in the banking district. I shut my eyes, then open them again. Where am I? Tokyo? Hamburg? New York? It doesn't matter. And they wonder why so few tourists visit the city. (Mathias Altenburg)

That's what author Matthias Altenburg, a Frankfurt native himself, wrote in 1999, in response to his self-posed question, "Why should anybody come here when it looks like everywhere else anyway?" But tourists do come to Frankfurt, and 1998 was a record breaking year with more than 2 million. Tourists come to Frankfurt neither for its tourist attractions nor because the city 'looks different' to any other place. They come to attend trade fairs and conventions, and to visit business associates.

'Business tourists' have been visiting Frankfurt since the 13th century, when the city first began hosting trade fairs of international importance. And for just as long, Frankfurt has also been a leading financial center. Today, Frankfurt is one of the world's leading trade fair locations, and, with over 350 banks, including the Central European Bank and the German Federal Bank, it is also one of the world's most important international financial centers (see Chapter 5). These elements, together with the conventions and congresses that have evolved into a crucial component of urban tourism, compose Frankfurt's contemporary tourism base. In fact, regular tourists play a very minor role in comparison.

Frankfurt's most valuable tourism prerequisite is its convenient location, based primarily on Frankfurt Airport (see Chapter 7). Tourism throughout the entire Rhein-Main region benefits from the airport as well. Even though regional tourism is influenced primarily by its larger cities, especially Frankfurt, the region contains other destinations that attract tourists as well. Most influential in this realm is health resort tourism. This sector, which also possesses a unique historical significance, is currently undergoing a period of restructuring. Despite the difficulties they have faced, spas continue to function as tourist destinations in the Rhein-Main region.

This chapter will discuss international tourism in Frankfurt and the Rhein-Main region. Tourism denotes highly differentiated value chains and a resulting heterogeneous market of travel related services. Destination determines both travel type and reason, and tourism service supply and demand can be expected to reflect structures that are dependent on, and characteristic of the region being considered. This chapter will demonstrate, on one hand, how international tourism serves as an indicator of the role of Frankfurt and the Rhein-Main region as a junction in global

D. Felsenstein et al. (eds.),
Emerging Nodes in the Global Economy: Frankfurt and Tel Aviv Compared, 213–235.

business and, on the other hand, how tourism is the result of driving forces in other sectors of the region, which are transforming the region's role within the European and global contexts. To this end, we will first examine basic data concerning tourist demand. It is well known that Germany has a decentralized urban system, and, as a result, international urban tourism is not concentrated in one single city, rather in approximately five. Based on its role as a business capital, however, Frankfurt occupies a unique position in the 'competition between cities' for international tourists. Next, this chapter will examine the industries that contribute most critically to the region's attraction of tourists: trade fairs, congresses and meeting centers - facilities that together attract great numbers of business travelers. It will also discuss the changing role of health resort tourism in the region's smaller cities, which once constituted an extremely prominent component of the tourist industry.

From the perspective of tourism, the most important element of a destination's infrastructure, aside from a good transportation infrastructure, is its range of overnight stays. On one hand, hotels in globalized regions are followers, responding to accommodation demands. On the other hand, they serve as a driving force behind international tourism by developing their own strategies. For this reason, the third focus of this chapter will be the structure of the region's hotel sector and the strategies employed by international hotel chains in order to restructure this sector.

This chapter will not, however, examine the entire scope of tourism-based service activities that have developed throughout the region; an extensive infrastructure of tourist advisory and arrangement services exists in the region as well. Consider, for example, the region's numerous airline offices and the offices of more than 60 foreign travel agencies, as well as the fact that the second largest package tour company in Europe - C&N (now Thomas Cook AG) - was formed there. Still, this chapter will focus primarily on tourism demand and the hotel sector.

While it is true that international tourism to the Frankfurt/Rhein-Main region is based mainly on business travel, the role of 'culture' as a tourist attraction must not be underestimated (see Chapters 10 and 12). The fact that the region is home to only a limited number of transnational company headquarters, which usually serve to attract, almost forcibly, a certain number of international business travelers, provides strong support for this contention. Trade fairs, conventions and congresses, which attract primarily business travelers to Frankfurt, are much more flexible attractions. The organizers of such events are becoming increasingly concerned with the cultural activities that the city has to offer, in order to differentiate their particular event from that of the competition. In an analogy to new urban politics (Häussermann and Siebel, 1993), one can regard this phenomenon as a 'festivalization'. This chapter will conclude with a critical look at the region's cultural activities and events that could possibly attract increased international tourism.

11.2 INTERNATIONAL BUSINESS TRAVEL AS THE BACKBONE OF TOURISM IN FRANKFURT

11.2.1 The Structure of Tourism

Almost 30 percent of the foreign overnight tourists who came to Germany in 1998 visited one of the 'top five' German cities: Berlin, Munich, Hamburg, Frankfurt and Cologne. In all five cities, however, the average duration of stay was short, usually less than two days (see Figure 11.1). The short stay and large number of foreign visitors reflect, not surprisingly, the important role played by business tourism in all of these cities. Still, the organizations responsible for tourism in these places have been unable to make detailed statements. A survey carried out by the recently privatized Frankfurt Tourism and Congress Company (TCF) found that 70 percent of hotel guests were traveling for business reasons. In Berlin, the figure was 50 percent, and in Hamburg, 40 percent. Statistics regarding same day visitors provide an even clearer picture. For example, while only 10 percent of Berlin's same-day visitors can be classified as business tourists, same-day visitors in Frankfurt account for an equal percentage as tourists who stay overnight. One reason for this is the city's close proximity to Frankfurt Airport, and the fact that the city is so well connected to virtually all other important European cities that even one-day meetings with international participants can be conveniently held in Frankfurt. Visitors from Paris, London, Stockholm and Rome can fly to Frankfurt in the morning, and fly home in the evening.

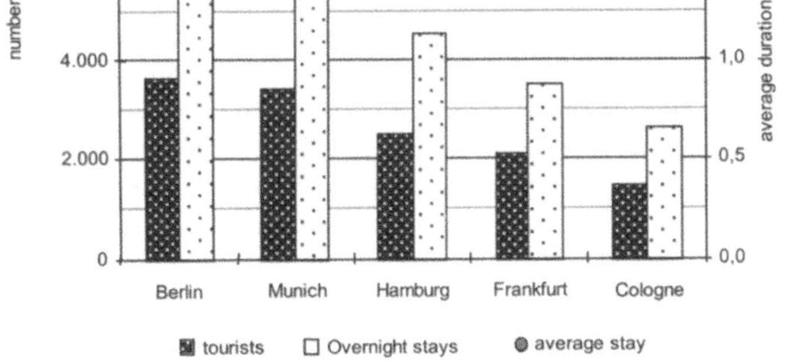

Figure 11.1 Total overnight stays, tourists, and average duration of stay in Germany's top-5 cities, 1998

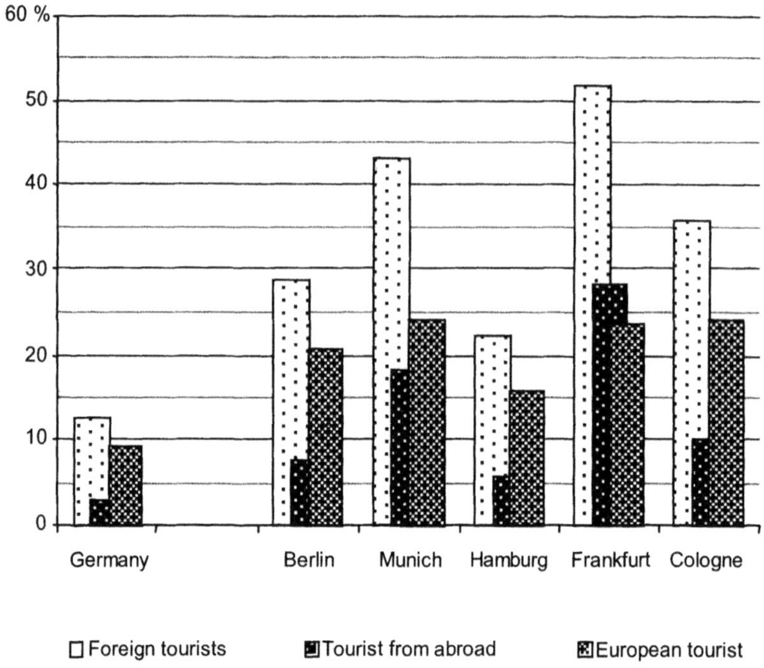

Figure 11.2 The share of overnight stays by foreign tourists in Germany's top five cities, 1998

Among Germany's top five cities, Frankfurt stands out as the city with the highest percentage of foreign guests (over 50 percent). In addition, the percentage of overnight stays by guests from other continents is higher in Frankfurt than in all other cities, and, at 1.68 days, the average duration of these stays is the shortest. What is not so obvious from Figures 11.1 and 11.2 is the fact that Frankfurt has the highest intensity of tourism, with 5.5 overnight tourist stays per inhabitant. These figures reflect the importance of business travel resulting from the global economic networks present in Frankfurt. Besides visitors from the United States and Great Britain, who account for a large portion of guests in all the cities in question, other cities are visited by people from neighboring European countries: Scandinavians in Hamburg, Scandinavians and Eastern Europeans in Berlin, Dutch and Belgian visitors in Cologne, and Austrians, Italians, and Swiss visitors in Munich. This also includes tourists from neighboring countries visiting these cities on weekend excursions. In fact, in terms of privately motivated tourism, Hamburg, Munich, and Berlin enjoy a considerable advantage over Frankfurt. Hamburg is a well established destination, with musicals attracting weekend tourists from all parts of Germany. According to regularly issued questionnaires, Berlin, Munich and Hamburg are by far the most popular destinations among tourists, while Frankfurt is located towards the bottom of the list. Tourism in Frankfurt benefits primarily from the city's role as a European traffic junction, and tourists from neighboring countries therefore play a less important role. As a result, only two neighboring countries are among the top ten nations whose citizens visit Germany the most. The countries of origin accounting for the most visitors are, in descending order, the United States, Great Britain, Japan, Italy and Spain. The ten most represented countries of origin also include the Arabian Gulf States and China. After a downturn in tourism in the mid 1990's, figures for visitors and overnight stays have started to climb over the past few years. With 2.1 million visitors and 3.5 million overnight stays, 1998 was a record-breaking year. Fluctuations in the numbers of visitors and over night stays from the United States and Japan reflect clear parallels between the economic situation in a tourist's country of origin and his or her travel activities (see Figure 11.3). This also applies to East Asian countries, albeit to a lesser degree.

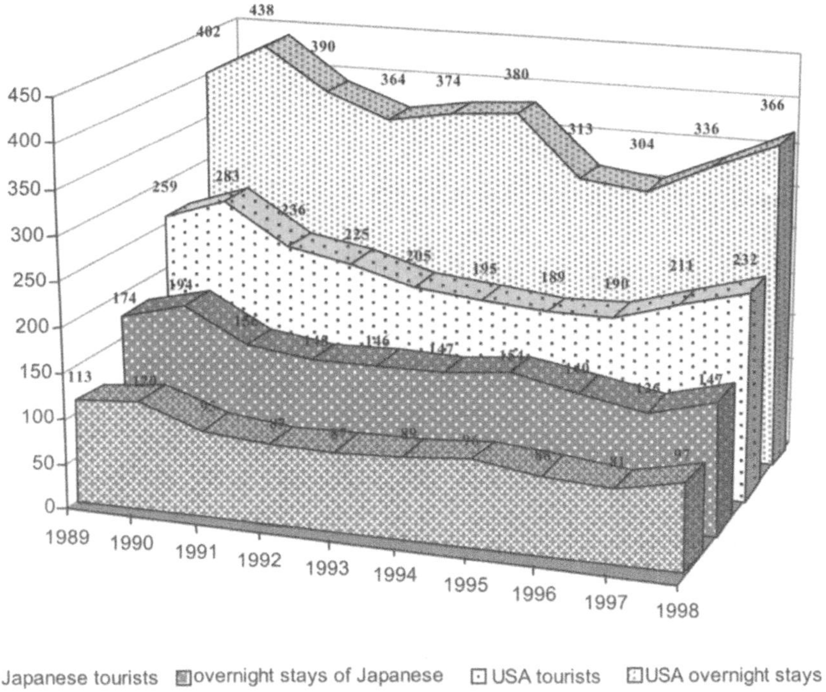

Figure 11.3 Number of visitors and overnight stays in Frankfurt from the United States and Japan, 1989-1998

Frankfurt's pattern of overnight stays during the course of the year provides further indication that business tourism is the city's most important type of tourism. This pattern is by far more stable in Frankfurt than in other large German cities or throughout Germany as a whole. Figure 11.4 indicates that spring and autumn constitute the annual high points of tourist activity in large German cities, as privately motivated city vacations are generally undertaken as shorter, second or third vacations of the year. The peak of Germany's overall tourism pattern is the summer, which is the primary vacationing season. Over the past few years in Frankfurt, trade fairs, conventions and congresses have been evenly distributed throughout the year, and this, in turn, has resulted in an even distribution of overnight stays.

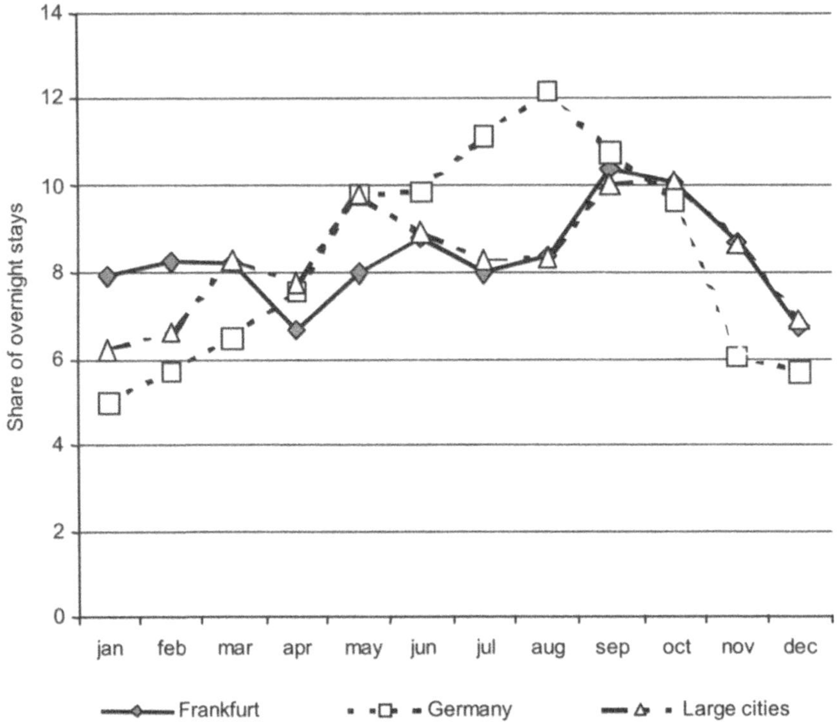

Figure 11.4 Seasonal variation of overnight stays in Frankfurt, as compared to other cities and the German average, 1998

Data regarding Frankfurt alone, however, does not provide a sufficient understanding of tourism in the Rhein-Main area as a whole. Unlike Berlin, Hamburg and Munich, Frankfurt is located in a more polycentric region, in which the large cities of Wiesbaden, Mainz, Darmstadt and Offenbach perform central functions. Naturally, this applies to tourism as well. Wiesbaden, Mainz and the health resorts around the edge of Taunus possess their own attraction for general and business tourists alike. These cities fulfill complementary functions alongside of Frankfurt, and a good example of this dynamic can be witnessed during large trade fairs.

Despite the existence of spas and health resorts in a few locations, this type of tourism no longer plays the central role it did in the past. For example, during the days of the German Empire, health resorts served primarily as meeting places for diplomats. Today, aside from a number of health resorts, the region's countryside plays a quantitatively minor role in Rhein-Main area tourism. The greatest influence on tourism in the Frankfurt/Rhein-Main area is undoubtedly big-city tourism. While the five large cities of Frankfurt, Wiesbaden, Mainz, Darmstadt and Offenbach account for approximately one-third of the region's population, they receive 45 percent of all overnight stays and 57 percent of total guests. Even more marked is the number of foreign guests visiting these large cities, especially Frankfurt: in fact, three out of every four foreign guests staying overnight in the region do so in Frankfurt (see Figure 11.5). Over the past few years, however, Frankfurt has been losing its lead, and the surrounding areas have made gains. The city of Offenbach and the district of Gross-Gerau, both of which are situated near the airport, have benefited from this dynamic.

Figure 11.5 Overnight stays in the districts of the Frankfurt/Rhein-Main region, 1998

Health resort tourism differs fundamentally from big city tourism. Health resorts in the region attract one-fifth of all overnight stays, and guests tend to stay for a longer period of time, averaging 6.5 days. Health resorts' share of foreign guests is extremely small - even lower than the total German average. In short, virtually nothing remains of the former international importance of spas. It should also be noted that spas closer to Frankfurt (Bad Vilbel, Bad Homburg and Bad Soden) possess a more 'city-influenced' guest structure, characterized by relatively short average stays and an above average percentage of foreign guests.

Tourism in the Rhein-Main region is dominated by Frankfurt. On the whole, Frankfurt's overnight guests include a high percentage of foreign guests, especially from the United States and Asia, and a short average duration of stay. Frankfurt is also at the top of the list when comparing numbers of foreign guests on the international level.

11.2.2 Tourist Destinations

Trade Fairs

The oldest 'tourist' destination in Frankfurt is its trade fair. Trade fairs have served as one of the most important magnets for international business travelers for centuries. In 1240 and 1330, Frankfurt received the Emperor's Trade Fair Privilege and, since then, has hosted autumn and spring trade fairs on a regular basis. Even then, trade fairs were important to tourism, as they resulted in a temporary doubling of the city's population. Today, approximately one-third of all business people staying overnight in Frankfurt (about a half million people each year) attend trade fairs. In 1997, over 2.3 million trade fair visitors were recorded - many of them same-day visitors - with close to 20 percent hailing from foreign countries. This figure can be compared to the almost 44,000 exhibitors, more than half of which are from foreign countries. Large trade fairs held in Frankfurt include the International Automobile Show, the Frankfurt Book Trade Fair and the Achema. Based on number of exhibitors, Frankfurt was by far the largest trade fair location in Germany in 1999. In terms of turnover, Frankfurt was second only to Düsseldorf, and in terms of number of visitors, it was second only to Hannover. These statistics reflect the stiff competition between trade fair locations (see Chapter 9).

Frankfurt's large number of foreign exhibitors highlights the international orientation of the city's trade fairs. Together with Cologne, Munich, Duesseldorf and Hannover, Frankfurt is engaged in global competition with leading trade fair cities like Paris, London, Milan and Birmingham. German trade fairs still lag behind these leading cities based on trade fair size (exhibitors, visitors and rented exhibit space), but they emerge as world leaders in terms of international exhibitors and visitors (Cuadrado-Roura and Rubalca-Bermejo, 1998). Competition on the international market, however, continues to grow, as many European and non-European cities are getting increasingly involved in trade fairs in order to better position themselves as international competitors. During trade fairs in Frankfurt, hotel rooms as far away as Limburg and Marburg (or throughout a 100 km radius around the city) are in demand. For example, 30 percent of overnight guests in Mainz hotels during trade fairs are fair participants (Schreiber, 1990).

Conventions and Congresses

After trade fairs, conventions and congresses are the second most important component of Frankfurt's tourism industry. The city has a 'congress industry' that produced a total of DM43 billion, reflecting total direct convention related expenditures, travel expenditures (DM8 billion), the monetary turnover of host buildings (DM10 billion) and indirect turnover generated in other branches (restaurants, retail trade, taxis, etc.). Turnover generated by congresses and conventions account for more than one percent of Frankfurt's Gross Domestic Product (German Convention Bureau, 1995). The importance of knowledge exchange, and communication has increased, along with the internationalization of business, the fast paced development of technology and increasingly close political relationships. A great variety of bodies serve as congress organizers, including associations, companies, political parties, state and local institutions, and scientific, cultural and religious organizations.

Competition within the congress industry is becoming increasingly intense. Not only has the demand for potential congress venues expanded, but so has supply, as more and more cities have come to recognize this burgeoning market. Organizers must take many factors into consideration when deciding where to hold a congress. They must ensure the existence of a reliable, extensive transportation system (airports, high-speed rail transportation, well connected highways, etc.), a sufficient number of diverse hotels, attractive cultural activities, and, of course, a modern convention center that meets their needs and expectations. In terms of these 'hard' location factors, German cities, including Frankfurt, enjoy an excellent reputation on the international market. In terms of 'soft' factors, however, things are not as rosy, as foreign convention participants have noted the absence of improvisation possibilities, hospitality and imagination in Frankfurt (German Convention Bureau, 1995). While a current analysis of the location choices of congress organizers is not yet available, Germany ranked fourth after the United States, France and Great Britain in the international congress market in 1997 (Hank-Haase, 1999), controlling a world market share of 5.5 percent. Berlin was the only German city ranked among the 25 leading congress cities, in thirteenth place. Among German cities alone, Frankfurt ranked sixth, behind Berlin, Munich, Cologne, and Bonn.

Still, the overall number of events in Frankfurt has increased by 25 percent during the last five years. The TCF has been compiling congress market statistics for Frankfurt for quite a few years. In 1998, Frankfurt was the site of over 55,000 conventions, 18 percent of which had an international orientation. In addition, more than half of all convention participants came from foreign countries. The majority of Frankfurt's conventions were single day events, while only 15 percent lasted more than one day. The opening of the Congress Center, located close to the fair grounds, resulted in a significant increase in the number of large events with over 2,000 participants (TCF, 1998).

Frankfurt's competitive advantage in hosting conventions and congresses lies to a great measure in its convenient location. Frankfurt airport is one of the most important centers of European air traffic, and the city's central location within the high speed train network must also be noted. In fact, 20 percent of all events in the area take place either at the airport itself or in the vicinity of the main railway station. Frankfurt's role as an international junction is another factor explaining the city's extremely high percentage of foreign convention participants (Hampel, 1999a). All this makes Frankfurt ideal for short international meetings. The situation is not ideal, however, when considering the role of tourism within the overall regional economy, as visitors tend to spend more time and money in the city only during larger, longer events.

A second element attracting convention and congress organizers is trade fairs, and the trend of scheduling trade fairs to coincide with conventions and congresses is on the rise. This includes everything from small branch-specific seminars of a specific exhibitor to international congresses. A good example of this phenomenon was the two-day international technical congress of the IAA, which had 400 participants. Many trade fair companies have integrated congress organization into their own sphere of work. In fact, Frankfurt's trade fair company also runs the new congress center. Along with the continuing growth of the market segment of trade fairs coinciding with conventions, and conventions coinciding with branch specific seminars, the position of congresses is becoming increasingly related to the position of trade fairs (AUMA, 1999).

A third location-oriented factor of conventions is the presence of resident businesses and institutions. With the European Central Bank itself located in the city, Frankfurt as a venue for the European Banking Congress, would seem a natural choice. The stock-broker association of the German book trade and the association of the German Automobile Industry also reside in Frankfurt, and both host large trade fairs and accompanying conventions. The University and other research establishments are also important location-oriented factors in Frankfurt (Hank-Haase, 1992).

Frankfurt's Congress Center, located on the fair grounds, is at the top of the list of convention venues in the city. In total, 70 suppliers offer 710 venues suited for events from up to 8,000 participants, including eleven relatively large venues that have auditorium facilities that can hold 1,000 people each. The new Congress Center also filled a market niche by offering a venue for events with over 2,000 participants, but an auditorium that can accommodate 20,000 people is still needed if Frankfurt wants to compete internationally for the market's largest events. Plans for an event auditorium in the 'Europa Quarter' near the fair grounds, where the freight station was once located, may provide a solution to this problem. However a major convention facility needs concomitant development in terms of hotel accommodation and the availability of hotels in Frankfurt is therefore of great importance to the city's convention industry.

Conventions in the Rhein-Main area, however, are not held only in Frankfurt. Other cities in the region are also making efforts to take part in the growth of the convention market and to attract well-paying visitors. This is true primarily for cities with no other potential tourist attraction, as current discussions regarding the construction of a convention center in Hanau illustrates. Health resorts are also trying to gain a foothold in the convention center market by offering combination business-health vacations. Large hotels in the health resort towns of Wiesbaden and Bad Soden provide accommodations primarily for convention visitors. Along with Frankfurt, Mainz and Wiesbaden are the largest convention center cities in the region. In Mainz, this is mainly due to the IBM training center located in the city (Schreiber, 1990).

Other Business Tourist Destinations

The other 40 percent of Frankfurt's business tourism can be categorized as classic individual business tourism. Due to the increasing globalization and internationalization of business, this type of tourism has expanded significantly over the past few years. Some cities have evolved into junctions within global networks, where the activities of large international companies are managed. In result, these cities require the high ranking service and telecommunication options that are integral to the performance of global business activities (Sassen, 1994). Business travel occurs between these global cities, that is, between finance centers and headquarters of multinational companies, as well as between global cities and regional headquarters of multinational companies. In addition, business travel between production centers throughout the world must also be taken into consideration. No detailed statistics exist documenting this steady stream of business travel. It can be assumed, however, that travel is greatest between global cities and between main headquarters and regional headquarters, as the importance of 'face to face' communication in decision-making (primarily at the middle and higher management levels) increases and becomes ever more complex (Shachar, 1995; Dicken, 1998).

Support for this assumption in Frankfurt and the Rhein-Main area can be found in tourist data and the regional business structure. As several chapters of this book illustrate, Frankfurt is Europe's most important financial center, an international node of high level services and an international management center. For example, 13 of the 50 largest American companies in Germany are located in the region, including Opel (in Rüsselsheim), Procter and Gamble (in Schwalbach) and Nike (in Mörfelden) (American Chamber of Commerce, 1999). Taking tourist demands into account, the large number of foreign visitors and the structure of this tourist segment supports the contention that Frankfurt, as a globalizing city, draws international business travel.

Culture and Health Resorts

Private tourism plays a minor role in Frankfurt. The city does contain buildings of historical importance (for example, Paul's Church and the Cathedral), and its wide array of cultural activities, including museums, opera, theater, and the renovated 'Alter Oper' (Old Opera House) are of a level comparable to the standards found in other similar large cities. However, despite these sites and the presence of attractions of international importance, such as the Museum of Modern Art and the Städel Museum, hardly any tourist agencies include Frankfurt in their program. The element missing is exciting tourist attractions, or 'events' - a term that has evolved as an industry buzzword. Some attempts have been made to introduce such attractions to Frankfurt. In the 1980's, the city invested in arts and culture under the leadership of Hilmar Hoffman, the head of the city's Department for Cultural Affairs. The old opera house that had been destroyed in the war was rebuilt, and now serves as an event venue for concerts and conventions. In addition, many museums were built on the southern bank of the Main River, and, together with the museums already present in the area, they formed the 'Museum River Bank'. Another major goal of that period was the reconstruction of the central part of 'old' Frankfurt, which had been destroyed during the war. The reconstruction of buildings from the Middle Ages at the Römerberg was meant to reveal a sort of 'medieval' heart of the city. Important exhibitions hosted by one of the museums built in the 1980's (the Schirn Museum) attracted visitors as well. In addition, two attempts were made to establish a permanent music festival (in Offenbach and Niedernhausen near Wiesbaden) during the 1990's, but both attempts failed. Currently, all hopes hinge on the establishment of an 'Urban Entertainment Center' to fill the gap, and it is believed that a centrally located shopping and entertainment district near the main railway station and the fair grounds should be developed. Among other components, two hotels, a multiplex movie theater, a shopping center and other types of entertainment establishments are being planned.

Today's efforts do not aim to compete with the already well known tourist attractions of Germany and Europe. Survey results show that German competitors alone possess an extremely significant advantage over Frankfurt in terms of visitor numbers (DFV, 1995): almost three-quarters of the people asked said that they preferred a trip to Hamburg, Munich, or Berlin, while only approximately 1.2 percent chose Frankfurt. Some have hoped that better city tourism offers would increase the low number of weekend hotel guests resulting from a structure based primarily on business tourism (Hampel, 1999b). New tourist attractions are especially needed in order to make the city more attractive for business tourists in general, and convention and trade fair participants in particular.

Despite the fact that Frankfurt is less attractive to tourists, 30 percent of the city's visitors are not business tourists. All in all, Frankfurt sees over 600,000 more tourists than any other city in the Rhein-Main area. This includes a high percentage of foreign visitors as well as tourists from overseas. It is normal to see Japanese tour groups in front of the Römer and in front of Goethe's house. Still, it is not the tourist attractions that draw foreign visitors to Frankfurt. The airport, however, does play an important role. Many tourists from the Far East either start or conclude their European or German tours at Frankfurt Airport. For overseas visitors, it is extremely important that Frankfurt offers hotels of several international chains. For example, Americans can lodge in the Hilton or Marriott as they are accustomed. Frankfurt also serves as a base for visiting other nearby tourist destinations, like Heidelberg, Rüdesheim, Mainz and Cologne.

Business tourism dominates the other cities of the Rhein-Main area as well. For example, Mainz receives the highest percentage of foreign guests after Frankfurt. Mainz also offers a look back over its long history, as well as a partially undestroyed medieval quarter, with a cathedral and other culturally significant buildings. The Mainz Carnival is also a very important event. Still, Mainz remains primarily an excursion destination or a place that tourists pass through. Private tourists usually visit Mainz as same-day visitors, and, in 1987 (more recent statistics do not exist), the city's share of private tourists stood at 12 percent (see Schreiber, 1990).

The history of health resorts is symbolic of the development of tourism in Wiesbaden, the second largest city in the Rhein-Main area. The city's first health resort, completed in 1810, was replaced with a more luxurious and larger building at the turn of the century in order to keep up with the growing need for social representativeness in the 'world health resort' city of Wiesbaden. Until the First World War, Wiesbaden was internationally known and adored by the European upper class as a tourist destination; its health resort became a pretext for visiting the city (Schürmann, 1995). This phase, however, ended with the First World War, and the city's tourism focus after the Second World War was on business motivated travel. The health resort reflected this change, and, after a number of renovations, it began functioning as a convention center in 1987. In fact, for several decades, health resort guests have accounted for less than 5 percent of guests (compared with 32 percent in 1910), while convention visitors have dominated the registers since the 1980's. Wiesbaden has established itself as a complement to the Frankfurt convention location, especially in the area of scientific and medical conventions. The completion of large hotels in the 1980's contributed to this development. This change in structure, however, resulted in a shortening of the average duration of stay in these hotels to the current 2.2 days per guest. This rate is the highest among the large cities of the Rhein-Main area, and can be attributed to the exceptionally long stays of health resort guests (in 1990, the average was 27 days per guest). In short, the number of guests has more than doubled since before the First World War, while the number of over-night stays has decreased by half (see Schürmann, 1995; Hank-Haase, 1992).

Wiesbaden reflects the long tradition of health resorts in the state of Hessen and the Rhein-Main area. The spas in Hessen had an international reputation from the 19th century until the outbreak of the First World War. Bad Nauheim, Bad Soden, Bad Homburg, and Wiesbaden were regularly visited by European royalty, especially Russian guests, and the orthodox chapels still standing in Bad Nauheim and Wiesbaden remain as evidence. Visiting health resorts had more to do with social and political relations than it did with medical necessity, and this sparked the construction of gambling casinos, ball rooms and luxury hotels. After the Second World War, health resort visits were transformed from social happenings into events financed by the public health care system. The proportion of private guests throughout Hessen's health resorts sank to under 20 percent, and virtually all of the resorts' guests were now German. Today, health resorts find themselves in yet a new phase. After the health care reforms of 1996, the number of recovering 'patients' paid for by the health care system sank dramatically, and health resorts have once again become increasingly dependent on paying guests. Healthy vacations have become the motto, and 'wellness' has become the buzz word - as it was during the previous century, a health resort visit should be something on which people gladly spend money. International guests are increasingly being wooed, and advertisements for 'luxury weekends' in Bad Homburg are run in Russia. This health resort, which is easily accessible from Frankfurt, also profits from demand in the metropolis itself, and in this way people are able to combine business travel and a health vacation. Gambling casinos also attract business tourists to health resort locations.

11.3 FRANKFURT/RHEIN-MAIN - A GLOBALLY BOUND HOTEL LOCATION

Considering the fact that the Frankfurt/Rhein-Main region serves both as a junction for international tourist traffic and a location for conventions, meetings and trade fairs, accommodation options for business tourists, convention visitors and those just passing through are a critical factor. For hosts of international conventions and seminars, the combination of meeting places, overnight accommodations and location convenience is of the utmost importance. In response to these demands, six Frankfurt hotels, along with the new Congress Center mentioned above, have joined forces within Convention Unlimited (C.U). This initiative combines local potential and facilitates cooperation in all aspects of the acquisition and implementation of international conventions and events. Convention Unlimited addresses the business needs of the event market in Frankfurt, while at the same time identifying decisive impulses in the sector as a whole.

The demands of hosts and tourists on overnight accommodation providers are highly differentiated. A wide variety of possibilities can be expected in Frankfurt/Rhein-Main in particular, as guests come from different countries with different motives. A closer look at Frankfurt's hotel selection provides revealing information regarding qualitative demands on one hand, and the status of the Frankfurt/Rhein-Main area among international hotel companies on the other. Brand name hotels stand in the foreground, including hotels that belong either to a chain or a corporation. Such hotels are integrated into a higher, single managerial unit and are subject to goal oriented decisions. Each individual hotel location reflects one piece of company strategy. In addition to the strategic plans of hotel operators, municipalities have their own reasons for being interested in serving as the location for such brand name hotels. The power of brand names has increased in the hospitality sector as well, and many guests, especially Americans and Japanese, associate brand name hotels with safety and reliability in upholding certain standards. For this reason, the presence of well-known hotel brand names is a valuable element of a location's tourism marketing.

11.3.1 The Hotel Supply

According to a study of the Frankfurt/Rhein-Main area's hotel market (Steinert 1998), the region has 558 hotels with over 20 rooms, each with its own bathroom, telephone and television. Among these hotels, 127 brand name hotels control over 52 percent of the region's combined total of 37,670 hotel rooms. In comparison, throughout Germany as a whole, the share of hotel rooms controlled by brand name companies is less than 30 percent of total overnight accommodation. Within the next 5 years, 3,000 to 5,000 new rooms will be added to the region's hotel room stock.

The largest share of hotels fall into the category of business and convention hotels, which means that they are set up to meet the needs of business travelers and that they generate most of their business through business tourism. Pure vacation hotels (resorts) and golf-course hotels are rare finds in the Frankfurt area, and do not characterize the large chain hotels in the region. Even in the surrounding area, in the moderate mountainous area of Taunus, Spessart and Odenwald for example, hotels are geared towards offering convention and meeting possibilities. In such areas, the combination of business travel and leisure activity plays an important role in marketing. The remaining hotels, which are mostly small, privately owned businesses (each with no more than 35 rooms), have no systematic structure that would allow them to be placed in any specific category. Such hotels are generally low budget, and, based on facilities and price, they are generally sought by blue collar business travelers, traveling salesmen and vacationers. Well known health resorts, like those in Bad Homburg and Wiesbaden, have modified their program in order to make themselves more attractive for business travelers, who, in many cases, like to take advantage of the well-maintained health resort atmosphere of the hotel buildings.

Table 11.1 Hotel companies in the Rhein-Main region, March 1998

Hotel Company	*Hotels in Rhein-Main*	*Hotels in Germany*	*Hotel Company*	*Hotels in Rhein-Main*	*Hotels in Germany*
Accor (F)	13	166	Intercontinental (USA)	2	11
Arabella Sheraton (D/USA)	4	18	Kempinski (Thailand)	1	9
Astron (D)	4	35	Marriott (USA)	1	6
Best Western (USA)	14	120	Maritim (D)	4	38
Choice (USA)	6	32	Queens (GB)	2	23
Dorint (D)	5	57	Ramada (USA)	5	23
Hilton (USA)	2	8	Steigenberger (D)	6	49
Holiday Inn (USA)	6	59	Treff Hotels (D)	7	72

Source: Steinert, 1998.

Almost all international hotel companies operating in Europe are represented in the region (Table 11.1). Of the sector's internationally important companies, only two luxury hotels in the highest category, the Four Seasons and the Ritz-Carlton, are not represented. Of the 20 hotel operators with the highest turnover in Germany, all except one had at least one hotel in the region in 1998, and many were running several hotels in the region. While five of these 19 companies are German, the rest are foreign, primarily American. Since the 1990's, the presence of foreign hotel companies has increased dramatically. In large cities, the number of rooms provided by new, often spectacular hotel buildings has increased considerably.

Six of the 20 hotel companies with the highest turnover in Germany (NGZ, 1999) are located in Frankfurt. In comparison to other cities, Frankfurt has the hotels with the highest turnover, while Berlin and Munich each have four of the top hotels. The hotel that has led the pack for years is the Sheraton Frankfurt, located at Frankfurt Airport itself. The Sheraton Frankfurt also places first in terms of the number of rooms (1,020), and is thus a top hotel in the region and one of largest such structures in Germany. All six of the highest turnover hotels in Frankfurt belong to chains, and are classified as upper class hotels (4 and 5 star). Two additional hotels - both recently constructed at the end of the 1990's - are expected to make the list of the top 20 highest turnover hotels within the next few years as well. In a nationwide comparison, Frankfurt hotels also rate high in terms of average occupancy. While average occupancy among Germany's top 200 hotels stands at about 64 percent, the occupancy rate among the Frankfurt hotels in the list range from 64.4 percent to 83 percent (NGZ, 1999).

11.3.2 Strategic Location Planning

This short introduction reflects Frankfurt's importance to hotel companies as a potential location, which has been the basis of the continuous influx of new hotels. In the context of restructuring, in which chain hotels displace smaller privately run hotels, internationally successful locations function as showcases. In such locations, companies demonstrate their presence and enter into direct competition with their competitors. Along with the business potential of such locations, strategic aspects concerning competition also come into play; this is where the eclectic theory of multinationals applies to the hotel sector (Dunning and Kundu, 1995).

From the perspective of globalization, this has special meaning. The current world-wide fusions and alliances between large hotel companies have been portrayed as an impact of globalization on the international hotel market (Go and Pine, 1995; Vorlaufer, 1993, 2000). For example, in 1998, the American hotel chain ITT Sheraton Hotels was acquired by Starwood International (ranked 7th worldwide in 1997), and in the same year, the German company Arabella Hotels began a joint venture with ITT Sheraton. In 1998, the luxury hotel company Ritz-Carlton acquired 99 percent of Marriott Hotels (ranked 5th in 1997), and the hotel chain Inter-Continental Hotels & Resorts was acquired by Bass Plc (ranked 2nd in 1997), which already owned the hotel chain Holiday Inn. Aside from elements of horizontal cooperation, vertical concentration within the complex system of tourism has increased as well, and Accor (ranked 6th in 1997) serves as a good example of this phenomenon. In addition to a number of different hotel chains, Accor also owns, among other things, the international travel agency Carlson Wagonlit Travel and, until recently, the rental car agency Europcar. Today, we can identify a growing tendency to form large, vertically organized multinational tour companies (Williams, 1995; Ioannides, 1998).

The Carlson Wagonlit Travel chain sells millions of plane and train tickets, overnight stays and rental cars each year. In light of the fact that Carlson arranges business travel for companies like Siemens, IBM and General Electric, and are more or less able to supply their own customers, the importance of such alliances is clear (Ruschmann, 1999). In such instances, 'company contracts' between large corporations and hotel companies are pivotal. The hotel company guarantees special prices and services for corporation employees, and the corporation, in turn, commits to using a certain number of rooms per year. Ideally, company contracts are made between corporations active on the global level and international hotel companies. A corporation's decision to cooperate with a hotel company is based on the presence of company hotels in the locations most important for that corporation's business. For this reason, each individual hotel location, which is part of a global network of locations, must be understood as a piece of overall strategy. Based on this fact, and in light of the international hotel companies represented here, it is clear that the region under discussion - not the city alone, but the entire region, including Mainz and Wiesbaden - is a strategic location. This assumption is also supported by the registers of many hotel chains, most importantly the international companies, which list themselves as being in the Frankfurt area by either adding 'Frankfurt' to the location name, or by listing the location as being situated in the city of Frankfurt itself. As explained succinctly by a manager of the Maritim hotel chain: "You've got to include Frankfurt." The Frankfurt region is also the location of important decision making centers, as the headquarters of seven of the ten leading hotel companies in Germany are located in this region, including Accor, Best Western, Holiday Inn, Marriott, the Kraus-Group and Intercontinental (Gessta, 1998).

Decision-making in terms of micro-location reflects trends reported in the United States and elsewhere (Go and Pine, 1995). With the exception of two airport hotels, Frankfurt's top hotels are located in the inner city (Figure 11.6). All remaining luxury hotels, with the exception of two exclusive traditional hotels, are located in the centers of Wiesbaden, Mainz, Offenbach and Darmstadt. In contrast to luxury hotels, middle class hotels often have locations outside of large cities as well. The favored locations of these hotels are the city of Offenbach and the area surrounding Frankfurt Airport. The hotel chains represented in this area cater to the upper-middle segment (3 star plus hotels). A large number of German hotel chains are represented at the airport, including many relatively young companies established during the second half of the 1990's. While the international companies in the middle and upper market segments are concentrated primarily in large cities, national companies are better represented outside of large cities, where they serve the needs of the upper middle class segment. This can be explained by differences between property prices inside and outside large cities. Many German hotel companies either started out in the building industry or are affiliated with a building company that took over the construction and financing of a hotel, and owns the real estate on which it stands. Such hotels are usually middle class family businesses, and the relatively inexpensive price of land outside of cities is preferred for obvious reasons. Within international companies, however, there is usually a functional division between the functions of hotel investment and hotel management. Hotel real estate is financed through private investors or funds, while hotel operators are responsible for running their hotels based on leases and management or franchise contracts. In this way, responsibility for the hotel project is divided between two experts (Clancy, 1998).

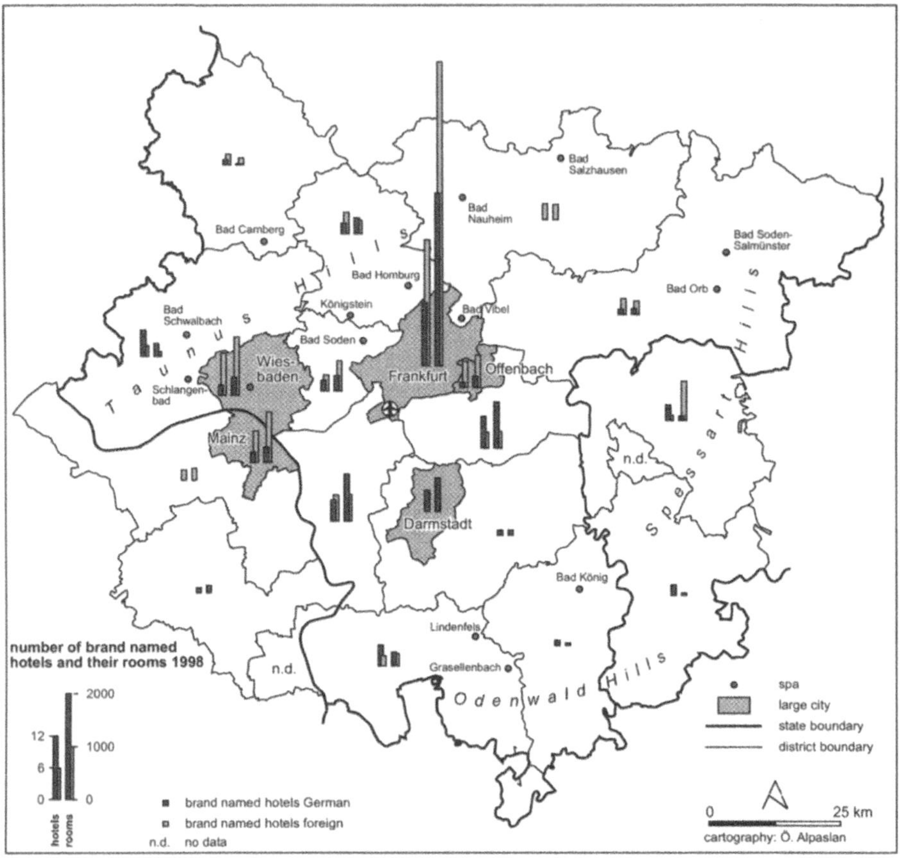

Figure 11.6 The spatial pattern of foreign and domestic brand name hotels in Frankfurt/Rhein-Main

An inner city location is a must for luxury hotels. Guests will only be willing to pay higher prices for overnight accommodations in the city in return for proximity to attractions such as the theater, the opera and shopping. Similarly, rent paid by hotel operators is higher in central locations than in outlying areas. This means that they must generate higher profit and therefore has an effect on the price of rooms. This, in turn, explains why only luxury hotels can consider operating in inner city areas. In Frankfurt, however, all properties suited to be considered by large hotel chains are already occupied. Still, Frankfurt appears on the wish-lists of international hotel chains time and again. For example, it is well known that Ritz-Carlton and Kempinski hotels are currently seeking a location in Frankfurt. Even companies that already have one location in Frankfurt have shown interest in opening up another (for example, Hilton and Arabella Sheraton). Demand is concentrated in the inner city of Frankfurt, as well as in locations near the airport. However, hotels also compete with businesses that are interested in the same locations for office space, which is often preferable due to the special considerations remanded by hotel property. Operators have adapted to this shortage in suitable property by seeking out already existing hotel structures and modifying them to suit their own needs. This has resulted in two-tracks of project development planning among hotel operators for finding and implementing new projects; while lower to middle segment hotels are usually constructed in the surrounding area, upper segment hotels are often based on the acquisition of existing buildings.

11.3.3 Future Plans

Despite the plethora of hotel companies in the region representing the upper-middle segment, two market segments are currently underrepresented: budget hotels on one hand, and true luxury hotels on the other. While the five star hotels operating in the region are luxuriously equipped and fulfill just about all international standards, they lack the magnetism and flair of world famous grand hotels. Plans for both underrepresented segments are currently in the works, and this will expand the choices offered by Frankfurt hotels in the future. Accor, for example, is currently constructing the budget and low-budget hotels 'Formule 1', 'Etap' and 'Ibis' throughout Germany, and Frankfurt will constitute a geographic center of this undertaking. There are also concrete plans for a project geared towards the highest market segment on the outskirts of the Frankfurt inner city, in which the city council of Frankfurt has a special interest. As was the case with the construction of the new Hilton in the inner city, no significant obstacles from the Town Planning Department are expected, as the city only stands to profit from the presence of world-renowned names such as Hilton, Intercontinental, Marriott and Hyatt. This new addition, and the brand-name images involved, will provide the location with an advantage that will serve to attract tourists. The internationality and worldliness projected by certain brand names is also projected onto the city itself. In this way, the international hotel companies represented in Frankfurt contribute to the tourism image of the city.

Until now, the Frankfurt/Rhein-Main region's hotel market has been strictly market driven, and its development has not been decisively affected by a series of tourism-related pilot projects. As supply has adapted itself to demand, which has been overwhelmingly international in nature, decisive impulses within the market have been significantly influenced by brand name hotels, and have come less from within the region itself than from the overall global hotel market. Impulses have either concentrated primarily on larger chain hotels or have been generated by them, and well known global brand names serving the uppermost segment dominate the industry. In contrast, middle class hotel operators, including a number of German hotel companies, act more or less defensively, emulating the standards of larger hotel companies. This is why no designer, artsy or other type of eccentric hotel has been opened in Frankfurt, as in other big cities in the region. A market gap definitely exists.

11.4 THE FINANCIAL METROPOLIS ON THE LOOKOUT FOR 'EVENTS' - RAMIFICATIONS FOR POLITICS

As discussed in previous sections, Frankfurt is not a destination for 'classic' city tourism. Two-thirds of all tourists who visit Frankfurt do not do so in their spare time. Tourism in Frankfurt profits from the function of the city as a European, and partly global travel and service junction. The strengths and advantages of Frankfurt's location in terms of international tourism undoubtedly lie in its infrastructure - its transportation connections and fair grounds, as well as its wide array of hotels and convention center possibilities. Its weaknesses, however, are also obvious, including its ordinary cultural activities and non-existent major tourist attractions.

Frankfurt's advantages attracting international business tourism, and those of the surrounding area, stand in stark contrast to the region's handicap of negligible tourist attractions. Frankfurt's image is that of a cold business and financial metropolis. So, despite the presence of a zoo, museums, theaters and an opera, as in any other big city, simple attractiveness is missing. Frankfurt does not have an Eiffel Tower, a Louvre, a Coliseum or a Buckingham Palace; it has no canals running through it and no idyllic mediaeval quarter. The Rhein-Main area has no Disneyland, and Taunus and Odenwald are not the Alps. In short, Frankfurt and its surrounding region are missing a certain special attractiveness - a uniqueness, and that cannot be changed. Frankfurt will never be able to compete with Paris, London or Vienna.

The absence of special attractions begs the question: can they be created? In a time of political 'festivalization', 'events' are important pretexts that can be used to convince someone to visit a city. It is a dazzling term that can be used to describe anything from a music festival to Expo 2000, and can refer to anything from concerts to the celebration of natural occurrences, like an eclipse. The goal of all such 'events', however, should be the same: to fulfill people's need for 'unforgettable experiences'. A specific event can lure tourists to a city in which they had previously been uninterested. Who would have ever thought of traveling to Bochum before the opening of the musical 'Starlight Express'? The work and achievements of Hilmar Hoffman, the magistrate head of the city Department for Cultural Affairs in the 1980's, serves as a useful example; as more money became available for arts and culture in Frankfurt, he rebuilt the old opera house, established the Museum River Bank and reconstructed the Römerberg as it appeared in the Middle Ages. In the 1990's, however, two attempts to bring musicals to the region (Offenbach and Niedernhausen) failed, despite the concurrent 'musical euphoria' in Germany. For quite a while, Frankfurt set its sights on a musical that would serve as a magnet, and this approach was most recently reflected in the planned Urban Entertainment Center. The positive experiences of Hamburg, Bochum and Stuttgart were a great source of hope, as the number of visitors to these cities grew after the opening of musicals. However, musicals suffer from the disadvantage characteristic of other events that are dependent on a certain craze; eventually, the craze subsides, the product becomes obsolete and the theater closes down. Cities that base their tourism strictly upon such fads are in danger of losing out in the long run.

This danger, however, does not pose much of a threat to Frankfurt. It was never the plan, nor could it ever be the plan, to base tourism solely on 'leisure' tourists, as the necessary infrastructure does not exist and hotels are undoubtedly focused on the needs of business travelers. The big problem is weekends, when city tourism should play a complementary role. It is also important to be able to offer business travelers and trade fair organizers an attractive framework for leisure activities. These 'soft' aspects of location are especially important for conventions and congresses. Travelers with business obligations during the day need to be offered special attractions during the evenings and on weekends. In addition to the direct positive impact that 'events' can have on tourism in a city, they can also impact a city's image and marketing ability. "Festivalization as media appropriate presentation of the city" (Häussermann and Siebel, 1993, p. 15) is becoming the most widespread strategy of the city. Festivals, taking place within specific time frames and fixed spaces, such as the Rheingau Music Festival, are very appropriate. Cities and regions concentrate on particular efforts for a short time, in order to turn them into media events to strengthen their position within international competition.

Frankfurt is less concerned with achieving fame than it is with shaking the image of a city of banking and skyscrapers, or with linking this image to more positive qualities, such as internationality and openness. Closing the gap between business metropolis and cultural province has become a theme woven into Frankfurt city politics. Enhancement of the city's leisure activities would improve not only the outer image of the city, but its inner image as well. Citizens would be able to identify more closely with their city and more investors would be attracted at the same time. One example of an activity focusing on the inner city is the annual Museum River Bank Festival, a street festival along the river bank that incorporates the museums in the area. Another example is the Skyscraper Festival, during which the upper floors of skyscrapers are opened to the public and people are entertained by an accompanying street festival. Activities geared towards outside the city, which are sponsored by the city administration, are less important.

So, while the politicians of Frankfurt are not directly involved with tourism, political activities in health resort cities are more intense due to the fact that these cities are much more dependent on tourism than are the larger cities. Supporting tourism in health resort cities is generally synonymous with supporting the economy. Regional cooperation, however, is not yet widespread. Now and then, a few joint productions of trade fairs in large cities are undertaken, and the Rheingau is also praised as a worthwhile tourist destination. Individual municipalities still tend to regard one another as competitors, however, and the Frankfurt region is still a long way from adopting a regional tourism policy, despite the fact that such a policy would make sense from a number of perspectives. Better cooperation between tourist industry suppliers and businesses in the region as a whole would, as Schreiber endorses (1994), even out the advantages and disadvantages among cities. Frankfurt is the destination of business tourists, while Rheingau and Taunus offer destinations with charming landscapes. Furthermore, in these resort towns, visitors can even do something positive for their health. Marketing the entire region as a destination could better highlight the wide range of tourism possibilities. On the whole, however, this chapter has shown that international tourism in the Frankfurt/Rhein-Main area is a business sector derivative, dependent on development in other sectors, such as finance, trade fairs, conventions and advanced services. Direct political management of international attractiveness would therefore be extremely difficult to carry out.

REFERENCES

Altenburg, M. (1999). Frankfurt. Blicke. *Die Zeit* no. 42, 14.10.1999, 49 f.

American Chamber of Commerce (1999). The top 50 U.S. companies in Germany. *Commerce Germany* 4/99, 12-15.

AUMA (Ausstellungs- und Messe-Ausschuss der deutschen Wirtschaft e.V.) (1999). *Die Messewirtschaft 1998/1999*. Berlin: AUMA.

Cuadrado-Roura, J. & Rubalcaba-Bermejo, L. (1998). Specialization and competition amongst European cities: A new approach through fair and exhibition activities. *Regional Studies 32*, 133-147.

Clancy, M. (1998). Commodity chains, services and development: Theory and preliminary evidence from the tourism industry. *Review of International Political Economy 5*, 122-148.

DFV Deutscher Fremdenverkehrsverband (Ed.) (1995). Städtetourismus in Deutschland. Grundlagenuntersuchung: Struktur, Bedeutung und Chancen. *Neue Fachreihe des Deutschen Fremdenverkehrsverbandes 7*. Bonn.

Dicken, P. (1998). *Global shift: Transforming the world economy*. London: Paul Chapman.

Dunning, J.H. & Kundu, S.K. (1995). The internationalization of the hotel industry - some new findings from a field study. *Management International Review 35*, 101-153.

German Convention Bureau (1995). *Der deutsche Tagungsmarkt 1994/1995*. Frankfurt am Main.

Gessta (Gesellschaft für Standortforschung mbH) (1998). *Der Hotelstandort Rhein-Main*. Frankfurt am Main: Gessta.

Go, F. & Pine, R. (1995). *Globalization strategy in the hotel industry*. London: Routledge.

Häussermann, H. & Siebel, W. (1993). Die Politik der Festivalisierung und die Festivalisierung der Politik. Grosse Ereignisse in der Stadtpolitik. In H. Häussermann & W. Siebel (Eds.), *Die Festivalisierung der Stadtpolitik. Stadtentwicklung durch grosse Projekte*. Opladen: Westdeutscher Verlag.

Hampel, G. (1999a). Kongress- und Tagungsdokumentation der Stadt Frankfurt am Main - am Beispiel des Jahres 1997. In M.Th. Schreiber (Ed.), *Tagungs- und Kongressmanagement (= Lehr und Handbücher zu Tourismus, Verkehr und Freizeit)* (437-457). München: Oldenbourg.

Hampel, G. (1999b). Weltoffen und gut gerüstet. Tourismus- und Kongressstandort Frankfurt am Main. *IHK Wirtschaftsforum / Mitteilungen der Industrie- und Handelskammer Frankfurt am Main 9/99*, 6-7.

Hank-Haase, G. (1992). Der Tagungs- und Kongressreiseverkehr als wirtschaftlicher Faktor in deutschen Grossstädten unter besonderer Berücksichtigung von Wiesbaden. *Materialien zur Fremdenverkehrsgeographie 27*. Trier: Geographische Gesellschaft Trier.

Hank-Haase, G. (1999). Stellung der Bundesrepublik Deutschland im internationalen Kongressmarkt. In: M.Th. Schreiber (Ed.), *Tagungs- und Kongressmanagement* (19-26). München: Oldenbourg.

Ioannides, D. (1998). Tour operators: The gatekeepers of tourism. In D. Ioannides & K.G. Debbage (Eds.), *The economic geographics of the tourist industry. A supply-side analysis* (139-158). London: Routledge.

NGZ (1999). Ranking der Top-Einzelhotels: 1998: Ein Glanzlicht. Umsätze rauf, Gewinne prima, Kosten stabil. *Neue Gastronomische Zeitung (NGZ)* Nr. 5/99, 34-49.

Ruschmann, D. (1999). Deutsche ohne Chance. Internationale Hotelketten erobern den deutschen Markt. Einheimische Hoteliers haben es schwer. *Wirtschaftswoche 43*, 21. Oct. 1999, 86-89.

Sassen, S. (1994). *Cities in a world economy*. Thousand Oaks, Can.: Pine Forge Press.

Schreiber, M. (1990). *Grossstadttourismus in der Bundesrepublik Deutschland am Beispiel einer segmentorientierten Untersuchung der Stadt Mainz*. Mainzer Geographische Studien 35. Mainz: Geographisches Institut Universität Mainz.

Schreiber, M. (1994). *Kongress- und Tourismusmanagement der Stadt Frankfurt am Main*. Mainzer Geographische Studien 40 (393-401). Mainz: Geographisches Institut Universität Mainz.

Schürmann, H. (1995). Kur- und Fremdenverkehr in Wiesbaden. Bedeutungs- und Konzeptionswandel im Spiegel städtebaulicher Entwicklungen. In G. Meyer (Ed.), *Das Rhein-Main-Gebiet. Aktuelle Strukturen und Entwicklungsprobleme*. Mainzer Kontaktstudium Geographie 1 (73-84). Mainz: Geographisches Institut Universität Mainz.

Shachar, A. (1995). Metropolitan areas: Economic globalisation and urban tourism. In A. Montanari & A.M. Williams (Eds.), *European tourism. Regions, spaces and restructuring* (151-160). Chichester: John Wiley & Sons.

Steinert, R. (1998). *Der Hotelstandort Frankfurt - Rhein-Main. Eine Untersuchung der Angebots- und Nachfragestrukturen auf dem Hotelmarkt*. Unpublished diploma dissertation.

TCF (Tourismus + Congress GmbH Frankfurt) (1998). *Kongress- und Tagungsdokumentation Frankfurt am Main*. Frankfurt/M.: TCF.

Vorlaufer, K. (1993). Transnationale Hotelketten: Entwicklung, Struktur und räumliche Ausbreitungsmuster. *Petermanns Geographische Mitteilungen 137*, 289-308.

Vorlaufer, K. (2000). Die Internationalisierung der Hotellerie: Determinanten, Strategien, Strukturen. In S. Landgrebe (Ed.), *Internationaler tourismus* (51-80). München: Oldenbourg.

Williams, A.M. (1995). Capital and the transnationalisation of tourism. In A. Montanari & A.M. Williams (Eds.), *European tourism. Regions, spaces and restructuring* (163-176). Chichester: John Wiley & Sons.

DANIEL FELSENSTEIN AND HANAN BARKAI

12. IDENTIFIYING GLOBALIZATION TRENDS IN THE CULTURAL INDUSTRIES OF TEL AVIV

12.1 INTRODUCTION

This study focuses on globalization trends in the cultural industries of the Tel Aviv metropolitan area. It is well known that global centers are often cultural service centers as well. London, New York, Paris and Moscow are all economic hubs in the global system but are also cultural centers. The centrality of a cultural node can be measured (like the centrality of any node in a system) through observing the flows into and out of that center (see above Chapters 1 and 6). The identification of flows gives a more dynamic view of the relations between nodes than do static rankings (Beaverstock *et al.*, 2000). In addition, attribute-based characterizations are particularly likely to under-identify 'emerging' nodes and the activities that take place within them. As such, a flows-based approach seems more appropriate for yielding insights into the way emerging nodes attempt to break into global networks using cultural activity as a vehicle of entry.

The existence of a thriving and globally active cultural industries sector is usually taken as an indicator of world city status along with other attributes such as command and control activity, advanced financial and business services and world-level tourism (Sassen, 1991; Government Office for London, 1996). However, the existence of a global cultural center is not independent of, and is invariably confounded by, these other attributes. In particular, the relationship of the arts sector to activities such as tourism and financial services, is difficult to unravel. The direction of causality can run both ways: cultural industries are both promoted and in turn promote other activities such as tourism. On the one hand, cultural activities are dependent on the existence of demand generated by other activities such as tourism or high-level business services. On the other hand, location decisions (for conventions, site selection and residence of high wage employees) may be contingent on the existence of local tourist and cultural attractions.

In the case of emerging nodes, the best way to capture these dynamics is through an analysis of flows. As noted in Chapter 1, 'emerging node' status can be identified through flow indicators, such as foreign investment, visitors, telecommunications networks, air passenger traffic and the like. In this chapter, we examine the particular case of flows related to the cultural industries of Tel Aviv. These can take one of the following forms. First, the *export flows* of local cultural goods that are sold abroad. These can either be receipts from sales of cultural services or receipts from *tourist-based demand* in the home country. In both instances, these flows are export-based and represent a major source of income for the exporting country.

D. Felsenstein et al. (eds.),
Emerging Nodes in the Global Economy: Frankfurt and Tel Aviv Compared, 237–254.

This income is often needed in order to pay for the second source of flows. These are the *import flows* of cultural goods from abroad. They represent payment abroad for cultural services provided locally. The size of this flow is also an indication of globalization in this sector.

Of the two sources of flows, the direct export and import flows are of greater relevance to the experience of Tel Aviv, than the indirect, tourist-based flows. As has been shown above (Chapter 10), the phenomenon of foreign tourists seeking local cultural attractions in the area of the performing arts is negligible in Tel Aviv. The city has not generally been considered a cultural or entertainment center. In addition, the dominance of Jerusalem and Nazareth as the major local cultural destinations and their relative proximity to Tel Aviv, serves to over-shadow the latter. Furthermore, the existence of a language barrier makes much local cultural activity inaccessible to tourists. In contrast, while the import and export-based flows are small, their trend seems to be rising.

In this chapter we have tried to assemble data on some of these flows from a variety of sources. Generally, this issue is treated as a sub-theme in the broader notion of the contribution of the leading cultural institutions to the metropolitan economy. In this chapter, we do not examine these impacts directly. Rather, we focus on evidence relating only to globalization trends in the arts industry. These trends are identified from a variety of data sources. Case study and institutional data are analyzed using both qualitative and quantitative approaches. It should be noted that the discussion presented here revolves around 'identifying' globalization tendencies. Some of these trends are not readily apparent and neither do they obviously emerge from the aggregate data. In the contest of the wider economic impacts of the cultural sector, they could be dismissed as marginal.

However, the justification for highlighting these incipient changes lies in more than just their aggregate effect. First, the existence of a thriving cultural sector is an important component in the global profile of a city. For a city with 'emerging node' status, such as Tel Aviv, the ability to promote and nurture a thriving cultural sector provides a further path for breaking into global networks. Second, the sheer economic weight of the cultural industries in many metropolitan economies means that this activity can no longer be dismissed as marginal or subsumed as part of a nebulous 'services' sector. It is therefore imperative to try and estimate the economic significance of the sector, when making the case that a thriving cultural sector is a cornerstone for global integration.

Finally, there is the issue of the merging of global social and economic forces (Scott, 2000). As cultural tastes become ubiquitous and cultural products become homogenized, the cultural industries would seem to be the battleground in which the two forces of economic and cultural globalization meet. If cultural products become available everywhere and if tastes converge around a single common denominator, this would seem to imply that emerging node economies will have a hard time asserting their position in increasingly homogenized (and cannibalized) markets. The wider issue then becomes, what can a node economy do in the face of these forces? On the one hand, correctly identifying global cultural trends would seem to be a key issue in breaking into global networks. On the other hand, does this imply that local cultural trends and products be considered parochial and provincial? While this is a dilemma beyond the remit of this paper, it does highlight the complexity of node economies harnessing cultural trends in order to improve their global position.

12.2 ECONOMIC AND CULTURAL CENTRALITY

Economic and cultural pre-eminence often go together. London and New York illustrate the case of world centers that combine these attributes. This does not mean that these two functions always occur in tandem: Edinburgh in the UK and Boston in the US are cases in point. However, London and New York are both global centers with all the ancillary flows of capital, information and people that this implies. As such, we can also expect large flows grounded in cultural goods and services of the type described above. It should be noted however, that centers of business and economic life that attract head office functions and high income visitors, do not necessarily develop into cultural nodes. In fact, the aura of a 'working' city is often enough to inhibit the development of a cultural sector. In this instance, Manchester and Chicago are examples. Interestingly however, in both cities economic restructuring over the last 30 years has seen a shift in emphasis towards a stress on (sports-based) culture: Manchester as the soccer capital of Europe and Chicago as the US basketball mecca.

The concentration of arts and cultural activities in urban centers is grounded in the logic of central place and agglomeration economies. Large cities usually have the minimum threshold demand to allow for the provision of specialized cultural tastes. The larger the city, the greater the volume of the cultural product it supplies and the more variety of cultural products it produces. This suggests that arts activity not only increases with city size but it also increases faster relative to the rest of the urban economy (Heilbrun, 1992). In this way, a disproportionately large share of cultural activity is found in the largest cities.

At the intra-urban level, cultural activities display clear tendencies to cluster expressed in the emergence of theater districts, artists quarters, museum complexes and the like. These translate into real-world locations in the big cities, such as Hollywood, Broadway and the West End. The advantages of clustering, expressed in labor pooling, specialized inputs and the existence of inter-activity spillovers lead to increasing returns whereby concentrations of cultural activity entrench their already dominant positions, thereby making it highly unlikely that other aspiring centers will ever catch them up. Aggregate evidence from the US shows that the cultural industries displayed a clear tendency towards increasing urban concentration in select locations throughout the 1970's and 1980's although a slight reversal of the trend was beginning to appear in the early 1990's (Heilbrun, 1996).

In cities such as London, New York and Los Angeles, the sheer magnitude of the cultural sector in economic terms is far from negligible. The arts sector in London for example, assumes a commanding position in the British economy. An estimated 140,000 Londoners are employed in the city's cultural industries and this sector contributes 5-6 percent of London's GDP (LPAC, 1991; LAB, 1996). This is nearly equal to the total product of London's manufacturing sector. More than a quarter of all national employment in the cultural industries can be found in London and the sector is a vital component in London's image as a global center.

Additionally, London is the most important tourist destination in the UK and one of the most important in Europe. Some 20 million people visited the city in 1994, half of them from overseas. The share of the tourists in the theater audience is about one third domestic tourist, one third overseas tourists and the remaining third - local population. In the summer these proportions change, and it is doubtful whether West End theaters could remain open throughout the summer, without overseas visitors (Hughes and Gratton, 1992). Surveys show that these visitors were the main reason for the increase in audiences during the 1980s. Evidence has shown that more than 10 percent of the overseas visitors point to the theater sector as the sole reason for their trip to London. A more careful look at the overseas audience shows it to be more interested in musicals than in classic plays: in the high season, 60 percent of the attendance at musicals is foreign visitors (14 percent locals) whereas in the audience for classic theater they comprise only 25 percent (40 percent locals). In this respect, the flows that make London a global cultural center are the (indirect) export-based flows: the demand generated by the flow of culture-seeking tourists.

New York is also a major target for tourists. Cultural tourism is less significant here, and was estimated at about twenty percent of the attendance in all cultural institutions (including non-profit, commercial, art galleries and auction houses) (Port Authority of New York, 1993). According to that survey, 41 percent of the respondents came from the NY metropolitan region, another 46 percent came from the rest of the country (10 percent neighboring states, 36 percent rest of the US - mainly Northwest and the South), and the rest - 13 percent - from abroad (thereof 7 percent Europe, 2 percent Canada). According to this survey, almost 60 percent of the visitors surveyed at performing arts events indicated 'attending cultural activity' as the main purpose of their visit. Twenty percent of the respondents that indicated other main purposes, reported that they extended the duration of their trip in order to attend cultural activity. This study estimates that the ancillary expenditure of these culture-motivated tourists was $1.1 billion per annum, and some $200 million were spent by those extending their trip, as mentioned above.

The flows that characterize the cultural industry in New York would therefore seem to be less grounded in tourism-related export-base than in London. However, the type of flow that distinguishes New York as a global cultural center would seem to be the direct export of cultural goods to other parts of the world. For example, Broadway productions and New York publishing houses are two typical global cultural trademarks that emphasize this role.

The cultural industries can also contribute to creating an independent image for a city. Edinburgh, for example, is a city with a high cultural profile that is not related to economic dominance. The Edinburgh festival (really a collection of nine disparate cultural happenings) plays a role in positioning the city as a node in the global cultural network. It promotes flows of visitors and income (over 20 percent of patrons are foreign tourists from outside the UK) and has a considerable economic impact. As a stimulant of economic activity it generates over 1,500 new jobs in the local economy and indirectly, over double that number in the Scottish economy (Smith and Jenner, 1998). Net benefits to the local economy (new local income) are estimated at over £30m p.a. and the equivalent figure for the Scottish economy is £120 p.a.

12.3 RESEARCH METHOD AND TOOLS

12.3.1 Data Sources

The basic unit of study in this chapter is the cultural institution. We analyze the cultural industries of Tel Aviv by assembling data on the cultural institutions in the following sub-sectors: theater, classical music (orchestras), opera and dance. This is a rather limiting definition of the 'cultural industries sector' and one concerned with the area of 'high' culture only. However, given the paucity of available data and the ubiquitousness of the institutions of popular culture, its use is justified here. We use two key sources for tracing globalization trends. The first is the annual reports of the Center for Information and Research in the Arts and Cultural Administration of the Israeli Ministry of Education. These reports present a set of income-expenditure accounts that cover all those cultural institutions that received public funding on an annual basis from 1991- 1996. Each institution is listed individually and those from Tel Aviv can be identified. On the basis of this data we have a description of all the Tel Aviv cultural institutions, by the four major cultural areas outlined above. For each institution, the source provides data on number of performances by location, sources of income (ticket sales, subsidies etc), number of employees and so on. This yields valuable fiscal data relating to income sources and attendance locally but it is rather limited on the subject of income and expenditure from abroad. However, it does supply us with a full set of 'trade flows' between regions, in that we have detailed data on Tel Aviv cultural institutions and their receipts from performances in Tel Aviv and the other five regions of the country.

We have therefore supplemented this data with a series of interviews with key personnel at the ten leading Tel Aviv cultural institutions. These included the Israel Philharmonic Orchestra, the Israeli Opera and a variety of theater companies and dance groups. The interviews yielded valuable qualitative information about trends in the globalization of the cultural industries in Tel Aviv, receipts and payments as a result of activities abroad, royalties and also the extent to which income and expenditures are generated in Tel Aviv. In addition, they provided detailed spatial information that was not available from the institutional source. Foremost amongst this was data relating to the spatial distribution of expenditures by institution, employees by place of residence and subscribers by place of residence.

On the basis of these two sources we estimate the contribution of the cultural industries to the Tel Aviv economy using an inter-regional input output (I-O) model. For the purpose of this chapter, the contribution of such an analysis is the regional decomposition of the economic impacts of the cultural industries. The input-output approach allows us to identify the inter-regional 'ripple-through' effect of income and employment change related to Tel Aviv cultural industries. However, the main utility of the regional I-O model stems from its ability to identify international flows of income related to the activity of Tel Aviv's cultural industries. The impacts of this sector are not simply disaggregated across the six regions of the country but a seventh 'region' is added to the model that represents the 'rest of the world'. This gives an indication of the extent to which the impact of the Tel Aviv cultural sector can be attributed to flows whose source is from outside the country. In this respect, the analysis adds a further dimension to the study of globalization trends in the cultural sector, allowing us to estimate that demand generated in Tel Aviv whose source is international.

12.3.2 Method

The analytical tool employed here is a multi-regional input-output model. This is the classic 'work-horse model' for estimating impacts (direct and indirect) and also disaggregating them across areas. This tool is increasingly used for estimating the role of the cultural industries on spatial units at the sub national level, such as regions or cities (Deloitte and Touche, 1993; Bryan *et al.*, 2000). The model used here is of a hybrid-type based on both survey and non-survey sources. It is based on the regionalization of the 1992 Israeli national input-output tables with on-going adjustment and modifications to the trade and technological coefficients. It contains 29 sectors (including households) and is calibrated for Israel's six regions. The model uses two direct column coefficient matrices. One is the standard input-output matrix for a given region and the other is a trade flow matrix. The two matrices are combined through multiplication and the output multiplier is derived through the classic Leontieff inverse $(I\text{-}A)^{-1}$.

Combining this with the trade flow matrix (C), yields an output multiplier of the form, $(I\text{-}CA)^{-1}C$. This gives the model its multi-regional perspective and allows for the estimation of 'reverse' and 'loop' flows of trade between the regions where the demand is initially generated and other regions[1]. This is particularly important in small economies such as Israel, where reverse flows (from destination region back to origin in response to demand generated at origin), can account for a significant part of inter-regional trade. As a regional forecasting and simulation tool, it has been extensively used and up-graded in the past and many of these applications and methodological extensions are described in the literature (Freeman *et al.*, 1990).

Recent development of the model has led to extending its use to analyzing impacts in service, entertainment and leisure sectors. This has signaled a break from traditional I-O applications to industrial impacts (Freeman and Sultan, 1997; Felsenstein and Freeman, 1998). The present variant of the model has been adapted to accommodate an analysis of the cultural industries. In order to effect this change, the model is disaggregated in the service sectors and left aggregated in other sectors of the economy such as industry and agriculture. Detailed data gathered from the ten leading Tel Aviv cultural institutions is incorporated into the model and an industry profile is constructed for each of the four major cultural areas identified above (theater, classical music, opera and dance). A final demand profile for each cultural activity is constructed drawing heavily on the survey data collected from each institution. This relates to the expenditure and income patterns of the cultural industries, trade flows data of receipts from performances outside Tel Aviv and employment and patrons by place of residence. The cultural industries appear as four separate rows and columns and as a result, the 25 sectors of the base model are expanded to 29. The basic transactions structure of the cultural industries is identified from the national I-O table where SIC 903 appears as 'theaters and orchestras'. The multi-regional structure of the model incorporates not only the demand flows from the origin region (Tel Aviv) outwards but also the feedback loops to the origin region from secondary demand created in other regions in their attempts to supply the demand generated by the origin region. These trade flows address a regional economic effect that is often overlooked in I-O studies and is particularly important in a small country like Israel. For our purposes, the addition of the 'rest of the world' as a seventh region in the model, allows us to identify and estimate the role of global (demand) flows in the impacts generated by the Tel Aviv cultural sector.

This analytic method provides us with following results relating to the extent and source of economic impacts generated by the cultural industries of Tel Aviv:

- an estimate of the overall impact of the cultural sector as measured by the multiplier. This multiplier expresses the relationship between the direct and total effects of the cultural industries. Total effects are measured as the direct, indirect (inter-industry) and induced (household) effects results attributable to change in the sector. A change in direct output, income or employment in the cultural industries will trigger-off rounds of secondary and tertiary change. The multiplier traces these economic effects until they evaporate in the local economy. In this chapter, the multiplier effect is calculated at two spatial scales, the (smaller) Tel Aviv multiplier and the (larger) national level multiplier.
- a disaggregation of these multipliers by individual types of cultural activity (theater, classical music etc.). This allows us to observe the contribution to the overall multiplier of the individual cultural activity.
- an inter-regional analysis of the impact of the Tel Aviv cultural industries on all other regions. This impact also includes all the feed-back loops needed to satisfy demand in the Tel Aviv region, as is likely to occur in a small country such as Israel.
- the inclusion of a 'rest of the world' table for trade flows, means that in addition to observing the regional contribution to the overall impact, we can also estimate that proportion of the impact whose source is abroad. This is taken as an indication of globalization tendencies in this sector. The variation in globalization trends across different cultural activities is also estimated. This allows us to identify those sub-sectors in the field of high-culture that are leading the incipient trend towards globalization.

12.4 FINDINGS

12.4.1 Describing the Aggregate Picture

In the first instance, it is important to establish the magnitude of the orientation of the cultural industries to Tel Aviv. While the vast majority of cultural institutions are located in the city and some forms of cultural expression such as opera, exist only in Tel Aviv, a more important indicator of economic impact is the place of residence of those employed in the cultural industries sector. The data show that Tel Aviv cultural institutions overwhelmingly employ Tel Aviv residents (76 percent of employees overall) and in some sub sectors such as orchestras, this figure rises to 82 percent (Table 12.1). Once the spatially contiguous central region is also included, this percentage rises to 95 percent of employees.

Table 12.1 Distribution of employment in Tel Aviv cultural institutions by region

	Total Employment in Tel Aviv Institutions	*Employees in Tel Aviv Cultural Institutions by Place of Residence*					
		Tel Aviv	*Center*	*Jerusalem*	*Haifa*	*North*	*South*
Theater	1199	911	240	24	24	–	–
Orchestras	185	152	32	1	–	–	–
Opera	323	248	51	14	5	4	1
Dance	206	156	41	5	4	–	–
Total	1913	1467	364	44	33	4	1

Source: Survey of Institutions

The significance of this finding lies in the fact that salaries form the single largest expenditure item of Tel Aviv-based cultural institutions. Overall, they account for 51 percent of total expenditure (Table 12.2). The remaining 49 percent covers production and operating expenses (the next single largest item accounting for 37 percent of all spending), debt financing, maintenance, publicity and administration. In certain sub-sectors, such as orchestras, this expenditure item accounts for over 80 percent of total expenditure. Thus, if the majority of employees in this sector live in Tel Aviv and the single largest budget item for these institutions is wages, the magnitude of the impact of the cultural industries in Tel Aviv can be appreciated. When all expenditure items are taken together (salaries, production, finance, management, publicity etc) then the share of this spending in Tel Aviv is over 80 percent (Table 12.2).

A further indication of the importance of the Tel Aviv cultural industries can be observed from observing the magnitude of the 'export' flows to places outside Tel Aviv (other regions in Israel and the rest of the world). Table 12.3 presents data on the income flows to Tel Aviv cultural industries from the 'export' of cultural services and products. As can be seen this varies greatly across sub-sectors. The theater sub-sector and to a lesser extent the dance sub-sector earn a sizeable amount of their income from the export of cultural services, mainly to other regions in Israel. Tel Aviv theater and dance groups regularly perform at venues outside Tel Aviv and the receipts from these performances account for 43 percent and 35 percent of their incomes respectively. Orchestras are far less export-oriented with only 17 percent of income from exports. Opera productions have to take place at the Tel Aviv Opera House and thus there is no export income in this sub-sector. As above, the implication of these export shares is that most of these flows are likely to be captured by the Tel Aviv economy. Salaries are the single largest expenditure item for all cultural sub-sectors and these go to employees whose are predominantly located in Tel Aviv. These flows are therefore likely to perpetuate the economic centrality of the Tel Aviv economy.

Table 12.2 Expenditure structure of Tel Aviv cultural institutions ($m, 1996)

	Total Expenditure	*Salaries*	*Production & Operating Expenses*
Theater	42.0	21.7	15.1
Orchestras	11.8	9.7	0.4
Opera	12.7	3.1	8.5
Dance	6.7	3.0	3.0
Total	73.2	37.5	27.0
% Total Expenditure in T.A.	80.4	78.5	79.5

Source: Survey of Institutions

Table 12.3 Income from performances: Tel Aviv cultural institutions ($m, 1996)

	Total Income	*Income from 'Exports' to other Regions*	*'Export' Income as % of Total*
Theater	17.9	7.4	43
Orchestras	10.2	1.7	17
Dance	1.8	0.6	35

Source: Survey of Institutions

A final indication of the extent to which the cultural industries are Tel Aviv-based, relates to the geographical impacts of cultural performances that take place in Tel Aviv. These are likely to cause inter-regional reverberations as demand for cultural output in Tel Aviv is met by producers located all over the country and even the world. In this manner, it is reasonable to expect some of the impact generated from Tel Aviv's cultural industries to filter through to other regions. This is especially likely to be the case in a small country such as Israel where distances are minimal and significant inter-regional trade flows are likely to exist.

These flows can be captured in a multi-regional input-output framework. Tables 12.4-12.6 illustrate the inter-regional impacts of cultural products and services produced in Tel Aviv. These are presented in terms of output impacts (Table 12.4), incomes (Table 12.5) and employment (Table 12.6). The figures in Table 12.4 represent the indirect inter-regional effects of a direct output impact of $53.8m generated by Tel Aviv cultural industries. The table shows the indirect and induced inter-regional effects generated by the initial output stimulus resulting from cultural goods and services generated in Tel Aviv. The initial stimulus of $53.8m expands in nearly three-fold in Tel Aviv (local multiplier of 2.9). Tel Aviv captures some two-thirds of the total effect in the country. Nationally, the indirect and induced effects sum to $231m, i.e. an output multiplier of 4.2. This is a large multiplier but it must be realized that its derivation might be upwardly biased. It is calculated as the total effect (direct, indirect and induced) divided by the direct effect. In this calculation, the large public subsidies directed to the various cultural sub-sectors serve to expand the value of the numerator in the multiplier term resulting in a large overall figure. The 'rest of the world' column is marginal to the aggregate picture and represents the output effect generated in Tel Aviv emanating from demand for Tel Aviv cultural goods and services, generated abroad. In 1996, only two sub-sectors generated revenues abroad (theater and dance) and the output effect generated in Tel Aviv comes from the spending of employees in these sectors who are predominantly Tel Aviv residents.

Table 12.4 Inter-regional output impacts of Tel Aviv cultural institutions[1] ($m 1996)

	Regional Distribution of Output						
	Tel Aviv	*Center*	*Jerusalem*	*Haifa*	*North*	*South*	*Rest of the World* [2]
Theater	79.4	10.5	3.5	9.5	5.2	5.9	.4
	(67)	(9)	(3)	(8)	(7)	(5)	
Orchestras	34.3	4.4	1.5	3.9	3.5	2.4	–
	(68)	(9)	(3)	(8)	(7)	(5)	
Opera	29.1	3.8	1.2	3.4	2.9	2.1	–
	(68)	(9)	(3)	(8)	(7)	(5)	
Dance	12.0	1.6	.5	1.4	1.1	.9	6.4
	(67)	(9)	(3)	(8)	(7)	(5)	
Total	154.8	20.3	6.7	18.2	12.9	11.3	6.8

(1) Percentages in parentheses.
(2) Impact in Tel Aviv of demand generated abroad.

The income impacts of the cultural industries show a similar picture of Tel Aviv primacy. In this case, the direct income effect of $25.8m generates indirect and induced impacts across the various regions nationally which sum to $56.7m (Table 12.5). The local (Tel Aviv) multiplier is 1.5, whereas the national multiplier is 2.2. Again, the vast majority of the indirect effect (over 70 percent) is captured by the

Tel Aviv region. Interestingly, \$3.5m of income effect is based in incomes derived from Tel Aviv- based institutions selling their services abroad and the fact that most of this earned income will be spent in Tel Aviv where most performers live.

Table 12.5 Inter-regional income impacts of Tel Aviv cultural institutions(1) (\$m 1996)

	Regional Distribution of Income						
	Tel Aviv	*Center*	*Jerusalem*	*Haifa*	*North*	*South*	*Rest of the World (2)*
Theater	19.8	2.3	0.9	1.7	1.7	1.3	.03
	(71)	(9)	(3)	(7)	(7)	(5)	
Orchestras	9.0	1.0	0.3	0.7	0.7	0.5	–
	(73)	(8)	(3)	(6)	(6)	(4)	
Opera	6.9	0.8	0.3	0.6	0.6	0.4	–
	(71)	(9)	(3)	(6)	(7)	(5)	
Dance	3.0	1.3	0.1	0.2	0.2	0.1	3.5
	(70)	(9)	(3)	(6)	(7)	(5)	
Total	38.7	4.4	1.6	3.2	3.1	2.3	3.53

(1) Percentages in parentheses.
(2) Impact in Tel Aviv of demand generated abroad.

Inter-regional employment impacts are presented in Table 12.6. Again, these results serve to underscore the primordial position of Tel Aviv's cultural industries. While total (direct and indirect) employment in Tel Aviv-based institutions is over 1900 employees, the four cultural sub-sectors generate a further 2578 jobs in indirect and induced effects. The inter-regional distribution of these jobs is displayed in Table 12.6. The employment multiplier nationally is therefore 2.4 and for the Tel Aviv economy it is 1.9. Thus, most of the indirect and induced employment effect is also captured by Tel Aviv.

Taken together, these findings illustrate two key points. The first relates to the magnitude of the inter-regional flows generated by the provision of cultural goods and services in Tel Aviv. The results above seem to show that the extent of these flows (or their 'trickle down' effect) is limited. Whatever the index of economic performance (output, income and employment), the general picture remains one of flows emanating from Tel Aviv that serve to perpetuate Tel Aviv's central position. In all instances, between 67-80 percent of all indirect flows have their source in Tel Aviv.

The second point relates to the seemingly limited extent of impacts whose source is abroad. The limits of this kind of analysis for identifying globalization trends however, should be noted. It is based on receipts for performances abroad for one year only. In addition, in the case where a large volume of performances does not result in any income (over expenses), then for the purposes of an analysis such as this, there is no economic effect. At the extreme, a cultural institution that performs abroad regularly on an exchange basis and is recognized as a flagship of local culture (such as the Israel Philharmonic Orchestra), will be not be considered as contributing to the globalization or export, of local culture. While this may be correct in the technical, accounting sense, it certainly misses the point. Clearly, an investigation of globalization in this sector therefore needs a finer-grained analysis in order to capture anomalies of this kind. It is to this issue that we now turn.

Table 12.6 Inter-regional employment impacts of Tel Aviv cultural institutions(1) ($m 1996)

	Regional Distribution of Employment						
	Tel Aviv	*Center*	*Jerusalem*	*Haifa*	*North*	*South*	*Rest of the World (2)*
Theater	1072	77	30	58	66	50	3
	(79)	(6)	(2)	(4)	(5)	(4)	
Orchestras	342	32	12	23	28	21	–
	(75)	(7)	(3)	(5)	(6)	(5)	
Opera	392	27	14	20	23	18	–
	(80)	(6)	(2)	(4)	(5)	(4)	
Dance	166	12	5	9	10	8	54
	(79)	(6)	(2)	(4)	(5)	(4)	
Total	1972	148	61	110	127	97	57

(1) Percentages in parentheses.
(2) Impact in Tel Aviv of demand generated abroad.

12.4.2 Indications of Globalization

We now present some more indirect indicators of globalization trends associated with the Tel Aviv cultural industries. The sources of these findings are both aggregate and qualitative. The aggregate data in Table 12.7 relate to audiences served abroad and incomes generated from receipts of payments abroad. As can be seen, the global activities of leading Israeli cultural institutions are limited and account for a few percentage points of both audiences served and incomes. It should be noted that while these data are national aggregates, the concentration of most publicly-funded non-commercial culture in Tel Aviv, means they are very representative of Tel Aviv.

The two sub-sectors that stand out as more globally-oriented are the classical music sector (as a result of the Israel Philharmonic Orchestra) and the dance sector (a result of the Israeli Ballet and the Bat Sheva dance troupes). In both these sectors receipts abroad account for over 5 percent of incomes and foreign audiences are over 8 percent of total audiences served.

Table 12.7 Audience and income generated abroad, by sub-sector, 1995

Sub-sector	*Audience Abroad*	*Income Abroad*
Theater	1%	1%
Orchestras	8%	7%
Dance	10%	5%
Opera	0%	0%
Total	4%	3%

Source: Center for Information and Research, Ministry of Education and Culture.

These figures however do not say anything about expenditures generated by global linkages. While comprehensive data on this issue are not readily available from institutional sources, the case of the Israeli Philharmonic Orchestra (IPO) may be suggestive. Table 12.8 shows the volatility of the relationship between performing abroad and net income from these performances. For example, the IPO, Israel's flagship cultural export, performed 43 times abroad in 1994 in front of audiences of over 100,000 with a net income of over 3m NIS. In 1995, the orchestra had only 9 performances abroad in front of much smaller audiences but netting two thirds of the 1994 income. In 1996, a similar volume of performances and audiences abroad failed to register any net income (income and expenditure cancelled out). This also can be observed in the findings relating to inter-regional impacts presented above (Tables 12.4-12.6) where, in 1996, only the theater and dance sub-sectors generated any economic impacts from their exports of cultural services to the 'rest of the world'.

Table 12.8 Performances, audience and income generated abroad; Israel Philharmonic Orchestra 1994-6

Year	*Performances Abroad*	*Audiences Abroad*	*Income Abroad (M NIS)*
1994	43	110,900	3.054
1995	9	20,500	2.010
1996	9	19,900	0

Source: Center for Information and Research, Ministry of Education and Culture.

When all the Tel Aviv institutions that serve export markets are individually identified from the aggregate (Ministry of Education) data, a similar picture emerges. Table 12.9 shows data for all these institutions in 1996. As becomes readily apparent, net income generated abroad is not necessarily related to the size of audience served or the prestige of the institution. In principal, the dance sub-sector seems to be the most efficient in terms of its global connections even though its public profile is lower than that of classical music. Overall however, the extent of all this activity in 1996 was marginal. Tel Aviv-based institutions played abroad to audiences of less than 100,000 in over 70 performances and netted less than 1 million NIS. When this total is compared to the figures for the Israel Philharmonic in previous years, its limited magnitude become apparent. Because of this limited size, these figures can be greatly influenced by the performance of a single large institution such as the IPO.

Table 12.9 Performances, audience and income generated abroad; all Tel Aviv- based cultural institutions, 1996

Sub-Sector	*Institution*	*Performances Abroad*	*Audiences Abroad*	*Income Abroad (Th NIS)*
Theater	Yiddish Theater	7	1,920	63.0
Theater	Aleh	1	68	0
Classical Music	Israel Philharmonic Orchestra	8	18,700	0
Classical Music	Israel Chamber Orchestra.	4	14,500	0
Dance	Israeli Ballet	11	8,000	277.6
Dance	Tnuatron	1	1,100	6.0
Dance	Bat Sheva	21	19,934	207.8
Dance	Ben Gal and Dror	17	6,202	190.0
Total		71	70,424	744.5

Source: Center for Information and Research, Ministry of Education and Culture.

Another reservation concerning this data relates the method of reporting. For example, in the case of income data, net income figures do not tell the whole story. In certain cases, especially in the theater sub-sector, a performance abroad can often be part of a festival or a cultural exchange program. Sometimes these arrangements do not include income from box-office sales. In other cases, there is a barter agreement between the hosts and the visitors. This makes the comprehensiveness of this data quite problematic when trying to compare it to other years or even to compare the same institution across different years.

12.4.3 Findings from the Qualitative Data

Due to the limits of the institutional data, interviews are an important source of supplementary information. They point to two types of orientation amongst Tel Aviv cultural institutions: a 'local' orientation and a 'global' orientation. These two approaches are to a certain extent, dictated by the language barrier. Because of this, theater tends to be a more locally-oriented activity while classical music and dance serve a more international audience.

The highest profile globally-oriented institutions are the IPO and the Israeli Opera. The former is world renown and gave about 30 performances abroad in 1998 that generated an income of 10 million NIS. However the expenditure on these performances was of similar magnitude and thus net income was minimal. On the import flows side, the IPO also hosts about 60 artists a year at a cost of about 9 million NIS. The total volume of import and export-based flows amounts to over 13 percent of the IPO's budget (Table 12.10).

The Israeli Opera offers about 8 productions a year. By nature, much of this activity involves large import-based flows. Only two of these are local productions; the rest are imports from abroad in various degrees. In 1998 for example, one production involved total import (performers, scenery, costumes etc) while five were a combination of local and imported inputs. Aside from direct payments abroad for royalties, stage scenery, payments to artists, producers etc which amount to one sixth of the annual budget of the institution, further import-related expenses are incurred relating to accommodation, shipping and the like. Together these flows can account for 20 percent of the Opera's budget (Table 12.10).

Table 12.10 Import and export-based flows related to leading Tel Aviv cultural institutions

Company	*IPO*	*Israeli Opera*	*Delal Dance Center*	*Cameri Theater*	*Gesher Theater*
Total Budget (1988, M NIS)	70	45	8.3	50	11
Of this: Importing artists etc.	9	7	2	0.5	-
Exporting Performances etc.	10	-	0.6	1.6	0.5
Royalties	0.3	0.2	-	2.4	0.6
Import & Export as % of budget	13.5	20	15.5		

Source: Interviews with directors of the institutions

For the locally-oriented institutions, their level of integration with global culture is based on receipts of royalties and salaries to (imported) foreign cast members. Thus while payment of royalties can be relatively high (for example, the Cameri theater) all other forms of flows that indicate a degree of globalization, are relatively limited (Table 12.10). In principle, the language barrier inhibits the internationalization of locally-oriented institutions. Income from tourists, royalty receipts and performances abroad and the ability to import foreign performers, are all limited. Tel Aviv cultural activity is thus strongly dichotomized in terms of its global visibility. On the one hand, leading representative institutions of Israeli culture abroad such as the I.P.O. and the Bat Sheva Dance troupe are Tel Aviv-based and associated with the city. On the other hand, in term of gross employment and income effects, the locally oriented Tel Aviv institutions, especially theater companies, have a more significant impact on the local economy.

12.5 CONCLUSIONS

On the basis of the above, we can point to the following conclusions. First, there is rather a large discrepancy between the (partial) picture painted by the institutional data and that suggested on the basis of in-depth interviews. This is probably due to the present system of reporting in the former that fails to reflect the international activities of the institutions. Looking at the volume of flow-based activity, it could be that for certain institutions, up to 30 percent of their activity is internationally related. If this is correct, then the sub-sectors of classical music, opera and dance are more integrated into global networks than we anticipated. Clearly, a static input-ouput based approach needs to be augmented with more qualitative data in order to get a fuller picture of globalization tendencies in this industry.

A second conclusion relates to the wide level of differentiation in terms of global activities, across sub-sectors. In this respect, the theater (which is a major source of export flows world-wide) is a particularly parochial institution in Israel. Attempts are being made at changing this (for example simultaneous translations and performances in English) but at present it would seem that language forms an insurmountable barrier to global integration. Other activities, such as classic music and dance would seem to have a much wider global reach. Some cultural institutions, such as the Israel Philharmonic Orchestra, have an international reputation and have functioned as cultural ambassadors for Israel for decades. Their global impact is not captured in economic terms but in terms of the global profile they have developed.

Third, the impact of the cultural industries on the micro-geography of Tel Aviv is negligible. Despite the logic of central place functions and agglomeration economies as described above, no 'theater district' or 'cultural quarter' has emerged in the Tel Aviv metropolitan area. Our survey and interview evidence with directors of cultural institutions did not yield any clear patterns of specialized input suppliers and unit costs savings arising from geographic clustering. Perhaps a minimum critical mass in this sector is still missing or perhaps the range of cultural sub-sectors is too diffuse to facilitate the emergence of a cultural agglomeration. Furthermore, key location decisions in recent years concerning the siting of major arts complexes such as the new Tel Aviv Opera House, the Delal Performing Arts Center or the Gesher Theater premises, seem to have been driven by short-run concerns over availability of premises and real estate considerations. These generally over-shadow any broader, strategic views of the role of cultural industries in urban development.

Finally, the use of cultural activities as a vehicle for effecting change outside the realm of the arts, has long been recognized. For example, in the area of urban regeneration, promoting culture and the arts have proven to be a popular platform for city marketing and place-selling (Bassett, 1993; Paddison, 1993). This has often taken the form of commercializing urban heritage or large-scale public investment in flagship cultural institutions in the hope of jump-starting lagging places. Some places have taken the route of selling their cultural brand-names in an effort to gain some form of competitive advantage in increasingly global markets (Scott, 2000). The Tel Aviv experience in high culture does not seem to match any of these trajectories. Building on the traditional Jewish presence in the performing arts, the main cultural institutions of Tel Aviv attempt to create a global presence in traditional markets (classical music, dance etc) often playing an ambassadorial role. We could interpret this as further evidence of the global 'signaling' in which an emerging node engages. As in the case of the tendency of high tech firms to go public abroad (Chapter 6), we can suggest that the globalization of Israeli cultural institutions is more to do with generating global visibility than with exporting a cultural trademark.

NOTES

1 The structure of the inter-regional input-output model is outlined in Freeman and Sultan (1997). The model combines an input-output (I-O) table and a trade flows (TF) table. The regional technological matrices are arranged along the diagonal of a $NM*NM$ matrix (with N regions and M sectors) with all off-diagonal values set to zero. The standard Leontieff, single region I-O formulation describes the inter-sectoral relationships as:

$$X=AX+Y$$

where X = gross output, A= direct I-O coefficients and Y = final demand.

The model integrates inter-regional trade flows into the above matrix formulation, in the following manner. A trade flow (TF) table is combined with the technological matrix such that matrix $C=C_m^{gh}$, i.e. the flow of goods in sector m between regions g and h. This matrix has the same properties as the $NM*NM$ matrix and has $N*N$ regional trade sub-matrices. As above all trade flows are along the diagonal.

Combining the two matrices through multiplication yields:

$$X=CAX + CY$$

This can be rewritten as:

$$(I - CA)X = CY$$

The Leontieff inverse of the above, showing the dependence of gross output on final demand can be written as:

$$X = (I - CA)^{-1} CY$$

The output multiplier (K_O) therefore is:

$$K_O= (I - CA)^{-1} C$$

REFERENCES

Bassett, K. (1993). Urban cultural strategies and urban cultural regeneration: A case study and critique. *Environment and Planning A, 25 (12)*, 1773-1788.

Beaverstock, J.V., Smith, R.G., Taylor, P.J., Walker, D.R.F. & Lorimer, H. (2000). Globalization and world cities: Some measurement methodologies. *Applied Geography, 20*, 43-63.

Bryan, J., Hill, S., Munday, M. & Roberts, A. (2000). Assessing the role of the arts and cultural industries in a local economy. *Environment and Planning A, 32*, 1391-1408.

Deloitte & Touche (1993). *The economic impact of the Arts in metropolitan Denver*. Denver, CO: Deloitte and Touche and the Colorado Business Committee for the Arts.

EU (1998). *Culture, the cultural industries and employment*. Brussels: Commission Staff Working Paper, SEC (98) 837.

Felsenstein, D. & Freeman, D. (1998). Simulating the impacts of gambling in a tourist location: Some evidence from Israel. *Journal of Travel Research, 37 (2)*, 145-155.

Freeman, D., Talpaz, H., Flesicher, A. & Laufman, O. (1990). A multi-regional input-output model for Israel and extensions: Methodology and experience. In D.E. Boyce, P. Nijkamp & D. Shefer (Eds.), *Regional science: Retrospect and prospect* (424-445). Springer Verlag Heidelberg.

Freeman, D. & Sultan, E. (1997). The economic impact of tourism in Israel: A multi-regional input-output analysis. *Tourism Economics, 3 (4)*, 341-359.

Government Office for London (1996). *Four world cities; A comparative study of London, Paris, Tokyo and New York.* London: Llewelyn Davis Planning.

Heilbrun, J, (1992). Art and culture as central place functions. *Urban Studies, 29 (2)*, 205-215.

Heilbrun, J, (1996). Growth, accessibility and distribution of arts activity in the United States, 1980-1990. *Journal of Cultural Economics, 20 (4)*, 283-286.

Hughes, H. & Gratton, D. (1992). The economics of the culture industry. In D. Whynne (Ed.), *The culture industry: The Arts in urban regeneration* (96-123). Aldershot: Avebury.

LAB (1996). *The Arts and cultural industries in the London economy.* London: London Arts Board.

LPAC (1991). *London; World city - the position of culture.* London: Comedia, London Planning Advisory Committee

Paddison, R. (1993). City marketing, image reconstruction and urban regeneration. *Urban Studies, 30 (2)*, 339-350.

Port Authority of New York (1993). *The Arts as an industry: Their economic importance to the New York-New Jersey metropolitan region.* NY: The Port Authority of New York and New Jersey.

Sassen, S. (1994). *Cities in a world economy.* Thousand Oaks, CA: Pine Forge Press.

Scott, A.J. (2000). *The cultural economy of cities; Essays on the geography of image-producing industries.* Thousand Oaks, CA: Sage.

Smith, C. & Jenner, P. (1998). *The impact of festivals and special events on tourism.* London: Travel and Tourism Intelligence, Economist Intelligence Unit.

SECTION V:

CONCLUSIONS

EIKE W. SCHAMP, DANIEL FELSENSTEIN
AND ARIE SHACHAR

13. EMERGING NODES IN A GLOBAL ECONOMY: A POSTSCRIPT

Rather than adopting a summative or reflective stance, this postscript attempts to take stock of the experiences of Frankfurt and Tel Aviv with a view to looking forward. We attempt to generalize about the conditions under which node economies emerge in order to provide a conceptual infrastructure for understanding similar processes in other locations. Despite the glorification of the global city phenomena, most places will never attain or even aspire to that pinnacle. Notwithstanding massive public investment, global image creating events (Expos, Olympics, World Fairs), flagship regeneration and place-marketing, most locations will never be able to compete with historical accidents, time-honored business practices and human capital skills acquired over long periods. Thus the maximum aspiration for emerging nodes would seem to be selective engagement with the global economy and a passage of entry via particular global networks. Locations are likely to connect with other locations as nodes in a global market place and grounded in specialization: logistics nodes, high tech nodes, international finance nodes, cultural nodes and the like. The multiplicity of routes into the global economy is thus varied and fascinating. We attempt to synthesize the experience of Frankfurt and Tel Aviv in order to highlight this diversity. In addition, we draw out some dominant themes that arise from the different studies presented above. These are given cursory attention here but potentially provide a wide research agenda for understanding the role of nodes in the global economy.

13.1 SYNTHESIZING THE EXPERIENCES

The preceding chapters present a kaleidoscope of specialized node activities, illustrating the multiple ways in which they evolve over time and the variety of place and sector-specific factors that have determined their emergence. From these experiences we can identify three principle forces at work. The first is the principle of increasing returns, both internal and external to the firm, currently operating in many sectors in the global economy. As noted by Krugman (1991) this is a factor freed of the constraints of both time and place and offers a rational choice explanation to networking processes and the emergence of nodes in the global economy. It also begs the question as to why these nodes have emerged over the last decade of the 20th century and not earlier? The second force relates to the role of specific historical and political environments and their role in node formation. This factor is intrinsically bound to a third force associated with the role of place: just

D. Felsenstein et al. (eds.),
Emerging Nodes in the Global Economy: Frankfurt and Tel Aviv Compared, 257–265.

how important is this in a global economy grounded in flows? We now deal with each of these in turn.

13.1.1 Pre-Conditions: The role of increasing returns

Increasing returns have been the source of intensive debate among scholars in a variety of scientific contexts. In the arena of the spatial analysis, the Krugman-type 'new economic geography' or 'new geographical economics' (Martin, 1999) both point to the interplay of decreasing transport and transactions costs and increasing returns to scale, working in favor of concentration in large urban agglomerations. The current lively debate in urban economics centers on the diversity and meaning of increasing returns in explaining growth of cities (e.g., Hansen, 2001; Ottaviano and Thisse, 2001). Others have emphasized the continuing and even increasing role of large transnational corporations in linking different places in the global economy (e.g., Martinelli and Schoenberger, 1991; Dicken, 1998). Whatever the focus, increasing returns invariably form the back-drop for these investigations.

Three separate and combinatorial forms of increasing returns can be noted: internal scale economies to the firm, external economies through proximity and network-based externalities. Scale economies internal to the firm are not sector-specific and diffuse into other sectors through technological and organizational innovation. New organizational forms are often adopted which allow for governing a multiplicity of activities across places. This is particularly prevalent in the service sector which is no longer restricted locally, regionally or nationally. A case in point is the Frankfurt airport company which has used internal economies of scale in order to become a continental, if not global force. Internal growth has been achieved through takeovers and mergers and external growth through strategic alliances (Chapter 7). Another case is the extension of the global accounting and advertising firms networks to Tel Aviv through merger and acquisition activity (Chapter 8). In addition, the global investment strategies of large international hotel corporations seem to point to a presence in emerging node locations. Thus global oligopolies are 'alive and well' as ever before (Martinelli and Schoenberger, 1991) and contribute to the re-interpretation of urban nodes and the formation of new ones.

Another area where increasing returns are of paramount importance is that of network-based externalities. With globalization as a process of networking and the global economy becoming a 'space of flows', non-local network externalities become increasingly important (Liebowitz and Margolis, 1994; Economides, 1996). Network membership can provide access to such externalities. While network externalities have only received minimal formal attention in this volume (for example, see Chapter 6), in most of the studies they are implicit and certainly deserve further attention. For example, the small high tech firms of Tel Aviv actively seek market advantages from global networking by going public on NASDAQ and attracting foreign investment. These pecuniary externalities are thus the basis for new processes of networking in the global economy. While it is generally assumed that globalization is advanced by the activities of large TNCs extending their internal network into emerging urban nodes in a 'top down' process, the Tel Aviv experience seems to suggest a 'bottom up' process of global networking through the efforts of small local firms.

Finally, the most obvious area of increasing returns for geographers and regional economists are local externalities, both as sector-specific localization economies and place-specific urbanization economies. The contemporary debate that evokes these externalities revolves around how to explain the spatial concentration of economic activities under globalization, and more specifically, the growth of cities. It refers to a variety of dimensions such as the size of public infrastructure that connects urban areas to the world (e.g. airports) or the size and quality of local labor markets, sector-specific advantages created by mainly informal local networking ('creative milieux' or 'untraded interdependencies') and the pecuniary externalities of market access (Henderson, 1988; Hanson, 2001). Most of the studies presented here refer to these externalities in one form or another. As noted at the outset, many urban places may attain urbanization economies but still not emerge as nodes in the global economy. The stories of both Frankfurt and Tel Aviv (two very different economic structures but both grounded in localization economies) would seem to underscore this point. Thus, it seems that increasing returns in a variety of forms play a decisive role in the emergence of global nodes. However, the minimum critical mass necessary to promote node activities would seem to have increased greatly over time. This makes it necessary to take into account specific historical processes in which increasing returns are embedded.

13.1.2 Changing Economic and Political Environments

Any answer to the question as to why nodes have emerged in their present configuration at the end of the 20th century ('why now'?) and why they have appeared in specific places ('why here'?) needs to be cognizant of the changing political and regulatory environment that has presented both constraints and opportunities for global integration. We note three major dimensions of political and economic change. The first is the confluence of political events of epochal importance over the last decade. The second is the emergence of new institutions that have facilitated global integration. The third relates to change in the regulative environment that has opened windows of opportunity for economic agents and enlarged the frame of their actions.

Some economic historians delimit a 'short 20th century' from the end of World War I till the political reorganization in Central Europe at the end of the 1980s resulting from the collapse of the socialist economies (Schwarz, 2000). The upshot of this has been fundamental change in the global political order. As a result, the 1990s have been a decade of unexpected political reorganization in the world regions that serve as the context for this volume. In Europe, German reunification after 1989 and the re-integration of Eastern Europe into a common political and economic European space has offered unexpected economic opportunity with enlarged markets and new political institutions. In the Middle East, the peace process initiated in 1993 caused an initial expectation of open regional borders and concomitant economic returns. These led to a partial removal of the Arab boycott on

Israel and an attendant exposure of the Israeli economy to global markets. This was later cemented by a steady rise in foreign direct investment in the Israeli economy over the second half of the 1990's (Chapter 4).

Several chapters in this book point to the evolution of local institutions as providing an enabling environment for firms to profit from these political changes. For example, the long term development of scientific and military research in Israel and the emphasis on skill formation and extensive social and business connections worldwide, gave rise to the emergence of a high technology firm cluster in Tel Aviv metropolitan area (Chapter 6). Similarly in the case of Frankfurt/Rhein-Main, two factors prepared the city for becoming a major European financial center. The first was the history of concentrating domestic financial activities in the city of Frankfurt in some part due to the location of the German Federal Bank. The second was the deepening political and economic integration in the European Union and especially the creation of the European Single Market in 1993 and the European Currency Union in 1994. Both of these were anticipated by firms long before they were announced in the 1980's. Thus, when potential member states of the European Currency Union started negotiating over the location of the European Central Bank, Germany had a strong case being the largest national economy in Europe and Frankfurt was conceived as an almost 'natural' location.

Changing technology and regulatory frameworks also helped re-fashion given political and economic environments. Over the 1990s, information technologies such as the Internet, cellular telephony and satellite communications gave a new meaning to the term 'information society'. These seemed to homogenize the process of globalization, removing barriers between remote places and giving rise to the formation of totally new sectors in the so-called 'New Economy'. Opportunities were created not only for high tech 'hot spots' such as Tel Aviv but, also, for financial centers. These capitalized on the development of financial products, instruments and markets. This process however was a double-edged sword, a fact that became apparent with the global slump of 2001. The new technologies both created the bubble economy and created the opportunities to undermine it as witnessed in the case of the effect of 'remote access' on the Frankfurt stock exchange (Chapter 5).

Major changes in the regulative environment accelerated the impact of the new technologies. The traditional arsenal of liberal economics such as deregulation, currency liberalization and privatization became the key words for changing regulatory structures aimed at curbing the perceived excessive activities of the nation state and enabling new growth opportunities for the private sector. Numerous examples of this process are outlined in this volume. In Germany, the gradual deregulation of financial markets during the 1990s allowed for the development of new financial products such as derivatives and new markets such as the 'Neuer Markt' (Chapter 5). Deregulation in business tax law saw the emergence of new fields for investment banking and served as an incentive for many foreign banks to locate in Frankfurt. Deregulation also extended to other activities, such as air traffic, road haulage etc.

In Israel, both economic integration and deregulation created new opportunities for the global networking of firms. Preferential trading agreements with the EU and

North America enlarged market access and foreign currency liberalization deregulated (financial) markets. In addition, innovative government activity helped jump-start the indigenous high tech sector through a string of new frameworks and instruments. De-regulation and targeted proactive government activity combined together in a variety of forms that ranged from standard public subsidies to R&D, through public-assisted venture capital funds to support for generic, pre-competitive technology and bi-national R&D agreements (Trajtenberg, 2000).

13.1.3 The Role of Place

The paradox of the node that owes its existence to a space of flows yet operates out of a concrete location, has been highlighted above (Chapter 1). The evidence on the importance of place-specifity in the emergence of the node, is however ambiguous. There is no doubt that some kind of idiosyncratic initial advantage contributes to the location of node activities. The increasing returns intrinsic to node development and the imperfect competition that characterizes the operation of new and fast-growing economic activities combine to offer an initial advantage to those places where related or supporting activities exist. This implies a cumulative growth process as illustrated in the inter-related emergence of node activities such as the airport, finance and the international hotel sector in Frankfurt/Rhein-Main. Similar inter-relationships appear between the high tech sector and the globalizing producer services in Tel Aviv. These processes can also largely be understood using the standard battery of explanations for agglomeration economies such as reduced transaction costs, urbanization economies and risk-minimization through labor market pooling (Krugman, 2001; Veltz, 1996).

This general argument can be augmented by a more focused view of the role of place-specificity. In a globalizing world of increasing complexity and uncertainty we can expect specific social relations between agents in geographical proximity to create specific external advantages. These are informal, hard to replicate, tied to a specific places and therefore untradable (Storper, 1997). This organization of 'economic reflexivity' becomes the major thrust of the emergence of some places as nodes in global networks. The indispensable existence of 'embeddedness' and social capital may be important ingredients in the emergence of node functions in Frankfurt and Tel Aviv.

For example, a recent study on knowledge generation and diffusion in the major sectors in the Frankfurt/Rhein-Main region, has come to the conclusion that neither 'traditional' knowledge systems in the field of chemistry or car manufacturing nor new sources in finance or biotechnology are embedded in local relationships (Schamp, 2002). Recent attempts on the part of local and state policy in the Frankfurt region to foster the generation of local social capital have met with mixed results. This is because the knowledge systems concerned extend to continental or even global networks. Additionally, anecdotal evidence from the Frankfurt finance sector suggests that there is little local infrastructure in human skill formation and research comparable to that of financial centers such as London or Paris. Urban and regional politics seem to have been unable, so far, to contribute to the formation of social capital that could support the diverse node activities in Frankfurt.

Thus it can be argued that place specific social capital per se is not a necessary condition for emerging nodes in the global economy. In some cases, however, it could become a major factor in anchoring node activities to specific places. The temporality and volatility of a node function means that even established places are under constant threat. For Frankfurt this is posed by the specter of being overtaken by London that should lead, according to some accounts to a more co-operative and less competitive division of labor between the two centers (Beaverstock, Hoyler, Pain and Taylor, 2001). However recent events only seem to undermine the self-confidence of the former. Deutsche Bank which is seen as a symbol of 'Finanzplatz Deutschland' has decided to relocate its main activities in investment banking to London while only maintaining an administrative presence in Frankfurt. In addition, the Frankfurt-based Dresdner Bank has been taken over by Allianz, the world largest insurance company located in Munich. In sum therefore, it would seem that the nodes featured in this volume seem to have been fashioned by both pre-conditions and changes in the political and economic environment. These have created the 'windows of locational opportunity' behind the emergence of these nodes in the global economy (Storper and Walker, 1989; Boschma, 1997). The territorial anchorage of these node activities is however still contested. The result is an ambiguous future for emerging nodes.

13.2 EMERGING THEMES

Three major themes on urban nodes emerge from this book. The first relates to the selective nature of incipient nodes. Frankfurt and Tel Aviv are not iconic 'global cities'. Nor are they likely to assume that position in the future. At most, they play selective node functions in global networks. In all the cases examined here, entry of the urban node into the global economy is via a few selective growth sectors and nearly always animated by foreign direct investment. A foreign presence in a domestic growth area would seem to be a pre-requisite for the entry of urban nodes into global networks. Selectivity is particularly pronounced at the intra-metropolitan level. Entry into global networks translates into a micro-geography in which only certain parts of the node location are really integrated into global activities. One of the paradoxes of the IT revolution is that it allows for distinct districts within a single metropolitan area to be connected together making for the development of mammoth city-regions. It also facilitates the selective connectivity between different parts of different metropolitan areas allowing for 'global' city-regions to develop.

This is illustrated in Frankfurt where different parts of the metropolitan region are incorporated into different global networks. When Frankfurt functions as a logistics node the airport area is linked into world-wide centers of distribution, hub locations and global transparks. In this case, Frankfurt as node communicates with other places functioning in a similar fashion such as Rotterdam or Atlanta GA. As a node in the global trade-fair network, the Frankfurt Messe district is connected to other similar locales in Birmingham, Milan and Paris. When Frankfurt operates as a major banking and finance node it means that the commercial downtown area of the city is connected to other similar districts in London (the City), Paris, Zurich, New York (Wall Street) and Tokyo. Tel Aviv demonstrates similar selectivity in both origin and destination. As a high tech node, those parts of metropolitan Tel Aviv tied into global networks are mainly the outer suburban industrial park clusters ranging from Herzelia in the north to Rehovot in the south. These enclaves are linked to a similar set of selective locations worldwide such as Silicon Valley, Cambridge, UK, the Research Triangle, NC and so on. In producer services networks, Tel Aviv as a node means that the agglomeration of accounting and advertising firms straddling the Ayalon freeway running through Tel Aviv and the new CBD are connected with similar clusters in New York (Madison Avenue), Brussels, Toronto and London (the West End).

The second theme relates to how endogenous is this growth process? Is it cumulative and self-fuelling? This also leads on to the question as to just how economically sustainable is the process? Do places emerge as nodes only to disappear just as fast as they arrive? If so, just how suitable a policy prescription is node-creation? Both the emergence of Frankfurt airport and the Tel Aviv high tech sector would seem to be good examples of an endogenous growth dynamic. However, the tourism stories from both places seem to suggest the opposite. As long as international tourism is mainly based on business travel, the growth trajectory of the tourism sector and the strategic decisions of global hotel companies would seem to be largely derived from reverberations emanating from global forces in other nodes.

Furthermore, endogenous growth processes are self-sustaining. As long as Germany had a regulated financial system which established barriers to entry for foreign competitors, a cumulative and re-enforcing process of geographical concentration of financial services took place in Frankfurt. This domestically-driven growth process was further promoted by the integration of German financial markets into the European area. Today however, it can be argued that this process has ostensibly ended. It has been replaced by Frankfurt as a center for trade and logistics and a growing necessity for 'upstream marketing functions' (Cornish, 1997). This has fostered a new endogenous growth process with Frankfurt as a node in global trade. This process however, is related to the same domestic context that contributed to Frankfurt's emergence as a financial center, i.e. Germany as a well-delimited market area where trade barriers still exist.

The third emergent theme is that of 'signaling'. Is foreign investment important of itself or simply a form of international recognition? Our evidence from Frankfurt and Tel Aviv points to the latter. Foreign presence is used as a form of flag-waving: an attempt to create a global presence and break into global networks. This also relates to the issue of 'image' versus concrete 'reality' in creating a global profile. A case in point is the volume of foreign banks present in the Frankfurt financial center. This assumes importance in the public debate on 'rating places' and Frankfurt's standing in these rankings. However, much of the foreign presence in Frankfurt is not actually involved in providing financial services to the German market at all. Another case in point is the public debate over the balance of foreign direct investment in Frankfurt which has been much more successful in attracting foreign investment than investing abroad (Chapter 2). From this perspective, Frankfurt has been the most attractive place in Germany for quite a long time.

Other aspects of signaling can be discerned with respect to firm behavior (Chapter 7). The Frankfurt airport company (FAG) wary of its global profile, changed its name to Fraport before going public. Several business associations representing the Frankfurt/Rhein-Main region have adopted a common logo in future, in order to project a common 'signal' and enable the region to penetrate global networks. Similar experiences have been reported above in relation to the behavior of Israeli high tech firms raising capital abroad (Chapter 6) and the role of Tel Aviv's arts sector in creating an international cultural presence (Chapter 12). Signaling can therefore be interpreted as an indicator of increasing information overflow in a globalizing world. In principal-agent theory, it is a classic means for overcoming information asymmetries (Sharpe, 1990). Both signaling and brand-naming offer access to global networks. For example, by using the NASDAQ exchange as an arena for generating global visibility, Tel Aviv high tech firms are not just generating a presence that reinforces their own competitiveness. At one and the same time, a similar effect is generated with respect to Tel Aviv's position as a high tech node. In this respect, firm-signaling is also place-signaling. However, due to the endogenous growth processes inherent in the emergence of nodes, the growth of the node over time becomes independent of the growth of the sum of the firms that initially comprised it. This is a dynamic process at present in formation. The challenge for the future lies in ensuring its sustainability.

REFERENCES

Beaverstock, J.V., Hoyler, M., Pain, K. & Taylor, P.F. (2001). *Comparing London and Frankfurt as world cities: A relational study of contemporary urban change*. London: Anglo-German Foundation for the Study of Industrial Society.

Boschma, R. (1997). New industries and windows of locational opportunity. A long-term analysis of Belgium. *Erdkunde 51*, 12-22.

Cornish, S. (1997). Product innovation and the spatial dynamics of market intelligence: Does proximity to markets matter? *Economic Geography, 73*, 143-165.

Dicken, P. (1998). *Global shift. Transforming the world economy*. London: Paul Chapman.

Economides, N. (1996). The economics of networks. *International Journal of Industrial Organization, 14*, 673-699.

Hanson, G.H. (2001). Scale economies and the geographic concentration of industry. *Journal of Economic Geography, 1*, 255-276.

Henderson, J.V. (1988). *Urban development: Theory, Fact and Illusion*. New York: Oxford University Press.

Krugman, P. (1991). *Geography and trade*. Cambridge MA: MIT Press.

Krugman, P. (2001). Where in the world is the 'new economic geography'? In G.L. Clark, M.P. Feldman and M.S. Gertler (Eds.), *The Oxford handbook economic geography* (49-60). Oxford: Oxford University Press.

Liebowitz, S.J. & Margolis, S.E. (1994). Network externalities: An uncommon tragedy. *The Journal of Economic Perspectives, 8*, 133-150.

Martin, R. (1999). The new 'geographical turn' in economics: some critical reflections. *Cambridge Journal of Economics, 23*, 65-91.

Martinelli, F. & Schoenberger, E. (1991). Oligopoly is alive and well: notes for a broader discussion of flexible accumulation. In G. Benko & M. Dunford (Eds.), *Industrial Change & Regional Development* (117-133). London: Belhaven.

Ottaviano, G.I.P. & Thisse, J.Fr. (2001). On economic geography in economic theory: increasing returns and pecuniary externalities. *Journal of Economic Geography, 1*, 153-179.

Schamp, E.W. (2002). Globalization and the reorganization of a metropolitan knowledge system: The case of research and development in Frankfurt/Rhein-Main. In R. Hayter & R. Le Heron (Eds.), *Knowledge, Industry and Environment: Institutions and Innovation in Territorial Perspective.* Aldershot: Ashgate (forthcoming).

Schwarz, H.P. (2000). Fragen an das 20. *Jahrhundert.Vierteljahrshefte für Zeitgeschichte, 48*, 1-36. Sharpe S. (1990). Asymmetric information, bank lending and implicit contracts: A stylized model of customer relationships. *Journal of Finance, 6594*, 1069-1087.

Storper, M. (1997). The regional world. Territorial development in a global economy. New York: Guilford.

Storper, M. & Walker, R. (1989). *The capitalist imperative. Territory, technology, and industrial growth.* Oxford: Blackwell.

Trajtenberg, M. (2000). *R&D Policy in Israel: An overview and reassessment.* Working Paper 7930, Cambridge MA, National Bureau of Economic Research.
Available: http://www.nber.org/ papers/w/7930

Veltz, P. (1996). *Mondialisation, villes et territoires.* L'économie d'archipel. Paris: Presses Universitaires de France.

INDEX

The GeoJournal Library

1. B. Currey and G. Hugo (eds.): *Famine as Geographical Phenomenon.* 1984 ISBN 90-277-1762-1
2. S.H.U. Bowie, F.R.S. and I. Thornton (eds.): *Environmental Geochemistry and Health.* Report of the Royal Society's British National Committee for Problems of the Environment. 1985 ISBN 90-277-1879-2
3. L.A. Kosiński and K.M. Elahi (eds.): *Population Redistribution and Development in South Asia.* 1985 ISBN 90-277-1938-1
4. Y. Gradus (ed.): *Desert Development.* Man and Technology in Sparselands. 1985 ISBN 90-277-2043-6
5. F.J. Calzonetti and B.D. Solomon (eds.): *Geographical Dimensions of Energy.* 1985 ISBN 90-277-2061-4
6. J. Lundqvist, U. Lohm and M. Falkenmark (eds.): *Strategies for River Basin Management.* Environmental Integration of Land and Water in River Basin. 1985 ISBN 90-277-2111-4
7. A. Rogers and F.J. Willekens (eds.): *Migration and Settlement.* A Multiregional Comparative Study. 1986 ISBN 90-277-2119-X
8. R. Laulajainen: *Spatial Strategies in Retailing.* 1987 ISBN 90-277-2595-0
9. T.H. Lee, H.R. Linden, D.A. Dreyfus and T. Vasko (eds.): *The Methane Age.* 1988 ISBN 90-277-2745-7
10. H.J. Walker (ed.): *Artificial Structures and Shorelines.* 1988 ISBN 90-277-2746-5
11. A. Kellerman: *Time, Space, and Society.* Geographical Societal Perspectives. 1989 ISBN 0-7923-0123-4
12. P. Fabbri (ed.): *Recreational Uses of Coastal Areas.* A Research Project of the Commission on the Coastal Environment, International Geographical Union. 1990 ISBN 0-7923-0279-6
13. L.M. Brush, M.G. Wolman and Huang Bing-Wei (eds.): *Taming the Yellow River: Silt and Floods.* Proceedings of a Bilateral Seminar on Problems in the Lower Reaches of the Yellow River, China. 1989 ISBN 0-7923-0416-0
14. J. Stillwell and H.J. Scholten (eds.): *Contemporary Research in Population Geography.* A Comparison of the United Kingdom and the Netherlands. 1990 ISBN 0-7923-0431-4
15. M.S. Kenzer (ed.): *Applied Geography.* Issues, Questions, and Concerns. 1989 ISBN 0-7923-0438-1
16. D. Nir: *Region as a Socio-environmental System.* An Introduction to a Systemic Regional Geography. 1990 ISBN 0-7923-0516-7
17. H.J. Scholten and J.C.H. Stillwell (eds.): *Geographical Information Systems for Urban and Regional Planning.* 1990 ISBN 0-7923-0793-3
18. F.M. Brouwer, A.J. Thomas and M.J. Chadwick (eds.): *Land Use Changes in Europe.* Processes of Change, Environmental Transformations and Future Patterns. 1991 ISBN 0-7923-1099-3

The GeoJournal Library

19. C.J. Campbell: *The Golden Century of Oil 1950–2050.* The Depletion of a Resource. 1991 ISBN 0-7923-1442-5
20. F.M. Dieleman and S. Musterd (eds.): *The Randstad: A Research and Policy Laboratory.* 1992 ISBN 0-7923-1649-5
21. V.I. Ilyichev and V.V. Anikiev (eds.): *Oceanic and Anthropogenic Controls of Life in the Pacific Ocean.* 1992 ISBN 0-7923-1854-4
22. A.K. Dutt and F.J. Costa (eds.): *Perspectives on Planning and Urban Development in Belgium.* 1992 ISBN 0-7923-1885-4
23. J. Portugali: *Implicate Relations.* Society and Space in the Israeli-Palestinian Conflict. 1993 ISBN 0-7923-1886-2
24. M.J.C. de Lepper, H.J. Scholten and R.M. Stern (eds.): *The Added Value of Geographical Information Systems in Public and Environmental Health.* 1995 ISBN 0-7923-1887-0
25. J.P. Dorian, P.A. Minakir and V.T. Borisovich (eds.): *CIS Energy and Minerals Development.* Prospects, Problems and Opportunities for International Cooperation. 1993 ISBN 0-7923-2323-8
26. P.P. Wong (ed.): *Tourism vs Environment: The Case for Coastal Areas.* 1993 ISBN 0-7923-2404-8
27. G.B. Benko and U. Strohmayer (eds.): *Geography, History and Social Sciences.* 1995 ISBN 0-7923-2543-5
28. A. Faludi and A. der Valk: *Rule and Order. Dutch Planning Doctrine in the Twentieth Century.* 1994 ISBN 0-7923-2619-9
29. B.C. Hewitson and R.G. Crane (eds.): *Neural Nets: Applications in Geography.* 1994 ISBN 0-7923-2746-2
30. A.K. Dutt, F.J. Costa, S. Aggarwal and A.G. Noble (eds.): *The Asian City: Processes of Development, Characteristics and Planning.* 1994 ISBN 0-7923-3135-4
31. R. Laulajainen and H.A. Stafford: *Corporate Geography.* Business Location Principles and Cases. 1995 ISBN 0-7923-3326-8
32. J. Portugali (ed.): *The Construction of Cognitive Maps.* 1996 ISBN 0-7923-3949-5
33. E. Biagini: *Northern Ireland and Beyond.* Social and Geographical Issues. 1996 ISBN 0-7923-4046-9
34. A.K. Dutt (ed.): *Southeast Asia: A Ten Nation Region.* 1996 ISBN 0-7923-4171-6
35. J. Settele, C. Margules, P. Poschlod and K. Henle (eds.): *Species Survival in Fragmented Landscapes.* 1996 ISBN 0-7923-4239-9
36. M. Yoshino, M. Domrös, A. Douguédroit, J. Paszynski and L.D. Nkemdirim (eds.): *Climates and Societies – A Climatological Perspective.* A Contribution on Global Change and Related Problems Prepared by the Commission on Climatology of the International Geographical Union. 1997 ISBN 0-7923-4324-7
37. D. Borri, A. Khakee and C. Lacirignola (eds.): *Evaluating Theory-Practice and Urban-Rural Interplay in Planning.* 1997 ISBN 0-7923-4326-3

The GeoJournal Library

38. J.A.A. Jones, C. Liu, M-K. Woo and H-T. Kung (eds.): *Regional Hydrological Response to Climate Change.* 1996 ISBN 0-7923-4329-8
39. R. Lloyd: *Spatial Cognition.* Geographic Environments. 1997 ISBN 0-7923-4375-1
40. I. Lyons Murphy: *The Danube: A River Basin in Transition.* 1997 ISBN 0-7923-4558-4
41. H.J. Bruins and H. Lithwick (eds.): *The Arid Frontier.* Interactive Management of Environment and Development. 1998 ISBN 0-7923-4227-5
42. G. Lipshitz: *Country on the Move: Migration to and within Israel, 1948–1995.* 1998 ISBN 0-7923-4850-8
43. S. Musterd, W. Ostendorf and M. Breebaart: *Multi-Ethnic Metropolis: Patterns and Policies.* 1998 ISBN 0-7923-4854-0
44. B.K. Maloney (ed.): *Human Activities and the Tropical Rainforest.* Past, Present and Possible Future. 1998 ISBN 0-7923-4858-3
45. H. van der Wusten (ed.): *The Urban University and its Identity.* Roots, Location, Roles. 1998 ISBN 0-7923-4870-2
46. J. Kalvoda and C.L. Rosenfeld (eds.): *Geomorphological Hazards in High Mountain Areas.* 1998 ISBN 0-7923-4961-X
47. N. Lichfield, A. Barbanente, D. Borri, A. Khakee and A. Prat (eds.): *Evaluation in Planning.* Facing the Challenge of Complexity. 1998 ISBN 0-7923-4870-2
48. A. Buttimer and L. Wallin (eds.): *Nature and Identity in Cross-Cultural Perspective.* 1999 ISBN 0-7923-5651-9
49. A. Vallega: *Fundamentals of Integrated Coastal Management.* 1999 ISBN 0-7923-5875-9
50. D. Rumley: *The Geopolitics of Australia's Regional Relations.* 1999 ISBN 0-7923-5916-X
51. H. Stevens: *The Institutional Position of Seaports.* An International Comparison. 1999 ISBN 0-7923-5979-8
52. H. Lithwick and Y. Gradus (eds.): *Developing Frontier Cities.* Global Perspectives – Regional Contexts. 2000 ISBN 0-7923-6061-3
53. H. Knippenberg and J. Markusse (eds.): *Nationalising and Denationalising European Border Regions, 1800–2000.* Views from Geography and History. 2000 ISBN 0-7923-6066-4
54. R. Gerber and G.K. Chuan (eds.): *Fieldwork in Geography: Reflections, Perspectives and Actions.* 2000 ISBN 0-7923-6329-9
55. M. Dobry (ed.): *Democratic and Capitalist Transitions in Eastern Europe.* Lessons for the Social Sciences. 2000 ISBN 0-7923-6331-0
56. Y. Murayama: *Japanese Urban System.* 2000 ISBN 0-7923-6600-X
57. D. Zheng, Q. Zhang and S. Wu (eds.): *Mountain Geoecology and Sustainable Development of the Tibetan Plateau.* 2000 ISBN 0-7923-6688-3

The GeoJournal Library

58. A.J. Conacher (ed.): *Land Degradation.* Papers selected from Contributions to the Sixth Meeting of the International Geographical Union's Commission on Land Degradation and Desertification, Perth, Western Australia, 20–28 September 1999. 2001 ISBN 0-7923-6770-7
59. S. Conti and P. Giaccaria: *Local Development and Competitiveness.* 2001 ISBN 0-7923-6829-0
60. P. Miao (ed.): *Public Places in Asia Pacific Cities.* Current Issues and Strategies. 2001 ISBN 0-7923-7083-X
61. N. Maiellaro (ed.): *Towards Sustainable Buiding.* 2001 ISBN 1-4020-0012-X
62. G.S. Dunbar (ed.): *Geography: Discipline, Profession and Subject since 1870.* An International Survey. 2001 ISBN 1-4020-0019-7
63. J. Stillwell and H.J. Scholten (eds.): *Land Use Simulation for Europe.* 2001 ISBN 1-4020-0213-0
64. P. Doyle and M.R. Bennett (eds.): *Fields of Battle.* Terrain in Military History. 2002 ISBN 1-4020-0433-8
65. C.M. Hall and A.M. Williams (eds.): *Tourism and Migration.* New Relationships between Production and Consumption. 2002 ISBN 1-4020-0454-0
66. I.R. Bowler, C.R. Bryant and C. Cocklin (eds.): *The Sustainability of Rural Systems.* Geographical Interpretations. 2002 ISBN 1-4020-0513-X
67. O. Yiftachel, J. Little, D. Hedgcock and I. Alexander (eds.): *The Power of Planning.* Spaces of Control and Transformation. 2001 ISBN Hb; 1-4020-0533-4 ISBN Pb; 1-4020-0534-2
68. K. Hewitt, M.-L. Byrne, M. English and G. Young (eds.): *Landscapes of Transition.* Landform Assemblages and Transformations in Cold Regions. 2002 ISBN 1-4020-0663-2
69. M. Romanos and C. Auffrey (eds.): *Managing Intermediate Size Cities.* Sustainable Development in a Growth Region of Thailand. 2002 ISBN 1-4020-0818-X
70. B. Boots, A. Okabe and R. Thomas (eds.): *Modelling Geographical Systems.* Statistical and Computational Applications. 2002 ISBN 1-4020-0821-X
71. R. Gerber and M. Williams (eds.): *Geography, Culture and Education.* 2002 ISBN 1-4020-0878-3
72. D. Felsenstein, E.W. Schamp and A. Shachar (eds.): *Emerging Nodes in the Global Economy: Frankfurt and Tel Aviv Compared.* 2002 ISBN 1-4020-0924-0

KLUWER ACADEMIC PUBLISHERS – DORDRECHT / BOSTON / LONDON

GPSR Compliance

The European Union's (EU) General Product Safety Regulation (GPSR) is a set of rules that requires consumer products to be safe and our obligations to ensure this.

If you have any concerns about our products, you can contact us on ProductSafety@springernature.com

In case Publisher is established outside the EU, the EU authorized representative is:

Springer Nature Customer Service Center GmbH
Europaplatz 3
69115 Heidelberg, Germany

Batch number: 10823905

Printed by Printforce, the Netherlands